S0-CAP-425

William Jessup University
Library
333 Sunset Blvd.
Rocklin, Ca 95765

Judaism and Christianity

Reference Sources in the Humanities Series
James Rettig, Series Editor

Journalism: A Guide to the Reference Literature. By Jo A. Cates.

Music: A Guide to the Reference Literature. By William S. Brockman.

On the Screen: A Film, Television, and Video Research Guide. By Kim N. Fisher.

Philosophy: A Guide to the Reference Literature. By Hans E. Bynagle.

Reference Works in British and American Literature: Volume I, English and American Literature. By James K. Bracken.

Judaism and Christianity: A Guide to the Reference Literature. By Edward D. Starkey.

724

JUDAISM AND CHRISTIANITY

A GUIDE TO THE REFERENCE LITERATURE

EDWARD D. STARKEY

LIBRARIES UNLIMITED, INC.
Englewood, Colorado
1991

Copyright © 1991 Edward D. Starkey
All Rights Reserved
Printed in the United States of America

No part of this publication may be reproduced, stored in a
retrieval system, or transmitted, in any form or by any means,
electronic, mechanical, photocopying, recording, or otherwise,
without the prior written permission of the publisher.

LIBRARIES UNLIMITED, INC.
P.O. Box 3988
Englewood, CO 80155-3988

Library of Congress Cataloging-in-Publication Data

Starkey, Edward D.
    Judaism and Christianity : a guide to the reference literature /
Edward D. Starkey.
    xii, 229 p. 17x25 cm.

    (Reference sources in the humanities series)
    ISBN 0-87287-533-4
    1. Judaism--Bibliography. 2. Christianity--Bibliography.
3. Bible--Bibliography. I. Title. II. Series.
Z6370.S78   1991
[BM45]
016.2--dc20   90-46212
                                                               CIP

Contents

Part I
THE REFERENCE LITERATURE OF
JUDAISM AND CHRISTIANITY

Part II
THE REFERENCE LITERATURE ON THE BIBLES
OF JUDAISM AND CHRISTIANITY

Preface

Every discipline continuously renews its reference literature to record new theories, revised theses, discoveries, deaths, and developments in the application of theory. New editions of standard works and new titles appear from time to time, while serials bibliographies index each year's outpouring of journal articles, monographs, and festschriften. This series, Reference Sources in the Humanities, takes as its purpose the identification, description, and organization of the reference literature of the humanities disciplines. The volumes in this series, emphasizing the Anglo-American reference literature of recent decades, are intended to serve the needs of undergraduates, graduate students, professors exploring adjunct disciplines, librarians building and using reference collections, and intellectually curious adults interested in systematic, self-guided study of the humanities.

Like bibliographic guides to the literature of any discipline, guides in this series are intended to serve various users in various ways. Students being initiated into the ways of a discipline can use these guides to learn the structure of the discipline's secondary literature, to find sources which will enable them to find definitions of specialized terms, to identify significant historical figures, to gain an overview of a topic, etc. Specialists may use them to refresh their memories about once familiar sources and to advise their students on approaches to problems. Librarians will use them to build and evaluate reference collections and to answer patron questions.

The volumes in the Reference Sources in the Humanities series are designed to serve all of these users and purposes. Each volume in the series is organized principally by reference genre, including types specific to each discipline. This will facilitate their efficient use by reference librarians, a group trained to think in terms of reference genre (e.g., encyclopedias, dictionaries, indexes and abstracts, biographical directories, bibliographies, etc.) within subject categories, when they seek a particular type of reference work in one of the humanities disciplines. Because no discipline's reference literature can completely convey its most recent discoveries, each volume also includes information on key journals and associations and research centers, the sources from which much of any discipline's new knowledge emanates and by means of which that knowledge is disseminated. While each of these guides describes the reference literature of its discipline as that literature presently exists, each also contributes to that literature's renewal and growth.

James Rettig
Series Editor

Introduction

The writing of reference books on religion is an ancient art — the Bible contains commentaries on itself. A massive number of such reference books exists, their publication spurred by the scholarly pursuit of religious studies in academia and by expression of the mature self-awareness of religious groups.

This great quantity of reference material is also widely dispersed. Few great libraries gather the universe of religious reference materials into a single collection. The library of a college or university related to a specific religion, in addition to general works on religion, can usually be counted on to have specific collection strength only in the works of that religion and perhaps related religious expressions. For comprehensiveness, the best one can do is to visit or live in a large city with many academic institutions and research centers. This spreading-out of reference resources on religion gives special importance to such consortia as the Boston Theological Institute Libraries.

This present bibliography identifies, describes, evaluates, and compares reference books dealing with Judaism and Christianity, and the Bibles of these two religious traditions, published in English through 1988. It will be useful for college students, seminarians, theological students, professors of religion, and the generally educated reader who seeks to know more about one of the religions covered or an aspect of it. I hope it will be especially useful to librarians, who must select and buy reference works and then locate them for patrons.

I have examined encyclopedias and dictionaries, handbooks, statistics sources, directories, yearbooks, biographical dictionaries, atlases, bibliographies, literature guides, abstracting services and indexes, databases, and quotation dictionaries, as well as commentaries and concordances to the Bibles. To make this book more useful to researchers unfamiliar with the field, I have included sections on important journals that specialize in Judaism or Christianity, and on key scholarly organizations and research institutes, many of which sponsor journals and other publications. I have attempted thorough coverage in areas where I could find little similar coverage of materials. I have chosen selective treatment either when the quantity of materials is so great as to exclude the possibility of comprehensiveness, or when recent directories or bibliographies have provided fuller lists. For both of these reasons, the second section of this bibliography, on the Bibles of Judaism and Christianity, is particularly selective.

I have limited treatment to works either originally written in English or translated into it. This is not to gainsay the importance of reference works in other languages but rather to take notice of the sheer quantity of works in all languages. To have attempted to annotate the important works in just French and German would have necessitated eliminating many works in English or increasing the length of this book inordinately.

Several bibliographies and guides published in the 1970s and early 1980s offer weaker coverage than the field requires, because their compilers included quantities of general works that cover religion only as a subdivision. With a few careful exceptions, I have not listed such general works, although I have included works on the great world religions in which Judaism and Christianity are given major treatment. Most of the works included pertain wholly to Judaism or a Christian denomination or to a broad theme common to one of these religions. I have avoided the minutely specific; thus, I have included encyclopedias of denominations and dictionaries of theology, but I have not examined bibliographies of specific persons. I have emphasized recency and included all reference works I could identify and examine, even the mediocre, from the 1970s and 1980s, since these are most likely to be available. Enough new reference works in this area are published to merit a review every decade. I have included older works, some from the nineteenth century, when they are recognized classics. Some have never been subsequently equalled. Others, even if less than definitive, continue to stand alone in their field. When possible, I have noted reprints of these. I have personally examined every work annotated, using the most recent edition I could locate.

The arrangement of entries is by type of reference work rather than by subject. Reference works on different religions and topics are interfiled. Although this arrangement is common to the publisher's series, and is based mainly on the intent to provide a service work for reference collections, further meaning can be drawn from it. It is a reflection of the pragmatic relationship of these two great religious traditions in the western world, especially in the United States where we have such organizations as the National Conference of Christians and Jews and such a commonly used expression as "the Judeo-Christian heritage." Both traditions are rooted in a single collection of scriptures which the Christians call the Old Testament and the Jews simply the Bible. The influence of this common book can be traced in such diverse places as the American legal system, the speeches of contemporary politicians, and given names and place names throughout North America. New reference works that treat the Hebrew Bible and the larger Christian Bible are often written by teams of Jewish and Christian scholars.

Reasons for treating reference works on the two religious traditions together can go beyond the pragmatic. For better and often for worse, the history of the two religions has been intertwined from the beginnings of Christianity. Indeed, Judaism gave birth to Christianity, and the first Christians were Jews. One of the more fertile products of contemporary New Testament study is the fuller understanding of the Jewish origins of Christianity. Simply put, Christians must study and understand Judaism not only out of a spirit of tolerance and respect but also to arrive at self-understanding. Jews always have the need to know and understand the numerically larger population of Christians, separated as they are into a variety of denominations, among whom Jews live and carry out their own religious life.

No better example can be found of the need to intersperse studies of the two religious traditions than the literature on the Holocaust. It is of obvious importance to Jews who must deal, as victims, with the implications of this hideous event, but its literature is never to be classified as a division of "Jewish studies."

Men and women brought up under the tutelage of every European Christian community except Anglicanism became involved in the Holocaust, and any self-understanding of contemporary Christianity must take this into account. One can trace the growing awareness of this by searching out the accounts of the Holocaust in reference works published between the 1950s and the 1980s.

Jews and Christians have everything to gain from learning from and understanding each other—the opposite has been tried in abundance and found dreadfully wanting. Let the prolific Talmudic scholar Jacob Neusner have the final word on the matter:

> The Jewish-Christian relationship was rarely characterized by charity of understanding on either side. Only in quite recent times, and primarily in America, have the two great religious traditions sought a constructive and mutually respectful way of living together.[*]

Charity based on mutual understanding has been a driving force behind this bibliography.

Reference works that are well conceived, well written, and published with care can serve as models to be followed in the production of similar works. The encyclopedias produced by the Brethren and the Catholics are such cases. Jewish scholars have offered well-wrought reference works in abundance. Jewish studies—that is, the academic focus on Judaism and its cultural expressions—is a mature, multidisciplinary science, with its origins dating specifically to work of Rabbi Leopold Zunz (1794-1886). From the nineteenth century, a sophisticated bibliography and corpus of other reference materials has grown up within Jewish studies. Aside from its evident value to Judaism, this is a model to the scholars of other religions who propose to examine their own traditions.

In the arrangement of materials within chapters, I have simply used the last name of the principal author, editor, or compiler, when available, from the title page. The indexes offer access by subject, with at least one entry for each work; by every author, editor, compiler, or translator listed; and by title and by series.

The time designations BC (Before Christ) and AD (Anno Domini, or Year of the Lord) are set aside in favor of the religiously neutral BCE (Before the Common Era) and CE (the Common Era). The terms "Old Testament" and "New Testament" prove more difficult; even Jewish writers still use both. In general I have used the term "Hebrew Scriptures" to refer to that collection Christians have traditionally called the Old Testament, but I have retained the expression New Testament. However where the expression Old Testament is called for by continued reference to the title of a work, I have kept it for clarity's sake.

Although the number of published religious reference books is vast, much yet remains to be accomplished. Whole areas of Judaism and Christianity have received only the most general treatment. Every denomination merits an encyclopedia or a handbook on its history, and its great theological themes, and a biographical dictionary of its revered leaders. Given the number of denominations, relatively few such works have been written.

---

[*]From p. 3 of Neusner's preface to *The Study of Judaism: Bibliographical Essays* (see entry 333).

I have a great many people to thank for their help on this work. Most are colleagues whose names I never learned. Throughout the gathering of materials, I was ever encouraged by the consummate skills and pleasant demeanor of reference librarians. The diverse places I visited, often while at conferences, include the Regenstein Library at the University of Chicago, and libraries at the Spertus College of Judaica in Chicago, the University of Illinois in Champaign-Urbana, Catholic University of America in Washington, Hebrew Union College in Cincinnati, Dallas Theological Seminary, and the Claremont Colleges near Los Angeles. In Indianapolis, I depended on Butler University, Marian College, the University of Indianapolis, and especially Christian Theological Seminary and the nearby Indiana University at Bloomington. In San Diego, I turned to the University of California in San Diego, Point Loma Nazarene College, and San Diego State University. I depended on, tried the patience of, and am especially grateful to personal friends and colleagues in two fine universities: Indiana University-Purdue University at Indianapolis and the University of San Diego.

To these many librarians and colleagues I owe much of the value of this work. A special note of gratitude is due the editor of the series, Jim Rettig, who offered constant encouragement and fine judgment, and who displayed patience above and beyond the call of dutiful editorship and friendship. I wish I could find someone on whom to lay blame for the errors and omissions sure to be found in this book but I cannot—I made them all myself.

My family will profoundly understand the words of James H. Evans who, in the preface of *Black Theology* (see 395), thanked his family "for enduring many months of barely audible muttering, one of the side effects of this kind of work." My wife, Paulette, and our children, Brendan and Eliane, endured not months but years of this, along with too many foreshortened vacations. To these three kind and loving persons, this work is dedicated.

Part I

The Reference Literature of Judaism and Christianity

1
Encyclopedias and Dictionaries

Because there is often confusion in the use of the words *encyclopedia* and *dictionary*, I have adopted a stringent, if arbitrary, practice in grouping the works in this chapter: all single-volume works are considered dictionaries and all multivolume sets are encyclopedias, regardless of the word used in the title.

I. General Encyclopedias on Judaism and Christianity

1. Cousins, Ewert, general ed. **World Spirituality: An Encyclopedic History of the Religious Quest.** 25 volumes projected. New York, Crossroad, 1985- .
    Relevant volumes published:
    1.1. Green, Arthur, ed. **Jewish Spirituality I: From the Bible Through the Middle Ages.** New York, Crossroad, 1985. 450p. index. (World Spirituality Series, vol. 13). LC 85-11287. ISBN 0-8245-0762-2.

    1.2. Green, Arthur, ed. **Jewish Spirituality II: From the Sixteenth-century Revival to the Present.** New York, Crossroad, 1987. 447p. index. (World Spirituality Series, vol. 14). LC 85-11287. ISBN 0-8245-0763-0.

    1.3. McGinn, Bernard, and John Meyendorff, eds. **Christian Spirituality I: Origins to the Twelfth Century.** New York, Crossroad, 1985. 502p. indexes. (World Spirituality Series, vol. 16). LC 85-7692. ISBN 0-8245-0681-2.

    1.4. Raitt, Jill, ed. **Christian Spirituality II: High Middle Ages and Reformation.** New York, Crossroad, 1987. 479p. indexes. (World Spirituality Series, vol. 17). LC 86-29212. ISBN 0-8245-0765-7.
    Twenty-five single-theme volumes are projected for this series, which will cover the entire field of human spirituality, including Asian, Amerindian, African, Hindu, Buddhist, Taoist, Confucian, Jewish, Islamic, Christian, and modern spiritualities. The board of editors is made up of outstanding contemporary scholars of religion, including many who collaborated on *The Encyclopedia of Religion* (see 2). The first volume on Christian spirituality, edited by McGinn and Meyendorff, contains thirty essays, each fifteen to twenty-five pages long, written by scholars of spirituality like Basil Pennington and Robert M. Grant. These volumes give witness to strong contemporary interest in spirituality, and will provide fine accompaniment to the Paulist Press series The Classics of Western Spirituality (Mahwah, NJ, 1978-) and *The Westminster Dictionary of Christian Spirituality* (see 130).

2. Eliade, Mircea, ed.-in-chief. **The Encyclopedia of Religion.** New York, Macmillan, 1987. 16 vols. index. LC 86-5432. ISBN 0-02-909480-1. Index volume (1987): ISBN 0-02-909890-4.

Seven years went into the making of this new encyclopedia, which contains 2,750 articles in its 16 volumes and 8,000 pages. It begs comparison with Hastings's *Encyclopaedia of Religion and Ethics* (see 5), produced in the first quarter of this century, and the Macmillan editors expect it to hold preeminent place among religion encyclopedias for the next half century. In the foreword, Joseph Kitigawa notes that Hastings concentrated on the theoretical aspect of religion, while this new effort includes also the practical and the sociological.

The scope is all-encompassing: "a system of articles on important ideas, beliefs, rituals, myths, symbols and persons that have played a role in the universal history of religions from Paleolithic times to the present day" (preface).

The international list of contributors is impressive. Mircea Eliade, the editor-in-chief, was one of the most erudite scholars on the history of religions this century has produced. He died in 1986, after writing the preface, and it is fitting that this encyclopedia is his monument. It will go far in introducing the advances in the knowledge of religions to a wide range of readers and students. Martin Marty (see 251), the prolific interpreter of the American religious experience, wrote the fifteen-page entry on Protestantism. The Roman Catholics Karl Rahner (see 121-123) and Yves Congar contributed "Vatican II" and "Christian Theology," respectively. Richard McBrien (see 156) wrote "Roman Catholicism," and Charles E. Curran, who has been relieved of all teaching responsibilities at Catholic University of America because of Vatican censure, wrote "Christian Ethics" (see also 98).

Although this is indeed an encyclopedia of all religions, including strong treatments of such world religions as Buddhism and Hinduism, and newer or often-overlooked movements such as the Unification Church, Voodooism, and Arctic religions, the coverage of Christianity and Judaism is especially good and up to date. It includes twelve subdivisions for "Christianity," eight for "Judaism," and four for "Christianity and Judaism." There are articles on major figures in both traditions: Moses, Miriam, Joshua, Jesus, Mary; and on scholars: Origen, Augustine of Hippo, Maimonides, Thomas Aquinas. There are also treatments of methodologies for understanding religious experience: structuralism, hermeneutics. "Anti-semitism" merits extensive treatment. "Holocaust" is divided in two: history and Jewish theological responses. Unfortunately, there is no mention of the growing Christian theological responses.

Excellent bibliographies, in list or narrative form, are appended to each article, and often have entries from the major scholarly languages. Frequently, the author of the article wrote a well-received monograph on the same subject.

Entries, arranged alphabetically, are broad in scope, and are often composite, that is, subdivided into articles. Thus, "Demons" is divided into an overview — which covers demonology in tribal cultures, Hinduism, Buddhism, Judaism, Christianity, and Islam — and psychological perspectives. Although the word stock is global, only the Latin alphabet is used, following the transliteration and romanization schemes of the Library of Congress where possible. The Gregorian calendar is used for all dates, which are given according to the common era (CE and BCE), except where a specific dating system has religious significance.

The superlatives are many and the drawbacks few, but they are to be found. An hour's reading usually reveals a typographic error. The fifty maps are clear in black-and-white. The absence of pictures (there are very few line drawings) is a major disappointment: "Icons," for example, has not a single picture. The integration of photographs with text in the *New Catholic Encyclopedia* (see 23) and the *Encyclopaedia Judaica* (see 25) is excellent, and it is sad that Macmillan did not pursue a like format—religion begs for the representative. Finally, strong as this encyclopedia is, it seems to lack the force of erudition that characterized the earlier Hastings work.

The index volume was published in 1987, a year after the main volumes. In addition to the full subject index, it contains a list of contributors, citing their articles; a list of the entries; a very useful synoptic outline of the contents, that is, a broad subject index (on Judaism, for example, one can find all the major articles, the supporting articles, and the biographical articles); and twelve pages of corrections covering each volume.

3. Hastings, James, ed. **Dictionary of Christ and the Gospels.** New York, Charles Scribner's Sons, 1906-08. 2 vols. indexes. LC 06-44352. Reprinted: Grand Rapids, MI, Baker Book House, 1973.

Hastings planned this and the subsequent *Dictionary of the Apostolic Church* (see 4) as supplemental to his *Dictionary of the Bible* (see 586). He meant to take the best scholarship of the age and make it available to preachers; indeed, he noted that most of the contributors were themselves preachers. There are indexes of subjects and of scripture, and there are lengthy bibliographies, mostly of works in English. The scholarship is dated, but Hastings reflects an age of theological giants when such subjects as the comparison of the birth of Jesus to the birth of Buddha were debated in lively manner.

4. Hastings, James, ed. **Dictionary of the Apostolic Church.** New York, Charles Scribner's Sons, 1919. 2 vols. index. LC 16-15591. Reprinted: Grand Rapids, MI, Baker Book House, 1973.

This British work followed Hastings's *Dictionary of Christ and the Gospels* (see 3) to complete coverage of the New Testament through the end of the first century CE. An ecumenical list of contributors included at least one Roman Catholic, Pierre Batiffol, but the editor was unable to transcend his times in all areas—the article "Woman" was written by a male, Henry Wheeler Robinson. There is a thorough overview of early twentieth-century scholarship: there are twenty pages on Paul and thirty-eight on the "Resurrection of Christ." There are indexes of subjects and of scripture texts. Bibliographies contain German and French entries, showing the influence of continental theology on Britain.

5. Hastings, James, ed. **Encyclopaedia of Religion and Ethics.** New York, Charles Scribner's Sons, 1908-27. 13 vols. index. LC 08-35833. Reprinted: London, T. & T. Clark, 1979-81. ISBN 0-567-06514-6.

This great work, like McClintock and Strong (see 9) before it and Eliade (see 2) after it, was produced in order to systematize and make available to the general, educated, reading public a prodigious body of new religious knowledge—in this case, developed in the last decades of the nineteenth century and the first decade of the twentieth. Hastings sought to include religions and ethics in their most comprehensive meaning: every religion, every ethical practice, theology, philosophy, and the relevant portions of anthropology, mythology, folklore, biology, psychology, economics, and sociology. The contributors were among the finest minds of the time: the psychologist James Mark Baldwin, the New Testament scholar Wilhelm Bousset, and the Greek scholar John Burnet, just to concentrate on one letter of the alphabet.

The entries are comprehensive and learned; subjects are often traced through many religions. "Adultery" is given fifteen pages of double-column fine print, subdivided into primitive and savage peoples, Buddhist, Egyptian, Greek, Hindu, Jewish, Muslim, Christian, Parsi, Roman, and Semitic treatments, each over a page long. Biographies are for the most part subsumed under movements, e.g., "Origen—see Alexandrian Theology."

There is very thorough treatment of Jewish and Christian topics. The Christian German biblical scholar Hermann Strack wrote "Anti-semitism," reviewing nineteenth-century European bigotry and refuting nine anti-semitic theses.

Some few line drawings and photographic plates were included in the first volume but not continued in the series, a distinct loss.

The immense amount of accurate historical detail in this work will never be replaced. While Eliade (see 2) updates this information and adds vast new perspectives, the two works should remain side by side.

6. Jackson, Samuel Macauley, ed.-in-chief. **The New Schaff-Herzog Encyclopedia of Religious Knowledge, Embracing Biblical, Historical, Doctrinal, and Practical Theology and Biblical, Theological, and Ecclesiastical Biography from the Earliest Times to the Present Day, based on the Third Edition of the Realencyklopadie Founded by J. J. Herzog and Edited by Albert Hauck.** New York, Funk & Wagnalls, 1908-14. 13 vols. index. LC 08-20152. Reprint: Grand Rapids, MI, Baker Book House, 1977. 15 vols. ISBN 0-8010-7947-0. Reprint includes Loetscher (see 8).

This is an encyclopedia with a noble lineage, as it is based on the *Real Encyklopädie für protestantische Theologie und Kirche*, originally edited by Johann Jakob Herzog and completed by Albert Hauck. The American edition follows the German subject headings, but the articles are condensed and updated, often by the original German contributor. Some new subjects, especially biographies, have been added by English-speaking scholars, where German coverage was lacking. The bibliographies are updated and broadened. Because of its close ties with the original, it can be regarded as a compendium of nineteenth-century German Protestant thinking, which, especially in the areas of church history, biblical studies, and theology, was one of the great creative periods of Christian intellectual history. For the first half of this century, this encyclopedia was definitive, and it is still invaluable as a historical reference tool.

Although its subject matter is "religious knowledge," implying broad coverage, the encyclopedia is informed by a Christian perspective. There are no articles on "Jews" or "Judaism," for example (though there is a cross reference to "Israel, History of"), but there is one on "Jews, Missions to the." There is a strong attempt at ecumenicity within Christianity; one of the best American Roman Catholic scholars of the period, James F. Driscoll, did editorial work and articles for the encyclopedia. Volume 13 contains a complete index, a bibliography bringing subjects down to 1914, and a conspectus of contributors and their articles. Loetscher (see 8) updates this pre-World War I work.

7. Lippy, Charles H., and Peter W. Williams, eds. **Encyclopedia of the American Religious Experience.** New York, Scribner's, 1988. 3 vols. index. LC 87-4781. ISBN 0-684-18062-6.

The whole of the North American continent falls within the purview of this work, though there is special emphasis on the United States. Essays cover virtually every aspect of United States religious history, including Native American, Asian, and Middle Eastern religions. Some 100 scholars from a broad range of academic disciplines, and including Mexicans and Canadians, contribute 105 topical and thematic essays averaging 17 pages and grouped in 9 areas: approaches to religion in America; contexts and backgrounds; Jewish and Christian traditions; religions outside the Jewish and Christian traditions; movements in American religions; American religious thought and literature; liturgy, worship, and the arts; religion and the political and social order; and the dissemination of American religion. Each essay is followed by an annotated bibliography. Cross references abound, and an extensive index of subjects, persons, publications, places, and events provides unified access to the whole. This thorough and readable work pulls together an immense body of knowledge of the American religious past and present, and will long be the authoritative compilation.

8.   Loetscher, Lefferts A., ed. **Twentieth Century Encyclopedia of Religious Knowledge.** Grand Rapids, MI, Baker Book House, 1955. 2 vols. LC 55-9824. Reprinted with Jackson (see 6).

This supplement to *The New Schaff-Herzog Encyclopedia of Religious Knowledge* (see 6) was put together by a large group of outstanding English-speaking religious scholars of the 1950s, mostly Protestants, but with a smattering of Catholics and Jews. The articles are short, but very well written, and include extensive bibliographic materials. It is reflective of its day: there is, for example, no article on the Holocaust, and the article on "Judaism, recent," written by a Jewish scholar, concentrates on the effects of the pogroms in turn-of-the-century Russia, without mentioning the later Nazi persecutions. In spite of the all-embracing title, this remains basically an encyclopedia —a very good one— of western Christianity.

9.   McClintock, John, and James Strong, eds. **Cyclopaedia of Biblical, Theological and Ecclesiastical Literature.** New York, Harper and Brothers, 1867-81. 12 vols. Reprint: Grand Rapids, MI, Baker Book House, 1981. LC 68-56007. ISBN 0-8010-6123-7.

This encyclopedia, the first of its kind in English, was produced as a result of a mid-nineteenth-century information explosion in biblical and historical religious studies. As such, it is the grandparent of Hastings (see 5) and Eliade (see 2). The contributors—their number was small—were immensely learned. Detailed bibliographies are appended to each article. There is no index to the set; at the end of each volume there is a list of articles contained in that volume. The abundant woodcuts are especially good; one can often understand a detailed point better from such a device than from a photograph. The scholarship is now very dated, but, from paging through these volumes, one can grasp the broad foundations on which the twentieth-century scientific study of religion has been based.

10.   Meagher, Paul Kevin, Thomas C. O'Brien, and Consuelo Maria Aherne, eds. **Encyclopedic Dictionary of Religion.** Washington, DC, Corpus Publications, 1979. 3 vols. LC 78-62029. ISBN 0-9602572-3-3.

This work was begun by the editorial staff of the *New Catholic Encyclopedia* (see 23) after it finished that work in 1966. In 1973, this group handed eleven thousand entries over to the Roman Catholic Sisters of Saint Joseph of Philadelphia, who completed the work, doubling the tally of entries. In its final form, it is thus the product of a large group of female scholars: fifty-six sisters are listed as "Summer Dictionary Staff." There is no scope note, but the reader soon learns that this is not an encyclopedic dictionary of religion in general, but rather of Christianity in particular, and more particularly of Roman Catholicism. Other religions are treated insofar as they impact Christianity. Thus, the article on Judaism is written by a priest/biblical scholar and is historical in nature, taking little account of Judaism as a major, contemporary, living world religion. This dictionary is the product of the post-Vatican II church—hence its ecumenical list of contributors—but its greatest strength lies in its definitions and explanations of minute and detailed aspects of Christian history, culture, liturgy, art, literature, etc. There are eleven pages of abbreviations of scholarly apparatus. The articles are signed, but there is no index by author.

11. Menachery, George, ed. **The St. Thomas Christian Encyclopaedia of India.** Trichur-1, India, The St. Thomas Christian Encyclopaedia of India, 1973-82. 2 vols. LC 73-905568.

Though this is basically a Roman Catholic work, the editors took an ecumenical approach, describing all Christian denominations in India, including Quakers, Mennonites, Pentecostals, the Salvation Army, Orthodox, and evangelicals. Christianity in the various regions of India receives coverage, as does Christianity in Pakistan. There are articles on each Catholic ecclesiastical division. Pictures, both black-and-white and color, though not of high quality, are spread throughout the text. An atlas section gathers together historical, linguistic, religious, and physical relief maps. The second volume is divided into two alphabets, major and minor articles, and focuses on the history of the Christianization of India. The evangelization by St. Thomas the Apostle, the earliest communities, the Syrian Orthodox Church, and the Malabar Christians receive extensive treatment. Although the organization of this extensive work is sometimes confusing, and the paper and pictorial quality are less than one could wish, there is no equivalent reference book offering such detailed treatment of Christianity in this large country.

12. Piepkorn, Arthur Carl, and John H. Tietjen. **Profiles in Belief: The Religious Bodies of the United States and Canada.** New York, Harper & Row, 1977-79. 4 vols. LC 76-9971. Vol. I: ISBN 0-06-066580-7. Vol. II: ISBN 0-06-066582-3. Vols. III & IV: ISBN 0-06-066581-5/set.

The first volume covers the Catholic and Orthodox traditions; the second, the main Protestant denominations; the third, the Holiness and Pentecostal movements; and the last, the evangelical, fundamentalist, and other Christian bodies. Piepkorn originally projected seven volumes, but died with only the first complete. Tietjen edited Piepkorn's massive notes for the next three volumes. The series contains extensive, scholarly essays on each religion, covering history, polity, worship, creed and doctrines, divisions, world impact, ecumenical relations, and statistics. Footnotes abound, and there are generous bibliographies. Although there is some disagreement over Piepkorn's understanding of the historical genesis of some denominations, the value of this reference work cannot be overstated. It is to be hoped that someone will finish the series, and cover Judaism and other religious traditions in North America in Piepkorn's thorough fashion, and thus supplement Melton (see 41) and Shulman (see 47).

II. Encyclopedias on Specific Religions

13. Bender, Harold S., and C. Henry Smith, eds. **The Mennonite Encyclopedia: A Comprehensive Reference Work on the Anabaptist-Mennonite Movement.** Scottdale, PA, Herald Press, 1955-59. 4 vols. LC 55-4563. ISBN 0-8361-1018-8.

In their attempt to provide "exhaustive coverage in all fields of Anabaptist-Mennonite history, theology, ethics and life," the editors produced an immense amount of historical and bibliographic coverage of this religious movement, in signed, scholarly articles. Biographies are abundant; the larger families in the movement are covered. There are entries for all known existing and extinct congregations, institutions, organizations, and publications in all countries. Two thousand known martyrs are included. For European information, the editors leaned heavily on the *Mennonitisches Lexikon* by C. Hege and C. Wolff (1913-), but the material on North and South America is all new. The work in its totality is inward-looking; the movement is rarely related to other religions or thought systems except where persecution is mentioned, as in the article on the Jesuits. Luther is covered, but not the Lutheran Church. Coverage of contemporary history is weak; an article on "Concentration camps" includes a passing reference to "the mass slaughter of Jews and detention of political prisoners and enemies of the [Nazi] regime," but states further that no German Mennonites were detained, although two Dutch Mennonites died in the camps.

14. Bodensieck, Julius. **The Encyclopedia of the Lutheran Church.** Minneapolis, MN, Augsburg, 1965. 3 vols. LC 64-21500.

The detailed, scholarly articles, signed by the outstanding Lutheran scholars of the 1960s, treat the Bible, doctrine, ethics, church history, Lutheranism on various continents, education, art, music, ecumenism, and famous Lutherans deceased by the time of publication. Some photos and prints are included. There is a good system of cross-references, but no index. Bibliographies are appended to some articles. There is occasional straying from matters Lutheran, as in the article on the French novelist Georges Bernanos. This authoritative source reflects one of the great theological and pastoral traditions of modern Christianity.

15. Brooks, Melvin R. **L. D. S. Reference Encyclopedia.** Salt Lake City, UT, Bookcraft, 1960-65. 2 vols. LC 60-44463.

Each volume is a complete alphabet; the second is actually a supplement. Brooks offers broad coverage of ecclesiastical history, biography, doctrine, and geography, drawing extensively from the holy books of the Latter Day Saints: the Bible, the *Book of Mormon*, the *Doctrine and Covenants*, and *Pearl of Great Price*. In addition to describing things Mormon, he adds information about non-Mormon churches, which is generally sympathetic if often not well researched. His sources are older and less-than-accurate reference books; for example, he includes an uncritical paragraph on Joanna the Popess, the female who is said to have occupied the papal throne in the Middle Ages, considered a legend by all modern, serious historians. There are few reference books on this largest of indigenous American churches; this work needs revising and updating to help fill the void.

16. Cathcart, William, ed. **The Baptist Encyclopaedia: A Dictionary of the Doctrines, Ordinances, Usages, Confessions of Faith, Sufferings, Labors, and Successes, and of the General History of the Baptist Denomination in All Lands with Numerous Biographical Sketches of Distinguished American and Foreign Baptists, and a Supplement.** Philadelphia, PA, Louis H. Everts, 1881. 2 vols. 1,324p. LC 41-30966.

16.1. Hayward, Elizabeth, comp. **Index to Names in "The Baptist Encyclopaedia."** Chester, PA, American Baptist Historical Society, 1951. 58p.

The vast majority of Cathcart's entries are biographies of "distinguished Baptists everywhere, living and dead," but he also includes events in Baptist history, confessions of faith, doctrines, practices, usages "peculiar to Baptists," principles, institutions, monuments, and achievements. Some five hundred pen sketches, principally of biographees, but also of buildings, are found throughout the work. A statistical table by state between 1770 and 1880 accounts for churches, ministers, and members.

17. Cox, Norman Wade, ed. **Encyclopedia of Southern Baptists.** Nashville, TN, Broadman Press, 1958. 2 vols. LC 58-5417. ISBN 0-8054-6501-4

17.1. Woolley, Davis Collier, ed. **Supplement.** Vol. 3., 1971. ISBN 0-8054-6511-1.

17.2. May, Lynn E. **Supplement.** Vol. 4., 1982. ISBN 0-8054-6556-1. Index to vols. 1-4, 1982. ISBN 0-8054-6562-6.

The first two volumes contain over four thousand articles by some nine hundred contributors, and were projected to assist Southern Baptists in their self-understanding as a group. There are pictures, bibliographies, and abundant cross-references. There is a particular richness in biographical information about Baptists from colonial times to the 1950s. State conventions, organizations, associations, institutions, publications, and agencies are covered, with a special emphasis on history. About one-fifth of the material is said to deal with general background: the history of Christianity, other denominations, other Baptist bodies, and the Bible. There is a very short article on "Judaism" and one on "Jews, home missions to." The article on Roman Catholicism offers a fair Protestant interpretation, stressing, in 1956, its "increasing isolation" (Pope John XXIII agreed). The supplements add over 2,400 articles, covering supplemental and omitted materials and new developments.

18. Daniel-Rops, Henri, ed. **The Twentieth Century Encyclopedia of Catholicism.** New York, Hawthorn Books, 1958-71. 150 vols. indexes. LC 58-14327.

Individual volumes, many translated from French, not published in sequence, offer monographic coverage of a wide variety of Catholic doctrines, as well as the Roman church's relation to art, science, literature, and other religions. As might be expected, the monographs are uneven both in quality and outlook. Earlier volumes reflect the liberal pre-Vatican II attitudes of French and American Catholics; later volumes are influenced by the developments during and subsequent to the Vatican II council. The *New Catholic Encyclopedia* (see 23) offers more consistent coverage.

19. Durnbaugh, Donald F., ed. **The Brethren Encyclopedia.** Philadelphia, PA, and Oak Park, IL, Brethren Encyclopedia, 1983-84. 3 vols. LC 84-2003. ISBN 0-936693-00-2.

The Brethren movement began at Schwarzenau/Eder in Germany, in 1708, and subsequently split into five major groups. All five contributed to this truly fine encyclopedia, which covers individual congregations, documents, institutions, periodicals, important writings, related religious movements, and historic sites and anecdotes of the Brethren. It is especially strong on biographies of leaders and major families. There is much attention to the thorough bibliographies which are appended to each article. The first two volumes hold the articles; the third contains maps, a chronology, statistics, lists of divisions, congregations, meetings, and ordained ministers, and a 254-page bibliography. The whole is a monument of Brethren scholarship, and could well serve as a model for similar reference works on other religions. The introduction gives a detailed overview of the genesis of the encyclopedia; its design; editorial processes; the construction of its articles, biographies, and bibliographies; and its use of cross-references and illustrations. In short, it is a blueprint for other works.

20. Harmon, Nolan B., general ed. **The Encyclopedia of World Methodism**, rev. ed. Nashville, TN, Abingdon Press, 1974. 2 vols. index. LC 76-312986. ISBN 0-687-11784-4.

This encyclopedia offers an enormous amount of detailed information on Methodist sites and historic shrines, educational and charitable institutions, hospitals, local churches of over two thousand members, and doctrine. There are multitudinous biographies of prominent figures in church organization. Excluded are those distinguished in fields outside the church – a distinct weakness, because Methodists have been United States presidents, members of Congress, and leaders in every field of endeavor. Appendixes list bishops, conference presidents, colleges and universities and their presidents, hospitals and homes, publishing agents, and membership statistics, and offer maps of United States conferences and a chronology of Methodism from the seventeenth century on. Photos of persons and institutions abound. Bibliographies are appended to some articles, but there are also thirty-five pages of bibliography in the second volume. The encyclopedia is inward-looking: while there is much biographical and historical material about the church, there is little about its immense influence on the world or its interaction with other religions, such as the *New Catholic Encyclopedia* (see 23) presents for Roman Catholicism. Such additional material may have doubled size and costs, but who would doubt the worth of the undertaking for this great branch of Christianity? Articles on doctrine tend to be short: two pages each for "Atonement" and "Trinity." There is no entry for "incarnation" and none for "Jesus," even in the index.

21. Herbermann, Charles George et al., eds. **The Catholic Encyclopedia. An International Work of Reference on the Constitution, Doctrine, Discipline, and History of the Catholic Church.** New York, The Encyclopedia Press, 1905-14. 16 vols. index. LC 07-11606.

    21.1.   Pace, Edward A., ed. **Supplement.** Vol. 17. New York, The Encyclopedia Press, 1922. LC 30-23167.

    21.2.   Hopkins, Vincent D., ed. **Supplement II.** Vol. 18, in 2 looseleaf sections. New York, Gilmary Society, 1950-58.

These densely packed volumes reflect the state of Roman Catholic scholarship in the first decade of this century. The encyclopedia attempts to go beyond being a church encyclopedia and "to chronicle what Catholic artists, educators, poets, scientists, and 'men of action' have achieved." It is a polemical and apologetic work, answering the charge that "Catholic principles are an obstacle to scientific research," and providing answers to "common misconceptions and serious errors" on Catholic subjects. A sense of history and worldwide geography prevails; its contributors came from around the world. It retains current value for its detailed coverage of historical topics, some of which was dropped by the *New Catholic Encyclopedia* (see 23). It is reflective of its age, however: a print of a river in Abyssinia shows a white missionary sitting on a raft being pushed by swimming natives. An exhaustive article on Luther emphasizes his personal, negative characteristics, but says little of his theology. The irenic Melanchthon merits a more sympathetic entry. The coverage of biblical criticism reflects the polemics of the age; the historical school is taken seriously, but Harnack, the great German Protestant, is attacked. The article on "Zionists" is sympathetic, but not so that on "Jews and Judaism."

In the decade when this was being written, the American Catholic church was recovering from a wrenching attack from Rome on its supposed support of the Modernist heresy, under the local title of "Americanism." Accordingly, the editors put aside the subject from the "A" volume and covered it under "Testem benevolentiae," Pope Leo XIII's letter of condemnation. By the time the "T" volume was prepared, many of the principals in the struggle had died, and an objective account could be attempted. Under pressure from readers of the early volumes, the editors added a full index.

22. Landman, Isaac, ed. **The Universal Jewish Encyclopedia.** New York, The Universal Jewish Encyclopedia, 1939-43. 10 vols. LC 40-5070. Reprint: New York, Ktav Publishing House, 1969. 10 vols. LC 77-86963.

    22.1.   Cohen, Simon D. **The Universal Jewish Encyclopedia: A Reading Guide and Index.** New York, The Universal Jewish Encyclopedia, 1948.

Growing anti-semitism in Europe and in the United States following World War I led to the formation of the National Conference of Christians and Jews. This encyclopedia was undertaken with a like sentiment in the minds of the founders of that organization: if people, especially Christians, could be brought to understand what Judaism is, there would be less persecution. Accordingly, there is an emphasis on the concerns of English-speaking Jews, as well as coverage of archaeology, art, Bible, ethics, history, Jewish literature, liturgy, philosophy, rabbinics, social institutions, and theology.

The history of the Holocaust is often divided into three stages: legal persecution in Germany from 1933 to 1939, ghettoization in 1939 and 1940 throughout occupied Europe, and extermination between 1941 and 1945. The publication dates of this work span all three periods, and bear witness to what was known in the Allied world prior to the collapse of the Nazis. A 69-page article entitled "Anti-Semitism" (hence published in the earliest volume) treats extensively the first phase in Germany, as well as anti-Jewish feeling in each modern European country, noting propaganda efforts launched outside of Germany by the Nazis. A 43-page article on "Germany" details extreme persecutions. By the time the authors wrote "Ukraine," they could report Eichmann's authority in the region in 1941, the machine-gunning of Jews there, and the wholesale deportation of Western European Jews to the Ukraine in September-October 1942, although there is nothing about the mass starvation imposed there by Stalin in the early 1930s. Photographs, smuggled to Allied countries, give some of the earliest visual evidence of the Holocaust.

In all, there are ten thousand signed articles, many accompanied by photographs and pictures. Bibliographies are extensive. The index, first published in 1944 as *The Seven Branched Light*, is not complete; its one hundred reading outlines lead to half the articles in the work. Twenty-three of the outlines are for biographical articles in particular fields.

In keeping with the ecumenical foundations of the work, Christian topics are well covered. There are articles on "Jesus of Nazareth" and "Jesus in Rabbinical Literature," as well as treatment of New Testament leaders, church fathers, popes, sects, doctrines, rites, and institutions.

This work is valuable for its historical articles, but is generally not credited with the same scholarly weight as the earlier *The Jewish Encyclopedia*, edited by Singer (see 26), or the later *Encyclopaedia Judaica*, edited by Roth (see 25).

23. McDonald, William J., ed.-in-chief. **New Catholic Encyclopedia.** New York, McGraw-Hill, 1967. 15 vols. index. LC 66-22292.

    23.1   Vol. 16: **Supplement 1967-1974.** Washington, DC; New York, Publishers Guild/ McGraw-Hill, 1974.

    23.2   Vol. 17: **Supplement: Change in the Church.** Washington, DC; New York, Publishers Guild/McGraw-Hill, 1979. ISBN 0-07-010235-X.

In the late 1950s, a revision of *The Catholic Encyclopedia* (see 21) was contemplated, but then cancelled, because changes in the Roman Catholic Church in particular and the world in general were so profound that it was felt the material in the early twentieth-century work could not be reworked in satisfactory fashion. Instead, this large and completely new encyclopedia was produced with seventeen thousand signed articles by forty-eight hundred scholars. Its scope is broad indeed, covering the doctrines, organization, and history of the church from the apostolic age through Vatican II. New developments in the study of scripture, theology, and patrology are treated extensively. Its coverage of church history is especially strong, though for some eras treatment in *The Catholic Encyclopedia* (see 21) is more lengthy. Each country and each archdiocese in the world is given an article although an American bias is evident: each diocese in the United

States receives treatment, and special attention is given to Latin America. Biographies of living people are excluded, except for the then-reigning pope, Paul VI (d. 1978).

Movements that have affected Catholicism are studied. There is fair treatment of other religions, especially Protestantism and Judaism, and of worship as a universal phenomenon, mythology, and comparative religion. Philosophy is amply covered, with an emphasis on Thomism. Psychology and psychiatry and the social sciences are studied, reflecting their growth since 1900. Education, so important to the American Catholic experience, is here. Art and music are broadly covered, not only as addenda to liturgies.

There are some three hundred maps and seventy-five hundred illustrations. There is an extensive cross-reference system, and an analytic index with 350,000 entries. Bibliographies are extensive, authoritative, and international in scope.

This encyclopedia seems also to be meant to serve as a general encyclopedia in Catholic schools, for there are treatments of nuclear physics, chemistry, and biology. Although there are ethical aspects to these sciences, there is little that is specifically Catholic in such articles as "Atmosphere, Physics of."

Throughout, there is an attitude of openness to human experience and history, coupled with the high scholarship evident in the older *Catholic Encyclopedia*. If openness has led to inclusion of possibly peripheral topics, this is a lesser weakness than its opposite. It should also be noted that there is little attempt to claim for Catholicism a lead in every field (a Catholic physics, a Catholic American literature), an annoying peccadillo of other works.

Some composite articles are monographic in length. The 10-part treatment of "Jesus Christ" would constitute a 150-page book. The Bible receives a like examination.

This is the most extensive Christian encyclopedia produced for readers of English so far in this century. Produced during and immediately after Vatican II, it can now be considered dated, because of the extraordinary developments in Catholicism since that Council. The supplement of 1974 contains 440 articles by 250 scholars, and attends to such topics as the ecumenical movement and pentecostalism, which received strong impulsion from the Council. The second supplement brings coverage to the beginning of the pontificate of Pope John Paul II, and studies change in two areas: the inner life of the church and the church's outreach, its ministry of justice and peace. An eighteenth volume, supplementing the set for the years 1978-88, was due in late 1989.

24. Patai, Raphael, ed. **Encyclopedia of Zionism and Israel.** New York, Herzl Press/McGraw-Hill, 1971. 2 vols. LC 68-55271. ISBN 0-0707-9635-1.

This extensive historical encyclopedia, with 3,000 articles by 285 contributors, covers events, decisions, congresses, and conferences. It includes statistics and much biographical material. There are ample cross-references, but no index. Individual entries lack bibliographies, but there is a six-page bibliographic appendix listing books only. The coverage of Zionism includes its history, ideologies, manifestation in major countries of the world, party formation, institutions, organizations, and men and women. There are many black-and-white photographs. Coverage of the land that now constitutes Israel begins in the middle of the nineteenth century. For up-to-date information on Israel, one must look elsewhere, but this encyclopedia is quite valuable for its presentation of history.

25. Roth, Cecil, and Geoffrey Wigoder, eds.-in-chief. **Encyclopaedia Judaica.** New York, Macmillan, 1972. 16 vols. index. LC 72-90254.

This is the major Jewish reference work in English for the latter half of this century. On its first page, its lineage is traced back to Singer (see 26) and Landman (see 22) as well as to

Hebrew, German, and Russian encyclopedias. Indeed, a direct ancestor is the *Encyclopaedia Judaica*, in German, which was completed only to the letter "L" before the Holocaust overtook its editors. It was in part to complete this latter work, as well as to render into English some of the material in the *Encyclopaedia Hebraica*, that the editors undertook this *Encyclopaedia Judaica*. In scope and depth, it stands beside the *New Catholic Encyclopedia* (see 23) and Eliade's *Encyclopedia of Religion* (see 2); in the English-language reference room, these are the three pillars of religious knowledge.

This encyclopedia takes into account the advances in Jewish studies in the twentieth century; the discoveries of ancient document collections, like the Dead Sea Scrolls and the Cairo Genizah; and new scientific perspectives, such as social and economic history, the history of Jews in Eastern Europe and in Moslem lands, Jewish art, and Jewish mysticism. An article simply entitled "History" offers a book-length historical overview of Judaism.

The Holocaust, Zionism, and the founding of the state of Israel receive much treatment. A good deal of original research went into the treatment of the Holocaust; this is the first major reference work to attempt an in-depth approach. A lengthy article is devoted to it, as well as many related articles such as "Holocaust and the Christian Churches" and "Holocaust, Rescue from." When countries, cities, villages, and persons are treated, any impact of the Holocaust on them is explained. For example, out of ten pages given to "Hungary," four are taken up with the effects of the Holocaust.

Biographies, including those of the living, play a major role. In order not to leave important persons out of the work, "capsule entries" are used. These are lists of prominent names at the end of subject entries, and are most useful for leading to further biographical research.

Bible books and topics receive lengthy articles, balanced between the traditional and modern critical approaches.

The entire encyclopedia, with twenty-five thousand entries, was written and edited during a five-year period so that, unlike many European works, it could be published at one time. Columns rather than pages are numbered, and the index refers to these column numbers. The index, with 200,000 entries, is placed in the first volume to emphasize its importance. Black-and-white illustrations appear on almost every page, and there are some color plates. In addition there are maps, charts, and diagrams. In addition to the index, the first volume contains supplementary lists: a hundred-year Jewish calendar (1920-2020 CE), a genealogical chart of Hassidism, a gazetteer for Israel, Hebrew newspapers and periodicals, plates on pottery, and a list of synagogues. For regular updates, see the *Encyclopaedia Judaica Year Book* (205).

26.   Singer, Isidore, managing ed. **The Jewish Encyclopedia: A Descriptive Record of the History, Religion, Literature, and Customs of the Jewish People from the Earliest Times.** New York, Funk & Wagnalls, 1901-06. 12 vols. LC 01-9359. Reprinted: New York, Gordon Press, 1976. ISBN 0-8490-2101-4.

Several major encyclopedias listed in this bibliography were planned and written following periods of great growth in scientific religious knowledge. *The Jewish Encyclopedia*, on the other hand, pulled into a system areas of knowledge wherein there was much disparate work that had never been brought together in modern times. Although Jewish studies traces its roots to the 1820s, this encyclopedia in a real sense stands at the beginning of its renaissance rather than in midcourse.

For this work, the vast matter of Judaism and Jewish culture was divided into three areas: (1) history, including biography, sociology, and folklore; (2) literature, including the Bible, the Talmud, and rabbinical writings, as well as jurisprudence, philology, and bibliography; and (3) theology and philosophy. Historical coverage was included for communities, including quite small European towns; for larger regions; and for countries. Jews in America and Russia merit special interest, because they were neglected in other studies. So also is biography emphasized.

Because scientific biblical studies had not yet been integrated with traditional interpretative methods, biblical books and stories generally receive three-fold treatment: (1) the statements of the text itself; (2) rabbinical (Talmudic and Midrashic) commentary; and (3) higher criticism. The New Testament is covered as Hellenic literature (as it was written, after all, in part by Jews). There is full treatment of the Talmud and later rabbinical literature. The encyclopedia also covers points of Jewish doctrine and systems of thought, since theology and especially Jewish medieval philosophy have "never yet received systematic treatment at the hands of Jews."

Line drawings and pictures abundantly benefit the reader. Hebrew, Arabic, and Russian words are romanized. There are musical scores for songs and hymns. Extensive bibliographies, with many works in German and Hebrew, are included for every entry. The work lacks an index, not a minor shortfall given the immense detail in the articles and the sometimes problematic subject headings. There is no article on Argentina, for example; one must search instead for "Agricultural Colonies (Argentine Republic)."

III. General Dictionaries on Judaism and Christianity

27.   Barrett, David B., ed. **World Christian Encyclopedia: A Comparative Study of Churches and Religions in the Modern World A.D. 1900-2000.** New York, Oxford, 1982. 1, 010p. indexes. LC 82-199409. ISBN 0-19-572435-6.

It is hard to imagine that the scope note, "a comprehensive survey of all branches of global Christianity," is an understatement, but it is. Twelve years in the making, instead of the projected three, this unique encyclopedia identifies 20,800 denominations among 8,990 separately identified peoples speaking 7,010 languages in 223 countries. Such varied statistical counts are included that each individual Christian is counted "in some 760 distinct absolute numbers" in the work, which surveys most of the quantifiable aspects of Christianity. The statistics were provided by the denominations themselves; therefore, there must be errors due to differences in interpretation. Many statistics were undoubtedly obsolete before they were published. However, Barrett notes that a system of counterchecks was included in the databases to catch egregious errors. One must conclude from the sheer quantity of angles of measurement that a preponderance of the numbers are indeed correct, at least for the 1970s.

The encyclopedia is divided into fourteen sections: (1) the status of Christianity in the twentieth century; (2) a chronology of world evangelization; (3) the methodology in enumerating Christians; (4) an ethnological classification of the cultures of the world; (5) how evangelization is quantified; (6) a codebook for statistical tables; (7) a survey of Christianity in 223 countries; (8) global, continental, and confessional statistics; (9) a dictionary; (10) a bibliography; (11) a full-color atlas; (12) a who's-who; (13) a directory of organizations, listed under 76 topics; and (14) indexes. The work does not cover archaeology, philosophy, dogma, ethics, or liturgy.

The seventh section, the longest, with 642 pages, offers for each country secular data; data on religious adherents, including non-Christians; an overview of non-Christian religions; an overview of Christianity; its relationship with the state; interdenominational organizations; broadcasting; a bibliography; and much additional data.

This work must be considered at least the beginning of the search for any inquiry including quantitative information. Its authority and quality place it firmly among the top dozen titles in this bibliography.

28. Bishop, Peter, and Michael Darton. **The Encyclopedia of World Faiths.** New York, Facts on File, 1988. 352p. LC 88-118151. ISBN 0-8160-1860-X.

After an introduction on the nature of religion in general, Bishop and Darton offer the general reader some twenty-two pages on Judaism, and more extensive coverage of Christianity. The treatment of Christianity is broken into essays on its development through the eleventh century, the Church of the East, Roman Catholicism, the Reformation churches, and other Protestant churches and Christian-related movements. A conclusion, on religion in the modern world, also treats both Judaism and Christianity. The many photographs are well-chosen and related to the text, which is not always true of handbooks and encyclopedias for a general readership. Short thematic essays are interspersed throughout the work; for example, an eight-page essay on death and afterlife interrupts the chapter on the Reformation. The editors add an extensive glossary, which relates each word to its religious origin, and a short bibliography of English-language works, divided by religion. An index gives subject access to the whole.

29. Canney, Maurice A. **An Encyclopedia of Religions.** New York, E. P. Dutton, 1921. Reprinted: Detroit, MI, Gale, 1970. 397p. LC 75-123370. ISBN 0-8103-3856-4.

Canney's work is now very dated but more scholarly than Pike (see 44). A bibliography lists 250 authoritative works on religion, and bibliographic additions to the entries refer to these. There are no entries on the subdivisions of Christianity, (for example, Anglicanism, Catholicism, or Lutheranism), but many societies are entered, such as the Jesuits, and the Guild of St. Matthew. There are no biographies. This work is very good for smaller societies, organizations, movements, and the gods of lesser-known religions.

30. Crim, Keith, general ed. **Abingdon Dictionary of Living Religions.** Nashville, TN, Abingdon Press, 1981. 830p. LC 81-1465. ISBN 0-687-00409-8.

Crim offers scholarly and sensitive entries on the historical development, beliefs, and practices of living religions in the traditions of Buddhism, Christianity, Hinduism, Islam, and Judaism. There is extended treatment of each major tradition, with cross-references between articles of shorter scope. Brief bibliographies are added to most articles. Some short creeds are quoted in full. There are articles on cross-traditional topics such as "Ethics" and "Monasticism." A guide to key entries lists articles closely related by religion, so that one is led from "Judaism" to "Moses," "Calendar," "Synagogue," and so forth, making this an excellent introductory work.

31. Cross, Frank Leslie, and Elizabeth A. Livingstone, eds. **The Oxford Dictionary of the Christian Church**, 2d ed. New York, Oxford, 1974. 1,518p. LC 74-163871. ISBN 0-19-211545-6.

31.1. Livingstone, Elizabeth A., ed. **The Concise Oxford Dictionary of the Christian Church**, 2d ed. abridged. New York, Oxford, 1977. 570p. LC 77-30192. ISBN 0-19-211549-9.

In the first edition (1957), Cross produced for the generally educated reader an immense compendium of factual information about Christianity as a whole, with emphasis on mainline western churches, especially in the United Kingdom, and on the nineteenth and twentieth centuries. Treatment of subjects is primarily historical. After each entry there are extensive bibliographies. The Bible is sidestepped, though not entirely, because of the abundance of reference books available on it. The second edition, during the production of which Cross died and Livingstone took over, incorporates the changes within Roman Catholicism and the change of rites and governance within the Church of

England. The second edition contains a list of popes and antipopes and over six pages of scholarly abbreviations. First-rank scholars from the Church of England and from the Roman Catholic and Protestant traditions contributed, but the articles are unsigned. Look elsewhere for more detailed information on things American; nevertheless, among single-volume reference books on Christianity, this holds primacy of place.

For ready reference, Livingstone produced the concise version, based on the 1974 edition, with shortened articles and no bibliographies.

32. Douglas, James Dixon, general ed. **The New International Dictionary of the Christian Church**, rev. ed. Grand Rapids, MI, Zondervan, 1978. 1,074p. LC 74-8999. ISBN 0-310-23830-7.

This dictionary looks broadly and deeply at Christianity from a definite, if unannounced, conservative, English-speaking Protestant viewpoint. There is very good biographical coverage of Protestant history. Entries are signed, and ample bibliographies enhance many articles. Almost two hundred scholars contributed, "Christian writers from many lands and denominations"; a handful are women, none appear to be Roman Catholic or Orthodox, and few are from the Third World. Articles on Judaism and non-Christian religions are generally learned, but not completely sympathetic—it is not necessary to point out the "faults" in religious doctrines that have had myriads of intelligent followers over centuries, if not millenia. The Holocaust is mentioned in "Jews, Missions to the," but not in "Judaism," where influences such as the 1967 Israeli-Arab war do receive brief attention. The great sea-change in the Roman Catholic Church is ignored by an Irish Baptist who wrote the article on Vatican II. Given the confines of a single volume, this is an erudite presentation of the evangelical Protestant tradition, but Cross's *Oxford Dictionary of the Christian Church* (see 31) is preferred for impartiality.

33. Ferm, Vergilius, ed. **An Encyclopedia of Religion.** New York, Philosophical Library, 1945. 844p. Reprint: Westport, CT, Greenwood Press, 1976. LC 75-36508. ISBN 0-8371-8638-2.

Ferm assembled a list of contributors that, while predominantly Protestant, included Jews and Roman Catholics and attempted to cover the whole gamut of world religions. The entries, initialed, are short but scholarly in tone, and contain brief bibliographies. There is broad treatment of Judaism by Jewish scholars, and an article on "Antisemitism," but there is no hint of the Holocaust in this 1945 publication: the population of world Jewry is listed as 15,700,000. There are biographies, including some for figures who, like Freud, impacted religion. Now badly dated, this has been supplanted by such single-volume works as Crim (see 30), Brandon (see 94), and Hinnells (see 36).

34. Ferm, Virgilius. **A Protestant Dictionary.** New York, Philosophical Library, 1951. 283p. LC 51-14412.

Ferm intended this widely available dictionary for general readers, but the brief definitions are not simplistic. Biblical terms are omitted, as are biographies of the living (as of 1951, of course). One can detect an emphasis on the origin and development of Protestantism in the United States. There are full-page treatments of important topics, but, while there are excellent thumbnail sketches of American Protestant thinkers like Walter Rauschenbusch, one really ought to go to a more comprehensive work for information on Martin Luther or John Wesley. There are cross-references, but no bibliographies.

35. Hill, Samuel S. **Encyclopedia of Religion in the South.** Macon, GA, Mercer University, 1984. 875p. index. LC 84-8957. ISBN 0-86554-117-5.

In fact, this is an encyclopedia of Christianity and Judaism in the American South. It contains articles on the religious histories of sixteen states, denominations, doctrines and movements, persons, sacred places, events, subject areas such as music and architecture, and even special features like roadside signs. Two appendixes contain articles on the colonial period and the present, though these might easily have been integrated with the rest. Coverage is extensive: there are nine pages on "Jews in the South," as well as articles on "Jewish folklore," "Jewish press," etc. There is good coverage of black churches and the civil rights movement. Doctrinal themes important to the South, such as sin, salvation, and atonement, are covered. Although the coverage is uneven (for example, the article on the "Electronic Church" could have been more exhaustive), there is an enormous amount of very useful and up-to-date research in this geographically targeted work.

36. Hinnells, John R., ed. **The Facts on File Dictionary of Religions.** New York, Facts on File, 1984. 550p. indexes. LC 83-20834. ISBN 0-87196-862-2.

The underlying structure of this excellent work becomes evident when one examines either the extensive bibliography or the synoptic index. Twenty-nine scholars were enlisted to write entries on thirty subjects, some geographical (meso-American), some major religions (Christianity, Judaism, Jainism). The entries, longer than is usual in a dictionary, were then aranged alphabetically. By using the synoptic index, one can introduce oneself to an unfamiliar area, as well as track down those few subject headings that defy imagination, e.g., "North America (Jews in)." An index by subject and personal name is also provided, necessary because of the size of the definitions. There are clear line drawings and a section of eleven maps, the specific names of which appear in the index. There are abundant cross-references to related subject headings and to bibliographic citations. Although Hinnells cites the growing awareness of religions of the world as the reason for the book, Christianity receives the most entries and the longest bibliography. Judaism is given ample, if shorter, coverage. The focus is on living religions; one should look elsewhere for better treatment of, for example, Greek polytheism. The level of scholarship is high, as is the readability. This is not as detailed as Crim (see 30) or Brandon (see 94), but it is more up to date than the latter. Hinnells also edited a companion work, *A Handbook of Living Religions* (see 149).

37. Kauffman, Donald T. **The Dictionary of Religious Terms.** Westwood, NJ, Fleming H. Revell, 1967. 445p. LC 67-22570.

This dictionary attempts to cover all religions, and includes "significant religious terms, symbols, rites, faiths, movements, orders, sites, ideas and people." Nevertheless, there is a tilt toward Christianity in many entries. Definitions are short and sometimes incomplete or idiosyncratic. "Drugs," for example, centers on a minister who successfully overcame heroin addiction, but ignores the ritual use of drugs in some religions. Kauffman is weakest in defining great movements (for example, "existentialism") and strongest in offering factual information about lesser-known phenomena. There are cross-references, but no bibliographic information. Most of the many short biographical sketches of deceased persons are of Christians. If a one-volume dictionary covering world religions is needed, Hinnells (see 36) and Brandon (see 94) offer more depth, but Kauffman has the largest number of entries.

38. Kennedy, Richard. **The International Dictionary of Religion.** New York, Crossroad, 1984. 256p. LC 83-27209. ISBN 0-8245-0632-4.

This device is meant for the general reader, and covers the dogmas and doctrines, organizations and hierarchies, leaders and founders, and nature of worship of major world religions. The definitions are not learned, and there is much padding with marginally related photographs. A half-page, for example, is spent on an entry on Trotsky, with a picture of him haranguing Red Army troops, but noting little relating to religion. Appendixes include the calendars of religions, ancient gods, a chronology of beliefs in historical context, readings from sacred scriptures, some minimal statistics, a global map of religious distribution, and a four-page bibliography. For coverage of Judaism and Christianity, there are a host of better works; for other religions, Brandon (see 94), Crim (see 30), Hinnells (see 36), or Bishop and Darton (see 28) are preferable.

39. Kerr, James S., and Charles Lutz. **A Christian's Dictionary: 1600 Names, Words, Phrases.** Philadelphia, PA, Fortress Press, 1969. 178p. LC 74-84542.

Kerr and Lutz cover the broad spectrum of Christianity, for the general reader, with their sixteen hundred entries, but the basis of their choice is not always clear. The French author Camus is included, but not Sartre. Pope John XXIII merits attention, but not the then-serving Pope Paul VI. Cross-references are few: under "Reformation," Luther, Zwingli, Calvin, and Knox are mentioned but not referred to their own entries. Kauffman (see 37) or Cross (see 31), with more and fuller entries, are preferred for quick reference.

40. Mathews, Shailer, and Gerald Birney Smith. **A Dictionary of Religion and Ethics.** New York, Macmillan, 1921. 513p. LC 21-16239. Reprint: Detroit, MI, Gale, 1973. LC 70-145713.

Along with Hastings's *Encyclopaedia of Religion and Ethics* (see 5), this can be regarded as a forerunner of *The Encyclopedia of Religion* published by Macmillan in 1987 (see 2). The contributors were American scholars and missioners, many connected with the University of Chicago, including Shirley Jackson Case, Franz Boas, and Edgar Goodspeed, as well as the two editors. There is an attempt to cover all religions historically rather than apologetically, but the majority of entries are specific to Christianity. Biographies for figures deceased at the time of publication are included. Longer entries are signed. Bibliographies are not added to entries, but a bibliography, prepared by a librarian, is appended to the book.

41. Melton, J. Gordon. **The Encyclopedia of American Religions,** 2d ed. Detroit, MI, Gale, 1987. 899p. indexes. LC 87-115312. ISBN 0-8103-2133-5.

41.1. **The Encyclopedia of American Religions. Second Edition Supplement.** Detroit, MI, Gale, 1987. 157p. LC 87-115312. ISBN 0-8103-2131-9.

Melton covers almost all religions practiced in the United States, including Islam, Eastern religions, and even witchcraft and satanism. The one area of exception is Native American religions, which, he notes in the preface to his first edition, deserve a reference book of their own. The great majority of the 1,350 religious groups he identifies are in the Judeo-Christian tradition.

The second edition of this encyclopedia is split into two parts. The first includes essays on the historical development of twenty-two major religious families and traditions. This is a distinct improvement over the first edition, with fifteen families, wherein Jews, Muslims, Hindus, Sikhs, Jains, Buddhists, Shintoists, and Zoroastrians were gathered under one "Eastern and Middle Eastern" heading, a useful grouping only in that it got everyone into the book. These have now been separated into four distinctive groups, in one of which Judaism stands by itself. A selective, up-to-date bibliography complements each essay. The second part, arranged in the same 22 families, contains directory information on the 1,350 churches, religious bodies, and spiritual groups, and includes names, addresses, contact persons, and descriptions of beliefs, history, organization, membership statistics, post-secondary educational facilities, publications, and bibliographic sources. Churches with no current address and defunct groups are included.

Melton is at his best in documenting smaller churches and splinter groups. Within the Adventist family, for example, he identifies seventy-three separate bodies. Within the western liturgical family, of which the Roman Catholic Church and the Protestant Episcopal Church of the U.S.A. are the largest communions, he describes an additional fifty-eight Old Catholic and Anglican groups. He offers relatively lean treatment of the mainline bodies such as the Roman Catholic Church; this is understandable, since the information is readily available in the directories he lists. However, it can be misleading; one index seems to be a thorough list of postsecondary institutions with religious affiliation, until one realizes that the 235 Roman Catholic colleges and universities in the United States have been omitted because the entry on this church notes that the information is available in *The Official Catholic Directory* (see 213) and the *Catholic Almanac* (see 207).

The second edition now has six indexes. A religious organizations and institutions index lists entries by all key words in names. The subject index is particularly valuable for bringing together apparently disparate groups which may share practices, such as baptism by immersion or pacifism. There are also indexes for publications, locations, personal names, and, as noted, postsecondary educational institutions. The indexes refer to page numbers for the first part and to entry numbers for the second.

Melton and his publisher plan to present inter-edition supplements; one had already been issued in 1985, for the first edition, when Gale took over the publishing. The 1987 supplement provides coverage of some two hundred additional religious groups, and updates information on some groups already included. Melton adds two new chapters, describing groups not falling into the twenty-two categories of the second edition.

Melton's encyclopedic directory, relying on the resources of his Institute for the Study of American Religion, has become the authoritative reference source for American religions. Piepkorn (see 12) remains valuable for understanding the doctrinal particularities of denominations, but here also Melton has weighed in with a related volume, *Encyclopedia of American Religions: Religious Creeds* (see 42).

42. Melton, J. Gordon, ed. **Encyclopedia of American Religions: Religious Creeds.** Detroit, MI, Gale, 1988. 838p. index. LC 87-30384. ISBN 0-8103-2132-7.

As a companion to his *Encyclopedia of American Religions* (*EAR*) (see 41), Melton gathered some 450 "Creeds, Confessions, Statements of Faith, and Summaries of Doctrine of Religions and Spiritual Groups in the United States and Canada" (title page). Creeds for Melton are "formal statements of belief to which members of a church are expected to give their intellectual assent" (Introduction). Arrangement of the creeds is by chapters that roughly parallel the *EAR*. A first chapter includes the five creeds of the early Christians, which the vast majority of present-day Christians accept. Over half of the remaining twenty-two chapters include the credal statements of various branches of Christianity. Other chapters cover Middle Eastern and Eastern religions, as well as metaphysical, spiritualist, ancient wisdom, Magick, and some unclassified groups. The Middle Eastern chapter includes both Judaism and Islam; the ten Jewish statements emanate from all four modern American Jewish groups: Orthodox, Conservative, Reform, and Reconstructionist.

The focus of the work is on religious groups currently functioning in the United States and Canada. There is no attempt to include the creeds of historical groups no longer practicing or groups outside North America. As with Melton's other works, Native American religions are also excluded. For each creed, Melton includes a title, the name of the group or groups to which it pertains, and the credal statement itself, as best as it can be found in English. He notes its origin, its ideas or emphases, variant readings, and relationships to other religious statements. Melton adds a key-word index which in a single alphabet joins the titles of the creeds and the names of the religious groups. Produced in large part from the files of the Institute for the Study of American Religion, this is a unique compilation.

43. O'Brien, T. C. **Corpus Dictionary of Western Churches.** Washington, DC, Corpus Publications, 1970. 820p. LC 78-99501.

The approximately twenty-three hundred unsigned entries emphasize the churches listed in the *1969 Yearbook of American Churches* (see 191) and treat objectively the churches themselves; their founding; confessional documents; terms of doctrine, worship, polity, and practice; theological themes; and people in the church. Entries are short for ready reference, but longer when called for: four-and-a-half pages on "Calvinism" follow two-and-a-half on "John Calvin." Statistics are given to suggest the size of churches. There are brief bibliographies, and three pages of reference works the editor relied on. Coming out of the Roman Catholic tradition, this is markedly more open than Catholic works of just a few years earlier, and boasts an ecumenical list of contributors.

44. Pike, E. Royston. **Encyclopaedia of Religion and Religions.** New York, Meridian Books, 1958. 406p. LC 58-8530.

Entries are short, making this more a dictionary than an encyclopedia. Of religions, Pike intends to cover "the founders…, the theological tenets and the philosophical concepts, the rites and ceremonies and practices, the sacred scriptures, the creeds and confessions of faith, the orthodoxy and heterodoxies, the churches, denominations, sects and schools of all the religions" (Introduction). The British flavor is useful: the article on Roman Catholicism has a history of that church in the United Kingdom. There are few cross-references and no bibliographies. Although Pike claims to avoid it, definitions start from a Christian viewpoint: "In Judaism there are no sacraments, only ceremonies and symbols, nor is there any creed or set of dogmas that must be accepted" (p. 216). Brandon (see 94) or Crim (see 30) are preferred.

45. Reese, William L. **Dictionary of Philosophy and Religion: Eastern and Western Thought.** Atlantic Highlands, NJ, Humanities Press, 1980. 644p. LC 78-12561. ISBN 0-3910-0688-6.

In his preface, Reese states that he offers "analyses of the thought of all major philosophers and religious leaders." The thought of each such leader is developed in a numbered sequence of paragraphs. When philosophical movements or major problems are defined, there are cross-references to the numbered paragraphs of individual thinkers. While the major works of each thinker are listed, there are no bibliographies of secondary materials. This work is very useful for its thumbnail summaries of ideas, but it is not as up-to-date as its publishing date might suggest. Karl Barth, Jacques Maritain, and Etienne Gilson are entered; Karl Rahner is not. "Vatican Council" describes only Vatican I (1869-70). There is no entry for historical criticism of the Bible, and only a very brief one on "Biblical criticism."

46. Riddle, Kenneth Wilkinson. **A Popular Dictionary of Protestantism.** London, Arco, 1962. 208p. LC 62-51341.

Riddle provides an historical introductory survey of Protestantism, and then lists, in ready reference format, information on persons, institutions, events, places, and doctrines. His interpretation of Protestantism is broad, including Anglicanism, but his information is slanted toward the Anglo-American experience, although there is some historical information on continental Protestantism. There are many cross-references, allowing one to survey a broad subject, but no bibliographies for further reference.

47. Shulman, Albert M. **The Religious Heritage of America.** San Diego, CA, A. S. Barnes, 1981. 527p. indexes. LC 81-3594. ISBN 0-498-02162-9.

Shulman's approach to gathering religions is historical; he includes over one hundred religions, living and dead, and makes no distinction between mainline churches and cults. He identifies each religion, gives a historical profile, traces the source of its name, describes the organizational structure, and outlines essential doctrines. Coverage is broad: mainline Protestants; Pietists; new migrants, including Roman Catholics and Eastern Orthodox; American sects; utopians; and "the American scene," a catch-all category that includes Satanists, Bahai, Buddhists, and the Salvation Army. Coverage is not as detailed as Melton (see 41), who identifies thirty-four Methodist groups to Shulman's one, or as Piepkorn (see 12). An essay on the diversity of religious expression in America is peripheral to reference use. Appendixes include the religious affiliations of United States presidents and members of the Ninety-seventh Congress. An appendix listing membership statistics sometimes gives figures different from those in the text.

48. Warshaw, Thayer S. **Abingdon Glossary of Religious Terms.** Nashville, TN, Abingdon Press, 1980. 94p. (Festival Series). LC 80-13121. ISBN 0-687-00472-1.

This is a short work indeed, the revised version of the glossary in Warshaw's handbook for teaching the Bible in literature classes. However, it is well done, and useful for the general reader of the humanities. It includes biblical, scholarly, and religious terms, and allusions from literature and art. It reflects critical scholarship in the conservative tradition, and has an American emphasis.

49. Wright, Charles Henry Hamilton, and Charles Neil, eds. **A Protestant Dictionary, Containing Articles on the History, Doctrines, and Practices of the Christian Church.** London, Hodder and Stoughton, 1904. Reprinted: Detroit, MI, Gale, 1972. 832p. LC 73-155436.

In their preface, Wright and Neil express admiration for Roman Catholic dictionaries produced in England and Germany, and then zestily state a Protestant turn-of-the-century position on virtually every aspect of Christian history and practice. The "Roman Catholic Church" of the Preface becomes "the Romish Church" in articles; High Anglicans are referred to as "Ritualists." Coverage includes the history of Christianity in the West and the Greek and Russian East, but not the Orient. There is nothing of India or Japan, but four columns cover the Roman Catholic "Index Expurgatorius" of books (an easy target subsequently laid to rest after Vatican II). Much has changed since these two nineteenth-century Protestant Charlies sallied forth against the Roman Catholic fortress in this delightfully tendentious work.

IV. Dictionaries on Specific Religions

50. Addis, William Edward, and Thomas Arnold. **A Catholic Dictionary: Containing Some Account of the Doctrine, Discipline, Rites, Ceremonies, Councils, and Religious Orders of the Catholic Church,** 17th ed. Revised by T. B. Scannell, P. E. Hallett, and Gordon Albion. Further revised by the staff of St. John's Seminary, Wonersh. London, Routledge & Paul, and St. Louis, MO, Herder, 1960. 860p. LC 21-3757.

This dictionary, first published in 1886, was originally intended to supply educated English-speaking Roman Catholics with a reference book that would counterbalance the Protestant dictionaries then available, some of which were openly hostile to Catholicism. It covers dogma; ritual; ancient, medieval, and modern church history; the Oriental rites (that is, those eastern churches in communion with Rome); religious orders; and canon law. Technical theological terms are rendered in Greek and Latin. Bibliographic references are abundant. The work was frequently revised throughout the twentieth century as new papal encyclicals were published, saints added to the calendar, and changes introduced to the liturgy. This is quintessentially a pre-Vatican II work, and could not have been easily revised after that event. Nowhere is this more evident than in the minimal articles on the Bible which stress canonicity, inspiration, and a history of the Church's opposition to lay reading (although, the authors note, this had been reversed by the twentieth century). No mention is made in any of the biblical articles of the encouragement by Pope Pius XII of scientific research on the Bible.

51. Alpher, Joseph, ed. **Encyclopedia of Jewish History: Events and Eras of the Jewish People.** New York, Facts on File, 1986. 288p. index. LC 85-23941. ISBN 0-8160-1220-2.

Rather than alphabetical, the format of this work is topical within a loosely chrono-logical framework. There are one hundred entries, each approximately eight hundred words long, that is, two facing pages. Each entry has a "key" (a visual summary), and a paragraph called "connections" that refers to related entries. Each page has five photo-graphs, and the editor has avoided cliché pictures. Good maps and diagrams are often present. This format is confusing when one wants quick reference, but is excellent for a leisurely overview. American Jews are covered in four entries, but the large Jewish commu-nities in Latin America and South Africa receive only passing notice. There are appendixes on Hebrew scripts, symbols in Jewish art, Jewish costumes, and paper cut crafts. There is a chronological chart of Jewish and world history. A ten-page glossary has extensive defini-tions, but alphabetizes "The Jewish Wars" under "T," making the entry unfindable and annoying to almost every user. Such minor mistakes aside, this is an excellent contem-porary overview of Judaism.

52. Attwater, Donald, ed. **A Catholic Dictionary,** 3d ed. New York, Macmillan, 1961. 552p. LC 58-5797.

This revised edition of *The Catholic Encyclopaedic Dictionary* was first published in the year Pope Pius XII died (1958), and it is impossible to read through it and foresee the great changes in outlook, if not in substance, that the Roman Catholic Church would adopt under Pope John XXIII and the Second Vatican Council. Biblical theology and criti-cism, and bodies of thought such as Christology, emanating from that council receive little notice. Articles on aspects of Catholicism are chauvinistic, and those on Protestantism are unsympathetic. It is hard to imagine that the article on the Jews was written after the phenomenon of Nazism. This dictionary remains useful only for preconciliar definitions of twentieth-century beliefs and practices of Roman Catholicism. Except for prominent saints, biography is excluded. Definitions are not historical. There is a decided emphasis on the English-speaking world, e.g., the article on "Opus Dei" does not mention the secular institute of that name, which was active in the Mediterranean countries earlier in the century and has now come into prominence in the church. There are no bibliographies. Appendixes contain abbreviations, the calendar of saints' feast days, the list of popes, and ecclesiastical modes of address. This effort has been surpassed by most reference works following the Catholic tradition since the early 1960s.

53. Ausubel, Nathan. **The Book of Jewish Knowledge. An Encyclopedia of Judaism and the Jewish People, Covering All Elements of Jewish Life from Biblical Times to the Pres-ent.** New York, Crown, 1964. 560p. index. LC 62-20063. ISBN 0-517-09746-X.

Ausubel's work, a tour de force for a single author, is intended for the general reader, and is arranged in encyclopedic format. He takes an historical, critical, and objective approach to many traditional facets of Jewish knowledge and culture. Except for "Moses," there are no specifically biographical entries; there is, however, a long article on "some architects of Jewish civilization." There are cross-references and an index of persons, as well as a general index, but no bibliographies. The word *Holocaust* is absent as an entry (note the 1964 publishing date), but there are long articles on anti-semitism, the Nazis, and the church and persecution. This book is especially useful for the Christian of any educational level who knows little about Judaism.

54. Benton, Angelo Ames, ed. **The Church Cyclopaedia: a Dictionary of Church Doctrine, History, Organization and Ritual, and Containing Original Articles on Special Topics, Written Expressly for This Work by Bishops, Presbyters, and Laymen. Designed Especially for the Use of the Laity of the Protestant Episcopal Church in the United States of America.** New York, M. H. Mallory, 1883. 810p. Reprinted: Detroit, MI, Gale, 1975. 810p. LC 74-31499. ISBN 0-8103-4204-9.

This was intended for the laity, "to enable them to judge for themselves, upon the many questions of fact, and doctrine, and government, in our communion, furnishing them the materials for forming such judgments, and for holding correct views thereon" (Preface). Its current usefulness lies in its histories of dioceses and lists of bishops in America. There are no cross-references, no bibliographies, and no biographical entries. Articles are signed.

55. Birnbaum, Philip. **Encyclopedia of Jewish Concepts**, rev. ed. New York, Sanhedrin Press, 1979. 722p. indexes. LC 64-16085. ISBN 0-88482-876-X.

Written for the contemporary English-speaking reader, this book is a compendium of the essential teachings of Judaism, arranged in dictionary format following the Hebrew alphabet. The key to the work is a topical index that divides the entries, often over a page in length, into twenty categories, including Bible, Torah, feasts and festivals, ethics, beliefs, law, history, education, Talmud, Kabbalah, and the Hebrew language. There is a complete English index with transliterated Hebrew words added, along with an exhaustive Hebrew index. The book is highly readable, and largely succeeds in spite of a complete lack of bibliographical materials and cross-references.

56. Bridger, David, ed. **The New Jewish Encyclopedia**, rev. ed. New York, Behrman House, 1976. 541p. LC 76-15251. ISBN 0-87441-120-3.

This is an encyclopedia in a single volume for the general reader. There are neither index nor bibliographies. Many black-and-white photographs accompany articles. Treatment is not exclusively of religious, or even Jewish, matters: there are articles on Jesus, Marx, and Freud. For a comparable work, somewhat older, see Werblowsky and Wigoder (86).

57. Broderick, Robert C., comp. **Catholic Concise Dictionary**, rev. ed. Revised by Placid Hermann and Marion A. Habig. Chicago, IL, Franciscan Herald Press, 1966. 330p. LC 66-14726.

The earlier editions, compiled by Broderick in 1944 and 1957, were based on the supposition that the language of the Catholic Church is for the most part static. This hardly proved to be the case, and, in light of Vatican II, Hermann and Habig revised Broderick's dictionary to include new definitions of old terms, Eastern rite terms, and biblical terms. This was new wine — but not enough of it — in an old skin. In 1966, the biblical renaissance was in its infancy in the American Catholic Church, and the great opening toward Protestant, and even European Catholic, biblical criticism was just beginning. Thus, there are no entries for form criticism or historical-critical schools. The entry for the "Index of Prohibited Books" does not mention its abrogation by the Vatican (June 14,

1966). This dictionary retains its value not for its revisions, which have been greatly surpassed by Broderick's *The Catholic Encyclopedia* (see 58), but for its coverage of earlier Latinate phrases. Because of the range of Catholic culture between the Councils of Trent and Vatican II, there will always be use for a dictionary that defines terms like *trination, denudation, delator,* and *flectamus genua.* There are forty-eight pages of appendixes with foreign words (although most Latin expressions are entered in the alphabet of main entries), abbreviations, a list of ecumenical councils and the doctrines they defined, patron saints, and a list of popes. Even with the revision, the scope is limited, as the title implies, to the Roman Catholic expression of Christianity.

58. Broderick, Robert C. **The Catholic Encyclopedia**, rev. and updated ed. Nashville, TN, Thomas Nelson, 1987. 613p. LC 87-1529. ISBN 0-8407-5544-9.

By the mid-1970s, Broderick, like many American Catholics, had changed considerably from pre-Vatican II years, when he could write in his preface to the *Catholic Concise Dictionary* (see 57) that language in the Catholic Church is static. In the introduction to the first edition (1976), he noted "great changes in language and definition of Church terms," and stressed the continuity of Judeo-Christian history and a broad spectrum of Christian experience. Thus, he included entries on Judaism and Protestantism, especially as they impact on Catholicism. There is, for example, a fair treatment of the "Lutheran-Catholic Dialogue," although there is a somewhat negative "Lutheranism" entry. Broderick is especially useful in recording new interests among American Roman Catholics in the decade following the publication of the *New Catholic Encyclopedia* (see 23). Many terms relating to Eastern Christianity are included, but the numerous Latin expressions are omitted. The few photographs from the 1976 edition are also omitted, although some decorative but not illustrative block prints remain. The substantive additions in the 1987 revision are several paragraphs on the Vatican II documents and on the new Code of Canon Law (1983), that body of laws covering the Latin (Western) division of the Roman Catholic Church, as well as a few articles on such contemporary topics as "Women, Ordination of," to which Broderick gave decidedly legalistic coverage. It lacks biographies and bibliographies, two distinct weaknesses. An additional weakness is the general lack of cross-references.

59. Brookes, Reuben S. **A Dictionary of Judaism.** London, Shapiro, Vallentine, 1959. 255p. LC 74-165070.

Brookes intended this short dictionary for Jews who wished to know more about their religion. Nevertheless, the definitions—quite basic and short—are very good for Christians who know little or nothing about Judaism. Brief biographical entries on a few great Jewish leaders are included. A bibliography of over fifty books is appended.

60. Bumpus, John Skelton. **A Dictionary of Ecclesiastical Terms, Being a History and Explanation of Certain Terms Used in Architecture, Ecclesiology, Liturgiology, Music, Ritual, Cathedral Constitution, Etc.** London, T. W. Laurie, 1910. 324p. Reprinted: Detroit, MI, Gale, 1969. LC 68-30653.

The terms are defined with a decidedly English and Anglican flavor, although "the Church of Rome" is sometimes alluded to. Architectural definitions refer to English cathedrals and chapels and French churches. Bumpus is especially valuable for obscure terms. Although there are many references to nineteenth-century studies in this older work, it is not outdated.

61. Burstein, Abraham. **The Illustrated New Concise Jewish Encyclopedia**, rev. ed. Edited by Robert Milch. New York, Ktav Publishing House, 1978. 174p. LC 78-8334. ISBN 0-87068-635-6.

Originally published in 1962 under the title *A New Concise Jewish Encyclopedia*, this work is actually a short-entry dictionary. Black-and-white photographs enliven every page. Coverage is a mixed bag. Some non-Jews (for example, Napoleon and Nasser) receive biographical sketches; others, who had more negative impact (such as Hitler and Eichmann) do not. There is no entry for the Holocaust and that on anti-semitism is but thirty-three words in a scant four lines. There is an entry for Islam, but none for Christianity. Roth (see 80) is a more reliable single-volume resource.

62. **A Catholic Dictionary of Theology.** London, Thomas Nelson, 1962-67. 2 vols.

Begun before Vatican II (1962-65), two volumes of a projected four were completed, giving us theology through the letters "Hea." Catholic doctrines are presented as they are drawn from the Bible and tradition, with special emphasis on the liturgical sources of theology. There are good bibliographies for each entry. Biographies of theologians who are little known in the United States are included. Although it is scholarly and progressive for its time, the change that occurred in Roman Catholicism with the second Vatican Council undoubtedly led the editors to abandon it. Those who have it will appreciate it for its outreach to other religions – "Buddhism" is quite sympathetic – and for its explanations of Catholic doctrines not accepted by Protestants, such as the "Conception, Immaculate" of Mary and her "Assumption."

63. de Haas, Jacob, ed. **The Encyclopedia of Jewish Knowledge.** New York, Behrman's Jewish Book House, 1938. 686p. index. LC 38-31458.

This single-volume encyclopedia, with six thousand entries, covers "Jewish history, incidents, experiences, persecutions, ideas, cultural efforts and the lives of great Jews" (Preface). Although the work is dated, biography is a special strength, and the volume has a synoptic index that allows the reader to identify biographees by country. Its awareness of Judaism is not total: there are no entries, for example, on the Hassidim or their founder, Rabbi Israel Baal Shem Tov. The four-page bibliography is now quite dated.

64. Demetrakopoulos, George H. **Dictionary of Orthodox Theology: A Summary of the Beliefs, Practices and History of the Eastern Orthodox Church.** New York, Philosophical Library, 1964. 187p. LC 63-13346.

The introduction to this work is a thumbnail sketch of the Orthodox faith, including a review of the first seven ecumenical councils. Cross-references are rare and there are no bibliographies. Definitions are often overly simple and abbreviated. There are no biographical entries. Some absences are surprising: there is no entry for the Virgin Mary, the mother of Jesus, but her feasts are noted. The term *Theotokos* (literally, "God-bearer," and referring to the Virgin) is defined, but without reference to the great struggle with Nestorianism in the fifth century. Likewise, the controversy over "Filioque," which ultimately separated the Eastern Church from the West, lacks historical treatment. Orthodoxy, one of the great poles of Christendom, needs a full, up-to-date, scholarly, historical reference work in English.

65. Fuerbringer, Ludwig Ernest, Theodore Edward William Engelder, and P. E. Kretzmann, eds. **The Concordia Cyclopedia: A Handbook of Religious Information, with Special Reference to the History, Doctrine, Work, and Usages of the Lutheran Church.** St. Louis, MO, Concordia Publishing House. 1927. 848p. LC 27-13940.

This single-volume work presents, from a Lutheran standpoint, general religious information, in a brief but comprehensive manner. Unlike some confessional reference works, e.g., *The Encyclopedia of World Methodism* (see 20), it is outward-looking; the reader of this 1927 work is not intended to learn solely about Lutheranism but about many matters, as viewed by Lutheran scholars. Polemics are strongly anti-Catholic, but one gets the sense that the writers could not help but admire their enemies: "Luther liberated millions from the shackles of the papacy; Loyola invented a machine to rivet the fetters anew and to bind the Church irretrievably to the ideas of medievalism."

66. Hardon, John A. **Modern Catholic Dictionary.** Garden City, NY, Doubleday, 1980. 635p. LC 77-82945. ISBN 0-385-12162-8.

Hardon was influenced in his choice of entries by *The New Catholic Dictionary* of 1929 (see 79). In more than five thousand entries, he attempts to define "every significant concept of the church's doctrine in faith and morals, ritual and devotion, canon law and liturgy, mysticism and spirituality, ecclesiastical history and organization." He pays special attention to Vatican II, which merits an entry while Vatican I does not. He is also strong on Catholic shrines and prayers. An appendix contains the post-Vatican II "Credo of the People of God," a list of popes, the Roman and Byzantine ecclesiastical calendars, and a list of religious communities in the United States. There are no bibliographies. The work is occasionally triumphalistic as when Hardon borrows the following expression from his 1929 predecessor: "the Vatican Library is presently making one of the greatest contributions to human thought." There is an entry on the papal encyclical *Divini Redemptoris* condemning communism, but none on Pius XII's *Divino afflante spiritu*, which laid out the road for the resurgence of critical biblical studies in the Roman Catholic Church. There is no general article on biblical criticism, and a negative entry on "form criticism" is given no more space than that on "fragrant odors." Some, but not all, mainline Protestant churches merit entries. Hardon is valuable for his presentation of contemporary conservative Catholicism. The dictionary contains terms not popular with liberals and often unknown to younger Catholics, such as *Limbo, Forty Hours,* and *Scapular.*

67. Harper, Howard. **The Episcopalian's Dictionary: Church Beliefs, Terms, Customs, and Traditions Explained in Layman's Language.** New York, Seabury Press, 1974. 183p. LC 74-12105. ISBN 0-8164-1166-2.

Harper covers points of doctrine, ritual, ecclesiastical clothing, festivals, architecture, church offices, and organization with clever definitions, often historical in nature. He has vowed not to underestimate lay persons' intelligence or overestimate their information. His coverage of things Episcopalian is excellent, but this work easily transcends the particular church. There is no bibliographic material; a few references would have been helpful to his intended readership.

68. Hyamson, Albert M., and A. M. Silbermann, eds. **Vallentine's Jewish Encyclopaedia.** London, Shapiro, Vallentine, 1938. 696p.

This scholarly, single-volume, English distillation of pre-war Jewish knowledge, liberal in outlook, includes much biographical material on the then-living as well as the deceased, and many articles on Jewish communities and development in Palestine, of which there is a two-color map. Black-and-white photographs are abundant. Two of its contributors were instrumental in producing the later *Encyclopaedia Judaica* (see 25).

69. Isaacson, Ben. **Dictionary of the Jewish Religion.** Englewood, NY, SBS Publications, 1980. LC 79-67485. ISBN 0-89961002-1.

Isaacson means this work for "the Jews of the Diaspora," that is, those not living in Israel, and especially for questioning youth. Treatment is reserved for things Jewish. Interaction between Judaism and other religions or thought systems is ignored; hence, there are no entries for Christianity or Marxism, although Freud is included. Biographical treatments are hagiographic. Bridger (see 56) or Werblowsky and Wigoder (see 86) are more useful single-volume works.

70.   Isaacson, Ben and Deborah Wigoder. **The International Jewish Encyclopedia.** Englewood Cliffs, NJ, Prentice-Hall, and Jerusalem, Masada Press, 1973. 336p. index. LC 72-13484. ISBN 0-13-473066-6.

Emphasizing the period since World War II, and prepared in Israel for Jews throughout the world, this encyclopedia covers "Judaism in all its manifestations: religion, history, literature, and culture" (Introduction). It is essentially introspective, and does not cover relationships between Judaism and other religions: there are no entries for Islam, Mohammed, the Quran, Jesus, or Christianity. The article on South Africa makes no mention of the problems of race. Many black-and-white, and some color, photographs are included. There are few bibliographic references. An index is provided. Roth (see 80) provides a more informed single-volume work.

71.   Langford-James, Richard Lloyd. **A Dictionary of the Eastern Orthodox Church.** London, Faith Press, 1923. 144p. Reprinted: New York, Burt Franklin, 1975. LC 72-82261. ISBN 0-8337-4210-8.

Langford-James was an Anglican with extensive acquaintance with Slavs and Greeks, partly as a result of contacts during the First World War. He interpreted sympathetically Orthodox customs, vestments, liturgy, and theology for British readers at a time of growing contacts between the Anglican and Orthodox communions. Orthodox discomfiture with papal claims and the Roman Church in general is often manifest. Biographies of great eastern saints are included. Appendixes include an eastern liturgical calendar (Julian), superimposed on a western (Gregorian) model and a bibliography, now badly dated. Demetrakopoulos (see 64) is a more recent work, but Eastern Orthodoxy needs a current, fuller reference treatment than either.

72.   Lieder, Walter. **Lutheran Dictionary.** St. Louis, MO, Concordia Publishing House, 1952. 47p. LC 53-222.

Lieder serves up brief definitions on biblical, historical, liturgical, and architectural items. The volume also covers church organizations and points from Luther's *Small Catechism.* Except for biblical references, there is no bibliographic material. Lieder can be harsh and opinionated: Islam, called "Mohammedan," is labeled a "fake religion." For short definitions of material not specifically Lutheran, one would more profitably turn to Cross (see 31).

73.   Lowery, Daniel L. **A Basic Catholic Dictionary.** Liguori, MO, Liguori Publications, 1985. 144p. LC 85-80600. ISBN 0-89243-241-1.

Like Harper (see 67) and Lieder (see 72), Lowery has produced for the laity of his church a dictionary covering Roman Catholic beliefs, liturgy, personalities, moral teaching, and some few terms not specifically Catholic. Lowery reflects the conservative wing of the contemporary church, often relying on the Code of Canon Law in his definitions. Hardon (see 66) is more comprehensive for a single-volume work on Catholicism.

74.   Lueker, Erwin L., ed. **Lutheran Cyclopedia,** rev. ed. Saint Louis, MO, Concordia Publishing House, 1975. 845p. LC 75-2096. ISBN 0-570-03255-5.

Unlike Bodensieck (see 14), an encyclopedia *about* Lutheranism, this is an encyclopedia about Christianity in general and, briefly, other religions, *for* Lutherans. In that sense, it follows Fuerbringer (see 65). There is no introduction and hence no exposition of scope; the book covers general religious terminology and Christian history. Brief biographies are particularly abundant. Entries are compact and intense, with much detail in small space. The bibliographies are excellent for a work of this size, and the many cross-references lead to thorough factual coverage of events and issues. Although on the whole more objective than the earlier 1954 edition, this dictionary acknowledges little about Judaism. "Anti-Semitism" receives a one-line definition, and there is not a hint of the Holocaust. "Zionism" mentions only "a flood of refugees from Hitler's concentration camps...."

75. Malloch, James M., comp., and Kay Smallzried, ed. **A Practical Church Dictionary.** New York, Morehouse-Barlow, 1964. 520p. LC 64-23926.

This dictionary is intended primarily for North American Episcopalians but, with objective articles on a wide variety of religions, historical events, and practices, it is useful to a broader readership. Definitions of such terms as *chapel royal, God's acre, nonjurors, nipperkin,* and *rood* give this work its Anglican flavor, but there is also treatment of *bar mitzvah,* the *Douay Bible, nirvana,* and *Siva.* Articles on religions are sympathetic, and there is progressive treatment of social problems like suicide and alcoholism. Coverage of biblical studies is much stronger than in Roman Catholic reference books of the period. Bibliographic references are not included with articles and definitions, but an appendix includes a short list, now dated, of reference works. Given the deep penetration of the churches of the Anglican Communion into the cultures of the English-speaking world, this dictionary is especially useful for readers of literature and history.

76. Markowitz, Endel. **The Encyclopedia Yiddishanica: A Compendium of Jewish Memorabilia.** s.l., Haymark Publications, 1980. 447p. index. LC 79-89973. ISBN 0-933910-02-9.

For Markowitz, the *Yiddishanica* of the title refers broadly to things Jewish; the purpose of this work "is to present a montage of Jewish trivia, facts and folklore." There are fourteen chapters covering, among other things, Jewish proverbs, Yiddish idioms, facts such as lists of actors, Jewish wit and humor, teachings from the Talmud, biblical jurisprudence, and the recent history of Judaism. Markowitz adds a short English-to-Yiddish lexicon and a two-page bibliography that includes only the titles and authors of his recommended books. This is a browsing rather than a reference book. From the title, one would think the author wished to give prominence to Yiddish, a language written in Hebrew characters, yet barely a Hebrew character exists in the work; almost all Yiddish words listed are transliterated to the roman alphabet. The Jewish Braille Institute of America has made this available in braille, on cassettes, and in large print.

77. Neufield, Don F. **Seventh-Day Adventist Encyclopedia.** Washington, DC, Review and Herald Publishing Association, 1966. 1,452p. (Commentary Reference Series, vol. 10). LC 66-17322.

Some seven hundred authors contributed over two thousand articles to this first encyclopedia for the Seventh Day Adventists (SDAs). Areas covered included church history; church organization and operation; institutions such as colleges, schools, sanatoriums, hospitals, publishing houses, health-food factories, orphanages, and old people' homes; biographies of six hundred deceased persons who were either famous SDAs or non-SDAs who influenced the movement; and beliefs and practices, especially where SDAs differ from other conservative Protestants. The work lacks an index.

78. Nevins, Albert J., ed. **The Maryknoll Catholic Dictionary.** New York, Grosset & Dunlap and Wilkes-Barre, PA, Dimension Books, 1965. 711p. LC 65-15436.

This dictionary for lay persons and nonspecialists was another attempt (see Hermann's and Habig's revision of Broderick, 57), to log the great changes in the Roman Catholic Church following Vatican II. Thus, there is a bow to Protestantism, a slight nod to Judaism, and a nascent attempt to incorporate changes in liturgy and in church discipline and organization. However, biblical studies gets scant treatment; the various schools of criticism are not mentioned, and the entire Protestant effort in biblical scholarship merits the kind but vacuous statement, "Other Christian non-Catholics had made great advances in ... their effort better to understand the Word of God" (p. 76). There is some welcome coverage of things Canadian. Uneven editing of entries by over two dozen writers, mostly from the Maryknoll community, left, for example, two similar entries for a tiny sect in British Columbia, one spelled "Doukhobors" and the other "Dukhobors." Ninety-six pages of appendixes cover Catholic abbreviations, forms of address, patron saints, a list of popes, biographies of deceased Catholics from the United States and Canada, and, unique to this book, a five-page list of American Catholic martyrs.

79. Pallen, Conde B., and John J. Wynne. **The New Catholic Dictionary. A Complete Work of Reference on Every Subject in the Life, Belief, Tradition, Rites, Symbolism, Devotions, History, Biography, Laws, Dioceses, Missions, Centers, Institutions, Statistics of the Church and Her Part in Promoting Science, Art, Education, Social Welfare, Morals, and Civilization.** New York, The Universal Knowledge Foundation, 1929. 1,078p.

This work was undertaken under the auspices of the editors of *The Catholic Encyclopedia* (see 21). Like that work, it has a broad spectrum and is very detailed. It names, for example, seventy-three geographical divisions to the Roman Catholic Church in China. It contains statistics, maps, line drawings, and photos. Judging from its title, there is little its editor did not think it would contain. It is of current interest primarily for historical detail and for the model it set for later Catholic dictionaries (see Hardon, 66).

80. Roth, Cecil. **The Concise Jewish Encyclopedia.** New York, New American Library, 1980. 561p. LC 79-27120. ISBN 0-452-00526-4.

Roth, an editor-in-chief of the *Encyclopaedia Judaica* (see 25), prepared this work as a ready reference for the general reader, and the choice of items and nutshell definitions bear the imprint of his immense scholarship. All Hebrew words are transliterated. Biographical material is abundant; biographies of non-Jews are indicated by an asterisk. Ample use of cross-references links the short entry items together. Roth eschewed pictures and bibliography to maintain brevity; for fuller treatment, one must turn from this fine small volume to larger single-volume works (see 81) or to the definitive *Encyclopaedia Judaica* (see 25).

81. Roth, Cecil, and Geoffrey Wigoder, eds.-in-chief. **The New Standard Jewish Encyclopedia,** 5th ed. Garden City, NY, Doubleday, 1977. 2,028 cols. (1,014p.). LC 76-21965. ISBN 0-3851-2519-4.

Although Roth and Wigoder cover every phase of Jewish life, literature, and thought from earliest times, they give special emphasis to three major events: the destruction of European Jewry, the establishment of Israel, and the emergence of the United States as the major diaspora community (a special American Advisory Board assisted the editors). Coverage includes prominent Jews, non-Jews (signaled by asterisks) who impacted Jewish history and scholarship, and Jewish communities in all countries and major towns, as well as summaries of Jewish history, literature, religion, philosophy, law, customs, festivals, and institutions. Conciseness is the primary aim; frequent cross-references give the reader access to related materials. Hebrew and Yiddish words are transliterated into the roman alphabet, and common English spellings are used except for contemporary Israelis; thus, "Moses" for the prophet but "Moshe" for the Israeli statesman/soldier. Black-and-white photos are abundant. Roth and Wigoder have produced the most scholarly, yet approachable, single-volume Jewish encyclopedia, which lacks only bibliographies for its credentials. For these one turns to the *Encyclopaedia Judaica* (see 25), of which Roth and Wigoder were also the editors-in-chief.

82.   Runes, Dagobert D., ed. **Concise Dictionary of Judaism.** New York, Philosophical Library, 1959. 237p. LC 58-59474.

Runes draws together theological, cultural, and biblical terms, biographies of prominent Jews from biblical times to the present, and a few organizations such as B'nai B'rith. Sixty-four black-and-white plates illustrate terms, but there are no bibliographies leading to further reading. The reader has a sense of incompleteness: there is little reference to persecution of Jews, and only minimal information on Israel.

83.   Schonfield, Hugh Joseph. **A Popular Dictionary of Judaism.** New York, Citadel Press, 1966. 155p. LC 66-24231.

Schonfield reflects the Orthodox tradition in this short work covering Jewish thought, customs, and usage. Biographical and historical materials are excluded. The author, a translator of the New Testament, counts the non-Jew among his readers, and thus refers to passages in the New Testament. He adds a basic bibliography of some twenty items. Hebrew terms are transliterated to the roman alphabet.

84.   Simpson, Matthew, ed. **Cyclopaedia of Methodism, Embracing Sketches of the Rise, Progress, and Present Condition, with Biographical Notices and Numerous Illustrations,** 5th rev. ed. Philadelphia, PA, Louis H. Everts, 1882. 1,031p. LC 28-15468.

This work is of great historical value, as it includes material on the chief facts, dates, and incidents connected with the rise of Methodism in England and America and its achievements in each state and in cities with populations of three thousand or more. Each annual conference is covered, as are seminaries, missions, schools, colleges, and universities. Biographical material is abundant, and there is an extensive bibliography of books written by ministers and other important churchmen. Of particular note is the extensive treatment of Methodism's response to slavery. A directory of foreign missionaries is appended.

85.   Wall, John N., Jr. **A New Dictionary for Episcopalians.** Minneapolis, MN, Winston Press, 1985. 179p. LC 85-51010. ISBN 0-86683-787-6.

In this dictionary for the general reader, Wall has, for the most part, stayed away from theology. He included words for Episcopalian services, vestments, church organizations, and the like. Where appropriate, he includes page number references to the *Book of Common Prayer.*

86.   Werblowsky, Raphael Jehudah Zwi, and Geoffrey Wigoder. **The Encyclopedia of the Jewish Religion.** New York, Holt, Rinehart and Winston, 1966. 415p. LC 66-10266.

Noting that "there is no dearth of encyclopedias of Jewish knowledge in English," the editors avoided "lists of Jewish Nobel prize winners" and focused on the religious aspects of Judaism: theology, philosophy, liturgy, ritual, religious institutions, and themes such as the influence of Judaism on other religions. The list of contributors includes some of the best Jewish scholars from the 1960s, but the articles are unsigned. There are several sets of black-and-white plates. Cross-references are extensive. For the Christian, or for the Jew who has been casual about his or her religion, this is the book to use for an excellent, scholarly, readable introduction.

87. Wigoder, Geoffrey, ed. **Encyclopedic Dictionary of Judaica.** New York, Leon Amiel, 1974. 673p. LC 74-12588. ISBN 0-8148-0598-1.

Planned as a ready reference complement to the *Encyclopaedia Judaica* (see 25), this work covers the Bible, Jewish communities throughout the world, prominent Jews within the Jewish context and as contributors to world culture, some non-Jews, and Jewish history and literature. There are maps, lists, charts, tables, and many illustrations, some in color.

88. Wright, Richard Robert, ed.-in-chief. **Centennial Encyclopaedia of the African Methodist Episcopal Church.** Philadelphia, PA, African Methodist Episcopal Church, 1916. 387p. index.

This is a mine of information on the African Methodist Episcopal (AME) Church, which was founded in Philadelphia in 1787. An historical essay and a chronology open the work, and are followed by hundreds of biographies of AME notables, women as well as men. An appendix includes "sketches and illustrations, churches, missionary societies, annual conferences, schools, etc." Portraits and photographs of institutions are plentiful. Ties with the church in South Africa are stressed. A list of delegates to a 1916 national congress is included, as is a complete index to the verbal sketches and illustrations in the work. This encyclopedia is important for two reasons: the intrinsic value of its information on the church, and the extrinsic value of its example. There are too few reference works on the Afro-American religious experience.

V. Encyclopedias and Dictionaries
on Religious Topics

89. Angeles, Peter A. **Dictionary of Christian Theology.** San Francisco, CA, Harper & Row, 1985. 210p. LC 84-48235. ISBN 0-06-060237-6.

Angeles intends to offer "readable and informal definitions of important Christian theological terms for the general reader and students of religion, literature and philosophy." The definitions, however, are idiosyncratic and anything but readable. They do give the Latin or Greek roots of terms, but most are overly brief and laden with jargon. One wonders if separate definitions for *prior, prioress,* and *priory* are really needed. "Anglicanism" gets a three-line historical definition, with no mention of its theology. The definition of *creationism* emphasizes that term's Roman Catholic use, and neglects the contemporary journalistic meaning, as in "creationism versus science." *Prophecy*, one of the most extraordinary and profound concepts in the Judeo-Christian tradition, merits only "the foretelling of things to come." "Magi, the" offers a definition based on medieval legend, without saying so, and takes no account of contemporary scholarship on the infancy narrative in the Gospel of Matthew. The definition of *historical method* is equally incomplete, and there is no entry for *form criticism.* Little account is taken of twentieth-century biblical theology in these definitions. This dictionary cannot meet the needs of the general reader; *The Westminster Dictionary of Christian Theology* (see 124) is much preferred.

90. Avi-Yonah, Michael, and Ephraim Stern. **Encyclopedia of Archaeological Excavations in the Holy Land.** Englewood Cliffs, NJ, Prentice Hall; Jerusalem, Masada Press, 1975-78. 4 vols. index. LC 73-14997. ISBN 0-13-275115-1, 0-13-275123-2, 0-13-275131-3, and 0-13-275149-6.

This is a translation and updating of the editors' Hebrew edition. They have examined 180 sites, the histories of which range from prehistoric times through the Crusades, and have gathered information on them from monographs and articles. They include some general, "composite" articles treating such matters as churches, megaliths, monasteries, synagogues, and specific areas like the Jordan Valley. There is a bibliography for each entry, and there are many illustrations, plans, line drawings, and monochromatic and color photographs. The end papers in volumes two through four are maps showing the sites covered by each volume. Each volume also contains chronological tables, lists of prehistoric and archaeological periods, and lists of kings and emperors. The paging is consecutive throughout the set, and the index in the fourth volume is comprehensive. Original contributors, whose work the editors carried into this English version, include some of the greatest mid-century biblical scholars: Roland de Vaux, William Foxwell Albright, and Nelson Glueck.

91.   Benner, David G., ed. **Baker Encyclopedia of Psychology.** Grand Rapids, MI, Baker Book House, 1985. 1,223p. LC 85-70713. ISBN 0-8010-3413-2.
     Benner has edited an encyclopedia on psychology from a conservative, evangelical Christian viewpoint, focusing on personality, psychopathology, psychotherapy, major systems and theories, and the psychology of religion. Articles range in length from short definitions to a few pages, and many offer explicit biblical and theological perspectives. Homosexuality, for example, is studied biblically and ranked as a sexual disorder, with appropriate treatment described. The explanation of *paraphilia* is "mankind's sinful nature." There are cross-references but no index, a distinct deficiency given the length of this work.

92.   Blunt, John Henry, ed. **Dictionary of Sects, Heresies, Ecclesiastical Parties, and Schools of Religious Thought.** Philadelphia, PA, J. B. Lippincott, 1874. 648p. index. Reprinted: Detroit, MI, Gale, 1974. LC 74-9653. ISBN 0-8103-3751-7.
     Cleobians, Colorbasians, Archontics, Hermogenians, Artemonites, and Ascodrugytae: all were second-century Christian heresies. This dictionary identifies forty heresies for the period 70-200 CE; a random search of nine in the index of the *New Catholic Encyclopedia* (see 23), which is generally strong on history, reveals that only two are mentioned there. Blunt, although over a century old and badly in need of reworking, has not been replaced, and is still quite useful. The classified table of contents lists Jewish sects (twelve in number), heathen religions, heretics referred to in the New Testament, early heretics (to 313 CE), later heretics (to 700 CE), medieval sects and heresies, continental sects of the Reformation, English sects, Scottish sects, American sects, Russian sects, church parties, and schools of thought. Blunt makes no effort at objectivity, and is therefore a lively read; the fanatical, licentious, anti-Christian, and iniquitous dot the wordscape of his colorful, if less ecumenical, age. Roman Catholics, for example, are "a sect originally organized by the Jesuits out of the relics of the Marian party of clergy and laity in the reign of Queen Elizabeth and further organized into a Donatist hierarchy by Cardinal Wiseman in the year 1850."

93.   Bouyer, Louis. **Dictionary of Theology.** Translated by Charles Underhill Quinn. New York, Desclee, 1965. 487p. LC 66-13370.
     Bouyer, a Calvinist turned Catholic, bridged the pre- and post-Vatican II eras, and was a leader in moving Roman Catholicism toward a thorough scientific and spiritual appreciation of the scriptures. This work, a translation from the 1963 French edition, treats doctrinal and theological points with definitions infused with biblical thought in a manner that many Catholic writers have yet to learn. In "Sex," for example, Bouyer develops concepts from the Hebrew scriptures and the New Testament, and mentions the positive contributions of Freud. Definitions are usually several paragraphs in length, one to two per page. There are references to biblical passages, to chief texts of Catholic doctrine, and to articles in the *Summa Theologica* of Thomas Aquinas. Other writers are mentioned only

for issues not treated by Thomas. Matters beyond doctrine, such as morality and history, are excluded. Bouyer is easier to digest than Rahner (see 121 and 122) and of higher quality than Hardon (see 66).

94.　Brandon, Samuel George Frederick, general ed. **A Dictionary of Comparative Religion.** New York, Scribner's, 1970. 704p. index. LC 76-111390. ISBN 0-684-15561-3.

Fundamental to this dictionary is its notion of comparative religion as an independent science, not "concerned primarily with the task of showing how other religions were destined to find their completion in Christianity" (Preface). The objective approach of the editors makes it especially valuable for its entries on Christian and Jewish topics. The entries, all signed and generally short, treat subjects as they relate to major religions. "Demon," for example, has a general introduction followed by an exposition of the demonology of nine religions. Bibliographies are abundant for a work of this size, and cross-references are extensive, "to show the interrelationships of topics and to facilitate comparative study." In this vein, and in addition to a general index, there is a synoptic index listing all entries relating to a major religion, which makes this book an effective introduction to each religion. Christianity and Buddhism receive the most entries. Important religions of smaller following receive single, comprehensive articles. There are minor problems with romanization of foreign alphabets: there is a cross reference to "Dukhobors," but the actual entry heading is "Doukhobors," quite a distance away. This is a quibble; the dictionary is first-rate scholarship and offers fascinating browsing.

95.　Brauer, Jerald C., ed. **The Westminster Dictionary of Christian History.** Philadelphia, PA, Westminster Press, 1971. 887p. LC 69-11071. ISBN 0-664-21285-9.

There is a strong attempt at objectivity in this work, but the editor admits to a larger proportion of articles on the twentieth century and on American churches than on other times and places. The intent is "to give an immediate, accurate, introductory definition and explanation concerning the major men, events, facts and movements in the history of Christianity" (Preface). While the editors are established church historians, many of the writers are younger academics. Entries are short and unsigned, with bibliographies appended only to the longest. There is an objective article on Judaism, but nothing specifically on the Holocaust. This is a well-done dictionary for introductory material; it needs updating to bring topics of current interest into perspective and to take account of the immense scholarship in biblical and historical studies of the past fifteen years.

96.　Burgess, Stanley M., and Gary B. McGee, eds. **Dictionary of Pentecostal and Charismatic Movements.** Grand Rapids, MI, Zondervan, 1988. 914p. (Regency Reference Library). LC 88-28341. ISBN 0-310-44100-5.

Although it does not purport to cover Pentecostalism in its worldwide applications, this thorough, ecumenical work does acknowledge the international scope of both Pentecostal and Charismatic movements. However, the book's central focus is on Great Britain and the United States. Its sixty-six contributors are drawn from evangelical and liberal Protestantism and Roman Catholicism. Many are women. Biographical entries cover persons of all types, and include frank treatments of Jimmy Lee Swaggart and Jim and Tammy Faye Bakker. Denominations, practices, books of the Bible, theological movements, and successful conferences all receive attention. Several entries are statistical studies. A brief bibliography is appended to each entry. Black-and-white photographs, especially of biographees, are frequent.

97. Campbell, Alastair V., ed. **A Dictionary of Pastoral Care.** New York, Crossroad, 1987. 300p. LC 87-20186. ISBN 0-8254-0834-3.

This broadly ecumenical and interdisciplinary work offers three hundred entries, by mostly British contributors, representing the mainline Christian denominations and Judaism and the fields of law, medicine, social work, teaching, philosophy, social psychology, and theology. A comprehensive theoretical background underpins the articles on theology, psychotherapy, counseling, and the nature and history of pastoral care. Basic information on the kinds of problems encountered is included, as are social and political topics such as pornography, poverty, and unemployment. Counseling is emphasized rather than such ministerial functions as preaching and the sacraments. Cross-references link articles, and each article is followed by a brief bibliography. There is a British tint to the whole; for example, British laws are mentioned where applicable.

98. Childress, James F., and John Macquarrie. **The Westminster Dictionary of Christian Ethics,** rev. ed. Philadelphia, PA, Westminster Press, 1986. 678p. index. LC 85-22539. ISBN 0-664-20940-8.

This is a major revision of Macquarries's *A Dictionary of Christian Ethics* (Philadelphia, PA, Westminster Press, 1967). It covers seven areas: (1) basic ethical concepts; (2) biblical ethics; (3) theological ethics; (4) philosophical ethics; (5) major non-Christian ethics; (6) psychological, social, and political concepts; and (7) substantial ethical problems such as abortion, war, unemployment. The number of contributors has doubled since the earlier edition, and the list is ecumenical, with offerings from Protestant, Anglican, Roman Catholic, Orthodox, and Jewish scholars. Many topics are new or treated far more extensively: war and peace, the environment, medicine, hunger, liberation. The articles are signed, and cross-references abundant, but bibliographies are too short and too infrequent, appended only to major articles. Some headings are idiosyncratic: one looks up "Roman Catholic Moral Theology" and is referred to "Modern Roman Catholic Moral Theology" and "Counter Reformation Moral Theology" (as well as "Moral Theology"). Like so many Westminster editions, this book is outstanding for its scholarship and readability. An ironic footnote: the entry on "Modern Roman Catholic Moral Theology" was written by Charles E. Curran, the Roman Catholic priest who was removed by the Vatican from his teaching position at Catholic University in 1986. In the entry, he capsulizes his views on legitimate dissent and in his bibliography he cites Pope John Paul II (as Karol Wojtyla).

99. Cully, Kendig Brubaker, ed. **The Westminster Dictionary of Christian Education.** Philadelphia, PA, Westminster Press, 1963. 812p. LC 63-11083.

Almost four hundred contributors, many with technical competence in fields other than religious education, wrote for this dictionary, and the result is uneven. Inspired by the need to update the *Encyclopedia of Sunday Schools and Religious Education* (New York, Thomas Nelson, 1915), Cully attempted to cover every aspect of Christian education. Thus, there is "clay modeling" and "doubt," "curriculum" and "India." "Bulletin boards" gets more space than "Norway," while "Books, religious" is shorter than either. A 1,277-item bibliography is included; it is now quite dated, and some items are only generally related to religious education. Westminster needs to update this one—the subject merits it—with a sharper editorial focus.

100. Davies, J. G., ed. **The New Westminster Dictionary of Liturgy and Worship.** Philadelphia, PA, Westminster Press, 1986. 544p. LC 86-9219. ISBN 0-664-21270-0.

This new work, the third edition of a work first published in 1972, as the *Dictionary of Liturgy and Worship*, takes into account the flourishing liturgical rejuvenation in Roman Catholicism, Anglicanism, and British Methodism, as well as contributions from the women's movement. It reflects a new interest in the human body with articles on dance, gesture, and posture. Groups of people, such as children, family, and the handicapped, are now covered. There is a 50 percent increase in churches treated. Bibliographies are appended to entries. Black-and-white photos are included, but they are darkly reproduced.

101. Dwight, Henry Otis, H. Allen Tupper, and Edwin Munsell Bliss, eds. **The Encyclopedia of Missions: Descriptive, Historical, Biographical, Statistical,** 2d ed. New York, Funk & Wagnalls, 1904. 851p. LC 4-27965. Reprint: Detroit, MI, Gale, 1975. LC 74-31438. ISBN 0-8103-4205-7.

   101.1. Bliss, Edwin Munsell, ed. **The Encyclopaedia of Missions: Descriptive, Historical, Biographical, Statistical.** New York, Funk & Wagnalls, 1891. 2 vols. index.

The second edition is an immense compendium of information about places, churches, and persons (deceased) relating to Protestant missions throughout the Americas, eastern Europe, Africa, Asia, and Oceania at the height of the colonial period. A ten-page article describes Roman Catholic missionary activity, and the Jews are covered as missionary objectives. Appendixes include a directory of foreign mission societies, the chronology of Protestant missions, a list of Bible versions in various languages, a list of missionaries who have translated the Bible, statistical tables of Protestant missions, and some statistics on Roman Catholic missions. The first edition included a gazetteer of mission stations, a listing of 269 Bible versions indexed by language and by geography, maps, bibliographies, and earlier versions of the statistical tables. Both editions contain unique information, and have great historical value for the study of empire as well as of religion.

102. Elwell, Walter A., ed. **Evangelical Dictionary of Theology.** Grand Rapids, MI, Baker Book House, 1984. 1,204p. LC 84-71575. ISBN 0-8010-3413-2.

This fine dictionary replaces Baker's *Dictionary of Theology* (1960), and contains twelve hundred entries by two hundred contributors, most of whom are evangelical Protestant males. Some are well-respected theologians like F. F. Bruce and Geoffrey W. Bromiley; many were trained at nonevangelical and non-Protestant institutions, and all were chosen for their sympathies for their subjects. Entries stress the theological dimension, but are written in popular language. Of the three entries on women, one was written by a woman, one by a man, and one by a married couple. "Counter-Reformation" offers a sympathetic treatment of its Catholic subject, and there is a penetrating analysis of Vatican II. "The Holocaust" gives a clear summary and, refreshingly, does not gloss over Christian reactions: "Many Christians as individuals helped Jews escape, but institutionalized Christianity failed both by silence and by lack of open, fearless, and concerted action to aid the oppressed." The two-page entry on "Sexual Ethics" attests to the currency of the work. Thorough, ecumenically drawn bibliographies, often including recent periodical literature, are appended to each article. This dictionary reflects a major body of Christian thought, and is more readable and less targeted to one thought system than Rahner and Vorgrimler (see 123).

103. Erickson, Millard J. **Concise Dictionary of Christian Theology.** Grand Rapids, MI, Baker Book House, 1986. 187p. LC 86-71158. ISBN 0-8010-3436-1.

Erickson intended this dictionary for students, especially those who may read his three-volume *Christian Theology* (Grand Rapids, MI, Baker Book House, 1986). While it is evangelical in outlook, coverage of Christian churches and lives is broad, and includes terms, events, movements, and theologians of the past and present. The 2,900 definitions are brief but masterful; more cross-references would have extended their value. For more extended treatments and different perspectives, one can turn to Rahner (see 121-123) or Elwell (see 102).

104. Ferguson, John. **An Illustrated Encyclopedia of Mysticism and the Mystery Religions.** New York, Seabury Press, 1977. 228p. LC 76-55812. ISBN 0-8164-9310-3.

Ferguson originally intended to confine himself to the ancient world, but expanded this fine work to encompass all ages and religions, including such modern developments as the work on art by C. G. Jung and neopentecostalism in the Roman Catholic Church. Christianity predominates, but there are entries on Jewish mysticism, and the religions of the East are well covered. Biographical entries on saints, heretics, artists, literary figures, philosophers, and psychologists are plentiful. Ferguson avoids the occult, demonology, magic, and witchcraft. Cross-references link articles that complement one another. Although he sometimes quotes whole poems, as in an article on Juan de la Cruz, Ferguson relied heavily on secondary sources for this work, and lists them in a ten-page bibliography.

105. Ferguson, Sinclair B., and David F. Wright, eds. **New Dictionary of Theology.** Downers Grove, IL, Inter-Varsity Press, 1988. 738p. (The Master Reference Collection). LC 87-30975. ISBN 0-8308-1400-0.

With signed articles by just under two hundred contributors, all seemingly Protestant, this fine theological dictionary includes essays on contemporary social, ecumenical, and intellectual topics such as Marxism and Christianity, sexuality, Shintoism and Christianity, the Holocaust, and African Christian theology, as well as ample coverage of the development of early Christian thought, medieval disputes, and Reformation and Counter-Reformation conflicts. Theologians, ancient and modern, from all branches of Christianity, are treated. Nowhere is the Protestant basis of the work explicitly stated (neither does Rahner identify his theological dictionary and encyclopedia (see 121-123) as Roman Catholic), although the preface notes that "the common standpoint of the editors and contributors is allegiance to the supreme authority of the Scriptures." In general, topics are grouped in larger categories for essays of broader scope; thus, homosexuality is covered in "Sexuality." The contributors append excellent bibliographies to each article, noting both classical twentieth-century works and quite recent books by Protestant, Catholic, and Jewish scholars. The use of cross-references is sophisticated. To the vast array of theological dictionaries and encyclopedias, this adds careful treatment of recent creative developments and directions, as well as a competent survey of past events and persons and perduring themes.

106. Harvey, Van A. **A Handbook of Theological Terms.** New York, Macmillan, 1964. 253p. LC 64-25193. ISBN 0-02-085430-7.

This solid work, meant for the general reader, covers systematic and philosophical theology, but excludes liturgy, the Bible, ethics, and ecclesiology. There are no biographies or bibliographies; but there are cross-references. Harvey intended in part to illuminate the differences between Roman Catholics and Protestants and among Protestants. There is little reference to the Eastern Orthodox. The selection of words is wise, and the definitions are objective, ecumenical, and readable, more easily understood than those of Rahner (see 121-123). See also 147.

107. Henry, Carl Ferdinand Howard, ed. **Baker's Dictionary of Christian Ethics.** Grand Rapids, MI, Baker Book House, 1973. 726p. LC 74-83488. ISBN 0-8010-4079-5.

The aim of this work is to be "authentically evangelical," and the 260 contributors who offered signed articles create a broad spectrum of evangelical Protestant scholarship. The choice of topics is wide-ranging, including historical questions such as the divine right of kings, and fair, if slightly dated, treatment of such contemporary issues as homosexuality and industrial espionage. Henry includes biographical sketches of ethicists, theologians, scientists, and philosophers. Six entries, including "Anti-semitism," cover Jewish matters. Some cross-references link articles on related topics, but a detailed index would have provided helpful access.

108.   Kaganoff, Benzion C. **A Dictionary of Jewish Names and Their History.** New York, Schocken, 1980. 266p. indexes. LC 77-70277. ISBN 0-8052-0643-4.

There are two parts to this unique, valuable, and fascinating dictionary. The first is an eleven-chapter history of Jewish names. The second, preceded by a four-page essay on determining the origins of family names, is the dictionary proper of selected Jewish names. Kaganoff holds that there were 75,000 Jewish names before the Holocaust. Through a series of symbols, names are identified as derived from geographical places, acronyms, abbreviations, personal characteristics, fancies, house signs, occupations, lineage, matronyms, patronyms, and "wife of." There is a bibliography, an index of all names mentioned in the book, and an index of subjects.

109.   Klenicki, Leon, and Geoffrey Wigoder. **A Dictionary of the Jewish-Christian Dialogue.** Ramsey, NJ, Paulist Press, 1984. 214p. indexes. (Stimulus Books, Studies in Judaism and Christianity). LC 83-62021. ISBN 0-8091-2590-0.

A Jewish view and a Christian view are presented for each of this book's thirty-four topics, including "Afterlife," "Antisemitism," "Church and synagogue," "Dogma," "Eschatology," "God," "Love," and "Personhood." Sometimes the topics are understood quite differently: "nomos," "torah," and "halakha," for example, are all translated into English as "law"; hence the great value of this fine work for promoting ecumenical discussions at all levels. Five Jewish and three Christian scholars collaborated on these essays, each several pages long. There is an index of Hebrew terms and a general index.

110.   Komonchak, Joseph, Mary Collins, and Dermot A. Lane, eds. **The New Dictionary of Theology.** Wilmington, DE, Michael Glazier, 1987. 1,112p. LC 87-82327. ISBN 0-89453-609-5.

The editors set out to present the developments in the Roman Catholic Church and its theology since the Second Vatican Council. They state that the dictionary is constructed around twenty-four topics which they believe "constitute the principal themes of the Christian vision of faith." Curiously, nowhere are these twenty-four topics listed. Presumably, they constitute the longest articles, from among those presented and signed by 170 contributors from throughout the English-speaking Catholic world. The writing quality of the contributions is uneven, and articles rarely reach the intensity of thought of Karl Rahner's definitions in his three works translated from German (see 121-123). Cross-references are abundant, and short bibliographies appear after each article.

111.   Metford, J. C. J. **Dictionary of Christian Lore and Legend.** New York, Thames and Hudson, 1983. 272p. LC 82-50815. ISBN 0-500-11020-4.

Metford defines *lore* as the learning and background knowledge associated with Christianity, and *legend* as "something to be read," a narrative which may be historical, traditional, or symbolic, without prejudgment as to its veracity. These, he notes, provide the essentials for Christian tradition in the visual arts, music, and literature. Thus, he includes materials on architecture, liturgy, the visible universe (fruits, flowers, colors), the Old and New Testament, apocryphal writings, the saints, the Byzantine heritage, changes in Catholicism and Anglicanism since Vatican II, and tales. Over forty different animals have entries. Unlike dictionaries of theology, this treats articles of faith "in the context of ordinary human experience." Along with reference material, Metford intended "to provide hours of informative browsing," and in this he is eminently successful. There are no bibliographies, a distinct weakness, since this work treats uncommon subjects. This is a unique and splendid work.

112.   Miethe, Terry L. **The Compact Dictionary of Doctrinal Words.** Minneapolis, MN, Bethany House, 1988. 224p. LC 86-12161. ISBN 0-87123-678-8.

Miethe briefly defines 550 words, some biblical (*Abba, Abomination of Desolation*), some theological (*Absolute, Adoptionism*), some historical (*Anabaptists, Antinomianism*), some philosophical (*Aristotelianism, Axiology*). Some entries, but not enough, have short bibliographies. There are also explanations of the non-Christian religions, too brief to be of value. Judaism gets six lines and no bibliography; Hinduism rates seven lines, two bibliographic citations, and a cross-reference. The choices for entries and bibliographies are idiosyncratic, reflecting Miethe's interests in medieval Catholic theology (he is a bibliographer of Augustine and Aquinas) and contemporary American Protestant conservatism.

113.   Muller, Richard A. **Dictionary of Latin and Greek Theological Terms: Drawn Principally from Protestant Scholastic Theology.** Grand Rapids, MI, Baker Book House, 1985. 340p. index. LC 85-70795. ISBN 0-8010-6185-7.

Drawing from both the Reformed and the Lutheran traditions, Muller defines the technical vocabulary used by late sixteenth- and seventeenth-century orthodox or scholastic theologians. Greek terms are alphabetized in their roman transliteration, given in Greek, and then defined. Muller stresses the Protestant genesis of this scholarly work, but he is too modest. Protestant orthodoxy has achieved a renaissance through such twentieth-century writers as Karl Barth, but in addition to this, many of the defined terms are universal to Christian theology.

114.   Negev, Avraham, ed. **Archaeological Encyclopedia of the Holy Land**, rev. ed. Nashville, TN, Thomas Nelson, 1986. 419p. index. LC 85-15276. ISBN 0-8407-7523-7.

Avi-Yonah and Stern (see 90) arranged their archaeological encyclopedia by existing site. Negev emphasizes the geographic names from the Bible, describes any excavations carried out in them, and traces their history from biblical times through the Arab conquest. He offers introductory articles on the archaeology of the Holy Land, on the methods of research in archaeology, and on prehistory. Like Avi-Yonah and Stern, Negev includes survey articles, covering such topics as baths and bathing, burial, and weapons and warfare. He adds a glossary; chronological charts of the royal lineages of Israel, Judah, Egypt, Assyria, Babylon, Persia, the Hellenic dynasties, Rome, and Byzantium; and a bibliography of ancient sources, but, unlike his colleagues, no modern works. Negev shares many contributors with Avi-Yonah and Stern.

115.   Neill, Stephen, Gerald H. Anderson, and John Goodwin, eds. **Concise Dictionary of the Christian World Mission.** Nashville, TN, Abingdon Press, 1971. 682p. LC 76-21888. ISBN 0-687-09371-6.

This is a very good work for charting the spread of Christianity outside the traditional western dominions. Unlike Dwight and Bliss (see 101) and Goddard (see 190), these editors have gone beyond Protestant missions in an "attempt to provide comprehensive information as to the entire process through which in the last five centuries Christianity has grown from a western to a universal religion." Subjects covered include persons and countries. Approximately two hundred scholars, from many denominations and parts of the world, contributed signed, objective articles with short bibliographies.

116.   O'Carroll, Michael. **Corpus Christi: An Encyclopedia of the Eucharist.** Wilmington, DE, Michael Glazier, 1988. 222p. index. LC 88-45354. ISBN 0-89453-687-7.

As he did in *Theotokos* (see 117) and *Trinitas* (see 118), O'Carroll has taken a major dogma of orthodox Christianity and, from a decidedly Roman Catholic viewpoint, treated the historical development of its great themes and the struggles to understand and redefine it. He treats extensively the Roman Catholic definition of *transubstantiation* (five pages) and the Council of Trent (nine pages), but also gives much time to Luther and the Lutheran-Roman Catholic dialogue, as well as to Bucer, Calvin, and Zwingli, often allowing them to speak in their own words. The bibliographic material after each entry is composed of a wide range of international scholarship, with books in German, French, Italian, and English. The index is merely a list of entries.

117.   O'Carroll, Michael. **Theotokos: A Theological Encyclopedia of the Blessed Virgin Mary,** rev. ed. with supplement. Wilmington, DE, Michael Glazier, 1983. 390p. LC 82-82382. ISBN 0-89453-268-5.

The title *Theotokos* ("God-bearer"), referring to Mary, the mother of Jesus, was a crucial dispute between orthodox Christians and Nestorians in the fifth century. In this work, O'Carroll includes articles on points of doctrine, fathers of the church, contemporary theologians, the Bible, songs and prayers, devotions, shrines and appearances, and fields of study such as archaeology. The work is Roman Catholic in origin and point of view, but O'Carroll strives for an ecumenical balance with articles on "Protestantism," "Ecumenism," "Anglicanism," and leading Protestant thinkers such as Barth. Articles are followed by excellent selective bibliographies in the major scholarly languages. Cross-references are abundant, but there is no index. The article titles from an eleven-page supplement to this edition are interfiled in the main alphabet of entries. Mariology as a scientific study is receiving increasing attention by Christian theologians, because of its ecumenical and feminist implications, and O'Carroll has provided the most widely used and usable reference work on the subject.

118.   O'Carroll, Michael. **Trinitas: A Theological Encyclopedia of the Holy Trinity.** Wilmington, DE, Michael Glazier, 1987. 220p. LC 86-45326. ISBN 0-89453-595-1.

As in his *Theotokos* (see 117), O'Carroll takes a major doctrine, which has seen renewed interest among Christian theologians of every kind, and in encyclopedia articles examines the development of the doctrine from New Testament times to the present. This tour de force is essentially Roman Catholic in outlook, but O'Carroll takes care to examine Protestant and Eastern Orthodox positions. His coverage includes theologians from church fathers to contemporary thinkers such as Barth, Rahner (see 121-123), and Kelly (see 242), as well as creeds, concepts, New Testament language, and omnibus articles such as "Recent Writers." Excellent, highly selective bibliographies accompany each article, and a master bibliography lists seventy-one major scholarly sources. O'Carroll uses cross-references abundantly to link related articles, but provides no index.

119.   Ollard, Sidney Leslie. **A Dictionary of English Church History.** Milwaukee, WI, Young Churchman, 1912. 673p. index. LC 13-1314.

Ollard attempts to synthesize, for the ordinary reader, the great advances in historical work on the English church achieved during the thirty-year period prior to 1912. "English" is meant literally here: the provinces of Canterbury and York are examined, but there is no coverage of Scotland, Ireland, America, or other English-speaking lands. The tone is Anglican throughout, but there is ecumenically minded treatment of Roman Catholicism.

120. Purvis, John Stanley. **Dictionary of Ecclesiastical Terms.** London and New York, Thomas Nelson, 1962. 204p. LC 65-51845.

Purvis includes terms relating specifically to the church and its structures. There is little theology; for example, there is no article on the Trinity or Jesus, but there are entries on "Trinitarian" and "Jesuit." Purvis includes many phrases of Latin origin still used in the Anglican and Roman Churches, and many British terms such as "month's mind" and "churchwarden." This is a serviceable, small work, but yields to Cross (see 31) for extent of coverage.

121. Rahner, Karl, ed. **Encyclopedia of Theology: The Concise Sacramentum Mundi.** New York, Seabury Press, 1975. 1,536p. LC 74-33145. ISBN 0-8164-1182-4. Reprinted: New York, Crossroad, 1982. 1,841p. LC 82-7285. ISBN 0-8245-0303-1.

Rahner placed great importance on producing reference works for the educated reader who is not a professional theologian: the student, the pastor, the lay person. This one merits a separate entry from Rahner's *Sacramentum Mundi* (see 122) because it is not simply a condensation of it. It does indeed have articles from that source, but Rahner added pieces from the *Lexikon für Theologie und Kirche* and the *Theologisches Taschenlexikon* as well as entirely new articles. Thus, post-Vatican II Roman Catholic theology is viewed from a more recent vantage point than in *Sacramentum Mundi*. While there are no biographical entries, systems such as Thomism, Aristotelianism, and Augustinianism are covered. Rahner dispenses with bibliographies in this work. As with many other Christian reference works, there is no specific mention of the Holocaust in the article on Judaism, only a reference to "the direst persecution in history, under National Socialism in Germany."

122. Rahner, Karl A. et al., eds. **Sacramentum Mundi: An Encyclopedia of Theology.** New York, Herder and Herder, 1968-70. 6 vols. index. LC 68-25987.

If a reference work be a compendium of what one does not need to remember but may need to look up, the editors claim the opposite for this modern summa of Roman Catholic theology: "to furnish the truths which should be the constant and vital possession of the believer." The list of contributors is "international"—read *European* here, as one looks in vain for an Oriental or African name—but the list is indeed a who's who of Roman Catholic theologians of the 1950s and 1960s, many of whom were theological advisors at Vatican II. Since most wrote seminal works on the topics they address in the encyclopedia, one can assume that the articles are accurate synopses of their thought. Any resurgence like that which accompanied and followed Vatican II gives rise to multitudinous developments; consequently, this work could already be considered dated. There are no articles on liberation or feminist theology, on Catholic pentecostalism, or on women. However, it is better to consider it fundamental rather than dated; "Political theology" by Johannes Metz serves as a prolegomenon to understanding the controversy over liberation theology. There are no biographies. Articles are signed, and the list of contributors identifies their articles so that one can read all the entries by a given theologian.

123. Rahner, Karl, and Herbert Vorgrimler. **Dictionary of Theology**, 2d ed. Translated by Richard Strachan, et al. New York, Crossroad, c.1981, 1985. 541p. LC 81-5492. ISBN 0-8245-0691-X.

Although genuinely a dictionary (the entries are short definitions), this work requires rigorous reading. Rahner, a Roman Catholic and one of the most influential theological advisors at Vatican II, is known for his philosophical theology, and the definitions here are intense. "Now," for example, contains allusions to the use of the word in Plato, Aristotle, Augustine, Meister Eckhart, Jaspers, and Kierkegaard. The title is incomplete: it is in fact a dictionary of Roman Catholic theology. A five-page entry on "Protestantism" outlines the theological positions of the Reformation churches and gives an unflinching—but not triumphal—Catholic response; one can study this and understand clearly what each side is saying. There are no bibliographic references except to the Bible, Denziger (*Enchridion symbolorum*, a compilation of Catholic dogmatic statements), and the documents of Vatican II. This edition is a translation of the tenth German edition of *Kleines theologisches Wörterbuch*, and is a complete reworking of a 1965 English translation. *The Westminster Dictionary of Christian Theology* (see 124) puts ideas into more scriptural and historical context, and is more accessible to the general reader. Rahner's dictionary is widely cited, in works stemming from the Protestant tradition as well as the Catholic, indicating the respect held for someone who so clearly understands and carefully enunciates the position of his own church.

124.   Richardson, Alan, and John Bowden, eds. **The Westminster Dictionary of Christian Theology.** Philadelphia, PA, Westminster Press, 1983. 614p. index. LC 83-14521. ISBN 0-664-21398-7.

This is based on Richardson's *A Dictionary of Christian Theology* (Philadelphia, PA, Westminster Press, 1969), and takes into account many new developments in theology in the intervening years, including pluralism, political theology, the psychology and sociology of religion, and the application to Christian doctrine of the kind of historical criticism which has been directed to the Bible. Biographical entries have been dropped, but there is an index of names: Wittgenstein is mentioned in six articles, Barth in almost seventy. Articles are signed, and the list of contributors reads like a who's who of prominent, contemporary, English-speaking theologians. In addition to new trends, there is thorough coverage of traditionally important terms: hence, "Incarnation" and "Ex opere operato" on the one hand, and "Marxist theology" and "Process theology" on the other. Bibliographies are very selective. At the same time readable and scholarly, this dictionary is more ecumenical than either Rahner (see 121-123) or Taylor (see 128).

125.   Roberti, Francesco, comp. **Dictionary of Moral Theology.** Translated by Henry J. Yannone; edited by Pietro Palazzini. Westminster, MD, Newman Press, 1962. LC 60-14828.

Intended to be a fresh examination of moral issues in the light of psychology, the social sciences, and twentieth-century papal statements, this dictionary, prepared by fifty-four priests and laypersons in Italy, reflects pre-Vatican II Italian Catholic thought, and is now dated because of developments in the biomedical sciences and new currents of Catholic thought since the Second Vatican Council. Introductory essays define *moral theology* and offer a historical overview of the science. An extensive bibliography lists works in English, German, Latin, French, Italian, and Spanish.

126.   Stoeckle, Bernard, ed. **Concise Dictionary of Christian Ethics.** New York, Seabury Press, 1979. 285p. LC 79-50666. ISBN 0-8245-0300-7.

These eighty-five signed essays and many more short entries reflect the Roman Catholic tradition. The entries are learned; some were translated from the German. There are good bibliographies of British, American, and translated continental works.

127.   Sutcliffe, John M. **A Dictionary of Religious Education.** London, S.C.M. Press, 1984. 376p. LC gb87-3113. ISBN 0-334-01968-0.

Sutcliffe ranges over all religious education, on different continents and in different faiths. He concentrates on methods of teaching, and identifies four categories for treatment: (1) description of the major religious teaching traditions; (2) summaries of the philosophical, theological, sociological, and psychological understandings of religious education; (3) outlines of curriculum and teaching methods; and (4) notes on resources for the teaching of religious education. His wide-ranging topics include countries, churches, devices, methods, techniques, skills, and special groups such as the handicapped. He includes an entry on Marx's influence. This work is more insightful and up to date than Cully (see 99).

128. Taylor, Richard Shelley, ed. **Beacon Dictionary of Theology.** Kansas City, MO, Beacon Hill Press, 1983. 559p. LC 84-175168. ISBN 0-8341-0811-9.

Taylor proposes "a scholarly dictionary frankly committed to a Wesleyan understanding of salvation" and a work "unabashedly evangelical and unabashedly Wesleyan." His 157 contributors, presumably all from this tradition, produced 954 articles written at the level of the general reader. There are abundant cross-references; Taylor reminds us that the intellectual chase through cross-references "is of infinitely greater consequence and more lasting benefit than could ever accrue from pursuing the fox or the possum," and further counsels the reader to move to a related article if he or she runs into "verbal fog." Short bibliographies are appended to the articles. There are no biographical entries, but this is not a weakness, because of the many encyclopedias treating individual theologians. This is a serviceable work, but not as powerful as Richardson and Bowden (see 124) or Rahner and Vorgrimler (see 123).

129. Turnbull, Ralph G., ed. **Baker's Dictionary of Practical Theology.** Grand Rapids, MI, Baker Book House, 1967. 469p. indexes. LC 67-18199.

The entries in this work are not in alphabetical order, but are arranged in a series of general categories: preaching, homiletics, hermeneutics, evangelism — missions, counseling, administration, pastoral, stewardship, worship, and education. "Preaching," to take one, has eleven subchapters, each with an extensive bibliography, and each done by a separate contributor. There are indexes of persons and of subjects.

130. Wakefield, Gordon S., ed. **The Westminster Dictionary of Christian Spirituality.** Philadelphia, PA, Westminster Press, 1983. 400p. LC 83-14527. ISBN 0-664-21396-0.

In line with the high quality of current Westminster dictionaries, this readable, ecumenical, and scholarly work treats subjects which are loosely covered in other reference works yet pertain to the very essence of Judaism and Christianity. The preface notes an even proportion among Protestant, Orthodox, and Catholic Christianity, with a favoring of the Western experience. The short, signed entries include schools, as in "Russian spirituality," and terms, as in "Death of God." Coverage is contemporary, with entries on Zen, Rastafarianism, feminine spirituality, black spirituality, liberation spirituality, and the Charismatic movement. Non-Christian religions are noted — Judaism, Islam, Buddhism — but the Amerindian is missing. Entries are signed and contain short bibliographies. This well-done work merits extensive re-creational reading.

2
Handbooks and Statistics Sources

I. Handbooks

131.   Barbour, Hugh, and J. William Frost. **The Quakers.** New York and Westport, CT, Greenwood Press, 1988. 409p. index. (Denominations in America, vol. 3). LC 88-10240. ISBN 0-313-22816-7.

The first part of this handbook, which surveys the Quaker movement from 1650 to 1987, is an extensive historical study, the first overview since 1942. A third of this study is devoted to the origins of the movement in England to 1700; the remainder covers the development of all the American branches and their confrontations over slavery, war, civil rights, and other social problems. The second part of the book is a biographical dictionary of prominent American Friends deceased before 1988. Each entry is accompanied by a bibliography with works by and about the biographee.

Three maps chart the growth of the meetings through 1890, and a table of membership figures covers the period from 1890 through 1982. A two-page chronology links Quaker events with other American religious facts. An index gives subject access to the whole work, which is completed by a six-page bibliographic essay structured along historical lines.

132.   Beaver, R. Pierce et al., consulting eds. **Eerdmans' Handbook to the World's Religions.** Grand Rapids, MI, William B. Eerdmans, 1982. 448p. index. LC 82-137503. ISBN 0-8028-3563-5.

After an introduction on the development of religion, this work covers ancient, primal, and living religions. Although the contributors, mostly British scholars, "write from a Christian concern to describe each faith 'as it is,' " the book is structured to point toward Christianity, wherein the word *fulfillment* is used to indicate its relation to other religions. A thirty-five page essay, "People of a Book," covers Judaism. Like other Eerdmans handbooks, this is replete with diagrams, special inserts, and color photographs. Beaver includes an index of subjects and a glossary, called a "rapid fact finder."

133.   Bent, Ans Joachim Van der. **Handbook: Member Churches**, rev. ed. Geneva, Switzerland, World Council of Churches, 1985. 289p. ISBN 2-8254-0725-9.

This is a companion volume to the *Directory, Christian Councils* (see 186), also published by the World Council of Churches (WCC). It is divided into three parts: (1) the history and description of the regional conferences and national councils; (2) a description of the various Christian world communions (churches); and (3) member churches listed by continent, subcontinent, and country. An appendix gives the constitution of the WCC (only two paragraphs) and its rules. There are indexes by country, by English name, and by non-English name if there is one. This is especially useful for finding information about churches outside the United States; American churches are amply covered by Melton (see 41), Mead (see 159), and Piepkorn (see 12).

134. Brackney, William Henry. **The Baptists.** New York, Greenwood Press, 1988. 329p. (Denominations in America, vol. 2). LC 87-15047. ISBN 0-313-23822-7.

Along with Robinson on the Unitarians and the Universalists (see 167), Brackney's work is part of Henry Warner Bowden's series Denominations in America, which updates and replaces the American Church History series done between 1893 and 1897. Brackney divides the work into two parts. The first part, an essay on Baptist history, identifies five central points, or "vertices," important to all Baptists: the Bible, the church, the ordinances/sacraments, voluntarism, and religious liberty. Extensive footnotes to this essay form a kind of bibliography. The second half of the work is a biographical dictionary, after the manner of Bowden's *Dictionary of American Religious Biography* (see 228), which includes sketches of Baptist leaders, each followed by a bibliography of works by and about the subject. Appendixes include a chronology from 1609 to 1979, statistics on the "International Baptist Family," and an 18-page bibliographic essay. There is an index to the whole work.

135. Brierley, Peter, ed. **UK Christian Handbook.** 1987-88 ed. London, MARC Europe, 1986. 649p. indexes. LC gb86-20591. ISBN 0-9476-9744-6.

Until the 1982 edition, the information contained in this work was spread among four publications. The 1982, 1984, and 1986-87 editions complement *The Church of England Year Book* (see 201) by covering all other Christian denominations. A series of short articles on the state of Christianity at home and in the missions is followed by a section of statistics and graphs on many denominations. A directory section lists Christian practitioners as diverse as "radio programme producers" and "book shops." Seven indexes do not lead to material in the book; rather, they list the membership of organizations such as the Evangelical Alliance.

136. Cardozo, Arlene Rossen. **Jewish Family Celebrations: The Sabbath, Festivals, and Ceremonies.** New York, St. Martin's Press, 1982. 268p. index. LC 82-5568. ISBN 0-312-44231-9.

Cardozo sought to recapture Jewish festival traditions for her family, and found that there was no guide. She wrote this one, explaining the origins of each festival and including recipes, blessings, songs, and family plays. Each blessing is given in Hebrew script, in romanized Hebrew, and in English. She covers the ancient fall, winter, and spring festivals, and includes two modern spring festivals: Yom Hasho'ah (Holocaust Day of Remembrance) and Yom Ha'atzma'ut (Israel Independence Day). There is a bibliographical essay called "Building the Family Bookshelf," an additional, extensive, more scholarly bibliography, and a glossary. Cardozo writes for assimilated Jews seeking to recover their heritage but, like Strassfeld (see 171), who offers deeper treatment, she can be read profitably by Christians who would like to understand both contemporary Judaism and the Jewish origins of their own religion.

137. Chapman, Colin Gilbert. **An Eerdmans' Handbook: The Case for Christianity.** Grand Rapids, MI, Eerdmans, 1981. 313p. index. LC 81-9704. ISBN 0-8028-3547-3.

Chapman offers an apologetic for Christianity for the lay reader rather than the advanced thinker. He begins with basic human questions, shows Christian answers to them, presents a Christian world view, tests it against other systems (some of which are of Christian provenance: Catholic scholasticism, deism, rationalism, atheism, agnosticism, mysticism, pantheism, Marxism, existentialism, and humanism), and, finally, presents the case for Jesus of Nazareth. The treatment of non-Christian thought systems is frequently simplistic, and there is no attempt to present or evaluate objectively a possible multiplicity of Christian responses. Abundant quotations and many color photos add a slick appearance. Authors are indexed, and there is a list of references.

138.   Cohen, Arthur A., and Paul R. Mendes-Flohr, eds. **Contemporary Jewish Religious Thought: Original Essays on Critical Concepts, Movements and Beliefs.** New York, Scribner's, 1987. 1,163p. index. LC 86-11856. ISBN 0-684-18628-4.

In compiling this handbook of contemporary Jewish theology, Cohen and Mendes-Flohr seek to avoid apologies—explanations of Judaism that allow non-Jews "to set the parameters of Jewish self-articulation"—and to produce a broad spectrum of Judaism, including Orthodox, Conservative, Reform, Reconstructionist, Zionist, non-Zionist, and secular Jewish thought. One hundred five contributors, including Emil Fackenheim, Jacob Neusner, Gershom Scholem, R. J. Zwi Werblowsky (see 86), and Geoffrey Wigoder (see 81 and 87), produced 6- to 16-page essays, each with 3 to 5 bibliographic citations, on 140 topics. A glossary includes terms, authors, historical movements, and events that appear at least twice in the essays. All Hebrew words are transliterated to the roman alphabet. Given the caliber of the contributors, and the pertinence and breadth of subjects treated, it is hard to dispute the compilers' contention that this "is not a group of separate and disconnected essays, but in itself constitutes a theological document of major importance."

139.   Cohen, Harry Alan. **A Basic Jewish Encyclopaedia: Jewish Teachings and Practices Listed and Interpreted in the Order of Their Importance Today.** Hartford, CT, Hartmore House, 1965. 205p. LC 65-16998.

After consulting the writings of some 100 Orthodox, Conservative, and Reform Jewish authorities, Cohen produced this handbook of Jewish teachings, with 155 entries, which with their subdivisions cover 350 themes. The teachings are ranked in order of importance under the categories "Elohim," "Torah," "Shema," "Mitzvah," "Shabbat," and "Yisrael." Cohen is aiming for a triple readership: rabbis and educators, Jewish men and women, and non-Jews who wish to learn what is especially valuable to Jews. Cohen lists 112 rabbinical citations, but does not offer a bibliography of the authorities he consulted. He does add Hebrew and English indexes, in which the most important articles are signaled with boldface type. Unlike any other Jewish reference work in English, this is similar to handbooks and dictionaries of Christian doctrine.

140.   Coxill, H. Wakelin, and Kenneth Grubb, eds. **World Christian Handbook 1968.** Nashville, TN, Abingdon Press, 1968. 378p. index.

Earlier editions were brought out in 1949, 1952, 1957, and 1962. This is the final edition, and the work is superseded by Barrett (see 27), who also worked on this edition. The handbook is divided into: (1) a section of nine essays on various churches and movements; (2) statistics, arranged by continent and then by country, of Protestantism, Anglicanism, Roman Catholicism, Judaism, and some world religions; and (3) a directory with addresses of ecumenical organizations and (by country) Protestant and Anglican bodies throughout the world.

141. Deedy, John. **The Catholic Fact Book.** Chicago, IL, Thomas More Press, 1986. 412p. index. LC 86-215323. ISBN 0-88347-186-8.

The time was when Catholic school children learned many facts about the religious culture of Catholicism in the western world; now even professionals may be ignorant of the matters noted in this work. What, for example, is a "minor basilica," and where is the nearest? There are thirty in the United States.

Deedy arranges his facts in seven sections: history; the basic beliefs; the teaching of the church, often including key paragraphs from papal encyclicals and conciliar documents; an organizational chapter covering movements, artifacts, institutions, orders, organizations, and communications; saints; famous Catholics; and a chapter of miscellany arranged alphabetically as a small dictionary. The index is particularly valuable for specific access to all this material. Deedy's work differs from Foy's (see 207) in that the latter offers systematic and complete information, while Deedy edits his to include what he thinks are highlights. His judgment is good and the book is useful to non-Catholics and Catholics alike.

142. Dollar, George W. **A History of Fundamentalism.** Greenville, SC, Bob Jones University Press, 1973. 415p. index. LC 73-176063.

The main part of Dollar's work is a monographic history of fundamentalism in the United States from 1875 through the early 1970s, but extensive additional sections give the work apparent reference value. A biographical index includes a capsule biography of every person mentioned in the history. This is valuable for researching fundamentalists, but sketches of nonfundamentalists are judgmental and prone to error. Dollar frequently calls liberal and neo-orthodox writers "apostates," and makes at least one egregious error when he identifies Martin Heidegger as a Jewish philosopher, which he was indeed not. Such mistakes bring into doubt Dollar's entire work. A bibliography includes works by fundamentalists and non- and antifundamentalists, and lists twenty-one theses and dissertations. An eight-page glossary is at its best in defining fundamentalist terms, and at its worst in dealing with other religions such as Buddhism. Most of the definitions are incomplete; for example, the theory of *inerrancy* should specify historical and scientific accuracy in the Bible. Fundamentalism is an important religious phenomenon in the United States, and needs better treatment than Dollar has afforded it. Some attention to it is given by Hill (see 35).

143. Donin, Hayim Halevy. **To Be A Jew: A Guide to Jewish Observance in Contemporary Life.** New York, Basic Books, 1972. 336p. index. LC 72-89175. ISBN 0-465-08624-1.

This thoughtful and readable work reviews basic Jewish beliefs, covers laws and observances, and provides a rationale for observance so that the Jew can live as a Jew in western society. Donin provides an index, and his bibliography of sixty-four items offers an excellent choice of supplementary reading.

144. Dowley, Tim, ed. **Eerdmans' Handbook to the History of Christianity.** Grand Rapids, MI, Eerdmans, 1977. 656p. indexes. LC 77-5616. ISBN 0-8028-3450-7.

This handbook, for the general reader, focuses on the development of the western Christian church and its missionary movements throughout the world. Eastern Christianity merits barely twenty pages after coverage of the first centuries of Christian development. Indeed, the sixty-six contributors seem to come from most branches of western Christianity, but not from the eastern tradition. Dowley has included time lines, maps, chronologies, charts and color photographs of art, architecture, and persons. Sidebars treat noteworthy persons and movements, and quotations from famous Christians, non-Christians, and anti-Christians gloss the pages. There are indexes of people and places. Chadwick and Evans's *Atlas of the Christian Church* (see 271) covers the same territory with better visuals and more scholarly depth, and pays attention to the East and the Third World.

145. Fu, Charles Wei-hsun, and Gerhard E. Spiegler, eds. **Movements and Issues in World Religions: A Sourcebook and Analysis of Developments Since 1945; Religion, Ideology, and Politics.** Westport, CT, Greenwood Press, 1987. 571p. index. LC 86-4634. ISBN 0-313-23238-5.

Fu and Spiegler gather twenty-one essays, each averaging twenty-six pages, by a wide range of religious writers, and group them in five divisions: interreligious conflicts; religion and politics in developing nations; religion and politics in developed nations; Marxism, religion, and politics; and the Holocaust: Christian/Jewish reflections. Although Buddhism, Hinduism, Islam, and Confucianism are studied, either Christianity or Judaism or both receive treatment in almost half the essays. The theme of the whole is the interrelation of religion and politics, as new religious currents develop and older traditions grow stronger. The essays cover the globe and its history over the past forty years, to examine both whole continents and persistent sore spots such as Northern Ireland, India and Pakistan, and Israel and the Arab countries. The two essays on the Holocaust examine current Jewish and Christian thinking. Extensive bibliographies, up to several pages, appear at the end of each essay, and several writers provide glossaries for their contributions. An index offers unified access to the whole.

146. **A Handbook of Christian Theology: Definition Essays on Concepts and Movements of Thought in Contemporary Protestantism.** New York, Living Age Books, published by Meridian Books, New York, 1958. 380p. LC 57-10852.

One hundred one terms of interest in the 1950s are defined in short essays by 71 writers, including some of the most outstanding of mid-century English-speaking Protestants: the Niebuhr brothers, Paul Tillich, Robert McAfee Brown, Jaroslav Pelikan, W. A. Visser't Hooft, and Thomas J. J. Altizer. The terms include classic Christian subjects, such as authority, death, the Incarnation, and the Trinity, as well as matters of emerging interest like neo-orthodoxy, ecumenism, Judaism (this essay contributed by a Jew, Arthur A. Cohen), and Thomism. At first the book appears dated, but the writers are good, and the topics still command debate and dialogue.

147. Harvey, Van Austin. **A Handbook of Theological Terms.** New York, Macmillan, 1964. 253p. LC 64-25193.

Harvey stresses that this is a word book, not a dictionary, and that therefore there are exclusions. The emphasis is on terms of systematic and philosophical theology; ethics, ecclesiology, works of literature, and the Bible are left out. Harvey is good at illuminating fundamental differences between Protestants and Roman Catholics and among Protestants. There are some cross-references, but no bibliographies. This essentially Protestant work is especially valuable for Roman Catholics, as the renaissance in Catholic theology has drawn from the work of such neo-Reformed theologians as Barth, Brunner, Bultmann, the Niebuhrs, and Tillich. Some essays, such as "Proofs for the Existence of God," run several pages. See also 106.

148. Hassan, Bernard. **The American Catholic Catalog.** New York, Harper & Row, 1980. 274p. index. LC 80-129756. ISBN 0-0606-3735-8.

Hassan was moved by such publications as *The Whole Earth Catalog* (Menlo Park, CA, Portola Institute, 1968-71) and *The Jewish Catalog* (Siegel, Richard et al. Philadelphia, PA, Jewish Publication Society of America, 1973) (see also 217) to produce this work and answer the question, "Just what is it that Catholics do?" Throughout, there is a concentration on ritual and worship. Hassan includes chapters on Christian initiation (baptism), the Mass and Eucharist, the rite of reconciliation (confession), matrimony, the anointing of the sick, ordination, the liturgical year, the saints, Mary, the spiritual life of

Catholics, music, and pilgrimage. For each rite, there is an explanation of what occurs, the new meanings intended by the post-Vatican II church, and a bibliography, making this a good introduction to the rituals of the church for Catholic and non-Catholic alike. A section of "yellow pages" (which are not, in fact, yellow) list such information as religious artists by state and Canadian province; associations and organizations for divers groups, such as black Catholics and deaf Catholics; book clubs and bookstores; colleges and universities; fraternities and sororities; houses of prayer; psychiatrists; and so forth.

149. Hinnells, John R., ed. **A Handbook of Living Religions.** New York, Viking Penguin, 1984. 528p. index. LC 85-243432. ISBN 0-7139-1626-5.

Meant as a companion to the *Facts on File Dictionary of Religion* (see 36), this handbook offers academic research on living religions to the general reader. Each religion is covered by an essay which starts with introductory information on its primary sources, its history, and the main assumptions of the scholarly study of it. The essay then covers the religion's main teachings, practices, popular traditions, and modern developments. The scholars add bibliographies, and often cite listed items in the essays. Of particular note is the thirty-six-page essay on Judaism, with eight pages of tables and maps, and a twenty-eight-item bibliography. Christianity is treated in sixty-six pages, with nine tables and a fifty-three-item bibliography.

150. **The Jewish People, Past and Present.** New York, Jewish Encyclopedic Handbooks, Central Yiddish Culture Organization, 1946-55. 4 vols. LC 46-7394.

Gershom Scholem, William Foxwell Albright, and Ashley Montagu are among the high-level contributors to this series, produced soon after the Holocaust in an effort to provide comprehensive and objective information on all aspects of Jewish life and thought. The first three volumes are a unit, with an index at the end of the third. Essays on Jewish history, demographic trends, agriculture, education, morals and law, social and political thought, and trends in spiritual life are accompanied by five hundred black-and-white and some color photographs. A fourth volume contains eleven monographs on the theme of Jewish life in the United States. Chronological tables and statistics are plentiful.

151. Keeley, Robin, organizing ed. **Eerdmans' Handbook to Christian Belief.** Grand Rapids, MI, Eerdmans, 1982. 480p. index. LC 82-7282. ISBN 0-8028-3577-5.

Meant for the general reader, this is a well-written handbook by an international group of contributors, many of them ecumenically minded evangelicals from the United Kingdom or British Commonwealth. The range of Christian beliefs is treated: revelation, God, Jesus Christ, ethics, and community. Contemporary issues are faced, including the creationism versus evolution controversy, new Christian communities, and God in world religions. There is a glossary and an index. Throughout, there are thumbnail sketches of prominent persons, movements, and events, with ample color photography. Treatment of "Jews and Christians" is very brief.

152. Keeley, Robin, organizing ed. **An Eerdmans' Handbook, Christianity in Today's World.** Grand Rapids, MI, Eerdmans, 1985. 384p. index. LC 85-6905. ISBN 0-8028-3618-6.

Keeley and his colleagues offer an impressionistic, rather than systematic or statistical, view of Christianity in the last quarter of the twentieth century. Their three sections present an overview of the main subgroups of Christianity, its impact on different geographical areas, and the application of Christian beliefs to contemporary situations. Meant for the general reader, this work has many color pictures, sidebars of special information, and diagrams showing how individual churches came to be. It is a browsing book rather than a strict reference work.

153. Klein, Isaac. **A Guide to Jewish Religious Practice.** New York, The Jewish Theological Seminary of America, 1979. 588p. index. (The Moreshet Series, no. 6). LC 78-12159. ISBN 0-87334-004-3.

Klein offers a digest of Jewish law "in the authentic spirit of the Conservative Movement," meant for the Jew in contemporary American society. He incorporates decisions reached by the Rabbinical Assembly Committee on Jewish Law and Standards, and covers daily prayer, blessings for various occasions, the Sabbath, holy days, fasts, the laws of mourning, dietary laws, marriage, circumcision, adoption, proselytes, divorce, and family purity. A widely read man, Klein is likely to quote the Christian scholar Paul Tillich in making a point. He includes a twenty-page bibliography with equal parts in English and Hebrew (with a romanized alphabet). Hebrew prayers are not romanized or translated. A detailed index gives access to the work, which goes far beyond other reference works in its serious study of daily life as a holistic expression of Jewish spirituality.

154. Kolatch, Alfred J. **The Jewish Book of Why.** Middle Village, NY, Jonathan David, 1981. 324p. index. LC 81-3274. ISBN 0-8246-0256-0.

154.1. Kolatch, Alfred J. **The Second Jewish Book of Why.** Middle Village, NY, Jonathan David, 1985. 423p. index. LC 84-21477. ISBN 0-8246-0305-6.

Kolatch offers, to the general Jewish reader, the answers to why specific laws, customs, and ceremonies evolved. His scope includes Reform, Conservative, and Orthodox Judaism. His first book answers some five hundred questions on childhood, marriage and divorce, death and mourning, dietary laws, garb, the synagogue, prayer, the Sabbath, and holidays throughout the year. A bibliography lists fifty-seven items for further reading. Kolatch's second volume offers "the attitudes of Jewish legal scholars on abortion, conversion, birth control, artificial insemination, organ transplants, smoking, proselytizing, intermarriage, traveling on the Sabbath, and Jewish-Christian relations" (General Introduction). The second bibliography adds 106 items. While the index in the first book is good, that in the second gives access to both books.

155. Mayer, Frederick E. **The Religious Bodies of America**, 4th ed. Revised by Arthur C. Piepkorn. St. Louis, MO, Concordia Publishing House, 1961. 598p. index. LC 61-15535.

This work grew out of the need in Mayer's seminary course for a systematic listing of America's religions. Twelve general sections give, for each church, an explanation of its foundation and main doctrines. Mayer's work reflects a less objective age in the study of American religion — his treatment of Judaism is woefully inadequate, and is found in the section on "anthropocentric and anti-Trinitarian bodies" — and his analysis is generally dated, but he began with the first edition in 1953 when little else was available. Piepkorn finished this edition and went on to do his own (see 12), which is on a higher plane of scholarship. Mayer and Piepkorn include an index and a short glossary, and bibliographic material follows each entry. Melton has specialized in identifying American religious bodies and has produced by far the best works (see 41, 42, 160, 193 and 247).

156. McBrien, Richard P. **Catholicism.** Minneapolis, MN, Winston Press, 1980. 2 vols. indexes. LC 79-55963. ISBN 0-03-056907-9.

McBrien intends to bridge the gap between conservative and liberal Catholics and between the pre- and post-Vatican II periods for the general reader without a theological background. Accordingly, this is a broad-based handbook covering the history, doctrines, and contemporary debates within the Catholic Church. There are detailed summaries at the ends of chapters, and the opposing views on controversial topics are given. A glossary and an index to personal names are useful, but the detailed subject index is most valuable.

157. McCollister, John C. **The Christian Book of Why.** Middle Village, NY, Jonathan David, 1983. 337p. index. LC 83-15111. ISBN 0-8246-0297-8.

McCollister was inspired by Kolatch's similarly titled books on Judaism (see 154) to provide an explanation of Christianity for the general reader. Like Kolatch, he does not take sides in controversies, but simply explains why each side believes as it does. He covers Jesus; basic beliefs; baptism and communion; public worship; prayer; marriage and divorce; festivals and seasons; holy objects and symbols; pastors, priests, and popes; and saints and sinners. A thirty-seven-item bibliography contains some scholarly and some popular studies. McCollister formulates questions on problems which are often quite real—"Why are so many Christians today at odds with the dogma of divine inspiration?"—but problems are sometimes manufactured to fit his format—"Why was Pope John XXIII accused of being too ecumenical?"

158. McDowell, Josh, and Don Stewart. **Handbook of Today's Religions.** San Bernardino, CA, Here's Life Publishers, 1983. 573p. index.

Four previously published books on cults, the occult, non-Christian religions, and secular religions make up the first four parts of this handbook. The fifth part is labeled "A Christian Approach to Comparative Religions." This is a tendentious work, and the authors maintain no scientific distance from their subject: "a cult is a perversion, a distortion of biblical Christianity and/or a rejection of the historic teachings of the Christian church." The entire history of post-biblical Judaism is summed up in a sixty-word paragraph covering Jewish culture in Babylonia, the Nazi persecution, and the foundation of Israel. However, of eight items in the bibliography on Judaism, six are by prominent Jewish scholars. Bibliographies of mixed value appear throughout the work, and the authors have included an extended glossary. Prepared for the Campus Crusade for Christ, this work exhibits the fundamentalist reaction to cults noted by Shupe, Bromley, and Oliver (see 435), among others. Beaver's treatment (see 132) of non-Christian religions, though infused with Christian presuppositions, is more informed and readable, and Nielson (see 162) offers far more objective and scholarly treatment.

159. Mead, Frank S. **Handbook of Denominations in the United States,** 8th ed. Revised by Samuel S. Hill. Nashville, TN, Abingdon Press, 1985. 320p. index. LC 84-24342. ISBN 0-687-16571-7.

Mead offers sketches of approximately one hundred separate Christian denominations, and brief treatment of Judaism, as well as other religions being practiced in the United States. Objective essays vary from one-half to several pages in length, and cover the beliefs, history, and directory information of their subjects. While more extensive essays on Judaism, Roman Catholicism, and Lutheranism can easily be located in other sources, Mead is especially useful for smaller denominations and divisions. Melton (see 41 and 42) and Piepkorn (see 12) give more details on more denominations and religions, but Mead's overview is current and worthwhile.

160. Melton, J. Gordon. **Encyclopedic Handbook of Cults in America.** New York, Garland Publishing Co., 1986. 272p. index. (Garland Reference Library of Social Science, Vol. 213). LC 83-48227. ISBN 0-8240-9036-5.

Melton, who established and directs the Institute for the Study of American Religion, and produced the *Encyclopedia of American Religions* (see 41), has identified some five hundred alternative churches, attempting through dispassionate analysis to arrive at the truth and eliminate erroneous judgment about cult life. This companion volume to his *Biographical Dictionary of American Cult and Sect Leaders* (see 247) offers a definition of cults; examines twenty established cults, such as the Jehovah's Witnesses and the Mormons;

provides an overview of the New Age movement, manifested primarily in eastern religions; studies sixteen "new" religions such as Hare Krishna, the Unification Church, witches, and neo-pagans; explores counter-cult groups; and analyzes the violence that often accompanies cult growth. There is an index of personal and group names. Bibliographic material accompanies each chapter, and there is an especially useful separate list of thirty-six basic items.

161. Mol, Hans J. J. et al. **Western Religion: a Country by Country Sociological Enquiry.** The Hague, The Netherlands, Mouton, 1972. 642p. indexes. (Religion and Reason Series, Vol. 2). LC 73-152083.

Mol and top scholars in the sociology of religion offer an essay for each western country, written at the undergraduate level. Each essay covers its subject country's religious history; denominational structure; religious beliefs, practices, and experiences; religion and class; religion and politics; and religion and education. Some also apply other sociological modes of inquiry, such as the family and religious practice. The essays are laced with statistical tables, and there are many bibliographic references.

162. Nielson, Niels C., general ed. **Religions of the World.** New York, St. Martin's Press, 1983. 740p. index. LC 81-51859. ISBN 0-312-67121-0.

Nielson and his colleagues bring contemporary scholarship to comprehensive (historical, geographical, political, and social) treatments of ancient and modern religions, and enliven their text with timelines, maps, and photographs of art and liturgies. Set-off features cover special ceremonies and events or offer portions of scriptures. The editors purport to emphasize the contributions of women. Treatments are more extensive than encyclopedia articles: Samuel Karff writes on Judaism in eighty-one pages and Alice Cochran describes Christianity in 103. There are annotated bibliographies for each religion at the end of the text. The bibliography on Christianity is sketchy, but has entries on women in the church; that on Judaism does not. A subject index is provided. Nielson has edited a thorough introductory work written in the naive dialect of textbooks.

163. Noll, Mark et al., eds. **Eerdmans' Handbook to Christianity in America.** Grand Rapids, MI, Eerdmans, 1983. 507p. indexes. LC 83-1656. ISBN 0-8028-3582-1.

This companion to *Eerdmans' Handbook to the History of Christianity* (see 144) emphasizes leaders, churches, and popular movements. There are four major historical divisions: the colonies; from the Revolution to the Civil War; the movement towards pluralism up through the 1920s; and the secular age from the Depression to the present. Top scholars (for example, Martin Marty, John Tracy Ellis, and J. Gordon Melton) were drafted to write on special subjects. Bibliographies are abundant, and there are maps, color diagrams, color photographs, and excerpts from key documents throughout. Noll adds indexes of people and of events, movements, and groups. In this series, Eerdmans has produced substantive reference materials in an attractive, contemporary format.

164. Parrinder, Geoffrey, ed. **World Religions: From Ancient History to the Present.** New York, Facts on File, 1983. 528p. index. LC 83-1510. ISBN 0-87196-129-6.

In twenty-one chapters, Parrinder introduces as many religions, living and defunct. Judaism and Christianity are each covered by essays treating their origins, historical development, modern problems, and trends. Well-chosen black-and-white photographs accompany the text. Strangely, the contributors, "specialists on the particular religions which they study," remain anonymous. A too-brief bibliography at the end of the volume offers about two dozen books for each religion. There is a full index. The new *Encyclopedia of Religion* (see 2) has more scholarly coverage of any religion treated herein.

165. Pearl, Chaim, and Reuben S. Brookes. **A Guide to Jewish Knowledge**, 2d ed., revised and expanded. Bridgeport, CT, Hartmore House, 1976. 142p. index. LC 76-25366. ISBN 0-87677-138-X.

For the general reader, this is a too-brief introduction to Judaism, covering the calendar, dietary practices, written sources of Jewish life and thought, the Hebrew language, Jewish history, and basic teachings. There is an index for access and a bibliography of English-language publications. In their effort to include "everything of fundamental importance" and to omit "the too complicated or advanced," the authors offer only cursory coverage of major aspects of Jewish life and history. They devote, for example, eight short paragraphs to the historical period from 1914 to the Yom Kippur War of 1973, which includes two world wars, the Holocaust, and the founding of Israel. Donin (see 143) provides more extensive guidance.

166. Pruter, Karl, and J. Gordon Melton. **The Old Catholic Sourcebook.** New York, Garland Publishing Co., 1983. 254p. indexes. (Sects and Cults in America: Bibliographical Guides, vol. 3; Garland Reference Library of Social Sciences, vol. 179). LC 83-47610. ISBN 0-8240-9111-6.

Old Catholic is used here as a generic name for groups whose origin can be traced to the Jansenist controversy in seventeenth-century France. In the United States, these groups now include national churches, homosexual churches, churches at odds with the dogma of Vatican I, and churches opposed to the liturgical reforms of Vatican II. The common thread is rupture with the mainstream of Roman Catholicism or (to a lesser extent) Anglicanism. This book is divided into an historical essay by Pruter, himself an Old Catholic bishop; a bibliography of 848 books and articles and 98 periodicals by Melton; a table of independent Old Catholic bishops, indicating their lines of succession and ordination dates; and a directory of 149 Old Catholic, Anglican, and Orthodox jurisdictions in the United States. This work stands alone as a research guide to this religious phenomenon.

167. Robinson, David. **The Unitarians and the Universalists.** Westport, CT, Greenwood Press, 1985. 368p. index. (Denominations in America, no. 1). LC 84-9031. ISBN 0-313-20946-4.

This well-indexed work is divided into two parts. The first, a history of the Unitarians and the Universalists, offers a summary overview, and traces the growth of the movements from their origins through the Transcendentalist controversy, the development of liberal religious tradition, and the union of the two churches in 1961, up to contemporary trends and issues. The second part is a 133-page biographical dictionary modeled after Bowden's *Dictionary of American Religious Biography* (see 228), and containing, for leaders of the movements, an outline of each subject's career, with birth and death dates; an exposition on the life; and a short bibliography of primary and secondary works. A chronology from 1742 through 1961 and a bibliographic essay on the movements follow the biographies. There are cross-references to the biographical entries from the historical and bibliographic sections.

168. Rosten, Leo, ed. **Religions of America. Ferment and Faith in an Age of Crisis. A New Guide and Almanac.** New York, Simon and Schuster, 1975. 672p. LC 74-11703. ISBN 0-671-21970-7.

In the first section of this work, Rosten asks questions of authorities of eighteen major denominations in America, including Jews, agnostics, the "unchurched," and scientists. The questions are specific to the religion addressed, and cover anything from doctrine to controversial topics such as attitudes toward homosexuality. The second section is an almanac containing "collations of facts, events, opinion polls, statistics, analyses and essays on the problems and crises confronting the churches today." It is a useful but already dated work, and one need only to look at it briefly to understand how perceptions on religions and their "crises" change in a dozen years. Rosten closes with a directory of the headquarters of major American religions and a glossary of religious terms.

169.   Roth, Cecil. **The Jewish Book of Days: A Day-by-day Almanac of Events from the Settlement of the Jews in Europe to the Balfour Declaration**, rev. ed. New York, Herman Press, 1966. 321p. LC 66-19768.

Roth, one of the eminent scholars responsible for the *Encyclopaedia Judaica* (see 25), originally published this work in 1930. He offers a daily accounting of Jewish history. This is often a sad tale of persecution and massacre; April 19th, for example, has been particularly unfortunate, with persecutions recorded in 1013, 1283, 1343, 1506, and 1903 CE. Roth adds a chronological index at the end, and completes the book with a list of "memorable events 1917-1948."

170.   Shulman, Albert M. **Gateway to Judaism: Encyclopedia Home Reference.** Cranbury, NJ, Thomas Yaseloff, 1971. 2 vols. index. LC 69-15777.

Although targeted by Shulman for Jewish homes, this handbook contains so much information that its possible use is much broader. Its entries are not alphabetized, but are instead incorporated into nine broad chapters covering Jewish literature; doctrine and beliefs; the calendar and holidays; ritual ceremonies; Jewish life; the synagogue; and sects, groups, and languages. The last chapters contain a biographical dictionary of famous Jews, an outline of Jewish history, and a directory of Jewish organizations arranged by type. A lengthy index — 125 pages — provides detailed access, but an outline of the very detailed chapters would have been helpful. Prayers are given in both Hebrew and English translation.

171.   Strassfeld, Michael. **The Jewish Holidays: A Guide and Commentary.** New York, Harper & Row, 1985. 248p. index. LC 84-48196. ISBN 0-06-015406-3.

Eleven Jewish festivals are each served by a chapter giving (1) the history, themes, and practices of the holiday; (2) the tradition, via a description of rituals and customs; (3) "Kavvanot," intentions for those seeking a contemporary approach or places to focus their observations; and (4) "Derash," interpretation. The wide margins of this beautiful book contain artwork by Betsy Platkin Teutsch and commentaries by five scholars. It will be difficult for a Christian reader, as the calendar used is entirely Jewish ("Yom Kippur falls on the tenth of Tishri"), but the reward is worth the effort. All Hebrew words are romanized except in the artwork. Six appendixes cover understanding the Jewish calendar, the Halakhah (Law) of the holidays, a Torah reading chart, common blessings in Hebrew, a glossary of Hebrew terms in English, and dates of the holidays between 5746 and 5760 (1985-2000 CE). For a somewhat easier read on the same subject, see Cardozo (136).

172.   Sutherland, Stewart et al. **The World's Religions.** Boston, MA, G. K. Hall, 1988. 995p. index. LC 87-35037. ISBN 0-8161-8978-1.

Fully a fourth of this large handbook is given over to a collection of essays on Judaism and Christianity. (Almost another quarter treats Islam.) Christianity receives the bulk of the treatment; of fourteen chapters, after an introductory one, five cover the historical development of European Christianity, another five treat its growth in Africa, North America, Latin America, India, and China, and a last looks at Christianity today. The treatment of Judaism, sparse but with fine writers, is determined by the presence of Christianity, with one chapter on the period before the coming of Jesus, and a single chapter of thirty pages on the entirety of the Jewish experience in the common era. Each essay of two dozen or so pages has a short bibliography of predominantly British publications; the contributors for the most part hold positions in British universities.

173. Thompson, Henry O. **World Religions in War and Peace.** Jefferson, NC, McFarland, 1988. 241p. index. LC 88-42516. ISBN 0-89950-341-1.

Thompson examines the history of ten world religions and the development of the concepts of conflict and peace in them. Of particular note is his examination of the "us versus them" attitude which seems prevalent in religious experience. An eighteen-page essay is devoted to Judaism, and an equal one to Christianity. The seventeen-page bibliography is not separated by religion. A full index offers access to the whole work.

174. Waskow, Arthur. **Seasons of Our Joy: A Handbook of Jewish Festivals.** Toronto, Canada, Bantam Books, 1982. 241p. LC 81-17552. ISBN 0-553-01369-6.

Written primarily for Jews interested in renewing their religious roots, Waskow's work begins with a preface called "Seasons of the Sun, Seasons of the Moon," explaining the meaning of the Jewish year. He then covers twelve feasts in as many chapters. For each feast, there is a passage on the mood of the day, a history of its celebration, formal preparation to be made for the day, an explanation of present-day celebration, new and emerging approaches for celebration, recipes, and a list of books and guides. Throughout the work, prints by Martin Farren and Joan Benjamin-Farren illustrate the themes of the feasts. Waskow adds five appendixes, including a short glossary, a bibliographic essay, and a list of the secular dates of Jewish feasts through the year 2009 CE.

175. Weiser, Francis X. **Handbook of Christian Feasts and Customs: The Year of the Lord in Liturgy and Folklore.** New York, Harcourt, Brace, 1958. 366p. index. LC 58-10908.

Weiser calls his work a compendium of "heortology," the science that explains the origin, meaning, development, and observance of feasts. He divides his matter into three parts: celebrations based on natural time (e.g., Sundays), commemorations of Christ's redemption (Christmas, Easter), and feasts of the fruits of the redemption (honoring the saints and Mary). The handbook is Roman Catholic in conception but ecumenical in inspiration; Weiser notes the Jewish origin of feasts when pertinent. The emphasis is on ancient and basic Christian celebrations; recent Roman Catholic feasts, such as that of the Sacred Heart, are omitted. For similar treatment of Jewish feasts, see Cardozo (136) and Strassfeld (171).

176. Zaehner, Robert Charles, ed. **The Concise Encyclopedia of Living Faiths,** 2d ed. London, Hutchinson, 1971. 436p. index. LC 70-878039. ISBN 0-09-107520-3.

Zaehner covers major living faiths, including Judaism, Zoroastrianism, and Jainism; he notes that these, although small in numbers, are great in world impact. The fundamental arrangement of the work is a division into religions of prophecy, which includes Judaism as basic, Christianity, Islam, and Zoroastrianism; and religions of wisdom, which includes Hinduism as basic, Jainism, Buddhism, Shinto, Confucianism, Taoism, and surprisingly, but well and fully justified, dialectical materialism. Each religion is treated by at least one essay covering the historical development of its principal beliefs. Christianity is given five essays and Buddhism three, since Zaehner concludes they are each the most prominent in their categories. The essays on Christianity treat the early church, the Eastern church, St. Thomas and the medieval church, Protestantism, and the Catholic Church since the Reformation. Each essay is followed by a selective bibliography, and Zaehner has provided an index to the whole work. The device of using longer essays by outstanding scholars — fourteen assisted Zaehner in this work — make this work more a handbook than the encyclopedia its name implies.

II. Statistics Sources

177. Carroll, Jackson W., Douglas W. Johnson and Martin E. Marty. **Religion in America: 1950 to the Present.** San Francisco, CA, Harper & Row, 1979. 123p. index. LC 77-20451. ISBN 0-06-065433-3.

There are four statistical essays in this work. Carroll leads off with "Continuity and Change: The Shape of Religious Life in the U.S., 1950 to the Present." Marty studies "Patterns of Religious Pluralism," and Johnson treats "Trends and Issues Shaping the Future." George Gallup presents an "Afterword: A Coming Religious Revival?" Eleven maps and twenty-two tables accompany these essays. There is an index to persons and churches.

178. Gallup, George, Jr., and Jim Castelli. **The American Catholic People: Their Beliefs, Practices, and Values.** Garden City, NY, Doubleday, 1987. 206p. index. LC 86-16576. ISBN 0-385-23122-9.

Gallup and Castelli used an "archaeological approach" in preparing this study; that is, they "dug into" two decades of Gallup polls (1965-1986) and examined data from thirteen studies, many of them commissioned for Protestant churches. The significant factors for the present work are that "Catholics" are self-defined and eighteen or more years old; that the number of Catholics who participated in most surveys was four hundred to five hundred, while the number of Protestants was over eight hundred; and that some older data was used if it involved core values not subject to sudden change. Catholics and Protestants are often compared here, but the data was insufficient to permit comparisons of Catholics and Jews. It was also insufficient, except in the case of Hispanic Catholics, to study Catholic ethnic differences. In all, Gallup and Castelli examine the religious beliefs and practices of Catholics and their opinions on economic, political, bioethical, and social issues, and on nuclear arms, education, and minorities, as well as the attitudes of Hispanic, teenage, and alienated Catholics.

179. **The Gallup Report**, 1965- . Princeton, NJ, Gallup Poll. Monthly. ISSN 0731-6143. Issues are numbered consecutively from 1965. Special reports on religion: February 1969 (no. 44), April 1971 (no. 70), December 1974 (no. 114), May 1976 (no. 130), August 1977 (no. 145), January 1981 (no. 184), June/July 1982 (no. 201-202), March 1984 (no. 222), May 1985 (no. 236), April 1987 (no. 259).

George Gallup, Sr., began asking Americans what they felt about things in 1935, and questions on religious subjects have been staples of his organization's polling from the start. In 1965, the Gallup organization began publishing *The Gallup Political Index*, whose name in 1967 became *The Gallup Opinion Index* and in 1981 *The Gallup Report*. In addition to individual questions on religious subjects, eleven special reports, often titled *Religion in America*, have been published since 1967, and George Gallup, Jr., who has written several books on religion in America, gave special attention to editing these issues. Except for the 1967 report, in each case an entire monthly number has been given over to Americans' perception of religious issues. Predominant issues for which polls have been formulated are how Catholics, Protestants, and Jews feel about themselves and each other; the influence of religion on American life and the political scene; church and synagogue attendance; financial support of religion; influence of television on religious behavior;

and the opinions of specific groups, such as clergy or college students, measured against the general public. The special report on religion published in December 1974 (no. 114) lists all Gallup news releases on religious questions published since 1935.

180. Quinn, Bernard et al. **Churches and Church Membership in the United States, 1980: An Enumeration by Region, State and County Based on Data Reported by 111 Church Bodies.** Atlanta, GA, Glenmary Research Center, 1982. 321p. LC 82-81978. ISBN 0-9144-2212-X.

This study, sponsored by several denominational research groups, "contains statistics for 111 Judaeo-Christian church bodies, providing information on the number of their churches and members for regions, states and counties of the United States" (Preface). It includes two Jewish, four black, and four Orthodox bodies. In all, it tallies 231,708 congregations with 112,538,310 adherents from statistics supplied by the church bodies themselves. Four tables show churches and membership by denomination, by region and denomination, by state and denomination, and by county and denomination. A fold-out map shows major denominational families by cities. Seven appendixes note particular situations in some regions, such as Alaska.

181. United States Department of Commerce and Labor. Bureau of the Census. Special Reports. **Religious Bodies: 1906.** Washington, DC, Government Printing Office, 1910. 2 vols.

181.1. United States Department of Commerce. Bureau of the Census. **Religious Bodies: 1916.** Washington, DC, Government Printing Office, 1919. 2 vols. indexes.

181.2. United States Department of Commerce. Bureau of the Census. **Religious Bodies: 1926.** Washington, DC, Government Printing Office, 1929. 2 vols. indexes.

181.3. United States Department of Commerce. Bureau of the Census. **Religious Bodies: 1936.** Washington, DC, Government Printing Office, 1941. 3 vols. indexes.

Until the practice was stopped after the special 1936 census of religious bodies in the United States, the Bureau of the Census produced a body of statistics of extraordinary importance to the historical study of American religion in general, and the development of religions and denominations in particular. Limited information was first published from the 1850 general census, followed by compilations from the 1860, 1870, and 1890 censuses. No tabulations were made from the 1880 census. Hence, *Religious Bodies: 1906* is actually the fifth compilation.

For the 1906 edition, a questionnaire was sent to all independent religious bodies and denominations in the country, asking of each its name, ecclesiastical divisions, organization, locations, year established, number of church edifices, seating capacity, value of church property, amount of debt incurred by the church, value of parsonages, language in which services are conducted, number of ministers and their salaries, number of communicants or members, and the number of Sunday schools conducted with the number of their teachers and "scholars." The introduction to the 1906 edition explains in detail the scope of the project, the methods pursued, the plan of the report, the classification of denominations from former census periods, the names and classifications of denominations used for 1906, and a list of denominations (the 1906 edition includes Buddhists, but not Hindus or Moslems, in addition to Jewish and Christian bodies). Part I of this edition contains the introduction, a summary, highly detailed "General Tables," and diagrams.

Part II includes the history, description, and statistics of each separate religious body; thus, the section on the Roman Catholic Church includes its history, a summary of its doctrine, an explanation of its "polity" or organization, a list of its works, and statistics by diocese.

The 1916 report was similar in structure to that of 1906, but added questions on the local names of churches, the number of church buildings in addition to the main edifice, and the amount of funds expended during the year for running expenses, repairs, benevolences, and other matters. An essay on the collection of the census data notes that the bureau maintained one card catalogue of 230,000 churches and another of 150,000 ministers. Eight hundred thousand returned schedules were checked against these catalogues. Difficulties encountered included a lack of accurate information, late responses, unwillingness to reply (perhaps engendered by a feeling that the government had no right to ask), and incomplete answers.

The format was again followed in 1926, with much updating of information under the "Works" and "Principal Events" sections for each denomination. For the first time, there appears a distinction between urban and rural statistics.

The 1936 edition appeared in three volumes, with Part II divided into two sections. The information, on 256 denominations or bodies, was first published in 78 separate bulletins. The complete list of denominations, in this last government census of religions within its territory, includes the names of denominations reported in 1926 but not in 1936, those existing before 1926 but not named therein, and new denominations.

182. Wilson, Samuel, and John Siewert, eds. **Mission Handbook: North American Protestant Ministries Overseas**, 13th ed. Monrovia, CA, Missions Advanced Research and Communication Center, 1986. 627p. indexes. LC 76-55223. ISBN 0-912552-55-7.

First published in 1953, this handbook offers statistical data on virtually all North American Protestant mission agencies and their overseas commitments, as well as analytical and interpretative material. The twelfth edition focused on the effort to evangelize "unreached peoples"—those with less than 20 percent committed Christians—in countries besides the United States and Canada. The thirteenth edition identifies some 764 agencies supporting 67,200 personnel with costs reaching one billion dollars. Data on United States and Canadian agencies are presented separately. Some information on the efforts of Roman Catholics, Latter Day Saints, and Jehovah's Witnesses is included as well. Based on a 1984 survey (reproduced at the end of the work) sent to every appropriate agency, the handbook includes directory information, data on distribution of overseas personnel, analysis of mission finance, and information on types of ministries. Each country of the world is listed, with names of and data on the agencies working in it. Three indexes arrange access to the information by state or province, by religious tradition, and by ministry activity. A short bibliography concludes the work.

3
Directories and Yearbooks

While general directories and yearbooks covering many religions or carefully defined topics are no more difficult to find than other reference materials, those treating specific religious bodies often present problems associated with complex publishing histories and, especially in Protestantism, church mergers carried out in an ecumenical spirit. Title changes are frequent, and the scope itself may change from year to year. In addition, these works are sometimes brought out by companies for whom the church in question is the sole source of business; and this leads to a tendency towards idiosyncratic formats. Nevertheless, such books are important and frequently unique sources of organizational, statistical, and biographical information. The student of the history of a denomination or religion does well to examine a full collection of its directories and yearbooks. While the listing here is by no means comprehensive, I have identified the directories and yearbooks of the major religious bodies.

I. General Directories and Yearbooks Covering Many Religious Communities

183. Beaver, Robert Pierce, ed. **The Native American Christian Community: A Directory of Indian, Aleut, and Eskimo Churches.** Monrovia, CA, Missions Advanced Research and Communications Center, 1979. 395p. LC 78-70999. ISBN 0-912552-25-5.

Beaver, in a major effort to collect information on Native American churches, opens with a survey of general statistical studies on Christianity done in the United States throughout the twentieth century by Protestants (see Beach, 270) and Roman Catholics. The scarcity of information led him to fill the lacuna with this ecumenical work covering Protestant, Catholic, and Orthodox communities among Native Americans. Extensive surveying, with statistics especially difficult to come by, eventually led him to project a total figure of slightly over 320,000 Native American Christians. He surveyed these Christians in the 1970s, and produced a series of directories covering denominational agencies, nondenominational societies and independent churches, and Native American urban churches, councils, service agencies, and educational ministries. There are Christian population reports by tribe and by state. A final set of tables covers Native American personnel, white personnel, and individual church statistics. This work offers essential information on the state of Christianity among Native Americans; it would be useful to have it updated with some regularity.

184. Braybrooke, Marcus. **Inter-Faith Organizations, 1893-1979: An Historical Directory.** New York, Edwin Mellen Press, 1980. 213p. (Texts and Studies in Religion). LC 79-91620. ISBN 0-88946-971-7.

Braybrooke begins with a sketch of the World Parliament of Religion held in Chicago in 1893, and traces the development of interreligious dialogue and "multi-logue" (that is, among more than two participants) in several areas, including academic matters, union of religions, peace through religion, and the initiatives of individual churches. He focuses particularly on the dialogues between Christians and Jews and between Christians and Muslims. Finally, he explores India as a meeting place of religions. Appendixes include a study of the World Fellowship of Faiths (Chicago, 1933) and a list of fifty-seven interfaith organizations. There is a seven-page bibliography, and extensive reference notes to the essays.

185. Butler, Francis J., and Catherine E. Farrell, eds. **Foundation Guide for Religious Grant Seekers,** 3d ed. Atlanta, GA, Scholars' Press, 1987. 172p. LC 87-9467. ISBN 1-555-40121-X.

Butler and Farrell list 407 foundations interested in offering grants for religious purposes, and give information on the grant-seeking process, facts about religious philanthropy, and building constituency support. They list foundations interested in funding religious organizations: Protestant, Catholic, Jewish, interfaith, and others. One appendix lists foundation libraries, and another is a bibliography of area foundation directories.

186. **Directory, Christian Councils,** 4th ed. Geneva, Switzerland, World Council of Churches, 1985. 244p. LC 86-221666. ISBN 2-8254-0846-8.

To facilitate communication among and provide basic information on ecumenical Christian councils throughout the world, this directory lists the regional ecumenical conferences and national councils affiliated with the World Council of Churches. Each conference and council is listed with its name and address, telephone number, cable address, chairperson, secretary, executive staff, number of members, founding date, basis of membership, aims, functions, activities, organization, subregional and local councils related to it, budget and sources, and ecumenical relationships. The organizational structure of the World Council is also included.

187. **Directory of Departments and Programs of Religious Studies in North America,** 6th ed. Macon, GA, The Council of Societies for the Study of Religion, Mercer University, 1989. LC 87-5568.

Schools in the United States and Canada (four hundred in this latest edition) buy space in this directory, which lists each school's address, chairperson, institutional setting, faculty, nature and size of the department, and admission requirements. Despite the title, Mexico is not represented. Appendixes include the names and addresses of all schools known to have programs (some twelve hundred). There is an index by state of participating schools, and an index of faculty.

188. **The Directory of Religious Organizations in the United States,** 2d ed. Falls Church, VA, McGrath Publishing, 1982. 518p. (A Consortium Book). LC 84-223812. ISBN 0-8434-0757-3.

This edition lists 1,628 organizations; since 328 were dropped from the 1,569 of the first edition, published in 1977, this is an actual increase of 387, or 31 percent. National churches are not listed, but their departments are, as well as professional associations, volunteer groups, government agencies, businesses, foundations, and fraternal societies. Each entry includes the name, address, telephone number, affiliation, chief executive, staff statistics, former names, purpose, and programs and projects of an organization. The arrangement is alphabetical by organization name. Indexes are missing and badly needed: a key-word index, an index by organization type, and one by religious affiliation. Entries are numbered but, with no indexes, the numbers serve little purpose.

189.   Geisendorfer, James V., comp. and ed. **Religion in America: A Directory.** Leiden, The Netherlands, E. J. Brill, 1983. 175p. LC 83-240687. ISBN 90-04-06910-0.

This directory is a simple listing of hundreds of churches and interdenominational and subdenominational organizations, giving the name, address, and sometimes chief officer and denominational affiliation, but not the telephone number or any explanation of work, purpose, or scope. Entries are alphabetical by the first word in an organizational name, and are not numbered. A key-word index would have eased access to all this information.

190.   Goddard, Burton L. **Encyclopedia of Modern Christian Missions: The Agencies.** Camden, NJ, Thomas Nelson, 1967. 743p. indexes. LC 67-29099.

This is a directory, not an encyclopedia. Goddard limits his coverage to Protestant agencies, but includes survey articles on the missionary efforts of the Roman Catholic and Greek Orthodox churches. Among the 1,437 entries he includes sending agencies, supporting agencies, evangelistic and broadcasting programs, Bible societies, significant mission periodicals, and training schools and colleges. Although much of this information is now quite dated—current through the mid-1960s—only the *Mission Handbook* of Wilson and Siewert (see 182) covers the same territory, and their interest is primarily statistical. Each entry for an organization contains the address, scope, purpose, activities, history, broadcasts, publications, income, number of workers in the field, and a bibliography. An "index of categories" lists subjects to which agencies pertain. For example, Japan has over ten dozen listed, and Albert Schweitzer had seventeen friends' societies supporting his work. A second index lists agencies that have secondary entries under other agencies.

191.   Jacquet, Constant H., ed. **Yearbook of American and Canadian Churches, 1916- .** annual. Nashville, TN, Abingdon Press. index. LC 16-5726. ISSN 0195-9043.

The eighty-sixth edition (1986) is fifty-fourth in the series, which has had a number of title changes since 1916. It describes the mainline churches in the United States and Canada, but notes it leaves out "a bewildering variety of sects and cults ... and other small religious bodies." Jewish, Muslim, Baha'i, and Buddhist groups are among those included. There are four sections: a four-year calendar with feast dates, a directory of churches, a statistical and historical section, and an index. The directory lists, for each entry, a church's national and international organizations, regional and local agencies, seminaries, colleges, periodicals, and service agencies. Statistics include current membership, number of churches and pastors, finances, trends, and developments, and a survey of religion in American life.

192.   Lea, Emma R. M., comp., and Alan F. Jesson, ed. **A Guide to the Theological Libraries of Great Britain and Ireland.** London, Association of British Theological and Philosophical Libraries, 1986. 321p. index. LC gb88-41755. ISBN 0-948945-00-1.

Lea and Jesson have gathered information on 397 collections of theological materials, mainly on Christian denominations, but also on Buddhism, Hinduism, Islam, and Judaism. Entries are arranged alphabetically by postal town and include, in table format, the name, address, and telephone number of the library; its history, date of founding and function, chief officers and number of staff, catalogues, number of volumes, classification system, publications by and about the library, rules of access, and availability of repro-graphic facilities. An index provides access by proper name of the library and by some generic divisions (such as abbey, bible college, cathedral, diocesan, parochial and public libraries), but, with the curious exception of the Society of Friends, libraries are not listed by religion or denomination. Thus, there is no way to identify all the Methodist or Jewish collections other than by proper name. For Britain and Ireland, this replaces Ruoss (see 195), who lists only eighty British theological libraries in his now very dated work.

193.   Melton, J. Gordon, with James V. Geisendorfer. **A Directory of Religious Bodies in the United States: Compiled from the Files of The Institute for the Study of American Religion.** New York, Garland Publishing Co., 1977. 305p. LC 76-52700. ISBN 0-8240-9882-X.

Melton provides an elaborate classification scheme, identifying 1,275 "primary religious groups" divided into 17 families. A *primary religious group* is that which claims the exclusive religious affiliation of its members; has at least two congregations, or 2,000 members, or membership extending throughout a multistate region; and has a unique point of view on at least one issue vital to its life. For bringing similar religious groups together for study, this classification is eminently successful, and Melton further refined it for additional reference works (see 41 and 42). The directory lists the groups alphabetically by official name, with cross-references from popular names. For each group, a headquarters address and, if possible, a publication is given. A five-digit number leads to a classification grouping religions with similar thought systems. The directory is more useful for smaller bodies than for mainline churches.

194.   O'Hara, Magdalen. **The Directory of Women Religious in the United States.** Wilmington, DE, Michael Glazier, 1985. 988p. index. LC 84-47752. ISBN 0-89453-528-5.

Noting an easily verifiable and "appalling lack of printed and written sources covering the work of women religious," O'Hara has produced "a profile by name, local address, order, and diocese of women religious in our own day" (Introduction). Limiting her scope to Roman Catholic sisters of Western and Eastern rites, O'Hara notes both that there are 109,000 such women in the United States and that she has included the vast majority. The main entry listing is by diocese, with religious houses and the sisters living in them identified. Each sister is again named in an index, with a cross-reference to her order and diocese of residence. Seven hundred orders for women are identified, 230 with less than 30 members, 230 with more than 300, and the remainder in between. Vicars are listed for each diocese. For information resources on women religious, see *Women Religious History Resources* (197).

195.   Ruoss, G. Martin. **A World Directory of Theological Libraries.** Metuchen, NJ, Scarecrow Press, 1968. 220p. indexes. LC 68-12632.

Based on a mail survey, Ruoss identifies 1,729 theological libraries as of 1967. These are arranged by continent, with subdivisions by state or province in Anglo-North America and by territory in Australia. Indexes by institutional name and by religious group facilitate entry to the work. Extensive abbreviations are used in the entries, which give the address, affiliation, and holdings of each library. Ruoss compiles and analyzes his survey results in an extensive essay at the beginning of the book, arranging numbers by religion, region, and date of founding (the oldest, the Dean and Chapter Library in Durham, England, was founded in 635 CE).

196. **A Sociological Yearbook of Religion in Britain, 1968- .** annual. London, S.C.M. Press. LC 75-216078. ISSN 0081-1777.

Each issue contains essays, using varying methods of sociological analysis, on a wide variety of religious phenomena in Great Britain. The essays are contemporary or historical, theoretical or empirical. Several issues contain supplements entitled "Bibliography of Work in the Sociology of British Religion." The initial bibliography was published by David Martin in *A Sociology of English Religion* (London, S.C.M. Press, 1967).

197. Thomas, Evangeline. **Women Religious History Resources: A Guide to Repositories in the United States.** New York, R. R. Bowker, 1983. 329p. index. LC 82-22648. ISBN 0-8352-1681-0.

The importance of this work for studying the contribution of women to religion in the United States cannot be overestimated. The first part is based on extensive surveying, and identifies 569 manuscript and archival sources for sisters (active workers) and nuns (contemplatives) of the Catholic, Orthodox, and Episcopal churches and deaconesses of the Lutheran, Methodist, and Mennonite churches. Arrangement is by state and by city within each state. Each entry contains the name, initials, denomination, and address of the congregation and archives, with a description of the community and its holdings. The second part is a twenty-five-page bibliography arranged by community name; the third, a table of founding dates of the United States communities; and the fourth, a biographical register of foundresses and major superiors. There is an index to the whole.

II. Directories and Yearbooks of Specific Religious Communities

198. **American Jewish Organizations Directory,** 11th ed. New York, Frenkel Mailing Service, 1982.

Formerly called the *American Synagogue Directory*, this work lists and gives addresses for synagogues, Jewish Community Centers, social service organizations, schools, research institutes, clubs, and fraternities and sororities. Synagogues are identified as Orthodox, Conservative, Reform, or traditional (a miscellaneous designation).

199. **Annual of the Southern Baptist Convention, 1845- .** annual. Nashville, TN, Executive Committee of the Southern Baptist Convention. index. ISSN 0081-3001.

This contains the constitution and bylaws of the convention and its annual proceedings, as well as reports of the agencies, committees, and associations; lists of elected officers; and a directory of pastors and ordained ministers. There is an index to the proceedings of the convention.

200. **Church of the Brethren Yearbook, Directory, Statistics, 1982- .** annual. Elgin, IL, Church of the Brethren General Board.

The first part of this annual is divided into a section on the organizational structure of the church, its related agencies, colleges, seminary, homes, hospitals, camps, and districts; a directory of congregations by district; and the official list of ordained and licensed ministers and lay preachers. The second part includes detailed statistical tables on church membership and finances.

201. **The Church of England Year Book: The Official Year Book of the General Synod of the Church of England, 1882- .** annual. London, Church Information Office. index. LC 72-622544. ISSN 0069-3987.

This yearbook contains the church calendar and two major divisions: the organization of the Church of England and that of the Anglican Communion, that is, the worldwide collection of churches associated with the Church of England, such as the Episcopal Church in the United States. The first part includes directory information on the General Synod, the Central Board of Finance, advisory committees, permanent commissions, the Convocations of Canterbury and York, and diocesan lists. The second lists Partners-in-Mission, autonomous churches and provinces of the Anglican Church, and churches with which the Church of England is more loosely affiliated. There is a list of organizations, a who's who, and a general index.

202. **Crockford's Clerical Directory: A Reference Book of the Clergy of the Provinces of Canterbury and York and of Other Anglican Provinces and Dioceses, 1858- .** irregular. Oxford, England, Oxford University Press.

The 1980-82 edition is the eighty-eighth. A companion volume to *The Church of England Year Book* (see 201), this offers biographical paragraphs on the bishops and clergy of the Church of England and of the Welsh, Scottish Episcopal, Irish, and overseas churches. There is an index of English, Welsh, Scottish, and Irish parishes.

203. **Directory of the American Baptist Churches in the U.S.A., 1973- .** annual. Valley Forge, PA, American Baptist Churches in the U.S.A. LC 73-646223. ISSN 0091-9381.

This companion to the *Yearbook of the American Baptist Churches in the U.S.A.* (see 220) contains the denomination's statistics, historical tables, lists of officers of church boards and committees, directories of affiliated and associated organizations, member churches, other Baptist bodies, nonsupporting churches, missionaries, and — the largest section — professional leaders, including persons in twenty-eight categories from pastors to musicians.

204. **Directory of the Ministry: A Yearbook of Christian Churches and Churches of Christ 1955- .** annual. Springfield, IL, Directory of the Ministry. index.

For the United States and Canada, this directory lists congregations, agencies, overseas missions, personnel, and statistics on schools, periodicals, radio and television programs, camps, and other organizations. There is an index of personnel. The twenty-eighth edition was published in 1986.

205. **Encyclopaedia Judaica Year Book, 1973- .** irregular. Jerusalem, Keter Publishing House. LC 72-90254. ISSN 0303-7819.

The *Encyclopaedia Judaica* was published in 1972 (see 25). Editions of the yearbook have been brought out for 1973-74, 1975-76, 1977-78, 1973-82 (a decennial book), and 1983-85. The intention was to make use of the "huge reservoir of textual and illustrative material ... assembled" for the encyclopedia and to provide an updated reference resource on the Jewish world. Two types of updating are included: ongoing events, and new discoveries about historical events, which are handled thematically in editions of the yearbooks. Obituaries, glossaries of new words, photographic essays, and regular features on such matters as Jewish-Christian relations, developments in Jewish communities throughout the world, and calendars of current and previous years are common to each edition. Each edition also has special features, such as the document collection in the decennial yearbook, which includes Egyptian President Anwar Sadat's 1977 address to the Knesset, Israel's parliament. Each yearbook has its own index and cross-references to articles in the *Encyclopaedia Judaica*.

206.   **The Episcopal Church Annual, 1882-** . annual. Wilton, CT, Morehouse-Barlow. LC 46-33254. ISSN 0071-1012.

The Episcopal Church in the United States consists of more than seventy-seven hundred parishes with three million members. This directory offers historical lists of statistics, conventions, and presiding bishops; the organization of the church; and a directory of its agencies, institutions, special ministries, periodicals, religious orders, dioceses, and clergy. The relation of this church to the Anglican Communion is noted, as well as ecumenical connections to other churches.

207.   Foy, Felician, ed. **Catholic Almanac, 1903-** . annual. Huntington, IN, Our Sunday Visitor. LC 73-641001. ISSN 0069-1208.

Foy packs an immense amount of useful information and documentation into this yearly offering. It includes special reports on contemporary issues; the news events of the past year; current information on the pope and the Catholic hierarchy; articles on church doctrine, the Bible, moral teaching, the liturgy, the saints, and the sacraments; the church calendar; reports on ecumenism and other Christian churches, on Judaism and Catholic-Jewish relations, on Islam and the "non-Abrahamic" religions; a glossary; highlights of church history; directories of organizations, institutes, social services, and communications; statistics on the church in the United States, Canada, and other countries; and honors, awards, and deaths. An extensive index keys the reader into all this data. The 1987 issue, a six-hundred-page paperback, offers unbiased coverage of the controversy over the removal of the Rev. Charles Curran from his teaching post at Catholic University in Washington and includes statements from the Vatican, the chancellor of the university, and Curran himself. Other 1987 documentation includes a letter from the bishops of the United Methodist Church, "The Nuclear Crisis and a Just Peace," and the Catholic bishops' letter, "The Challenge of Peace: God's Promise and Our Response."

208.   Greenberg, Martin Harry. **The Jewish Lists: Physicists and Generals, Actors and Writers, and Hundreds of Other Lists of Accomplished Jews.** New York, Schocken, 1979. 327p. indexes. LC 79-14349. ISBN 0-8052-3711-9.

Greenberg, like many other observers, was struck by the sheer number of Jews prominent in public and artistic life, and quotes Hannah Arendt in attributing this phenomenon to the existence of Jewish literacy and cultural unity since antiquity. He develops lists of the celebrated in public life, the professions, business, social science, physical science, arts and entertainment, motion pictures and television, and sports, and has a separate chapter on prizes (Nobel, Pulitzer, and Olympic). Roman Catholics and Jews seem bent on developing such lists (see Siegel and Rheins 217), but Greenberg does it with a twinkle in his eye when he lists Jewish spies, gangsters, and revolutionaries.

209.   Guerriero, Elio, ed. **Catholica: The World Catholic Yearbook 1987.** San Francisco, CA, Ignatius Press, 1988. 400p. LC 88-659940. ISBN 0-89870-179-1. ISSN 0896-5994.

This work is translated from *Catholica: Annuario della Parola e della Vita della Chiesa* (Milan, Italy, Jaco Book, 1987), and is the first in a series put out by Catholic publishers in Italy, Germany, France, Spain, and the United States. Although this is not an official publication of the Roman Catholic Church, it does present an anthology of that church's official thought. The preface is by Joseph Ratzinger, head of the Congregation of the Doctrine. Three sections cover the speeches and writings of the pope; statements of bishops of Africa, America, Asia, and Europe on contemporary issues; and the life of the church in Africa, America, Asia, and eastern Europe. This last includes coverage of church people in specific situations such as hospitals, universities, missions, and, in the eastern bloc, labor camps. A final feature is "The Man of the Year," who, for 1987, was Jean

Vanier, the Canadian who founded the L'Arche movement of communities for the mentally handicapped. Current events are not comprehensively covered, and controversy, such as the struggle of liberation theology to find a home in the church, is avoided. Publication, in November 1988, comes almost a year after the year under review.

210.   Himmelfarb, Milton, and David Singer. **American Jewish Yearbook, 1899/1900- .** annual. New York, The American Jewish Committee and Philadelphia, The Jewish Publication Society of America. index. LC 99-4040. ISSN 0065-8987.

210.1.   Solis-Cohen, Elfrida C. **American Jewish Yearbook: Index to Volumes 1-50: 1899-1949 (5660-5709).** New York, Ktav Publishing House, 1967. 375p.

This yearbook reviews Jewish affairs in the United States and other countries, and offers directories of national Jewish organizations, federations, community councils, welfare funds, and periodicals. The organizations listed encompass community relations, overseas aid, religion, education, social and mutual benefit, social welfare, Zionism, and pro-Israel sentiment. Periodicals are listed by state, and include some not covered by Rogow (see 448). Obituaries of deceased Jews of prominence are included, as are calendars of feasts for the coming several years. There is an index. Also included is the annual report of the Jewish Publication Society of America. Solis-Cohen's work indexes the first fifty years of this standard record of American Judaism.

211.   Japhet, Roger, ed. **The Jewish Year Book, 1896/97- .** annual. London, Jewish Chronicle Publications. LC 14-2382. ISSN 0075-3769.

This annual, which antedates its American counterpart by a few years (see 210), contains detailed calendars for observances; directories of Anglo-Jewish institutions and of international Jewish organizations; statistics; lists of Jews who have received British aristocratic titles; a who's who; and an index to the whole. An ample book list contains titles of current and classic interest.

212.   **LCA Yearbook, 1985- .** annual. Philadelphia, PA, Board of Publication of the Lutheran Church in America. LC 86-644171.

From 1963 through 1984, this was entitled *Yearbook: Lutheran Church in America*. Each yearbook contains short notes on the history of the church during the preceding year and the liturgical calendar for the coming year. Directory information, covering the United States and Canada, includes the general administration of the church, with the executive council, administrative divisions, boards, and synods of the church; a list with addresses of the thirteen separate (as of 1984) Lutheran bodies in North America; addresses of all LCA congregations, seminaries, colleges and universities (with chief faculty), hospitals, social service agencies, campus ministries, and the locations of English-language Lutheran services overseas and of sign-language services in the United States and Canada. The list of ordained ministers includes separate mention of the newly ordained and those removed by death or resignation. Other personnel listings includes deaconesses, military chaplains, and lay persons in professional service to the church. An index to the yearbook is placed among the first pages and is called the "contents."

213.   **The Official Catholic Directory, 1886- .** annual. Skokie, IL, P. J. Kenedy. LC 1-30961. ISSN 0078-3854.

Covering the United States, Puerto Rico, the Virgin Islands, Guam, the Caroline and Marshall Islands, and, briefly, Canada and Mexico, this directory contains an immense amount of information about the Roman Catholic Church, but not all of it is easily accessible. There are three sections. The first lists the hierarchy of the global church, and the third offers brief statistics and main addresses for the Catholic Church in Mexico and Canada. The second section, by far the largest, gives a detailed listing of the church's structure in the United States by diocese. However, to find information, for example, the address of an organization, one must know in advance to which diocese it pertains. There are no indexes, except for a list of all living clergy in good standing and a necrology, which link the living and the recently deceased to their dioceses. The national governing bodies of the church are listed: the Vatican representation to the American Church, the National Conference of Catholic Bishops, and the U.S. Catholic Conference. Overseas missions are included. Archbishops, bishops, and abbots are listed alphabetically and by seniority. Lay sisters and brothers are not included unless they are officers of their orders and congregations or of institutions.

214. **Orthodox Church in America Yearbook & Church Directory, 1971- .** annual. Syosset, NY, Orthodox Church in America. LC 86-643468. ISSN 0145-7950.

With over a million members, the Orthodox Church in America is the largest independent Russian Orthodox church in North America. The four divisions of this annual include a listing of the church administration, a directory of parishes by diocese, a personnel directory of clergy and stewards, and an index of parishes.

215. Proc, Alex. **Yearbook of the Orthodox Church, 1978- .** annual. Munich, Germany, Verlag Alex Proc. 309p. indexes.

Though an annual, this is published in different languages in different years. It is divided into three parts: (1) autocephalous churches; (2) churches not yet autocephalous but whose bishops possess apostolic succession; and (3) indexes of all bishops in office and of other names and places. The listing for each church includes an historical outline, the head and members of its synod, other members and bishops, theological institutions, publications, and its dioceses in its primary country and those, around the world, that are attached to it. Since jurisdiction in one Orthodox church frequently overlaps the geography of another, this is a valuable vehicle for understanding the extent of each church.

216. Rosen, Oded, ed. **The Encyclopedia of Jewish Institutions: United States and Canada.** Tel Aviv, Israel, Mosadot Publications, 1983. 501p. index. LC 83-186126. ISBN 0-9131-8500-0.

Rosen's almost four thousand entries include synagogues, congregations, temples, community centers, schools, colleges and universities, women's organizations, service agencies, national organizations, lodges, fraternal associations, museums, libraries, hospitals, nursing homes, and senior citizens' residences. Entries are arranged by state or province, and then alphabetically under local community, and include address, telephone number, affiliation, accreditations, goals, services, activities, programs, member statistics, employee statistics, history, publications, facilities, achievements, and officer and chief staff names. There is an index by name, but not by type of institution. Rosen offers more information about each organization than *Who's Who in American Jewry* (see 260), but the latter lists more organizations and includes a directory.

217. Siegel, Richard, and Carl Rheins, comps. and eds. **The Jewish Almanac.** New York, Bantam, 1980. 622p. index. ISBN 0-5530-1265-7.

This work contains much information, some of greater and some of lesser importance, some popular and some serious. Thus, there is a list of Hassidic masters and a list of American Jewish gangsters, a list of best-selling Jewish music and a list of Jewish Nobel Prize winners (eighty-five as of the publishing date). Facts, photos, and figures abound. Much of the information is contained in other sources, but not in a convenient single book and not juxtaposed quite like this. All persons, things, and events are indexed.

218.   Tillem, Ivan L., comp. and ed. **The Jewish Directory and Almanac, 1984- .** annual. New York, Pacific Press. LC 85-644354. ISSN 0742-2385.

This yearly compendium emphasizes Jewish social issues, and contains sections on demographics, the year in review, current issues (for example, from 1986: Soviet Jewry, Ethiopian Jewry, Nazi war criminals, church-state issues, genetic diseases), notes on the Holocaust, current issues in Israel, historical notes (including reprints of newspaper pages), biographical sketches, the Torah, liturgical cycles, media, and sports. An extensive section of "yellow pages" covers the United States and Canada.

219.   **Year Book & Directory of the Christian Church (Disciples of Christ).** Indianapolis, IN, Office of the General Minister and President, 1986.

This contains directories of governing bodies, ministers, congregations by state, and missionaries; reports of the General Assembly, the General Board, divisions, and councils; statistics of each congregation; and documents, including the "Design for the Church," and the "Guide to General Assembly Actions."

220.   **Yearbook of the American Baptist Churches in the U.S.A., 1907- .** annual. Valley Forge, PA, American Baptist Churches in the U.S.A. index. LC 73-647495. ISSN 0092-3478.

This is the official record of the governance of the American Baptist Churches in the U.S.A. and includes summaries of activities of the Office of the General Secretary and of the Boards of Educational Ministries, National Ministries, International Ministries, and Ministers and Missionaries Benefits. There are also financial reports and the minutes of the biennial meeting of the American Baptist Churches in the U.S.A.

4
Biographical Sources

221. Anderson, Joy, general ed. **The American Catholic Who's Who.** Washington, DC, National Catholic News Service, 1911, 1934/35-1980/81. LC 11-10944. ISSN 0364-6394.

The 1980-81 edition (the twenty-third and last), contains six thousand entries, some two thousand more than the edition of 1978-79. This is explained in part by the inclusion of prominent Canadian Catholics. There is a geographical list of entries, a necrology, and, for some biographees, references to previous editions where more information can be found. There are also geographical lists of the members of the National Conference of Catholic Bishops (American) and the Canadian Conference of Catholic Bishops.

222. Arrington, Leonard J., ed. **The Presidents of the Church: Biographical Essays.** Salt Lake City, UT, Deseret Book, 1986. 460p. index. LC 85-31117. ISBN 0-87579-026-7.

Arrington leads a group of sympathetic yet scholarly authors who examine the lives of the thirteen Presidents of the Church of Jesus Christ of Latter-Day Saints, in essays averaging thirty-five pages. A photograph of the subject precedes each essay except that of Joseph Smith. Bibliographies follow each essay, and contain citations from non-Mormon as well as Mormon scholars. Arrington has added an index to the whole work.

223. Asplund, John. **The Universal Register of the Baptist Denomination in North America, For the Years 1790, 1791, 1792, 1793, and part of 1794.** Boston, MA, J. W. Folsom, 1794. Reprint: New York, Arno Press, 1980. 93p. (The Baptist Tradition). LC 79-52581. ISBN 0-405-12448-1.

"...[A]s I had not any certain abode, property or possession, wife, children, relations, or other things to entangle my mind," Asplund journeyed mostly on foot, over 7,000 miles visiting 250 churches and 15 associations in 1790 and 1791. "[T]o remedy the former defects and to get further information," he made another tour in 1792-94, visiting 550 churches and 24 associations and meeting 300 preachers. By state and locality (many can hardly be called towns), he lists each church, the association to which it belongs, the foundation date, its ordained preachers, and the number of members for each year. He covers such groups as Particular Baptists, General Baptists, Seventh Day Baptists, black churches, and Indian churches. He lists candidates for the ministry and diminutions from the ministry by death, excommunication, and resignation; gives extracts from association minutes for the years covered; adds a summary account of the Baptists in North America; and has statistics on Baptist churches and ministers in Europe, Asia, Africa, and America outside the United States. This is an historical resource of prime importance for the study of the second largest religious group in America, but it also transcends that worthy denomination and makes for fascinating browsing.

224.   Attwater, Donald. **The Penguin Dictionary of Saints**, 2d ed. Revised and updated by Catherine Rachel John. Hammondsworth, England, and New York, Penguin, 1983. 352p. LC gb84-17488. ISBN 0-1405-1123-7.

Attwater, the scholar who worked with Herbert Thurston to update *Butler's Lives of the Saints* (see 258), here provides a quick reference to the lives of better-known saints, as well as lesser ones which "reading and travel might bring you across." British and Irish saints are given special attention. He has fewer entries than Farmer (see 236), and ignores Russian and Eastern saints except for the truly famous. A readable introduction, an eight-page glossary with meaty definitions of terms relating to sainthood and church history, a list of saints' emblems, and a bibliography of thirty-five works for further reading add substance. However, Farmer's entries are on the whole fuller, and he adds bibliographic material to each entry, which Attwater does not.

225.   Bacote, Samuel William, ed. **Who's Who Among the Colored Baptists of the United States.** Kansas City, MO, Franklin Hudson Publishing, 1913. Reprinted: New York, Arno Press, 1980. 307p. index. LC 79-52588. ISBN 0-405-12455-4.

Bacote has furnished laudatory biographical sketches of 128 prominent black men and women Baptists living at the time of writing. Photographs accompany the entries, which are in random order and accessible by an index in the front of the book.

226.   Barker, William Pierson. **Who's Who in Church History.** Grand Rapids, MI, Baker Book House, 1977. 319p. LC 74-85306. ISBN 0-8010-0705-4.

Barker's criteria for inclusion, outside of general fame, are three: persons who identified themselves as Christians, who had an effect on the ministry of the church, and who are no longer living. He gathers a wide range of persons, not all saints, from the early church fathers until present times, and includes Catholics, Anglicans, Protestants, and a few, such as the tragic Michael Servetus, who managed to offend everyone. Barker's colorful and tight prose captures salient features: "Swiss Protestant Barth dropped his blockbuster Commentary on the Epistle to the Romans in 1918, shattering forever the blithe liberalism of western Protestantism and launching a muscular system of Biblically-based thinking" (p. 31).

227.   Benedictine Monks of St. Augustine's Abbey, Ramsgate (UK), comps. **The Book of Saints: A Dictionary of Persons Canonized or Beatified by the Catholic Church**, 5th ed. rev. New York, Thomas Y. Crowell, 1966. 740p. LC 66-22140.

Produced and revised since 1921, this work gives short sketches of all those considered saints (*canonized*) or blessed (*beatified*, a stage on the way to canonization), who are honored in a country, diocese, or order of the Roman Catholic Church. The compilers make no claim to original research, except in the case of Benedictine saints, but do maintain objectivity, separating fact from legend and taking into account the latest scholarship in the field of hagiography. Saints from churches not in union with Rome (for example, the Russian Orthodox) are not included; for coverage of these, see Holweck (239). For each saint, the sketch includes name and surname or appellation; religious order, if any; present state of cult; date of feast; year of death; and chief features of the life. There is no bibliographic material.

228.   Bowden, Henry Warner, and Edwin S. Gausted, advisory ed. **Dictionary of American Religious Biography.** Westport, CT, Greenwood Press, 1977. 573p. LC 76-5258. ISBN 0-8371-8906-3.

This pioneering and well-wrought dictionary contains 425 biographies of American religious leaders who died before July 1, 1976. In the editor's own words, entries are not limited to predominantly Protestant "ordained white clergymen," but include women, Indians, blacks, Asians, laymen, theists, freethinkers, transcendentalists, and cultists. However, most biographees are from mainline churches. Each entry offers the vital statistics of the subject's life, a narrative with interpretative judgments, and a bibliography containing up to six books by the subject, references from nine standard biographical directories like the *Dictionary of American Biography* (New York, Scribner, 1928-37) and up to five book-length biographies about the subject. Useful appendixes list each biographee by denomination and by place of birth. The index is particularly strong on events and organizations.

229. Brown, John Thomas. **Who's Who in Churches of Christ: Biographical Sketches and Portraits of Ministers and Other Leaders.** Edited by E. W. Thornton. Cincinnati, OH, Standard Publishing, 1929. 299p.

Brown died while writing this or, as the editor notes, "the pen of the author unexpectedly dropped from his hand." Over fourteen hundred short biographical sketches of ministers and leaders are included here, many accompanied by black-and-white photographs. Brown includes a theological introduction on the development of the Churches of Christ.

230. Code, Joseph Bernard. **Dictionary of the American Hierarchy 1789-1964.** New York, J. F. Wagner, 1964. 452p.

After an extensive bibliographic introduction to the history of the American Roman Catholic hierarchy, Code identifies nearly one thousand bishops, including all native-born Americans raised to the episcopate, apostolic delegates from the Vatican to the United States, non-Americans who served in the United States before being nominated bishop outside the country, and non-American vicars apostolic of Hawaii and Guam after these became American territories. Each biography contains full name, birth and death dates, names of parents, higher education, diocese of origin, dates of ordination to priesthood and consecration to episcopate, and works by and about each bishop. No fewer than thirty-three appendixes include chronologies, necrologies, lineage, episcopal families (bishops listed according to which bishop consecrated them), non-American bishops residing in the United States, and lists of bishops attending the plenary councils of the American hierarchy. There is no more extensive historical compilation on this subject.

231. Comay, Joan. **Who's Who in Jewish History: After the Period of the Old Testament.** New York, David McKay, 1974. 448p. index. LC 73-93915. ISBN 0-679-50455-9.

Comay's scope is the whole of Jewish history from approximately the second century BCE. She includes Jews who contributed to this history and to Jewish thought, as well as some prominent non-Jews such as Arthur James Balfour. The living are omitted, except for a few very prominent Jewish and Israeli leaders in office during the book's compilation. An essentially popular treatment, the book has many black-and-white photographs and some in color. Bibliographies are lacking, always a loss. Comay offers this startling statement: "for the reader's convenience cross references have been kept to a minimum." A thematic index serves as a key, and a glossary and a chronology from 134 BCE assist the non-Jewish reader.

232. Deen, Edith. **Great Women of the Christian Faith.** New York, Harper, 1959. 410p. index. LC 59-12821. ISBN 0-06-061849-3.

This collection includes biographies of Protestants, Anglicans, and Roman Catholics in three chronological sections: the second to the seventeenth centuries, the eighteenth through twentieth centuries, and, rather like an appendix, women of both these periods who were not yet included. The accounts are hagiographic — adjectives such as "valiant," "selfless" and "inspiring" abound — but finding biographical information on women is in general so difficult that this work is to be counted a valuable contribution. A bibliography contains just under a hundred sources, and there is an index.

233.   Delaney, John J. **Dictionary of American Catholic Biography.** Garden City, NY, Doubleday, 1984. 621p. LC 83-25524. ISBN 0-385-17878-6.

Delaney, a prolific writer on matters Catholic (see 234 and 235), here provides, for the general reader, biographical sketches of deceased American Catholics who made contributions either to the church or to the nation. He states that all his information is taken from secondary sources, but does not offer these in a bibliography. Each sketch contains date and place of birth, educational background, important positions held, important works, and death date. A series of appended lists includes important events in the history of American Catholicism between 1513 and 1984, Catholic justices of the United States Supreme Court, and Catholics who served in presidents' cabinets.

234.   Delaney, John J. **Dictionary of Saints.** Garden City, NY, Doubleday, 1980. 647p. LC 79-7783. ISBN 0-385-13594-7.

This work, Roman Catholic in viewpoint, contains brief sketches of five thousand saints and near-saints, that is, all the saints in the Roman Calendar, the church's official list. Delaney has been careful to cull those dropped from the calendar because of insufficient evidence. In some cases, legendary material is included, but is so labelled. Saints of the Eastern Church which is in union with Rome are included, but those recognized exclusively by the Greek or Russian Orthodox churches are not. The saints are arranged alphabetically, with feast day listed at the end of each sketch. Delaney's appendixes include lists of saints who are patrons of causes and places, their symbols in art, a chronological list of popes and world rulers, the Roman Calendar, and the Byzantine (Eastern Rite) Calendar. For short sketches, Delaney covers more of the Catholic world than Farmer (see 236) or Attwater (see 224), who tend to emphasize the saints of the British Isles.

235.   Delaney, John J., and James Edward Tobin. **Dictionary of Catholic Biography.** Garden City, NY, Doubleday, 1961. 1,245p. LC 62-7620.

Fifteen thousand persons, all deceased, are treated in thumbnail sketches, including date and place of birth, important positions held, summary of work, and date and place of death. Coverage includes those who contributed to the life of the church, those who made contributions to other human endeavors, and some who were inimical to the church. Cross-references link alternate names. Bibliographies are scarce, added only for major figures. Appendixes list popes, emperors, and other great figures. The scope is international, but in 1961 for the most part that meant European and American.

236.   Farmer, David Hugh. **The Oxford Dictionary of Saints**, 2d ed. New York, Oxford University Press, 1987. 478p. index. LC 86-19263. ISBN 0-19-869149-1.

The first edition (1978) covered all English saints, including those who died abroad and foreigners who died in England; all saints for whom there is a cult in England; and important saints of Ireland, Scotland, and Wales. It generally excluded Eastern saints. This second edition adds the important Easterners, both Greek and Russian, as well as the earliest martyrs of the Christian church, and updates several dozen essays. Each sketch of a saint is based on scholarly sources, and gives name, dates (when known), an outline of the life and works, and a brief but solid bibliography. Appendixes contain sketches of thirteen unsuccessful candidates for canonization, principal patronages (wherein we learn that St. Francis of Assisi is the patron of ecologists, St. Jerome of librarians, and St. Barbara of gunners), and iconographical emblems. An index lists places in Great Britain and Ireland associated with specific saints, and a calendar gives the feast days of the saints listed in the volume. Farmer includes modern Roman Catholic saints, as well as pre-sixteenth-century figures, who are also venerated by Anglicans. Although the coverage emphasizes England, the excellence of the scholarship and bibliography make this the best single-volume reference work in this area.

237.   Hatfield, Edwin Francis. **The Poets of the Church: A Series of Biographical Sketches of Hymn-Writers with Notes on Their Hymns.** New York, A. D. F. Randolph, 1884. 719p. LC 12-28654. Reprint: Boston, MA, Milford House, 1972. 719p. index. LC 78-133349. ISBN 0-87821-028-9. Also reprinted: Detroit, MI, Gale, 1978. LC 78-19045. ISBN 0-8103-4291-X.

Hatfield offers sketches of two pages each for approximately two hundred musical poets, principally American and British hymnwriters of the eighteenth and nineteenth centuries, although there are some from earlier centuries. Hatfield does not add any bibliographic material, but does give an index of hymns.

238.   Hoehn, Matthew, ed. **Catholic Authors: Contemporary Biographical Sketches 1930-1947.** Newark, NJ, St. Mary's Abbey, 1948-52. 2 vols. LC 48-2039. Reprinted: Detroit, MI, Gale, 1981. LC 81-183250. ISBN 0-8103-4314-2.

Hoehn includes 620 authors, living and dead, American and foreign, if at least one work of each has been translated into English. The great are here (Jacques Maritain, Evelyn Waugh) as well as the truly obscure. Sketches range in length from a few lines to several columns. This work, created by a librarian with library reference shelves in mind, can be likened to the biographical dictionaries published by the H. W. Wilson Company.

239.   Holweck, F. G. **A Biographical Dictionary of the Saints.** St. Louis, MO, B. Herder, 1924. 1,053p. LC 24-20782. Reprinted: Detroit, MI, Gale, 1969. LC 68-30625.

From "Aaron of the Nuts" to "Zwentibold of Lorraine," Holweck has attempted to note briefly all who have been and are venerated in the Christian church, not for the purpose of glorification or hagiography, but for historical truth. Fancies, forgeries, and romances are named as such. In his sweep, he includes Eastern saints from the Church of Russia, the Monophysite Coptic Church, Arians, and Nestorians, offering an outline of each saint's work, notes on the liturgical cult, and, wherever possible, a bibliographic notation. His sources are primarily nineteenth-century scholarly works. This is more comprehensive, if more dated, than the works by Farmer (see 236) and the Ramsgate Benedictines (see 227), which are both essentially Roman Catholic in scope.

240.   John, Eric, ed. **The Popes: A Concise Biographical History.** New York, Hawthorn Books, 1964. 496p. index. LC 64-12422.

This work offers sketches, varying in length from a column to several pages, on all popes from Peter (according to Roman Catholics, the first pope) to Paul VI, who was elected in 1963. The chronology is divided into eight periods, each with an historical introduction by Douglas Woodruff. Though the sketches are somewhat hagiographic, tending to glorify the lives of these men, controversies are not skirted, especially by Woodruff. Bibliography is scanty and left to the end of the work. There is a complete index. Black-and-white and color portraits and woodcuts are plentiful.

241. Kalberer, Augustine. **Lives of the Saints: Daily Readings.** Chicago, IL, Franciscan Herald Press, 1983. 495p. LC 74-10761. ISBN 0-8199-0539-9.

This book is meant, as its title notes, for daily reading on the lives of the saints, a spiritual device widely practiced in Christendom, especially Catholic Christendom, until the recent past, and a practice meant to be revived by the publishers. The work has reference value because it contains, in addition to the better-known ancient, medieval, and early modern saints, more recent saints, such as the American Frances Cabrini, and many lesser known "Blesseds," those who have passed through the first stage toward sainthood, such as Andre Bessette and Theresa Ledochowska. Black-and-white photographs are added when available. The biographical sketches are laudatory, but not unpleasantly so or stretched to fiction, a fault common to the genre in the past.

242. Kelly, J. N. D. **The Oxford Dictionary of Popes.** New York, Oxford University Press, 1986. 347p. index. LC 85-15599. ISBN 0-19-213964-9.

Having noted a void in the literature, Kelly, an Anglican scholar, with "cool but not unsympathetic detachment," provides page-long sketches of popes from St. Peter (whose standing as a pope other Anglicans might dispute) to John Paul II, covering family background, prepapal career, and activities in office. He includes antipopes as well and, in an appendix, the illusive Popess Joan, said to have reigned sometime in either the ninth, tenth, or eleventh century. Bibliographies with each sketch contain primary and secondary sources. Kelly opts for a chronological arrangement of his subjects, but provides an alphabetical list at the beginning of the book and a generous, seventeen-page index. In comparison with John (see 240), Kelly is the more scholarly; yet Kelly, a practiced interpreter of Christian doctrine to the educated general reader, is eminently readable.

243. Kleinz, John P. **The Who's Who of Heaven: Saints for All Seasons.** Westminster, MD, Christian Classics, 1987. 334p. LC 87-071420. ISBN 0-87061-136-4.

Hagiography among Christians is the biography of those deceased who are considered to have achieved heaven. Kleinz, a priest and journalist, intends this work for the general reader, but does not sacrifice seriousness, scholarship, and a good writing style. His biographical sketches originally appeared as newspaper articles. He divides them into sections on Mary, the mother of Jesus; role models for Catholic priests; missionaries; foundresses of women's religious communities; Jesuits; and saints of the early and medieval church. In addition to treating many who are official saints of the church, Kleinz includes some who have not yet arrived, and indeed who have been controversial in recent times, such as Teilhard de Chardin, who was under censure even when he died in 1955 but whose ideas influenced thinkers at Vatican II.

244. Kolatch, Alfred J. **Who's Who in the Talmud,** rev. ed. Middle Village, NY, Jonathan David, 1981. 216p. LC 64-24891. ISBN 0-8246-0263-3.

Kolatch's work is both more and less than its name implies. It is a popular introduction to the Talmud, and includes a definition of the work, a very brief overview of each of its sixty-three tractates, ten pages of terms, and overbrief biographical sketches of the many persons instrumental in the Talmud's transmission. There are no indexes, few cross-references, and not a single bibliographic reference. Kolatch has not standardized the English spelling of names with a more authoritative source such as the *Encyclopaedia Judaica* (*EJ*) (See 25). Although no other recent work is similar to this, one's time is better spent with the *EJ*.

245. Leete, Frederick De Land. **Methodist Bishops: Personal Notes and Bibliography with Quotations from Unpublished Writings and Reminiscences.** Nashville, TN, Parthenon Press, 1948. 457p. LC 48-15027.

Leete gathers biographical and bibliographical materials on 250 Methodist bishops from the Methodist Bishops' Collection, which includes letters, books, sermons, addresses, essays, and lectures; records of origin, ancestry, and descendants; and unpublished biographies and autobiographies. Leete's divisions include biographies of and bibliographies for each bishop, a list of books containing writings by or about Methodist bishops, general works on the episcopacy in Methodism, quotations from episcopal correspondence, portions of unpublished manuscripts, and reminiscences. Leete provides access to the whole through an index.

246. Littauer, Fred, ed. **National Directory of Christian Artists,** 1986 ed. San Bernardino, CA, Praise Ministry Associates, and Eugene, OR, Harvest House, 1985. 264p. indexes. LC 85-80487. ISBN 0-89091-490-2.

Littauer lists 236 conservative Christian individuals and groups, mostly performers, in five major categories: speakers, evangelists, individual musicians, musical groups, and visual artists. For each artist or group, he gives a name and address, a photograph, and a brief description, followed by a note on type of people ministered to, titles or subjects of work, publications, quotations about the artist or group, geographical area of ministry, and fee range. Since the editors do not endorse those included, a list of references is given for each. Littauer adds an alphabetical list of all artists included, as well as a cross-reference index, since many of the artists are multitalented.

247. Melton, J. Gordon. **Biographical Dictionary of American Cult and Sect Leaders.** New York, Garland Publishing Co., 1986. 354p. index. (Garland Reference Library of Social Science, vol. 212). LC 83-48226. ISBN 0-8240-9037-3.

Melton here provides biograpical sketches of 213 American sect or cult founders and leaders whom he regards as responsible for diversity in American religion. All were deceased prior to 1983. Each sketch contains birth and death dates and places, higher education, marriages, principal activities, and a bibliography of works by and about the individual. Appendixes list the biographees by sect, by birthplace, and by original religious background, and there is an index of all proper names mentioned. Nowhere else is information on such a diverse group of people gathered in one book.

248. Moyer, Elgin. **Wycliffe Biographical Dictionary of the Church.** Revised and enlarged by Earle E. Cairns. Chicago, IL, Moody Press, 1982. 449p. LC 81-22578. ISBN 0-8024-9693-8.

This is an update of Moyer's *Who Was Who in Church History* (Moody Press, 1968), and includes three hundred new biographees in its over two thousand entries. Ecumenical in scope, it covers Protestant, Roman Catholic, and Eastern deceased church leaders including blacks and evangelicals, who are often overlooked in other works. Martin Buber, the Jewish philosopher, is included. Arrangement is by chronological outline, which includes three subdivisions for each of the three major divisions of western history. Each entry is a short sketch containing birth and death dates, principal activities, and main books by the subject person. No bibliographic sources are included, a weakness.

249.   Nadell, Pamela S. **Conservative Judaism in America: A Biographical Dictionary and Sourcebook.** New York and Westport, CT, Greenwood Press, 1988. 409p. index. (Jewish Denominations in America). LC 87-31782. ISBN 0-313-24205-4.

Conservatism, a movement of the center between Orthodox and Reform Judaism, now numbers a million and a half adherents congregating in some eight hundred synagogues. Nadell has written the biographies of 130 professional, administrative, and intellectual leaders of the movement, deceased and living: mostly rabbis, and a lone woman. Nadell also includes the leaders of the Reconstructionist movement (seventy-seven thousand members in fifty-five synagogues as of 1987), since most spent a major part of their careers in Conservatism. Each biographical sketch is concluded with a three-part bibliography listing the subject's writings, works he edited or translated, and works about him. Nadell adds an introduction on the general development of Conservatism and Reconstructionism; notes on the movement's three prominent institutions, the Jewish Theological Seminary of America, the Rabbinical Assembly, and the United Synagogue of America; twelve appendixes, which list historically the leaders of Conservative institutions; a glossary; and a sixteen-page bibliography listing official publications, the writings of leaders, memoirs and biographies, synagogue histories, and secondary sources. This scholarly work concludes with a full index of names of persons, places, and organizations.

250.   Parbury, Kathleen. **Women of Grace: A Biographical Dictionary of British Women Saints, Martyrs and Reformers.** Stocksfield, Northumberland, England, and Boston, MA, Oriel Press, 1985. 199p. LC 85-141016. ISBN 0-85362-213-2.

Parbury divides this work in two. The first part is a biographical dictionary of religious women from earliest times to 1845. In this part, she includes some generic groups such as recluses and royal nuns. At times she includes women for whom there is only a minimal trace, such as "three women recluses of York," but the trace itself is worthy of preservation. This part has as an appendix a list of noble families whose daughters became nuns. The second part is an alphabetical listing and historical description of monastic houses for women. Parbury includes both Roman Catholic and Anglican holy women, even though in the sixteenth and seventeenth centuries these were on opposite sides of a brutal, and often fatal, struggle. She adds no bibliographic materials to the biographies or the histories of nunneries, and this weakens the book, but she does list some forty-six "books of reference" at the end.

251.   Peerman, Dean G., and Martin E. Marty. **A Handbook of Christian Theologians,** enlarged ed. Nashville, TN, Abingdon Press, 1984. 735p. LC 84-16879. ISBN 0-687-16563-6.

Of the thirty-eight essays in this handbook, twenty-six are reprinted without change from a 1965 edition. This earlier edition excludes, albeit apologetically, Roman Catholics, and treats only Berdyaev as representative of the Orthodox tradition. The enlarged edition includes five Roman Catholics in its twelve additional essays but, like the earlier version, covers only theologians in the Euro-American academic tradition. The essays average eighteen pages, and include a brief biography and a hefty introduction to the thought system of each theologian. Only two bibliographic entries are appended to each essay: a book by and a book about the subject. The essays are written by experts, some of whom are themselves worthy of inclusion in a similar volume. Biographical notations on these contributors are included in an appendix. This handbook packs an enormous amount of factual and introductory material into its seven-hundred-plus pages, but leaves the reader arguing for more: more theologians, especially women and third-worlders, more bibliography, and even more about each subject theologian.

252.   Polner, Murray. **American Jewish Biographies.** New York, Facts on File, 1982. 493p. index. (A Lakeville Press Book). LC 80-27105. ISBN 0-87196-462-7.

Polner offers page-long biographies of over four hundred distinguished Jews in American life (Maurice Sendak, Jill Clayburgh, Artur Rubinstein) and notables in American Jewish life (Menahem Mendel Schneerson, Balfour Brickner, Nathan Perlmutter). Bibliographies accompany most entries, and an appended bibliography lists four dozen sources for American Jewish life. The index is full, but lacks entries by field, so that one cannot find all the rabbis or film directors.

253.   Rosenbloom, Joseph R. **A Biographical Dictionary of Early American Jews: Colonial Times Through 1800.** Lexington, KY, University of Kentucky Press, 1960. 179p. LC 60-8517.

Rosenbloom enters every person identifiable as a Jew in America before 1800, although he notes that some 20 percent of the Jewish population remains obscure and unknown. He includes Canadians up till 1783. Variant surnames are reduced to a uniform listing, and some multiple entries to what is probably the same person are cross-referenced. Each entry includes known birth and death dates, a thumbnail biography, and reference to at least one published or unpublished source of information. The listings reveal a rich ethnic background, with names from England, Germany, Spain, and Portugal. In sum, Rosenbloom estimates there were "no more than 4,000 Jews, 1,500 of whom were born in America."

254.   Scheuritzel, Paul, ed. **Episcopal Clerical Directory.** New York, The Church Hymnal Corporation, 1985. Biennial. LC sn84-12118. ISSN 0160-5445.

Formerly called *The Clerical Directory of the Episcopal Church*, the 1985 edition (the thirtieth) contains over fourteen thousand biographies of active and retired Episcopal clergy in good standing, and notes that eleven thousand have updated their entries with recent information. There are, unfortunately, no indexes by institution, diocese, or geographical location.

255.   Schwarz, J. C., ed. **Who's Who in the Clergy: Vol. I 1935-36.** New York, the author, 1936. 1,222p.

255.1.   Schwarz, J. C., ed. **Religious Leaders of America: Vol. II 1941-42.** New York, the author, 1941. 1,147p.

In his first volume, Schwarz included over 7,000 Protestants, Catholics, and Jews from an American clergy estimated at 250,000. He changed the title in the second volume to take into account religions that have leaders but no formal clergy. For the second volume, no estimate is given of how many names were added or dropped. When a leader chosen for the second volume did not return Schwarz's survey, the name is listed with reference to the earlier volume. These volumes, undoubtedly planned as the inauguration of a regular series, remained the only attempt at wide-ranging, ecumenical, biographical reference until Marquis published the first *Who's Who in Religion* in 1975 (see 261).

256.   Segal, Igal. **Who's Who in World Jewry: A Biographical Dictionary of Outstanding Jews,** 7th ed. New York, Who's Who in World Jewry, 1987.

Segal includes biographies of over six thousand Jewish men and women from more than seventy countries in this work, the first edition of which was in 1955. He includes a special section identifying Soviet *refuseniks*, those who seek to emigrate but have been refused exit visas. Segal's work makes a fine companion to Polner (see 252) and *Who's Who in American Jewry* (see 260) for global biographical coverage of Jewish subjects.

257. Smith, William, and Henry Wace, eds. **Dictionary of Christian Biography, Literature, Sects and Doctrines: Being a Continuation of "The Dictionary of the Bible."** Boston, MA, Little, Brown, 1877-87. 4 vols.

Basing their work on the great eighteenth- and nineteenth-century collections of primary sources of Christianity, the editors conjoin the efforts of ninety-nine British scholars to provide objective information about all persons from the first eight centuries of Christian history about whom anything is known. Special attention is given the church history of England, Scotland, and Ireland. Wace and Piercy attest to the exactitude of the scholarship of this work when they note in the preface to their abridged version (see 259) that it contains biographies of no fewer than 596 men whose name is John.

258. Thurston, Herbert, and Donald Attwater, eds. **Butler's Lives of the Saints: Edited, Revised and Supplemented.** New York, P. J. Kenedy, and Westminster, MD, Christian Classics, 1956. 4 vols. indexes. LC 56-5383.

Alban Butler published his work between 1756 and 1759. Thurston thoroughly revised this, streamlining the florid eighteenth-century style and adding information from nineteenth-century scholarship, and published his edition with Attwater's help between 1925 and 1938. The current edition, published in 1956, excised about a tenth of the 1925-38 work and added entries for new saints. Thus, while the original Butler included 1,486 saints, the 1956 edition covers 2,565, with each saint receiving a biographical sketch from a paragraph to four pages long. Arrangement is by saint's feast day, and follows the calendar of the year. Indexes are thus essential, and each volume, covering three months, has its proper index, while the fourth volume has a comprehensive index for the year. Scholarly bibliographies are appended to each saint's biography. Appendixes include a memoir of Alban Butler and an essay on the process of beatification and sanctification, both by Thurston, and a list of the recently (through the early 1950s) beatified.

259. Wace, Henry, and William C. Piercy, eds. **A Dictionary of Christian Biography and Literature to the End of the Sixth Century A.D. with an Account of the Principal Sects and Heresies.** London, John Murray, and Boston, MA, Little, Brown, 1911. 1,028p. LC 12-1409.

In order to provide a manageable variant of Smith and Wace's four-volume *Dictionary of Christian Biography, Literature, Sects and Doctrines* (see 257), Wace and Piercy drop lesser-known persons and limit coverage to the first six centuries of Christendom, thereby excluding the growth of the Teutonic church. The remaining articles, often updated from the earlier masterpiece, remain lengthy and learned; that on St. Athanasius, for example, is nineteen columns. The bibliographies appended to each article contain popular and scholarly works as well as works newer than those listed in the earlier set. The editors note the ecumenical attitude toward this early twentieth-century work, which brought contributions from both Roman Catholic and Protestant scholars.

260. **Who's Who in American Jewry, 1980 Edition: Incorporating The Directory of American Jewish Institutions.** Los Angeles, CA, Standard Who's Who, 1980. 726p. LC 80-645196. ISSN 0196-8009

There are over six thousand biographies of Jews distinguished in some field or in Jewish life, in what the editors claim is the first dictionary of Jewish biography in half a century. They missed some notables, however, such as David Riesman and Jill Clayburgh, who were treated by Polner (see 252). The directory section contains ten thousand organizations, synagogues, educational institutions, youth groups, libraries, periodicals, hospitals, and camps, giving the name, address, and telephone number for each as well as information on affiliation and purpose. Rosen (see 216) offers more information for the organizations he covers, but this work lists many more organizations.

261. **Who's Who in Religion,** 3d ed. Chicago, IL, Marquis Who's Who, 1985. 439p. LC 76-25357. ISBN 0-8379-1603-8.

The basic biographical facts and vital statistics are given for seven thousand church officials, educators, and lay leaders, four thousand of whom are new to this edition. This edition is, however, considerably shorter than the second (1977), with its eighteen thousand religious leaders, or the first (1975) with sixteen thousand, and so should be used in conjunction with one or both of these. Some names are cross-referenced to other Marquis publications, such as *Who's Who in America.* The scope is limited to the United States; therefore, Christians and Jews make up the vast majority of entries.

262. **Who's Who in the Methodist Church.** Nashville, TN, Abingdon Press, 1966. 1,489p. LC 66-26876.

262.1. Clark, Elmer T., ed. **Who's Who in Methodism.** Chicago, IL, Marquis, 1952. 860p. LC 52-8040.

The earlier work, the more international in scope of the two, contains approximately fifty thousand names with biographical sketches. The 1966 version includes twenty-five thousand American church officers, Methodists of distinction in non-church fields such as government, and Methodist leaders in world Christianity outside the United States.

263. Williams, Ethel L. **Biographical Directory of Negro Ministers,** 3d ed. Boston, MA, G. K. Hall, 1975. 584p. index. LC 74-34109. ISBN 0-8161-1183-9.

After combing the national organizations and national committees of churches and the National Black Catholic Clergy Caucus, Williams offers biographical sketches of 1,442 ordained black clergy, 799 of which are new to this edition. There is a geographical index as well as a list of sources by denomination. Reproduced from the typewritten page, it is somewhat difficult to read, but few reference works are available on the immense contributions of blacks to American religious life, and this is a major resource.

264. Witherspoon, Eugene Daniel, Jr., comp. **Ministerial Directory of the Presbyterian Church, U.S., 1861-1967.** Doraville, GA, Foote & Davies, 1967. 648p. LC 68-3645.

264.1. Scott, Eugene Crampton, comp. **Ministerial Directory of the Presbyterian Church, U.S., 1861-1941.** Revised and supplemented, 1942-50. Atlanta, GA, Hubbard, 1950. 798p.

Witherspoon brings to date Scott's works, published in 1941 and revised in 1950, by updating the information on persons named in Scott, adding new biographees, and dropping the biographies of those no longer in the denomination. Biographies primarily give information about activity within the church. Witherspoon adds a bibliography of twenty-nine biographical works used by Scott in the preparation of the earlier editions.

265. Woodbridge, John D., general ed. **Great Leaders of the Christian Church.** Chicago, IL, Moody Press, 1988. 384p. index. LC 87-34974. ISBN 0-8024-9051-4.

For the general reader, Woodbridge offers sketches of sixty-four Christian leaders from Peter (Woodbridge declines to use "Saint") to Billy Graham. Each sketch contains a brief chronology, an introductory assessment, a review of the subject's activities and writings, and a reproduction of a painting or photograph of the subject. Additional photographs aptly capture the subject's life, such as the scenes of Irish monasteries for (St.) Patrick. The range of Christians covered includes Jewish Christians (Peter and Paul), Easterners (Ignatius of Antioch and Origen), medieval Westerners (Boniface, Bernard of Clairvaux, Thomas Aquinas), and Protestants and Catholics of the Reformation period

(Hus, Luther, Ignatius Loyola, Francis Xavier). After the Reformation, there are no more Easterners; after Blaise Pascal, no more Catholics. Billy Graham is the only living subject. Each subject receives a good bibliography of English-language books from a wide range of Christian sources. Woodbridge concludes the work with an index of personal and place names.

266.   Young, Henry J. **Major Black Religious Leaders: 1755-1940.** Nashville, TN, Abingdon Press, 1977. 173p. LC 76-51731. ISBN 0-687-22913-8.

    266.1.   Young, Henry J. **Major Black Religious Leaders Since 1940.** Nashville, TN, Abingdon Press, 1979. 160p. LC 79-11646. ISBN 0-687-22914-6.

Young's purpose in offering sketches of twenty-six black religious leaders in these two works is to elucidate the religious foundations of their active lives. Biographical material is brief and incomplete; Young neglects to note, for example, in which church and when Jesse Jackson was ordained a minister. Liberation is the predominant theme of the first volume, with coverage from Nathaniel Paul and Richard Allen to Marcus Garvey, since the leaders of this period had to respond to slavery or its aftermath. The fourteen sketches of the second volume are divided into groups covering social activism, the Nation of Islam and black Christian nationalism, the theology of nonviolence, and black theology as an end in itself. Both books would have been much improved by more careful biographical coverage, indexes, and bibliographies of sources for each person treated.

5
Atlases

267.   al-Faruqi, Isma'il Ragi A., ed., and David E. Sopher, map ed. **Historical Atlas of the Religions of the World.** New York, Macmillan, 1974. 346p. index. LC 73-16583. ISBN 0-02-336400-9.

Al-Faruqi notes that the most research in historical religious geography has been done for Christianity and for the biblical period. For other world religions, including Judaism, the scholarship is still elementary, while for such traditional religions as the African it is nonexistent. Fourteen scholars contribute text to accompany sixty-five small, monochrome maps. Judaism receives eighteen pages and thirteen maps, wherein there is particularly good coverage of movements of Jewish population groups in the last century. Christianity is also depicted, in thirteen maps, among them one showing the Nestorian and Roman Catholic presence in Asia during the Middle Ages. An appendix with chronologies of the great religions curiously leaves out Judaism. Indexes cover subjects and proper names.

268.   Anderson, Charles S. **Augsburg Historical Atlas of Christianity in the Middle Ages and Reformation.** Minneapolis, MN, Augsburg, 1967. 68p. indexes. LC 67-11723. ISBN 0-8066-1317-3.

Anderson supplies thirty-two multicolor maps, covering the period from 600 to 1648 CE, as working tools for students rather than for advanced scholars. A text outlining the historical period accompanies each map, and there are indexes for both the plates and the text. Anderson has a knack for putting in just the right amount of detail so that the maps are uncluttered and understandable. One can use this in conjunction with a general atlas for more detail when needed.

269.   Bahat, Dan. **Carta's Historical Atlas of Jerusalem: An Illustrated Survey.** Jerusalem, Carta, 1983. 96p. index. LC 83-168743. ISBN 965-220-020-4.

After an overview of this pivotal holy city, Bahat offers clear monochrome maps, architectural cutaway drawings, and black-and-white photographs, all accompanied by a readable text, separated into twelve historical periods from the time of the Canaanites to the post-1967 reunification. Bahat views the history of the city from the vantage point of an Israeli. A table of contents and a general index have been added; earlier editions, browsable works of just over fifty pages and with a slightly different title, did not have these access points. A map of the modern city, with its own index of streets, sites, and institutions, closes the atlas.

270.   Beach, Harlan Page, and Charles H. Fahs, eds. **World Missionary Atlas: Containing a Directory of Missionary Societies, Classified Summaries of Statistics, Maps Showing the Location of Mission Stations Throughout the World, a Descriptive Account of the Principal Mission Lands, and Comprehensive Indices.** New York, Institute of Social and Religious Research, 1925. 251p. indexes.

> 270.1.   Beach, Harlan Page, and Burton St. John, eds. **World Statistics of Christian Missions: Containing a Directory of Missionary Societies, a Classified Summary of Statistics, and an Index of Mission Stations Throughout the World.** New York, Committee of Reference and Counsel of the Foreign Missions Conference of North America, 1916. 148p.

> 270.2.   Dennis, James S., Harlan Page Beach, and Charles H. Fahs. **World Atlas of Christian Missions.** Maps by John G. Bartholomew. New York, Student Volunteer Movement for Foreign Missions, 1911. 172p. indexes.

> 270.3.   Beach, Harlan Page, ed. **A Geography and Atlas of Protestant Missions: Their Environment, Forces, Distribution, Methods, Problems, Results and Prospects at the Opening of the Twentieth Century.** New York, Student Volunteer Movement for Foreign Missions, 1901-03. 2 vols. 571p.

The 1925 and last edition of Beach's work, based on the annual reports of mission societies for 1923, contains four major sections: a directory of missionary societies by continent of origin; the statistics of Protestant missions, especially noting their growth since 1900, and including figures for foreign staff, general education, higher education, medical facilities and medical education, philanthropic work, and Bible distribution; twenty-four maps, mostly of Protestant mission stations, arranged by continent and country; and general descriptive notes on what today would be considered the Third World but in 1925 comprised Latin America and a series of empires: British, French, Japanese, and American. Beach includes extensive introductions and explanatory notes for each section. The 1925 edition, unlike earlier editions, contains relatively little information on Roman Catholic missions, because by publication date there had been no post-World War I studies of the field. A map on Roman Catholic and Greek Orthodox missions is reprinted from the 1911 edition. The directory does list thirty-three mission societies, in thirteen countries, whose purpose was work among the Jews. The scope of the work excludes mission work in Europe, although a map of the continent is included. Anglo-America is also omitted except for missions to Indians, Eskimo, and Asians. Four indexes provide access to the wealth of information: of mission societies, of mission stations, of mission societies by their initials, and of geography.

Copies of these now-dated works are rare, but provide unique information on the spread of Christianity in the early part of this century. The directory information was updated by Goddard (see 190), but no new atlas of the missions has come forth. While many of the churches covered by the various editions of this atlas are now considered indigenous—that is, self-supporting both in finances and local personnel—mission activity persists as a dominant theme in most branches of Christianity, and any new atlas will have to take into account attempts to reconvert such "Christian" lands as northern Europe.

271.   Chadwick, Henry, and Gillian Rosemary Evans, eds. **Atlas of the Christian Church.** New York, Facts on File, 1987. 240p. index. LC 86-32894. ISBN 0-8160-1643-7.

Chadwick and Evans divide this atlas into six historical and thematic periods, and offer forty-two maps, a scholarly yet readable text, a chronological table, an index of subjects, and an excellent bibliography. Two hundred thirty-nine photos in color and sixty-three in black-and-white avoid visual clichés and enhance the text. Much original thinking went into the design of this book. The color maps offer a fresh view, often seemingly from a satellite's eye rather than in traditional Mercator projection. The bibliography includes scholarly works; those published in French or German are accompanied by citations to English translations. Two themes emerge as one pages through this atlas: the spread of Christianity and its breaking up and gathering together again. Although the editors state that they could not include lesser-known manifestations of Christianity, they do capture its variety, by shifting their focus to cover, among other areas, the Third World, Christians in contemporary wars, the Orthodox churches, and the varieties of the nineteenth-century American experience. One would have a fine, small, reference library for Christianity if one were to include this atlas on a shelf with Cross (see 31) and Barrett (see 27). It joins the Facts on File series which includes Matthews's *Atlas of Medieval Europe* (see 288), Rogerson's *Atlas of the Bible* (see 667), and de Lange's *Atlas of the Jewish World* (see 273).

272.   Cornell, Tim, and John Matthews. **Atlas of the Roman World.** New York, Facts on File, 1982. 240p. LC 81-19591. ISBN 0-87196-652-2.

Although this work addresses the rise of Christianity as only part of its scope, it, like van der Heyden and Scullard (see 283), offers much to the student of Christianity and Judaism. There are fifty-four intelligible, full-color maps, and many color photos of scenes and art objects. Time charts trace the development of Rome from the 800s BCE to the 500s CE. A bibliography of several hundred works devotes a section to the rise of Christianity, and there is a gazetteer and an index. This is most useful for its good maps and contemporary photography, but it does not have the scholarly depth of van der Heyden and Scullard.

273.   de Lange, Nicholas. **Atlas of the Jewish World.** New York, Facts on File, 1984. 240p. index. LC 84-10102. ISBN 0-87196-043-5.

This fine atlas and handbook offers forty-eight multicolored, clear maps that are not overburdened with detail. It has three major divisions: the historical background, the cultural background, and the Jewish world today. The last systematically covers Jewish communities on all the continents, and gives better attention to the influential South African and the large Latin-American Jewish communities than does Alpher (see 51). De Lange has added fifteen essays on special topics, including the Bible, the Hebrew language, and the New York and Paris Jewish communities. There is a lengthy gazetteer, an index, a bibliography with notations through 1983, and a chronological table. More detailed maps of the Holocaust and the growth of Israel would be welcome (but see Gilbert, 277). There are many photographs, most in color, not chosen by the author, but generally well suited to the text.

274.   Emmerich, Heinrich. **Atlas Hierarchicus.** Modling, Austria, St. Gabriel-Verlag, 1968. 76p. LC 71-653123.

Emmerich maps Roman Catholic ecclesiastical circumscriptions throughout the world and shows dioceses, archdioceses, and abbeys for each country. Eastern churches united with Rome are included. Information on each diocese includes its foundation date, ecclesiastical rank, square kilometers, square miles, total population, Catholic population, and numbers of parishes, prelates, priests, seminarians, brothers, sisters, colleges, schools, converts, and baptisms. Statistics are taken from the 1967 edition of the *Annuario Pontificio*, the church's official yearbook and directory, published by the Vatican. Religious orders of men (but not of women) are included. English and French predominate, although explanations of local situations may be in German, French, Italian, or Spanish where pertinent, and regions of the Third World are offered up in the predominant western language of an area. Thus, notes and maps of North Africa are in French, while English is used for southern Africa. There are alphabetical lists of territories and of ecclesiastical circumscriptions.

275. Freitag, Anton, with Heinrich Emmerich and Jakob Buijs. **The Twentieth Century Atlas of the Christian World.** New York, Hawthorn Books, 1963. 198p. index. LC 63-17035.

This is essentially a Roman Catholic work, divided chronologically into six chapters. A short one, with no maps, covers Protestant missions. There are twenty-nine multicolor maps, but this is not enough: a single map of the Mediterranean region contains dots for Christian communities of the first six centuries, with dots color-specified for each century; the result is confusing. Six hundred thirteen black-and-white photographs accompany the maps and text, and extensive notes at the end of the book explain the photographs in detail.

276. Gaustad, Edwin Scott. **Historical Atlas of Religion in America**, rev. ed. New York, Harper & Row, 1976. 189p. indexes. LC 76-25947. ISBN 0-06-063089-3.

Gaustad presents a formidable cartographic and statistical study, divided into four sections: (1) religion in America, 1650-1800; (2) 1800-1975, colonial and larger noncolonial bodies; (3) additional noncolonial bodies; and (4) special aspects, including Indians, Jews, Afro-Americans, Alaskans, and Hawaiians. Four appendixes cover denominational distribution in 1650, 1750, 1850, and 1950. Four indexes cover the author and title of works mentioned, places, religious bodies, personal names, and subjects. Much statistical information is presented, and many bibliographic sources are cited in each section. Maps are more detailed than in Gaustad's 1962 edition; some include county breakdowns. A full-color map shows denominational distribution in 1970, and another depicts Catholic-Protestant dominance throughout the nation county by county.

277. Gilbert, Martin. **Atlas of the Holocaust.** New York, Macmillan, 1982. 256p. index. LC 81-675599. ISBN 0-02-543380-6.

The 316 maps "show, in chronological sequence, the destruction of each of the main Jewish communities of Europe, as well as acts of resistance and revolt, avenues of escape and rescue, and the fate of individuals" (Introduction). Gilbert (see 278) brings human reality and individuality out of statistics by showing on maps the journeys of individual deportees and communities from their homes to death camps. Thus we can see that on January 11, 1943, 750 Jews were sent from Westerbork, Holland to Auschwitz, Poland and on another map that here a mother and child were shot and there four Jews were hanged. The book is replete with black-and-white photographs, and text explains the maps. There is an extensive bibliography of published and unpublished sources. Useful detail is sometimes omitted, as when maps of Europe do not show the 1940s boundaries of countries, but this is a minor drawback. The final maps, which treat survivors and list the dead, are numbing: Norway—1,000 survivors, 728 dead; Poland—225,000 survivors, 3,000,000 dead, and so forth. This is one of the best reference books listed in this bibliography, although one of the hardest in which to sustain reading.

278. Gilbert, Martin. **Jewish History Atlas**, 3d ed. Cartography by Arthur Banks and T. A. Bicknell. New York, Dorset, 1985. 128p. LC 77-8252. ISBN 0-88029-057-8.

Gilbert, a prolific author and now the official biographer of Winston Churchill, currently has thirteen historical atlases to his credit, including the Macmillan *Atlas of the Holocaust* (see 277). He has a talent for making history and statistics come to life by plotting them on maps. Thus, from figures on a battle map, one learns, for example, that during the American Civil War twelve hundred Jews fought for the Confederacy and six thousand for the Union. This atlas contains 124 monochromatic maps, many depicting aspects of Jewish history little known to contemporary Christians and Jews, such as "The Khazar/Jewish Kingdom 700-1016 A.D." Gilbert may annoy some readers by employing "B.C." and "A.D.," rather than the neutral "B.C.E." and "C.E." While the map "Christ in Palestine" was dropped for this edition, "The Preaching of St. Paul" was not. The bibliography of eighty books was not updated from the second edition (1976), and the work lacks an index.

279. Grant, Michael. **Ancient History Atlas**, 3d ed. Cartography by Arthur Banks. London, Weidenfeld and Nicolson, 1986. unpaged. 87 maps. index. LC gb87-9492. ISBN 0-297-78874-4.

Grant, a widely published British scholar who frequently has brought the ancient world to the contemporary reader, here assembles eighty-seven black-and-white maps covering the political, economic, cultural, and religious life of antiquity from the early second millenium BCE to the reign of Justinian in the sixth century CE. Although only a half dozen of these maps are specific to the Hebrew world and the rise of Christianity, almost every map deals indirectly with these subjects. Thus, on map 58, "The Roads of the Roman Empire," the reader can trace the journeys of St. Paul, St. Ignatius of Antioch, or the much later St. Jerome. Particularly useful and unique are Grant's specialty maps, such as "Rainfall in the Mediterranean" and "The Religious Centres of Greece," and plans for cities such as Pompeii and Rome. There are several maps of Roman Britain.

280. Halvorson, Peter L., and William M. Newman. **Atlas of Religious Change in America: 1952-1971.** Cartography by Mark C. Nielsen. Washington, DC, Glenmary Research Center, 1978. 95p. LC 78-67653. ISBN 0-914422-09-X.

Because religious matters are no longer of question on the United States Census (but see 181), this atlas fills the gap by comparing studies done in the early 1950s and 1970s for the growth or decline of thirty-five denominations, which comprise 80 percent of religious preference in the United States. Each denomination is depicted in four maps: adherents by county in 1951; in 1971; percent change over the time; and "shift-share," that is, "a ratio that shows the extent to which a denomination has changed its share of the total religious adherence in a county between 1952-1971." The numerical and spatial change of each denomination is thereby charted. The maps are analyzed for each denomination. There are four additional maps showing national patterns for all denominations and a brief bibliography.

281. Hammond, Nicholas G. L., ed.-in-chief. **Atlas of the Greek and Roman World in Antiquity.** Park Ridge, NJ, Noyes Press, 1981. 56p. LC 81-675203. ISBN 0-8155-5060-X.

Like Cornell and Mathews (see 272) and van der Heyden and Scullard (see 283), this covers the world in which Judaism and Christianity flourished—from the neolithic age to the sixth century CE. There are forty-six monochrome maps and a gazetteer, but no text. Van der Heyden and Scullard (see 283) is the more scholarly.

282. Hawes, Gordon K., comp., and Stanley Knight, cartographer. **Atlas of Man and Religion.** Oxford, England, The Religious Education Press, 1970. 127p. LC 78-653717. ISBN 0-08-006999-1.

This is an idiosyncratic work that briefly addresses world religions and world organizations, but mostly treats Christianity. It opens with narrative sections on "the world in which we live," the impact of Christianity on the West, the background of Christianity, the United Nations, and the World Council of Churches. Forty-one maps follow, arranged to mirror the structure of the preceding essays. These include seventeen world maps, dealing with such general topics as food supply, climate, and animal husbandry. The arrangement is confusing: a map on the spread of Christianity and Islam in the late ninth century CE is followed by one treating Palestine in the times of the Hebrew scriptures. Littell (see 287) gives a clearer cartographic exposition of Christianity, and Gilbert (see 278) is preferable for Judaism.

283.   Heyden, A. A. M. van der, and H. H. Scullard. **Atlas of the Classical World.** New York, Nelson, 1960. 221p. indexes. LC 60-1130.

There is little direct treatment of Christianity or Judaism in this fine volume, largely because it was conceived as a companion to van der Meer (see 289), but the seventy-three maps and multitude of black-and-white photographs deal with a world in which Judaism was both a nation-state and a nation in diaspora, and into which Christianity was born. If one is to understand the Bible as a historical document, one must know something about the classical world. About a sixth of the work deals with the period during which Christianity was the official religion of the Roman Empire. There is an index.

284.   Karta. **Atlas of Israel: Cartography, Physical and Human Geography**, 3d ed. New York, Macmillan, 1985. 232p. LC 85-675163. ISBN 0-02-905950-X.

284.1.   Israel. Department of Surveys. **Atlas of Israel**, 2d ed. Jerusalem, Survey of Israel, 1970. LC 76-653754. ISBN 0-444-40740-5.

While these two works are different editions of the same publication, all editions are useful to have, and are quite different from each other. The first, published in Hebrew in 1956, contained 101 maps and reflected the armistice of 1948. The second, published in 1970, included the Golan Heights and the Sinai, territories occupied after the 1967 Six-Day War. To gain a more international readership, only English was used, and some materials of a local nature in the first edition were dropped. This edition contains twelve historical maps, from pre-history to modern times. There is a bibliography of over a thousand cartographic sources on Israel. The third edition is claimed to be bilingual, but is not entirely so; all place names are in Hebrew, but only the larger are printed in English. The color cartography and the Landsat photography are extraordinary. A particularly interesting plate details world Jewish emigration to Israel.

285.   Jedin, H., Kenneth Latourette, and Jochen Martin. **Atlas zur Kirchengeschichte: Die christlichen Kirchen in Geschichte und Gegenwart.** Freiburg im Breisgau, Germany, Herder, 1987. 235p. index. LC 88-130060. ISBN 3-4512-0869-5. Reissue of 1970 ed.

This exception to the "English-only" rule for this bibliography is based on the assumption that an atlas can be studied profitably by a reader who knows little or no German. The title is translated *Atlas of Church History: The Christian Churches in History and the Present Time*. The preparers of this atlas rank among the greatest historians and geographers of Christianity and Judaism in the twentieth century, and include the American Latourette. The editors and cartographers have prepared 257 maps and graphs, accompanied by eighty-three pages of commentary (in German, of course) with much statistical information. Arrangement of the maps is historical, and the scope of the work is worldwide. The concentration is on mainline churches including the Roman Catholic, Orthodox, Lutheran, Reformed (and Presbyterian), Baptist, Methodist, and Congregational, and organizational charts are included for many churches. Much unique information for the Americas is contained on such maps as "Missions in Venezuela and Columbia up to 1817" and "The Indian Missions from 1567 to 1861 in the Territories Presently Considered the U.S.A." The editors added a detailed gazetteer.

286.   Laor, Eran, comp. **Maps of the Holy Land: Cartography of Printed Maps, 1475-1900.** New York, Alan R. Liss, and Amsterdam, The Netherlands, Meridian Publishing, 1986. 201p. indexes. LC 86-15298. ISBN 0-8451-1705-X.

Laor has collected maps of the Holy Land since the late 1940s, and lists 1,185 in this cartobibliography descriptive of the collection named after him at the Jewish National and University Library in Jerusalem. He adds a fifteen-page biographical dictionary of cartographers and printers, and a bibliography of fifty reference works. With its twenty-three full-color and many black-and-white reproductions, this is an eminently browsable work, and an index of personal names and a chronological index of the maps provide for more specific access. Printed on high-gloss paper, this is at once a work of high scholarship and great beauty.

287.   Littell, Franklin Hamlin. **The Macmillan Atlas History of Christianity.** Cartography of Emanuel Hausman. New York, Macmillan, 1976. 176p. index. LC 75-22113. ISBN 0-02-573140-8.

This is a history of the spread of Christianity, with a large number of small, mono-chromatic maps interspersed with the text. Line drawings, done from photographs, are included. There is no bibliography. Littell notes the importance of Jewish and Islamic history to Christianity; he includes information on the Jews of Ashkenaz, Jewish messian-ism in the thirteenth to eighteenth centuries, the expulsion of the Jews from Iberia, and their repression in the sixteenth and seventeenth centuries. Splinter groups, such as the Mennonites and Doukhobors, are covered, as are new religions, such as Baha'i, and inde-pendent African Christian movements. Littell also juxtaposes Christianity and ideologies such as Marxism and Nazism.

288.   Matthews, Donald. **Atlas of Medieval Europe.** New York, Facts on File, 1983. 240p. index. LC 82-675303. ISBN 0-87196-133-4.

This is a companion to T. Cornell and John Matthews's *Atlas of the Roman World* (see 272). The medieval world is thought by some to be synonymous with the Christianity of the period, and, indeed, this atlas is replete with sections such as "Christendom on the Move." Jewish life in Western Europe was also very rich in the Middle Ages, but there is scant notice of it in this work. Islam, which shared a frontier with Christianity across the entire Mediterranean, is given more due. As with Cornell and Matthews, the color maps are excellent. There is a chronological table covering from the 300s CE to the 1500s; a glossary; a bibliography; a gazetteer; and an index.

289.   Meer, Frederic van der. **Atlas of Western Civilization**, 2d rev. ed. English version by T. A. Birrell. Princeton, NJ, D. Van Nostrand, 1960. 240p. index. LC map60-339.

Van der Meer has not produced an atlas of the development of western civilization with battles, kings, and political frontiers. Instead, the focus is on the development of thought, art, and religion, from Homer to the establishment of the United Nations. Many of the fifty-two maps, each representing an epoch or a particular aspect of western culture, pertain directly to Christianity, as with the map of "Paleo-Christian Monuments." This is a companion to the *Atlas of the Early Christian World* (see 290), and, in the manner of that volume, van der Meer includes 977 well-chosen black-and-white photographs. Neither work has been truly superseded.

290.   Meer, Frederic van der, and Christine Mohrmann. **Atlas of the Early Christian World.** Translated and edited by Mary F. Hedlund and H. H. Rowley. London, Nelson, 1959. 216p. indexes. LC map58-7.

Much scholarship went into identifying dioceses, archdioceses, monuments, castles, monasteries, ruins, writers, and writings by century, and placing these on forty-two finely detailed, color maps that cover the period from the post-apostolic age, ca. 80 CE, to 600 CE. There are maps showing the spread of monasticism, the travels of Augustine, and Christianity in western Europe, as well as detailed layouts of Rome, Jerusalem, Constantinople, Ravenna, and Alexandria. Indexes cover places and geographical features, persons, and inscriptions. Copious notes explicate 614 black-and-white photos (taken in the 1940s and 1950s) of sites, ruins, roads, harbors, and mountain passes. As a pictorial presentation of the development of Christianity, and especially when used with its companion volume (see 289), this remains unsurpassed.

291. Smith, George Adam. **Historical Atlas of the Holy Land**, 2d ed. London, Hodder and Stoughton, 1936. 61 plates. index. LC map38-46.

In 1936, the Holy Land was the British Mandate of Palestine. Smith's color maps cover the period from 1400 BCE to the twentieth century, and offer good coverage of ancient political divisions, climate, and vegetation. There is a chronological table running from ca. 4,000 BCE to 4 BCE.

292. Vilnay, Zev. **The New Israel Atlas: Bible to Present Day**. Maps by Carta, Jerusalem. Translated by Moshe Aumann. Jerusalem, Israel Universities Press, 1968. 112p. LC 79-653239.

With his main focus on modern Israel, Vilnay has produced 114 maps divided into four sections: (1) modern Israel, featuring climate, roads, railways, and the like; (2) the struggle for independence, with seventeen maps covering military clashes from 1920 to the Six-Day War in 1967; (3) the history of the country from the biblical period through the British mandate; and (4) proposals for a Jewish state, covering the political developments leading up to the creation of the country. The second and fourth sections could have been combined after the third for a more even chronological flow. The third section is of special interest to readers of the Bible; some fifteen maps cover the biblical period and are entirely oriented toward the Hebrew and early Jewish peoples. The maps are not always clearly explained by the accompanying text. A few maps are in color, but the monochrome are often difficult to read, since opposing forces and diverse movements are depicted by various shades of the same color. Vilnay adds an extensive gazetteer of modern towns and villages.

293. Wardin, Albert W., Jr. **Baptist Atlas.** Cartography by Don Fields. Nashville, TN, Broadman Press, 1980. 63p. LC 79-52541. ISBN 0-8054-6551-0.

Although Wardin admits he lacks comprehensive coverage of non-American Baptist groups, he does attempt to cover all Baptist groups in the United States, including mission organizations and their fields of work throughout the world. Twenty-seven maps and many tables and graphs illustrate statistics. Sections cover the beginning of the movement, its development in the United States, a classification of Baptist bodies, a regional geography of Baptists in the United States, and world mission activity. Wardin adds a thorough bibliography of statistical sources on Baptists, complementing abundant references in the text.

6
Bibliographies, Literature Guides, and Catalogs

I. Literature Guides and Bibliographies of Many Religious Communities

294.   Adams, Charles Joseph, ed. **A Reader's Guide to the Great Religions**, 2d ed. New York, Free Press, 1977. 521p. indexes. LC 76-10496. ISBN 0-02-900240-0.

The second edition of this collection of critical bibliographic essays contains two chapters on Judaism and one on Christianity. "Early and Classical Judaism," by Judah Goldin was updated from the first edition, and "Medieval and Modern Judaism" by Seymour Cain is wholly new. The chapter on Christianity, prepared for the first edition by H. H. Walsh, was updated by Jaroslav Pelikan. There is a useful appendix on "The History of the History of Religions" by Charles Long. The authors, for the most part limiting their recommendations to works in English, have made their choices on the basis of utility and availability to the generally educated reader as well as to graduate students, teachers, and librarians, and they evaluate the works they list and relate them to general frameworks of thought. Indexes allow access by subject and by author, compiler, translator, or editor. The overly brief table of contents does not analyze the chapters; each of the chapters on Judaism contains eight major divisions and that on Christianity has twelve, along with subdivisions.

295.   Barber, Cyril J. **Introduction to Theological Research.** Chicago, IL, Moody Press, 1982. 176p. LC 81-22531. ISBN 0-8024-8625-8.

Like Sayre and Hamburger (see 318), Barber prepared his bibliography for a course meant to introduce students to resources for the study of Christianity and the Bible. In a series of fifteen bibliographic essays, he evaluates many reference works on religion. Two useful features are the photoreproductions of pages of selected resources and the exercises at the end of each chapter. A serious drawback is Barber's uncritical recommendation of reference works already a century old. Though bibliographic records indicate that Barber added an index, the copy reviewed did not have one.

296.   Barber, Cyril J. **The Minister's Library.** Grand Rapids, MI, Baker Book House, 1974, 1983. 2 vols. indexes. Vol. 1: LC 73-92977. ISBN 0-8010-0598-1. Vol. 2: LC 80-148664. ISBN 0-8010-0830-1.

Barber is thinking here of a large personal library that will serve a minister in his or her primary activity: preaching. In his first volume, he offers instruction on setting up, cataloging, and classifying, according to the Dewey Decimal System, such a library. He then presents an extensive book guide, covering doctrine, devotion, pastoral theology, social and ecclesiastical theology, missions, Christian education, and comparative religions. Each book receives an annotation as well as a classification and Cutter number. Barber is forthright in declaring the annotations to be evaluative from a conservative and evangelical point of view. Outstanding books in this category receive an asterisk for recommendation, and books departing from this line, i.e., when written by liberal Protestants or Roman Catholics, are also signaled. Barber's second volume collates four supplements to the first. There is only a subject index to the first volume, and only separate author and title indexes to the second.

297. Barrow, John Graves. **A Bibliography of Bibliographies in Religion.** Ann Arbor, MI, Edwards Brothers, 1955. 489p. index. LC 55-8299.

Basing this work on this 1930 Ph.D. dissertation at Yale, Barrow includes only published, monographic bibliographies which list printed works. Although most entries are on Christianity, he attempts coverage of other religions, and lists seventeen pages of Jewish bibliographies. His chapters include periodicals, catalogs, the Bible, church history, church fathers, the Catholic Church and its orders, the Reformation, sects, missions, religious education, sermons, liturgy and music, and individuals. A chapter of miscellaneous items covers atheism, ars moriendi (the art of dying well), heresy, prophecy, psychology and religion, and social services. Within chapters, bibliographies are listed under subject headings by publication date. In an appendix, Barrow lists bibliographies he did not personally examine and titles he could not verify. The work is accessible through a title index, an author index, and an extensive subject index. Smith (see 319), upon examining Barrow's dissertation, predicted it would be definitive when it was published.

298. Bollier, John A. **The Literature of Theology: A Guide for Students and Pastors.** Philadelphia, PA, Westminster Press, 1979. 208p. index. LC 78-10962. ISBN 0-664-24225-1.

Intending to assist Catholic and Protestant theological students and pastors, Bollier annotated 543 reference sources on Christianity and Judaism, including works covering general knowledge like Sheehy's *Guide to Reference Books* (10th ed.: Chicago, IL, American Library Association, 1986) and *Books in Print.* (New York, Bowker, 1948-). These latter may be helpful to those unacquainted with library research, but their inclusion limits the number of titles dealing specifically with religion. Bollier's divisions are traditional: general works, Bible, systematic theology, denominational works, and practical theology. The annotations are learned, often giving the bibliographic history of the work at hand. There is a combined author/title index which does not always include name changes, e.g., *Religion Index* (see 470 and 476) must be sought out as the former *Index to Religious Periodical Literature.* Although the work is intended to be a guide to research, there is no mention of online databases.

299. Borchardt, C. F. A., and W. S. Vorster, eds. **South African Theological Bibliography/Suid-Afrikaanse Teologiese Bibliografie.** Pretoria, South Africa, University of South Africa Press, 1980, 1983. 2 vols. Vol. 1: ISBN 0-86981-185-1. Vol. 2: ISBN 0-86981-300-5.

Borchardt and Vorster cite South African books, journal articles, dissertations, theses, and university series, arranging their entries under the broad headings of the Bible, systematic theology, history, practical theology, the science of religion, missiology, apologetics, and sects. Although the introduction and table of contents are in both English and Afrikaans, the titles of the entries are in the language of publication. The editors include an author index in each volume and, in the second volume, a subject index in English. For a bibliography of South African church history, see Hofmeyr and Cross (401).

300.   Branson, Mark Lau. **The Reader's Guide to the Best Evangelical Books.** New York, Harper & Row, 1982. 207p. index. LC 81-48205. ISBN 0-06-061046-8.

Branson limits his coverage to the decades from 1950 to 1980, with emphasis on more recent publications, and divides his work into (1) popular books on the Christian life and (2) the Bible, the church, and the world. An introduction to each topic highlights the most significant books, and throughout the work prominent evangelicals offer lists of books influential on their lives. The range of writers is wide, from the very popular to such noted Protestant scholars as Karl Barth, Oscar Cullmann, Jaroslav Pelikan, and the Roman Catholic Hans Kung. Barth and C. S. Lewis have the most entries in the author index.

301.   Brunkow, Robert deV., ed. **Religion and Society in North America: An Annotated Bibliography.** Santa Barbara, CA, ABC-Clio, 1983. 515p. indexes. (Clio Bibliography Series, no. 12). LC 82-24304. ISBN 0-87436-042-0.

Brunkow draws 4,304 entries, published in 600 periodicals (mainly between 1973 and 1980) from volumes 11 to 18 of *America: History and Life* (Santa Barbara, CA, Clio Press, 1964-), covering topics on the history of religion in the United States and Canada since the seventeenth century. Organization is by general topic, including education, government and politics, health, labor, revivals, Sabbatarianism, negative impulses (anti-Catholicism, anti-Mormonism, anti-semitism, racism), and the major religious traditions. He excludes articles on Native American religions uninfluenced by European traditions. In addition to an author index, there is an extensive "Subject Profile Index," in which key terms and a historical period for each entry are linked to form a subject profile and then rotated so the complete subject profile appears after each key term.

302.   Burr, Nelson R., ed. **A Critical Bibliography of Religion in America.** Princeton, NJ, Princeton University Press, 1961. 2 vols. (Religion in American Life, vol. 4). LC 61-5383. ISBN 0-691-07107-1.

Burr here produces an unusual bibliography, in that its narrative format on the development of the American religious experience can be read as an end in itself. Before Burr put himself to the task, no comprehensive bibliography of books on the subject had been attempted. The work is divided into five general parts: bibliographical guides; the evolution of American religion; religion and society; religion in the arts and literature; and intellectual history, theology, philosophy, and science. Burr covers all religions established in America, including those from the East, Judaism, and American creations such as deism and Mormonism. Since they are integrated in the narrative, citations are minimal: author, title, place of publication, and date. There are no indexes, a fact which seriously weakens the work as a reference tool. The best access is through the detailed table of contents. Burr offers extensive treatment of some minorities such as blacks, but for contributions to religion by American women, one must look to later bibliographies such as Bass and Boyd (see 373) and Richardson (see 426). This is the seminal work upon which later bibliographies, such as Sandeen (see 317), were built.

303.   Burr, Nelson R., comp. **Religion in American Life.** New York, Appleton-Century-Crofts, 1971. 171p. index. (Goldentree Bibliographies in American History). LC 70-136219. ISBN 0-3901-5607-8.

Burr, who earlier produced the first comprehensive bibliography on religion in America (see 302), here briefly annotates over 1,600 books, journal articles, and dissertations on the many different religions and denominations; on the interplay of American religion with politics, sociology, education, science, art, and literature; and on theology and special ministries. This is a fine working tool, with extra-wide margins and blank pages for notes, meant for undergraduate use. An author index is included. The work is somewhat dated, as evidenced by the brief section on "death of God" theology.

304.   Chernow, Barbara A., and George A. Vallasi, series eds. **The Reader's Advisor: A Layman's Guide to Literature**, 13th ed., 6 vols.

>   Volume 4: William L. Reese, ed. **The Best in the Literature of Philosophy and World Religions.** New York, Bowker, 1988. 801p. indexes. LC 57-13277. ISBN 0-8352-2148-2.

The format of the series is the evaluative bibliographic essay, followed by annotated lists of the best works in print as determined by the scholars writing the subject essays, followed in turn by biobibliographies of great writers in the field under study. Four chapters, covering "Judaism," "Early Christianity," "Late Christianity," and "The Bible and Related Literature," make up fully a third of this volume. A last chapter on "Minority Religions and Contemporary Religious Movements" covers nineteenth- and twentieth-century expressions of Christianity as well as non-Judeo-Christian new religions. Title and subject indexes, as well as a name index that includes both authors and names used as subjects, provide ease of access. This bibliography is highly useful to the layperson and the librarian for quick access to the main themes in a thinker's work, as well as the important titles by and about him or her. The overview of the Bible, prepared by staff editors, contains much recent material. However, a chronology of English language versions, unchanged from previous editions of the work, ends in 1970, thereby missing some widely used translations published since.

305.   Crysdale, Stewart, and Jean-Paul Montminy. **La Religion au Canada: bibliographie annotée des travaux en sciences humaines des religions, 1945-1970/Religion in Canada: Annotated Inventory of Scientific Studies of Religion, 1945-1972.** Quebec, Canada, Les Presses de l'Université Laval, and Downsview, Ontario, Canada, York University, 1974. 189p. indexes. (Histoire et Sociologie de la Culture, no. 8). LC 75-506956. ISBN 0-7746-6687-0.

Two separate bibliographies, with separate author indexes, are here presented. Both offer extensive abstracts covering topics, methods, and findings. Though both present empirical studies with formal research designs, Crysdale notes that French-Canadian social scientists have tended to deal with the general aspects of religion, while Anglo-Canadians focus on the more specialized and quantitative. The French bibliography covers anthropology, ethnography, folklore, social history, psychology, and sociology. The English encompasses those areas and adds economics, demography, political science, political sociology, and social geography.

306.   Farris, Donn Michael, and Raymond P. Morris. **Aids to a Theological Library: Selected Basic Reference Books and Periodicals.** rev. ed. n.p., American Theological Library Association Library Development Program for the American Association of Theological Schools, 1969. 95p.

A revision of a 1958 edition, this ecumenical work includes Jewish, Roman Catholic, Eastern Orthodox, and Protestant materials, as well as those reflecting both liberal and neoconservative schools of thought. There is an emphasis on selection tools and bibliographic resources rather than on an ideal, well-balanced collection. The work is divided in two, with the first section covering monographs and reference tools, including some general reference works, and the second treating scholarly periodicals.

307.   Freudenberger, Elsie, and John T. Corrigan. **Reference Works in the Field of Religion 1977-1985.** Haverford, PA, Catholic Library Association, 1986. 65p. index. LC 87-101762. ISBN 0-87507-037-X.

Freudenberger's 158 entries, with full descriptive but not evaluative or comparative annotations, were originally published in the "Religious Reference Works" column of

Catholic Library World. She cites works on world religions in addition to Christianity and Judaism, but all titles are in English. She adds a combined author/title index. Primarily a selection guide for librarians, this booklet has the virtues of being short, excellent, and recent.

308. Gorman, G. E., and Lyn Gorman. **Theological and Religious Reference Materials.** Westport, CT, Greenwood Press, 1984, 1985, 1986. 3 vols. indexes. (Bibliographies and Indexes in Religious Studies, nos. 1, 2, 7). Vol. 1: LC 83-22759; ISBN 0-313-20924-3. Vol. 2: LC 83-22759; ISBN 0-313-24779-X. Vol. 3: LC 86-380; ISBN 0-313-25397-8.

When this four-volume set is completed, it will be the standard English-language bibliography of religious reference works for the remainder of this century. The Gormans have taken a comprehensive approach to providing an annotated bibliography for students, practicing clergy, and scholars. The result is international, multidisciplinary, and interdenominational. General reference works are included when considered pertinent. Even the definition of *reference books* is broad: useful textbooks and topical surveys are included. Coverage is not restricted to recent or widely available titles—published catalogs of individual libraries, for example, are included.

The first volume contains a fine essay by John B. Trotti on the study and use of theological literature. Thereafter, it is divided between general reference materials and biblical studies. Volume two covers systematic theology and ethics, church history, missions and ecumenism, and religious orders. The third volume focuses on practical theology, encompassing liturgy and worship, homiletics, education, counseling, and sociology. The final volume will treat comparative religion and the non-Christian religions.

Each volume contains separate author, title, and subject indexes, with the author list including editors and translators and the title index giving British and American variants and foreign originals. The preface is repeated, with specifics for each volume, so that each can stand as a self-contained unit. The publisher exhibits a curious ambivalence as to whether the series is a unit or four separate bibliographies. The Gormans use a single, consecutive alphanumeric system for the entries, but Greenwood has printed only the series title on the spines, and declined to number them, so that to shelve the set together is to give the impression of having four copies of the same work.

Just shy of six thousand entries in the first three volumes, the series can be regarded as definitive, and will probably be superseded only by online sources.

309. Hadidian, Dikran Y., comp. **Bibliography of British Theological Literature 1850-1940.** Pittsburgh, PA, The Clifford E. Barbour Library, Pittsburgh Theological Seminary, 1985. 455p. (Bibliographia Tripotamopolitana, no. 12). LC 85-26839. ISBN 0-931222-11-7.

Hadidian provides an extensive list by author of British imprints, mostly first editions, for the period covered. He includes an essay, "Introduction to the British Theological Scene 1850-1940," with its own hefty bibliography. Coverage is broad, including, for example, Sir Richard Burton's travelogues, and translations such as Martin Niemoller's *From U-Boat to Concentration Camp.* Hadidian notes that some of his materials are not to be found in the *National Union Catalog Pre-1956 Imprints* (London, England, Mansell, 1968-80. See also **711**), the British Museum's *General Catalogue of Printed Books* (London, England, Trustee of the British Museum, 1959-66. See also **684**), or their supplements. Bibliographic citations are short, and include for each author the title, place, and date publication of each work. There are no avenues of access beyond the author listings.

310. Karpinski, Leszek M. **The Religious Life of Man: Guide to the Basic Literature.** Metuchen, NJ, Scarecrow Press, 1978. 399p. indexes. LC 77-19338. ISBN 0-8108-1110-3.

Over two thousand works, of which some six hundred deal with Judaism or Christianity, receive brief and for the most part nonevaluative annotations. Karpinski aims at students of religious life in its broadest definition, and includes studies of the religions of antiquity, Asian religions, native religions, and the occult. Monographic historical and thematic surveys are included along with reference materials. The scope is so broad that, although one can profitably use this as a checklist for beginning research, one must immediately move on to a more specific bibliography. There is a combined title/author index and a separate periodical index.

311. Kennedy, James R., Jr. **Library Research Guide to Religion and Theology: Illustrated Search Strategy and Sources,** 2d ed., rev. Ann Arbor, MI, Pierian Press, 1984. 59p. index. (Library Research Guides Series, no. 1). LC 84-61723. ISBN 0-87650-185-4.

For the advanced undergraduate and graduate student, Kennedy provides instruction on researching a religion term paper, from choosing and narrowing a topic to finding and evaluating books, periodical articles, current information, and quotations. This revised version of the 1974 edition includes information on other guides to religious study published in the past ten years (Kepple, see 312; Bollier, see 298; McCabe, see 355), and updates an extensive bibliography of finding tools. The revision also contains information on searching *Religion Index* (see 476).

312. Kepple, Robert J. **Reference Works for Theological Research: An Annotated Selected Bibliographical Guide,** 2d ed. Washington, DC, University Press of America, 1981. 283p. index. LC 81-40350. ISBN 0-8191-1680-7.

312.1. Kepple, Robert J., and John R. Muether. **Reference Works for Theological Research: Supplement of Additions and Changes.** Philadelphia, PA, Westminster Theological Seminary, 1986. 47p.

Intended for both student and instructor, this work is divided in two, the first part treating general and general religious or theological works, and the second twenty-one subfields of theology. Kepple acknowledges McCabe's *Critical Guide to Catholic Reference Books* (see 355), and avoids duplication except where Roman Catholic works are important to the study of Christianity as a whole. He includes many general, nonreligious reference works, including national bibliographies, dissertation-finding tools, and writing and publishing aids; this practice weakens his coverage of materials relating to theology. There is no treatment of online databases in the 1981 edition. An index combines authors, editors, titles, and alternative titles, giving broad access to this fine guide. Kepple published brief supplements in 1981/82 and 1983. The 1986 supplement replaces these, and a third edition is expected.

313. Mitros, Joseph F. **Religions: A Select, Classified Bibliography.** New York, Learned Publications, 1973. 435p. index. (Philosophical Questions Series). LC 77-183042. ISBN 0-9121-1608-0.

Mitros covers the methods of studying religions, general reference works, non-Christian religions, Christianity, patristic studies, the scriptures, and journals. Only thirteen pages are set aside for Judaism, while half the book is given to Christianity, its history, and its denominations. Some important works are annotated. Mitros includes an index of authors.

314. **Religious & Inspirational Books & Serials in Print 1987**, 5th ed. New York, Bowker, 1987. 1,826p. indexes. LC 78-63633. ISBN 0-8352-2320-5.

Drawn from the massive Bowker databases from which the Books in Print series is produced, this work lists 61,204 books from some 3,000 publishers. Each book is listed with full bibliographic citation in an author, a title, and a subject index with over six thousand subject headings and over five thousand cross-references. Although all the world's religions are covered, since most of the books in the database are written in English, there is a predominance of works on aspects of Christianity and Judaism. The subject index uses Library of Congress subject headings, commonly used in American libraries; for convenience, a subject area directory groups the subject headings under forty-eight broad categories.

In addition to the books, 3,606 serials and periodicals are listed, with full bibliographic citations, in both title and subject indexes, the latter grouping the entries under 162 broad subject categories.

Completing the work, a key to the abbreviated names of publishers and distributors includes editorial and ordering addresses and telephone numbers.

This work is a great convenience to students of religion, but, because its publishing frequency is planned for every two years, the searcher had best check the newest edition of *Books in Print* (New York, Bowker, 1948-) and *Forthcoming Books* (New York, Bowker, 1966-) or *Ulrich's International Periodicals Directory* (New York, Bowker, 1932-) for the most up-to-date information on availability and ordering of a book or periodical.

315. **Religious Books 1876-1982.** New York, R. R. Bowker, 1982. 4 vols. LC 83-6028. ISBN 0-8352-1602-0.

With 130,000 titles under 27,000 subject headings, this is claimed by Bowker to be "the most comprehensive bibliography of books on religion for North American usage" (Introduction). The importance of this claim, however successful, is underscored by the following very true statement: "In North America, there are few truly comprehensive library collections in religion."

Bowker assembled this bibliography from its book publishing records, augmented by the Library of Congress's *National Union Catalog* and other sources. It is primarily a subject index, using Library of Congress subject headings. Each book has a full bibliographic citation under the first subject heading assigned to it by the Library of Congress. Author and title entries are brief and refer to the full subject citation.

When developing a comprehensive bibliography, this should be used in conjunction with *Religious & Inspirational Books and Serials in Print 1987* (see 314) and the most recent edition of the *Subject Guide to Books in Print* (New York, Bowker, 1957-).

316. **Religious Books in Print: A Reference Catalogue.** London, J. Whitaker, 1986- . ISSN 0305-960X.

Over 18,000 titles from British publishers and from overseas publishers but available in Britain are listed, both in a single alphabet for authors, titles, and key words, and in an index with 18 classifications and 127 subsidiaries. Each entry includes author, title, subtitle, editor, translator, size, number of pages, illustrations, series title, price, publisher, date of publication, and International Standard Book Number (ISBN). Children's books are excluded. The listings are predominantly on Christianity, but one of the eighteen sections on "Non-Christian Religions and Ideologies" includes some five hundred titles relating to Judaism.

317. Sandeen, Ernest R., comp., and Frederick Hale. **American Religion and Philosophy: A Guide to Information Sources.** Detroit, MI, Gale, 1978. 377p. indexes. (American Studies Information Guide Series, vol. 5). LC 73-17562. ISBN 0-8103-1262-X.

Sandeen and Hale briefly annotate 1,639 entries to books and articles, including "key primary documents," arranged in 21 chapters following a rough chronology and including general works, Amerindians, Catholicism, major Protestant denominations, Judaism, utopian groups, religion in the South, missions, new religions, movements in the twentieth century, and the various American philosophical movements. Access is eased through separate subject, author, and title indexes. Inevitably, the larger churches and movements get more space: there are twenty-six entries for Mormonism but over a hundred for Roman Catholicism. Since emphasis is on the recent, with most publications dating from the 1960s and 1970s, this can be used as a complement to Burr's comprehensive work (see 302).

318. Sayre, John L., and Roberta Hamburger, comps. and eds. **Tools for Theological Research,** 7th ed. Enid, OK, Seminary Press, 1985. 120p. index. LC 85-11979. ISBN 0-9128-3222-3.

Intended primarily for seminary students taking a course of the same title, this work is divided into two parts. The first covers one hundred basic works, almost half of which are general reference materials. The second covers what Sayre and Hamburger consider to be supplementary resources for religious studies. The annotations are thorough, accounting for the persistent popularity of the many editions of this booklet. The editors add an index of authors and titles.

319. Smith, Wilbur M. **A List of Bibliographies of Theological and Biblical Literature Published in Great Britain and America 1595-1931: with Critical, Biographical, and Bibliographical Notes.** Coatesville, PA, the author, 1931. 62p. index. LC 32-15205.

Smith identifies, describes, and arranges chronologically separately published bibliographies of biblical and theological literature in English. He excludes church history, for which he refers the reader to Case (see 381). An index provides access by author and title. A unique feature is a biographical note for each author (often but a few words, as bibliographers on the whole lead obscure lives). Smith's contribution is valuable for its historical material; he himself points to Barrow (see 297) for comprehensiveness.

320. Society of American Archivists, Religious Archives Section. **Religious Archives in the United States and Canada: A Bibliography.** Chicago, IL, Society of American Archivists, 1984. 17p. ISBN 0-931828-62-7.

This bibliography of articles on archives and archival practices covers the Baptists; Brethren; Church of Christ, Scientist; Jews; Latter-Day Saints; Lutherans; Mennonites; Methodists; Moravians; Presbyterians; Roman Catholics; and the United Church of Canada. A general list of forty articles on church archives precedes these chapters.

321. Trotti, John, ed. **Aids to a Theological Library.** Missoula, MT, Scholars Press, 1977. 69p. (American Theological Library Association Library Aids, no. 1). LC 76-54173. ISBN 0-89130-127-5.

Originally published as the *Library Check List*, this pamphlet was revised several times to reflect the association's expansion to include Roman Catholic libraries and its growing interest in Judaism and other world religions. Current through 1974, it contains basic monographs and general reference works in addition to religious reference books. Trotti cites some important foreign-language sources. Arrangement is by type of reference work; there are no indexes. Citations are not numbered or annotated. Though still useful, it has been superseded by Bollier (see 298) and Kepple (see 312).

322. Walsh, Michael J. et al., comps. **Religious Bibliographies in Serial Literature: A Guide.** Westport, CT, Greenwood Press, 1981. 216p. indexes. LC 81-312. ISBN 0-313-22987-2.

This covers 178 serial bibliographic tools, including some of general scope such as *Abstracts in Anthropology*. Most, however, are specific to the study of religion. There is a subject index, and a title index which includes superseded and alternate titles. Each entry includes title with standard abbreviation, subtitle, bibliographic details, publishing history, arrangement, coverage, comments, publisher's name and address, and International Standard Serial Number (ISSN).

323. Wilson, John F., and Thomas P. Slavens. **Research Guide to Religious Studies.** Chicago, IL, American Library Association, 1982. 192p. (Sources of Information in the Humanities, no. 1). LC 81-22862. ISBN 0-8389-0330-4.

All religions are within the scope of this two-part work, and its intended readership is primarily librarians. The first and largest part is a series of five authoritative bibliographic essays by Wilson on the study of religion, the history of religion, Western religions, religious thought and ethics, and scientific study of the religious experience. Full bibliographic citations of works mentioned—all in English—follow each essay. In the second part, Slavens annotates a highly selective list of reference works covering religion in general, mysticism, sacred books, and particular religions. One hundred five works on Christianity are listed, as well as thirty on Judaism. Slavens's selection seems haphazard: *Catholic Periodical and Literature Index* (see 457) is treated, but not *Religion Index One* (see 470); *New Testament Abstracts* (see 722) is here, but not *Old Testament Abstracts* (see 723). Although compiled in the 1980s for librarians, no mention is made of online databases. Given the immense scope of the theme, Wilson's collection of essays provides librarians with the more valuable selection tool. The title/author index includes all works listed in both sections.

II. Library Catalogs

324. **A Bibliography of the Catholic Church Representing Holdings of American Libraries Reporting to the National Union Catalog in the Library of Congress.** London, Mansell, 1970. 572p. ISBN 0-7201-0134-4.

Drawn from the materials gathered for *The National Union Catalog, Pre-1956 Imprints* (London, England, Mansell, 1968-80, see also 711), this work holds sixteen thousand main entries, and added entries for documents emanating from and arranged according to the administrative, judicial, and legislative organizations of the Roman Catholic Church. Each entry includes a location symbol for a library in North America. Nonliturgical entries include publications of the Vatican Chancery, congregations, and commissions; papal bulls, encyclicals, epistles, registers, and treaties; and documents and reports from papal legates. The ten thousand liturgical entries reflect the state of the liturgy in the church before Vatican II, and is "probably the largest organized listing of Western liturgical materials ever assembled" (Foreword).

325. **Dictionary Catalog of the Missionary Research Library: New York.** Boston, MA, G. K. Hall, 1968. 17 vols. LC 74-169177.

The Missionary Research Library, founded in 1914 by Charles H. Fahs (see 270), contains over one hundred thousand books, periodical titles, reports, and archival collections, listed in this catalog by author, title, and subject. The seventeenth volume lists the periodicals separately, along with reports from mission churches, hospitals, and other institutions. Emphasis is on Protestant missions outside the United States, but works on Roman Catholic missions, on missions within Europe, and on missions to Amerindians are not lacking. A Chinese index is not included, but many Chinese works are in the main catalog with romanized titles. An unusual strength is the inclusion of periodical articles by important authors.

326.   Friends Historical Library of Swarthmore College. **Catalog of the Books and Serials Collections of the Friends Historical Library.** Boston, MA, G. K. Hall, 1982. 6 vols. ISBN 0-8161-0376-6.

The Friends Historical Library attempts to gather all works by and about the Quakers. It has holdings, mostly American and British, from the mid-seventeenth century to the present, the particular strength being historical material on the slavery issue and Quaker aid to blacks. The catalog lists forty thousand books under title, author, and subject entries in a single alphabet. The final volume includes three separate listings for serials, broadsides, and tracts. Serial holdings include proceedings of yearly meetings, newsletters, annual reports of institutions, children's magazines, and journals about social issues.

327.   Harvard University Library. **Catalogue of Hebrew Books.** Cambridge, MA, Harvard University Press, 1968. 6 vols. LC 68-22416.

327.1.   **Catalogue of Hebrew Books. Supplement.** Cambridge, MA, Harvard University Library, 1972. 3 vols.

The 1968 collection lists the forty thousand titles of this great Hebraica collection. The first four volumes are an author and subject listing in the Latin alphabet, and the final two volumes contain a Hebrew-alphabet index of titles. The 1972 supplement adds thirteen thousand new titles, with the first volume arranged by classification number, the second by author and subject, and the third by Hebrew title. Yiddish books are not included in these sets.

328.   Hebrew Union College, Jewish Institute of Religion, Library. **Dictionary Catalogue of the Klau Library.** Cincinnati, OH, and Boston, MA, G. K. Hall, 1964. 32 vols. LC 65-1601.

Founded in 1875 and now containing one of the greatest Jewish collections, the Klau Library by 1964 held some 200,000 items, with particular strengths in general materials on the Jews and Judaism, the Bible, the ancient Near East, Jewish music, Spinoza, and fifteenth- and sixteenth-century Judaica and Hebraica. The catalog contains twenty-seven volumes of subjects, authors, and titles in the roman alphabet, and five volumes of titles in the Hebrew alphabet.

329.   Library of the Ecumenical Centre. **Classified Catalog of the Ecumenical Movement.** Boston, MA, G. K. Hall, 1972. 2 vols. LC 73-155601. ISBN 0-8161-0925-7.

329.1   **Supplement.** Boston, MA, G. K. Hall, 1981. 517p.

This catalog reflects the holdings of the library of the World Council of Churches in Geneva, Switzerland as of the end of 1971. It lists 52,000 books and pamphlets and 1,350 periodicals, of which 750 were then current. Individual periodical articles are included in the catalog. The library at the time also housed eight thousand boxes of archival materials, but only published works are included in the bibliography. These consist chiefly of works of ecumenical relevance published between 1500 and 1900, works on the movements of the early twentieth century, World Council of Churches documentation, documents of world confessional families, treatments on the ecumenical movement as expressed on all continents, works for and against Christian unity, proceedings and reports on discussions from church union negotiations, ecumenical theology, biographies of leading figures, and works on Vatican II and non-Catholic reactions to it. The arrangement of all this material is by Dewey classification number, and there is a fourteen-page breakdown of the 280.1 to 280.9 schedules. An index of authors, with reference to their entries, is given at the front of each volume. The 1981 supplement adds twelve thousand titles.

330. New York Public Library, Reference Department. **Dictionary Catalog of the Jewish Collection.** Boston, MA, G. K. Hall, 1960. 14 vols. LC 60-3398.

> 330.1. New York Public Library, Reference Department. **Dictionary Catalog of the Jewish Collection. First Supplement.** Boston, MA, G. K. Hall, 1975. 8 vols. LC 75-647729.

The main set includes 270,000 entries, including periodical articles, from all divisions of the library, including the Jewish Division, which alone contains over 100,000 volumes. The preface notes that "the collection is strong in biography, bibliography, and other reference works; the history of the Jews in all countries; Bible commentaries; the archaeology of Palestine; medieval and modern rabbinic, philosophic and kabbalistic texts; social studies and belles lettres; newspapers and periodicals." In the main set, the first eleven volumes contain roman and Cyrillic works interfiled. Volumes twelve and thirteen are Hebrew entries, and volume fourteen, Yiddish and Ladino. The supplement has six volumes of roman and Cyrillic entries and two of Hebrew, covering some forty thousand works added to the collection between 1961 and 1973. Judaica and Hebraica added to the NYPL collection after 1973 are accessible through the computer catalog, *Dictionary Catalog of the Research Libraries.*

331. Rowe, Kenneth E., ed. **Methodist Union Catalog: Pre-1976 Imprints.** Metuchen, NJ, Scarecrow Press, 1975- . LC 75-33190. Vol. 1: ISBN 0-8108-0880-3. Vol. 2: ISBN 0-8108-0920-6. Vol. 3: ISBN 0-8108-1067-0. Vol. 4: ISBN 0-8108-1225-8. Vol. 5: ISBN 0-8108-1454-4. Vol. 6: ISBN 0-8108-1725-X.

By 1987, Rowe had reached the letter "I" in volume 6 of the author listing of this massive collection of imprints, dating between 1729 and 1975 on Methodist history, biography, doctrine, polity, missions, education, and sermons. The holdings of over two hundred libraries have been searched, including the major Methodist collections in the United States, Great Britain, Canada, and several European countries. All Methodist bodies are covered. Books, pamphlets, and theses are included; periodicals are not. Up to twelve location symbols are given for each entry. In all, twenty volumes including one hundred thousand entries are projected for the series. Additional index volumes are planned for subjects and titles and for additional entries found too late to be included in the early part of the alphabet.

332. **Shelf List of the Union Theological Seminary Library, New York.** Boston, MA, G. K. Hall, 1960. 10 vols. LC 61-4932.

This extraordinary bibliography lists the majority of the library's 365,000 items as of the 1960 publication date. Excluded are a collection on British history and theology from the sixteenth through the eighteenth centuries, and the collection of general and general/ theological periodicals. Arrangement is by the seminary's own classification scheme; there is no author or title access. The preface cites several articles describing the classification scheme, and notes that a copy of the scheme and its supplements is available from the library. The classification letter "G" is of particular note, since under it are gathered the writings of important theologians.

III. Bibliographies of Specific Religious Communities

333. Anti-Defamation League of B'nai B'rith. **The Study of Judaism: Bibliographical Essays.** New York, Ktav Publishing House, 1972. 229p. LC 72-79129. ISBN 0-87068-180-X.

Six bibliographical essays by Jewish and Christian scholars constitute this study. Coverage includes Judaism in New Testament times, rabbinic sources, Judeo-Christian relations, modern Jewish thought, the contemporary Jewish community, and the Holocaust. The introduction was written by the prolific Jacob Neusner. The work is now somewhat dated, but is still a useful opening to Jewish studies.

334. Bergman, Jerry. **Jehovah's Witnesses and Kindred Groups: A Historical Compendium and Bibliography.** New York, Garland, 1984. 370p. index. (Garland Reference Library of Social Science, no. 180, and Sects and Cults in America: Bibliographical Guides, no. 4). LC 83-47603. ISBN 0-8240-9109-4.

An enormous amount of fugitive material is published by the various Jehovah's Witness groups, with pamphlets often having initial press runs of one to three million. Bergman attempts to capture as much of this as possible, often against the express wishes of secretive officials, and he also lists a good deal of the literature against or simply about the Witnesses. He distinguishes between books, booklets (eight to twenty-five pages), and tracts (two to six pages). After a useful introduction, he divides his unnumbered and unannotated entries into five areas: official Watch Tower Bible and Tract Society literature, material associated with the Russell movement, material about the Witnesses, offshoots of the movement, and aspects of the movement outside the United States. Bergman notes that the Witnesses are a valuable phenomenon for study, not only as a religious group, but also because of their positive influence on freedom of speech and conscientious objection in the United States.

335. Bjorling, Joel. **The Churches of God, Seventh Day: A Bibliography.** New York, Garland, 1987. 296p. index. (Bibliographies on Sects and Cults in America, no. 8, and Garland Reference Library of the Humanities, no. 362). LC 87-67. ISBN 0-8240-8537-X.

Bjorling has identified 1,627 books, pamphlets, periodical articles, tracts, and leaflets, which he divides into eight chapters covering the history of Sabbatarianism; the Bible Sabbath Association; various Churches of God, Seventh Day; Herbert W. Armstrong's Worldwide Church of God; groups that splintered from Armstrong's church; and the Sacred Name movement. The entries, unannotated, are indexed by author. Each chapter receives an extensively footnoted introduction, and in two appendixes Bjorling examines Sabbath observance and the names of God which these groups have seized upon.

336. Bonk, Jon. **An Annotated and Classified Bibliography of English Literature Pertaining to the Ethiopian Orthodox Church.** Metuchen, NJ, Scarecrow Press, 1984. 116p. index. (American Theological Library Association Bibliography Series, no. 11). LC 84-10547. ISBN 0-8108-1710-1.

The Ethiopian Orthodox Church refused to accept the dogmas defined by the Council of Chalcedon in 451 CE; like other monophysite churches and the Nestorians, it has remained on the borders of Christian consciousness ever since. With evaluative annotations to 570 entries, which include books, periodical articles (from both journals and magazines), encyclopedia entries, and dissertations, Bonk provides access to materials on this fascinating expression of Christianity, which was influenced by Judaism in a unique manner. Five sections cover general works, history, teaching and practice, liturgy and scripture, and organization and government. Bonk combines authors and subjects in a single index.

337.   Brickman, William W. **The Jewish Community in America: An Annotated and Classified Bibliographical Guide.** New York, Burt Franklin, 1977. 396p. index. (Burt Franklin Ethnic Bibliographical Guide, no. 2). LC 76-30284. ISBN 0-89102-057-8.

In nearly 850 entries, with evaluative annotations on works in English, Hebrew, Yiddish, Ladino, German, French, Hungarian, Polish, and Russian, Brickman covers 300 years of Jewish life in America. He annotates historical works, bibliographies, biographies, and recent monographs, and covers "family life, society, religion, economics, industry, politics, education, literature, culture and foreign relations." A 124-page appendix contains the English text of documents pertaining to Jews in America, ranging from letters from the Dutch East India Company to Governor Peter Stuyvesant to papers from the first two decades of the twentieth century.

338.   Brisman, Shimeon. **A History and Guide to Judaic Bibliography.** Cincinnati, OH, Hebrew Union College Press, and New York, Ktav Publishing House, 1977. 352p. (Jewish Research Literature, vol. 1, and Bibliographica Judaica, no. 7). LC 77-26149. ISBN 0-87820-900-X.

Brisman distinguishes Hebraica from Judaica: the first encompasses works written in Hebrew characters, no matter what the language (Hebrew, Yiddish, Ladino, Judeo-Arabic, or Judeo-Persian). The second is the collection of books written on Jewish themes in any language in non-Hebrew characters. In this first of a projected three-volume series, Brisman includes Hebraica chapters on general bibliographies, catalogs of collections, bio-bibliographical works, and subject bibliographies, and Judaica chapters on bibliographies, bibliographical periodicals, indexes to Jewish periodicals and monographs, and miscellaneous Jewish biographical works.

339.   Brisman, Shimeon. **A History and Guide to Judaic Encyclopedias and Lexicons.** Cincinnati, OH, Hebrew Union College Press, 1987. 502p. index. (Jewish Research Literature, vol. 2, and Bibliograpica Judaica, no. 11). LC 87-25969. ISBN 0-87820-909-3.

In the second of his projected three-volume series, Jewish Research Literature, Brisman offers "detailed bibliographical, biographical, historical, and genealogical data on more than 360 Judaic encyclopedias and lexicons, written in more than a dozen languages" (Preface). He covers inclusive works (section 1), works on specific subjects (sections 2 to 5), general Jewish biographical works (sections 6 to 8), and books dealing with the communities and personalities of the Diaspora (section 9). Extensively footnoted bibliographic essays highlight each chapter, and are followed by entries listed chronologically and including summaries with bibliographic, organization, content, and editorial notes on each work. One index leads the reader to the texts of the essays and their notes, a second to the separate entries. Brisman also includes an extensive bibliography of monographic and periodical materials used to prepare this work.

340.   Crown, Alan David. **A Bibliography of the Samaritans.** Metuchen, NJ, Scarecrow Press, 1984. 194p. index. (American Theological Library Association Bibliographic Series, no. 10). LC 84-1386. ISBN 0-8108-1693-8.

Crown emphasizes contemporary articles from 213 periodicals, in all Western scholarly languages (including Latin), in his 2,806 unannotated entries on this Jewish sect. Since entries are arranged in a single alphabet by author, access is gained through the classified subject index, divided into eighteen categories covering Samaritan history, theology, folklore, language, music, social conditions, arts, medicine, and science. Crown stresses his attempts at accurate bibliographic citations, laying to rest some longstanding bibliographic ghosts. For some rare items, entries give annotations along with the name of a holding library.

341. Cutter, Charles, and Micha Falk Oppenheim. **Jewish Reference Sources: A Selective, Annotated Bibliographic Guide.** New York, Garland, 1982. 180p. indexes. (Garland Reference Library of Social Science, no. 126). LC 82-15434. ISBN 0-8240-9347-X.

Capturing especially the many publications in Jewish studies brought out in the 1970s and early 1980s, Cutter and Oppenheim divide their 371 annotated entries into two sections: (1) general reference books and (2) subject reference works and basic monographs. The latter division provides bibliographic coverage for anti-semitism; art; biblical studies; calendars; crafts; cults; genealogy and names; history; the Holocaust; Israel; Jewish literature and languages; socialism and radicalism; legends, folklore, and humor; music and songs; rabbinical literature; women; and Zionism. The authors include both scholarly and popular works, and provide separate author and title indexes. Some Hebrew works, with titles romanized, are annotated. The reader will find this the basic bibliographic introduction to Jewish studies.

342. Durnbaugh, Donald F., and Lawrence W. Schultz. **A Brethren Bibliography, 1713-1963: Two Hundred Fifty Years of Brethren Literature.** Elgin, IL, Brethren Press, 1964. 177p. index. (In Brethren Life and Thought, vol. 9, nos. 1/2, Winter/Spring 1964.

Durnbaugh, who edited *The Brethren Encyclopedia* (see 19), and Schultz aim for a comprehensive compilation of publications by Brethren authors, and include all Brethren authors prior to 1900. Authors from the present century are selected on the basis of their relevance to Brethren life, history, and teaching. Excluded are non-Brethren authors and Brethren authors from India, Nigeria, China, and Ecuador. Unpublished materials, theses, and dissertations are also omitted. Arrangement is by year of publication and, within a year, alphabetical by author. Important publications are briefly annotated, and location symbols are given for pre-1900 materials. The authors include a checklist of Brethren authors of secondary importance.

343. Edelheit, Abraham J., and Hershel Edelheit. **The Jewish World in Modern Times: A Selected, Annotated Bibliography.** Boulder, CO, Westview Press, and London, Mansell, 1988. 569p. indexes. LC 87-35200. ISBN 0-8133-0572-1.

Following an eight-page introductory essay on "The Outline of Modern Jewish History," this work has two parts: "The Jewish World" and "The Jewish Community." The first covers the periods of Jewish history, religious trends, cultural trends, anti-semitism, public affairs, the Holocaust, and Zionism and Jewish nationalism. The second examines nine general localities throughout the world, and concludes with an unannotated list of bibliographies and guides. In all, the Edelheits identity 2,170 English-language books, which entries they annotate, and journal articles and pamphlets, which for the most part are not annotated. Advanced means of access include separate author, title, and subject indexes and extensive cross-references. A four-page glossary follows the bibliography. The Edelheits have produced an up-to-date and thorough bibliography of English-language works on the Holocaust (see 394), and have here drawn together much contemporary publishing on a wide range of Jewish topics.

344. Ellis, John Tracy, and Robert Trisco. **A Guide to American Catholic History**, 2d ed. Revised and enlarged. Santa Barbara, CA, ABC-Clio, 1982. 265p. index. LC 81-17585. ISBN 0-87436-318-7.

Ellis is the dean of historians of the American Roman Catholic Church. The 1,258 entries in this work cover guides; general works; studies in diocesan, sectional, and parish history; biographies, correspondence, and memoirs; religious communities; education; special studies; periodicals; and historical societies. There is an index of authors, titles, and subjects. This work updates Vollmar (see 370).

345. Flake, Chad J., ed. **A Mormon Bibliography 1830-1930: Books, Pamphlets, Periodicals and Broadsides Relating to the First Century of Mormonism.** Salt Lake City, UT, University of Utah Press, 1978. 825p. index. LC 74-22639. ISBN 0-87480-016-1.

Flake offers bibliographic descriptions for more than ten thousand entries. The subtitle states what is included; excluded are individual newspaper and periodical articles, manuscripts, maps, and prints. Locations are given, but there are no annotations. Titles in non-roman alphabets are transliterated. There is an index of entries by year. Flake expects omissions to be discovered and calls for supplements, but this excellent work is the definitive basis for future Mormon bibliography.

346. Frank, Ruth S., and William Wollheim. **The Book of Jewish Books: A Reader's Guide to Judaism.** Cambridge, MA, Harper & Row, 1986. 320p. index. LC 86-45014. ISBN 0-06-063008-6.

Chapters in this guide to current books for the general reader cover the Bible, children's books, history, the Holocaust, Israel and Zionism, Jewish living, Jewish thought, literature and the arts, personalities, prayer books, women's issues, and reference sources. Annotations to the entries, selected for their excellence or because they are the sole offerings in an area, are commendatory. Frank and Wollheim have included a six-page glossary and a single index of authors and titles. The chapter on "Reference and Resources" includes lists of Jewish bookstores in the United States and Canada, out-of-print book searchers, book-related organizations, and major Jewish libraries.

347. Gurock, Jeffrey S. **American Jewish History: A Bibliographical Guide.** New York, Anti-Defamation League of B'nai B'rith, 1983. 195p. index. LC 83-71207. ISBN 0-8846-4037-X.

Reflecting the growth in American Jewish historiography since the mid-1950s, Gurock has produced six scholarly bibliographical essays covering 850 works, which works are then listed in a formal bibliography with complete citations. Author and title indexes provide access to the whole. The first and last essays are thematic, covering introductory and general reference works and special topics such as American Zionism, interracial relations, and American Jewish women's history. The middle four essays survey the work on four periods of American Jewish history. There is also a five-page essay on suggested future research directions. Gurock succeeds "for the novice scholar and the intelligent layman" in capturing the breadth, depth, seriousness, and objectivity of recent American Jewish historiography.

348. Herman, Edward, comp. **Jewish Americans and Their Backgrounds: Sources of Information.** Chicago, IL, Office for Library Service to the Disadvantaged, American Library Association, 1976. 28p. LC 76-350113. ISBN 0-8389-5461-8.

Herman emphasizes juvenile and general adult reader materials in descriptive annotations to thirty-seven bibliographies, three directories, forty-one periodicals, thirteen Jewish professional associations, and two Jewish library associations. The work is now dated, but most of the listings are not found in similar bibliographies.

349. Hillerbrand, Hans Joachim, comp. **A Bibliography of Anabaptism, 1560-1630.** Elkhart, IN, Institute of Mennonite Studies, 1962. 281p. indexes. LC 66-35203.

With the goal of compiling an exhaustive scholarly bibliography of Anabaptism during the Reformation, Hillerbrand lists 4,611 unannotated entries under three general divisions: areas; persons; and topical studies, which includes origins, general histories, disputations, theology and piety, hymnology, and martyrology. There are author and title indexes. Library locations in the United States and Europe are given for many entries. Springer and Klassen (see 365) take up where Hillerbrand leaves off, that is, with the foundations of the Mennonite movement in 1631.

350. **The Jewish Experience in America: A Historical Bibliography.** Santa Barbara, CA, ABC-Clio, 1983. 190p. index. (ABC-Clio Research Guide, no. 1). LC 82-22823. ISBN 0-87436-034-X.

A companion to *Religion and Society in North America: A Bibliography* (see 301), and, like it, culled from the database of the American Bibliographical Center, this work contains abstracts to 827 articles in 42 languages from over 2,000 journals published between 1973 and 1979. All non-English titles are rendered in English, and all abstracts are in English. The whole Jewish experience in North America is explored and accessed through a subject profile index, wherein four to six key terms for each entry are linked and rotated so that each is somewhere first in the alphabetical listing.

351. Kaplan, Jonathan, ed. **International Bibliography of Jewish History and Thought.** Munich, Germany, K. G. Saur, and Jerusalem, Magnes Press, 1984. 483p. indexes. LC 84-188389. ISBN 3-598-07503-0.

The Magnes Press and The Hebrew University in Jerusalem also published this work under the title *2000 Books and More.* To offer a basic reading list of up-to-date scholarship for anyone interested in Jewish history and Jewish studies, Kaplan listed and annotated 2,190 works in 6 sections: general, the biblical period, the medieval period, the modern period, and Jewish communities throughout the world. The works listed are in Hebrew, English, German, Spanish, Portuguese, and French. Kaplan provides access through two author indexes, one in the Hebrew and one in the roman alphabet.

352. Karkhanis, Sharad. **Jewish Heritage in America: An Annotated Bibliography.** New York, Garland, 1988. 434p. indexes. (Reference Library of Social Science, vol. 467). LC 88-25935. ISBN 0-8240-7538-2.

Karkhanis, a Hindu, became fascinated with the wealth of Jewish history, and made yet another attempt to get at the vast literature (see Brickman 337 and Gurock 347). His seven sections cover reference, historical perspectives, anti-semitism, religious trends, intellectual and literary trends, sociological impact, and political activism. Each except the first is divided into sections on books and articles. In all, Karkhanis annotates 323 books and 777 articles from 88 popular and scholarly periodicals dating from 1925 to 1987. He thus updates Marcus (see 466) from 1969 to 1987 on some journals. He excludes autobiographies and biographies, poetry, and fiction. There is some overlap with Brickman and Gurock, but Brickman includes works in many languages, while Karkhanis concentrates on English productions; where Gurock notes books, Karkhanis includes articles. Moreover, Karkhanis included materials from the 1980s that neither of the other compilers had at his disposal.

353. Kohn, Gary J., comp. **The Jewish Experience: A Guide to Manuscript Sources in the Library of Congress.** Cincinnati, OH, American Jewish Archives, 1986. 167p. index. (Monographs of the American Jewish Archives, no. 11). LC 86-17305. ISBN 0-87820-014-2.

Kohn, who worked for some time in the Manuscript Division of the Library of Congress, produced "a compilation of as comprehensive a list of sources as possible in the Manuscript Division" (Introduction). He divides it into three parts: 126 collections of Jewish individuals and organizations (including two Marxes: Groucho and Karl); (2) Jewish individuals and corporations represented with materials throughout the collections (there are ten thousand in the division); and (3) subjects. Kohn provides a complete index of all persons and organizations referenced in the work. Beyond some indexes to individual collections, this valuable work is the sole access to these materials.

354. Lubetski, Edith, and Meir Lubetski. **Building a Judaica Library Collection: A Resource Guide.** Littleton, CO, Libraries Unlimited, 1983. 185p. index. LC 83-900. ISBN 0-87287-375-7.

The Lubetskis intend to assist academic librarians in obtaining published resources to support the growing interest in Jewish studies. The first part of their work is a bibliographic guide for the selection of books, periodicals, microforms, dissertations, pamphlets, public documents, manuscript and archives sources, and media materials. All Hebrew characters are romanized. The second part is a worldwide directory of publishers, bookdealers, antiquarians, and media publishers and distributors.

355. McCabe, James Patrick. **A Critical Guide to Catholic Reference Books,** 3d ed. Englewood, CO, Libraries Unlimited, 1989. 323p. index. (Research Studies in Library Science, no. 20). LC 89-2835. ISBN 0-87287-621-7.

McCabe identifies over fifteen hundred reference works treating Catholicism, most in English, but many in the European scholarly languages as well as Latin. He divides them into sections on general works, theology, the humanities, the social sciences, and history. Originally a Ph.D. dissertation, this work includes full descriptive and evaluative annotations, and often citations to and quotations from review articles on a book in question.

356. Mickler, Michael L. **The Unification Church in America: A Bibliography and Research Guide.** New York, Garland, 1987. 227p. index. (Sects and Cults in America, Bibliographical Guides, vol. 9, and Garland Reference Library of Social Science, vol. 211). LC 83-48225. ISBN 0-8240-9040-3.

An introduction by J. Stillson Judah covers the beliefs of the Unification Church (UC); the life of the Reverend Sun Myung Moon; the growth of the church in the United States, Korea, and Japan; and the difficulties the UC faces. The bibliography portion lists materials, published in the United States between 1960 and 1985, and falling into three categories: materials produced by the church, including the complete speeches given in the United States by the Rev. Moon and materials produced by UC affiliates; responses to the church in popular literature; and scholarly treatments and government documents. The last category includes theological, sociological, psychological, and legal works, as well as theses and dissertations, and notes general materials on new religious movements which also cover the UC. Excluded are ephemera and newspaper articles. In all, Mickler identifies 1,826 items and provides an author index to them. He does not annotate the citations, but does preface each of his six chapters with a bibliographic essay.

357.   Moyles, R. G. **A Bibliography of Salvation Army Literature in English (1865-1987).** Lewiston, NY, Edwin Mellen Press, 1988. 209p. index. (Texts and Studies in Religion, vol. 38). LC 88-8964. ISBN 0-88946-827-3.

In 1865, William Booth began his soup-to-salvation movement to save the "submerged tenth" of English society. Moyles, who has written on the history of the Salvation Army in Canada, attempts to collect all the available literature produced by the Army and written about it in English since its foundation. He identifies more than two thousand works, and divides them into nine sections on history of the movement, social service, promoting the "war" for salvation, use of music, Salvationist biography, autobiography, creative prose and poetry by members, creative literature about the Army, and portraits and photographs. Moyles excludes ephemera and individual pieces of Army music.

358.   Oppenheim, Micha Falk. **The Study and Practice of Judaism: A Selected, Annotated List.** Brooklyn, NY, Torah Resources, 1979. 78p. indexes. LC 79-20390. ISBN 0-9603100-0-2.

Intending to reach the Jew newly awakened to his or her roots, Oppenheim lists and annotates some five hundred books and pamphlets that reflect the growing body of mature Torah literature written originally in English or in both English and Hebrew. These he divides into sections on Tanach; Mishnah, Talmud, and Halakhah; prayer; ethics; festivals; Hassidim; the philosophy of Judaism; biography; and history. To accompany this broad subject access, he adds author and title indexes.

359.   Prince, Harold B., comp. and ed. **A Presbyterian Bibliography: The Published Writings of Ministers Who Served the Presbyterian Church in the United States During Its First Hundred Years, 1861-1961, and Their Locations in Eight Significant Theological Collections in the U.S.A.** Metuchen, NJ, Scarecrow Press, 1983. 452p. indexes. (American Theological Library Association Bibliography Series, no. 8). LC 83-10116. ISBN 0-8108-1639-3.

"The Presbyterian Church in the United States" is that denomination which was established in the Confederate States in 1861 and has been predominantly in the South ever since. Prince's 4,128 entries, some with contents notes and annotations, all with location symbols, include works by and about the church's ministers. Entries are arranged in a single alphabet by author, and Price eases access to the list by providing an index of the ministers, an index of persons who are not ministers, and a subject index. He notes the strong contributions by women, as listed in the second index; beginning in 1965, the church ordained women, but this is outside Prince's scope.

360.   Pritchett, W. Douglas. **The Children of God/Family of Love: An Annotated Bibliography.** New York, Garland, 1985. 177p. index. (Garland Reference Library of Social Science, vol. 209, and Bibliographies on Sects and Cults in America, no. 5). LC 83-48223. ISBN 0-8240-9043-8.

Pritchett notes that the Children of God is the most organized religious group to grow out of the counter-culture movement of the 1960s and 1970s, and he offers a useful twenty-page chronological introduction. He divides his 1,728 entries — most of which, in spite of the title, are not annotated — into 3 chapters. The first is given over to the published letters of David Berg, founder of the Children of God, to his church. The second includes such Children of God publications as letters, magazine articles, books and booklets, posters and tracts, periodicals, children's literature, and cassette tapes. The final chapter covers secondary materials, both scholarly and journalistic. Pritchett adds an author index.

361. Rowe, Kenneth E., comp. and ed. **United Methodist Studies: Basic Bibliographies**, 1987 rev. ed. Nashville, TN, Abingdon Press, 1987. 80p. LC 87-11495. ISBN 0-687-43110-7.

To provide students with a list of the best resources for studying United Methodist history, and to identify the minimum library standards to support such historical coursework, Rowe listed, but did not annotate 903 works. The entries are arranged in eight sections covering general resources, history, doctrine, polity, audiovisual resources, works for children and youth, works for new and continuing adult members, and basic history for students. The great majority of works listed are books, although some few key articles, as well as a section on periodical titles, are included. Rowe does not provide an index, a serious omission.

362. Schwartz, Bertie. **The Atid Bibliography: A Resource for the Questioning Jew.** New York, United Synagogue of America, Department of Youth Activities, 1977. 153p. indexes. LC 77-153082.

Schwartz gives the lay reader short, descriptive annotations to 1,100 entries arranged under some 25 subject headings, with additional access through separate title and author indexes. She includes non-Jewish works when pertinent to Jewish topics.

363. Shields, Steven L. **The Latter Day Saint Churches: An Annotated Bibliography.** New York, Garland, 1987. 281p. index. (Bibliographies on Sects and Cults in America, vol. 11, and Garland Reference Library of Social Science, vol. 337). LC 87-19835. ISBN 0-8240-8582-5.

Shields identifies over one hundred different Latter Day Saint organizations and movements that have functioned since Joseph Smith led his church; of these, fifty are still in operation. The two largest are the Latter Day Saints (Mormons), headquartered in Utah, and the Reorganized Latter Day Saints, established in Missouri. The bibliography is not organized by author or church, but rather by the chronological divisions of the movement. Thus, there are five sections: general; the original church (1830 to 1844, the date of Smith's death); dissident movements during Smith's life; the non-extant churches founded during the fragmentation period (1844 to the mid-1860s); and the six churches founded during this period (virtually all extant movements have a background in one of these six).

Shields identifies and annotates 1,538 English-language items, including books, pamphlets, and periodicals representative of the history and theology of each church. Individual periodical articles are not included. Historical notes head up each section. Shields complements Flake's massive work (see 345), though some items are duplicated. This work is intended primarily for non-Latter Day Saint researchers, but it is difficult to use. Shields provides an author index, but no access by subject except for the name of a specific church or movement, often named after the leader (for example, Strang, Young, Cutler, Bickerton, Hendrick). Thus, if one wanted to research contemporary plural marriage, one would have to know that polygamist practices occur primarily among the Priesthood groups, splintered off Brigham Young's Mormons.

364. Shunami, Shlomo. **Bibliography of Jewish Bibliographies**, 2d ed., enlarged. Jerusalem, Magnes Press, Hebrew University, 1965. 997p. index. LC he65-1493.

364.1. **Supplement.** Jerusalem, Magnes Press, Hebrew University, 1975. 464p. index.

Shunami has produced the major Jewish bibliography of bibliographies of this century. This second edition, following 29 years after the first, contains 4,751 entries; an additional 2,108 are found in the supplement. In the main, the bibliographies are monographs, but some are periodical articles or appendixes to other works. They are arranged by subject, with chapters for reference works, the Bible, Talmudic and Midrashic literature, liturgy, Jewish literature, Jewish languages, Jews and gentiles, sociology, sects, secular sciences, Zionism, Israel, history by country, the Holocaust, biography, Hebrew typography and books, and personal bibliographies. Works in many languages are listed, although English and Hebrew predominate. All authors and editors are listed under subject headings and in the subject indexes in the roman alphabet. Cyrillic titles are romanized, but Hebrew ones are not. Lengthy, detailed indexes give access to subjects and authors in both the main volume and the supplement.

365. Springer, Nelson P., and A. J. Klassen. **Mennonite Bibliography 1631-1961.** Scottdale, PA, Herald Press, 1977. 2 vols. indexes. LC 77-9105. ISBN 0-8361-1208-3.

This thorough work, which drew from earlier Mennonite bibliographies, and takes up where Hillerbrand left off (see 349), is arranged geographically: volume I covers Europe, Latin America, Asia, and Africa; volume II treats North America. The 28,155 entries include books, periodicals, pamphlets, dissertations, festschriften, symposia, book reviews, and encyclopedia and periodical articles. There are indexes to authors, subjects, and the book reviews. Much of the material cited is in German. Location symbols for twelve Mennonite libraries are added to citations. This can be used in conjunction with Bender and Smith's *The Mennonite Encyclopedia* (see 13).

366. Starr, Edward Caryl, ed. **A Baptist Bibliography: Being a Register of Printed Material By and About Baptists; Including Works Written Against the Baptists.** Rochester, NY, American Baptist Historical Society, 1947-76. 25 vols. LC 47-11981.

"Monumental" can easily become a cliché in the evaluation of reference literature. Not so here. Starr attempts to include the works of all Baptist authors from 1609 onwards who wrote in any language about Baptist topics, as well as books "of general theological, philosophical, historical and social content." Works on science or novels by Baptists are excluded, but works written against Baptists or their positions do appear. At least one location symbol accompanies each entry. Starr includes the citations of W. T. Whitley (see 371), but goes far beyond this work, as Whitley was unable to visit the great American collections at Brown University and the American Baptist Historical Society.

367. Steinbech, A. Alan. **The Jewish Book Annual,** 1942- . annual. New York, The Jewish Book Council of the National Jewish Welfare Board. LC 44-6602. ISSN 0075-3726.

From its origin, this annual was meant to be a cultural exchange for the three Jewish linguistic groups in the United States — English, Hebrew, and Yiddish — and has included reviews, overviews, and extensively annotated bibliographies. Its first ten volumes featured separate sections for the three languages, with short English summaries of the Hebrew and Yiddish, but these divisions subsequently were dropped in favor of interweaving the languages, a feature which remains in current practice. The twenty-fifth volume has a cumulative index of volumes 1 to 25, and the fortieth indexes volumes 26 to 40. Recent annuals contain literary studies and list the National Jewish Book Awards.

368. **The Study of Judaism: Bibliographical Essays.** New York, Ktav Publishing House for the Anti-Defamation League of B'nai B'rith, 1972. 229p. LC 72-79129. ISBN 0-87068-180-X.

Jacob Neusner wrote the introduction to this fine bibliographic handbook to Jewish studies. Six essays follow: "Judaism in New Testament Times," by R. Bavier; "Rabbinic Sources," by J. T. Townsend; "Judaism on Christianity: Christianity on Judaism," by F. Talmage; "Modern Jewish Thought," by F. Rothschild and S. Siegel; "The Contemporary

Jewish Community," by Lloyd Gartner; and "The Holocaust: Anti-Semitism and the Jewish Catastrophe," by Henry Friedlander. Each author uses his own bibliographic style. A fine introduction, but much has been done since 1972.

369. Trinterud, Leonard J., comp. **A Bibliography of American Presbyterianism During the Colonial Period.** Philadelphia, PA, Presbyterian Historical Society, 1968. unpaged. index. LC 70-128.

Trinterud identifies twelve distinct Presbyterian groups that functioned in the American colonies, and arranges 1,129 items, with full bibliographic citations but no annotations, under the names of these groups. Each group has separate sections devoted to works by members of the group and to works about the group by nonmembers. Trinterud gathered much information from Charles Evans's *American Bibliography* (Chicago, IL, the author, 1903-59), and adds the Evans number, when available, to each entry. He also includes works that Evans missed and works that were printed in Great Britain.

370. Vollmar, Edward R. **The Catholic Church in America: An Historical Bibliography**, 2d ed. New York, Scarecrow, 1963. 399p. index. LC 63-7466.

Vollmar includes 5,794 entries, some with brief, descriptive annotations, on all aspects of American Catholic history. Theses and dissertations are here included; his first edition in 1956 lacked them. There is a thirty-page overview of American Catholic historiography. Vollmar adds a subject index. Ellis (see 344) considerably updates this work.

371. Whitley, William Thomas. **A Baptist Bibliography: Being a Register of the Chief Materials for Baptist History, Whether in Manuscript or in Print, Preserved in Great Britain, Ireland, and the Colonies.** London, Kingsgate Press, 1916-22. 2 vols. LC 17-17988. Reprint: Hildesheim, Germany, and New York, G. Oims, 1984. 2 vols. in 1. LC 85-100802. ISBN 3-4870-7456-7.

"The Colonies" of this title could not include the United States in 1837, the terminal year of Whitley's coverage, and indeed he was unable to visit the great Baptist libraries at the American institutions now known as the American Baptist Historical Society and Brown University. Starr's bibliographic masterpiece (see 366) does include America's multitudinous Baptist imprints, as well as the global work through the mid-twentieth century, but Starr only begins with 1609 imprints, whereas Whitley goes back to 1526, to the very origins of the Reformation. Whitley's arrangement is chronological, hence the importance of his four indexes: by author; by anonymous pamphlets; by district; and by institutions, principles, and doctrines.

372. Wolff, Zipporah. **A Sampling of Books on the Jewish Heritage.** Jerusalem, Department of Torah Culture, Ministry of Education and Culture of the State of Israel and the Department for Torah Education and Culture in the Diaspora of the World Zionist Organization, 1976. 92p. LC 77-353917.

For serious Jewish students seeking their roots, Wolff lists slightly under two hundred books. The ample descriptive and evaluative annotations are divided into chapters on the Bible; the Misnah and Talmud; Musor (ethics), Kabbalah (mysticism), and Hasidism; prayer; the Sabbath and festivals; philosophy and theology; history and the Holocaust; and general and miscellaneous materials. Although this bibliography is now dated, the books listed are classic choices for any bibliography, and the annotations are of such excellence as to maintain its current value.

IV. Bibliographies of Specific Religious Topics

373. Bass, Dorothy C., and Sandra Hughes Boyd. **Women in American Religious History: An Annotated Bibliography.** Boston, MA, G. K. Hall, 1986. 155p. index. (American Women in the Twentieth Century Series). LC 86-22397. ISBN 0-8161-8151-9.

Bass and Boyd provide evaluative, and sometimes lengthy, annotations to 568 reference works, monographs, and journal articles. Entries are divided into seven chapters: general works; Protestantism; Roman Catholicism; Judaism; Afro-American religion; Native American religions; and utopian, communitarian, millenarian, and other alternative religious movements. Works entered were published prior to 1986, pertain only to the United States, and are in English. Keeping a historical emphasis, the compilers include some important primary sources. Although Richardson covers black women in religion through 1980 (see 426), Bass and Boyd have produced a unique comprehensive work.

374. Bent, Ans J. Van der. **A Guide to Essential Ecumenical Reading.** Geneva, Switzerland, World Council of Churches, 1984. 44p. LC 84-670112. ISBN 2-8254-0791-7.

In a bibliographic essay, Van der Bent notes recent major ecumenical histories, reference works, and general reading on the World Council of Churches, unity, church and society, missions and evangelism, dialogue, international affairs, interchurch aid, development, racism, education, women, laity, youth, renewal, and communication. He includes biographies and anti-ecumenical literature, but excludes devotional literature, hymnbooks, books on bilateral dialogues, church union negotiations, national and regional committees of churches, and ecumenical theology. This essay is followed by a bibliography, in list form, with complete citations for the works mentioned.

375. Bent, Ans J. Van der. **Six Hundred Ecumenical Consultations, 1948-1982.** Geneva, Switzerland, World Council of Churches, 1983. 246p. indexes. LC 83-212561. ISBN 2-8254-0764-X.

Van der Bent offers brief descriptions and bibliographic information on 633 ecumenical consultations organized by the various divisions, departments, and secretariats of the World Council of Churches (WCC). He organizes these according to the three-fold structure of the WCC: Faith and Witness, Justice and Service, and Education and Renewal. He excludes consultations that produced little or no records or papers; assemblies of the WCC and world conferences of Faith and Order, Church and Society, and World Mission and Evangelism; regular meetings of commissions and committees; and seminars and training conferences. Van der Bent provides indexes by place of consultation, by theme of consultation, and by topic.

376. Blasi, Anthony J., and Michael W. Cuneo. **Issues in the Sociology of Religion: A Bibliography.** New York, Garland, 1986. 363p. index. (Garland Bibliographies in Sociology, no. 8). LC 86-1292. ISBN 0-8240-8585-X.

This thorough, scholarly bibliography is organized around issues treated and discussed in sociology, rather than by religious organization or person. Thus, there are three broad chapters: structures, processes, and disciplinary conceptualizations. There are no annotations to the 3,582 entries but chapters, sections, and subsections are given introductions. Blasi and Cuneo include books, articles, dissertations, and theses in the major scholarly languages, and index their work by subject and author.

377. Bowman, Mary Ann, comp. **Western Mysticism: A Guide to the Basic Works.** Chicago, IL, American Library Association, 1978. 113p. indexes. LC 78-18311. ISBN 0-8389-0266-9.

Bowman seeks to balance the interest in Eastern mysticism by making readers aware of the Western tradition, by encompassing Western Christian, Eastern Orthodox, and Jewish sources. Some of the citations to 532 English-language sources are briefly annotated. Coverage is limited to the common era, and thus excludes ancient Hebrew mysticism. Chapters of unequal length cover the history, practice, and experience of mysticism, oriental mysticism in the West, and mysticism in literature. A final chapter contains 321 entries on primary sources. Bowman provides author/title and subject indexes. An eight-page appendix listing items recommended for purchase by librarians is unnecessary; the same end could have been accomplished by signaling the original entries with asterisks.

378. Breslauer, S. Daniel, comp. **Contemporary Jewish Ethics: A Bibliographical Survey.** Westport, CT, Greenwood Press, 1985. 215p. indexes. (Bibliographies and Indexes in Religious Studies, no. 6). LC 85-9895. ISBN 0-313-24594-0.

379. Breslauer, S. Daniel, comp. **Modern Jewish Morality: A Bibliographical Survey.** Westport, CT, Greenwood Press, 1986. 241p. indexes. (Bibliographies and Indexes in Religious Studies, no. 8). LC 86-12145. ISBN 0-313-24700-5.

These two works are complementary studies of the theoretical and the practical, and Breslauer structures both in the same manner: an in-depth introduction followed by an extensive, annotated bibliography of multilingual works, primarily published between 1968 and 1983, with access through separate title, author, and subject indexes. The first part presents the confrontation between Jewish ethics and other philosophical systems and, within Jewish ethics, between the traditional and the contemporary. Here Breslauer gathers materials from the Reform and Conservative movements, from Yeshiva University studies, from scholarly articles and books, and from traditional Hebrew ethical writings. The second volume aims to present "a unified picture of modern Jewish moral reflection" on biomorality, sexual morality, the family, education, feminism, the elderly, the dead, war and peace, race, capital punishment, poverty, business ethics, interreligious dialogue, and conversion to Judaism.

380. Cargas, Harry James. **The Holocaust: An Annotated Bibliography.** 2d ed. Chicago, IL, American Library Association, 1985. 196p. indexes. LC 85-20069. ISBN 0-8389-0433-5.

Cargas, who identifies himself as a "post-Auschwitz Catholic," devotes fourteen chapters to evaluation and annotation of some five hundred books on the Jewish Holocaust, all written in English and published in the United States. This selective bibliography is designed for American high school, college, and university courses and libraries. The useful fifteenth chapter, by librarian Dan Sharon, offers students research help with sections on subject searches, reference works, and periodicals on the Holocaust. Cargas provides an author/title index and a regional index that identifies works by country and by concentration camp. For more detailed and extensive bibliographies of the Holocaust, see Robinson and Friedman (429), Robinson (428), Laska (411), Szonyi (438), and Edelheit and Edelheit (394).

381. Case, Shirley Jackson, ed. **A Bibliographical Guide to the History of Christianity.** Chicago, IL, University of Chicago, 1931. 265p. index. LC 31-29796. Reprint: Ann Arbor, MI, University Microfilms, 1970.

The 2,512 entries in this work are arranged into chapters covering Christianity in general, the Roman Empire, Western Europe, the British Isles, Eastern Christianity, the

Americas, and new fields. Were it compiled by a lesser person, it would be dismissed as too dated, but Case was a seminal thinker, and the bibliography is itself a study in historiography, a compendium of scholarship on the development of scholarship on Christianity.

382. Chadwick, Owen. **The History of the Church: A Select Bibliography.** 3d ed. London, The Historical Association, 1973. 52p. (Helps for Students of History Series, no. 66). LC 76-381345. ISBN 0-8527-8183-0.

Chadwick, a master British historian, produced this excellent bibliography as an introduction to basic works for history students. It is more up-to-date than Case (see 381). Books in German and French, as well as English, are listed, but whenever available, the English translation is noted. The evaluative and comparative annotations make reading this an end in itself: "by a clear-headed Jesuit" and "a study mainly of the Netherlands, but casting a sunset light over the whole."

383. Chase, Elise. **Healing Faith: An Annotated Bibliography of Christian Self-Help Books.** Westport, CT, Greenwood Press, 1985. 199p. indexes. (Bibliographies and Indexes in Religious Studies, no. 3). LC 85-929. ISBN 0-313-24014-0.

Chase, a frequent reviewer for *Library Journal*, provides evaluative annotations for 723 books published since 1970, creating a bibliography which "explores ways in which Christianity and psychology openly intersect each other." Three broad divisions govern arrangement of entries: spiritual psychodynamics, family and developmental issues, and the wider community. Within subdivisions of these, arrangement is not alphabetical, but "designed to create a smooth narrative flow between annotations and to juxtapose books with diverse theological views on similar subjects." Because of this and overlap of subject matter, similar books may be located in any of the divisions; hence the need for a good subject index, which, with separate title and author indexes, is indeed provided. In a lucid and engaging preface, Chase explains the nature of this literature.

384. Choquette, Diane, comp. **New Religious Movements in the United States and Canada: A Critical Assessment and Annotated Bibliography.** Westport, CT, Greenwood Press, 1985. 237p. indexes. (Bibliographies and Indexes in Religious Studies, no. 5). LC 85-9964. ISBN 0-313-23772-7.

Choquette, librarian of the New Religious Movements Research Collection in the Graduate Theological Union Library in Berkeley, emphasizes Hinduism, Buddhism, Sikhism, Sufism, Neo-Paganism, Witchcraft, and the Human Potential Movement in this bibliography, the starting point of which is the counter-culture movements of the 1960s. Nevertheless, there is material on the Peoples Temple Christian Church, the Jesus Movement, Jews for Jesus, and the Unification Church, as well as a section on "Christian and Jewish Responses to New Religious Movements." Arrangement is by scholarly discipline. There are author/title and subject indexes, and a list with addresses of publishers of materials on the new religious movements.

385. Cohen, Susan Sarah, ed. **Antisemitism: An Annotated Bibliography. By the Vidal Sassoon International Center for the Study of Antisemitism, The Hebrew University of Jerusalem.** New York, Garland, 1987. 392p. indexes. (Garland Reference Library of Social Science, vol. 366-). LC 87-11842. ISBN 0-8240-8532-9.

Anti-semitism is here defined as antagonism toward Jews and Judaism expressed in writing, the visual arts, or action. Having combed some four hundred periodicals and collections for materials, Cohen and the staff of the center identify and descriptively annotate 1,255 books, dissertations, theses, and articles published through 1985, covering history, psychology, sociology, anthropology, literature, and art. In what is planned as an ongoing bibliography, the editors identify works about anti-semitism rather than expressions of it, although a list of anti-semitic periodicals is appended to the main bibliography. A second appendix lists bibliographies on the topic published before 1984. The editors include works dealing with gentile philosemitism, Jewish responses to anti-semitism, and Jewish self-hatred. Four areas of coverage are so voluminous that the editors note careful limitations: the Holocaust period, Soviet Jewry, Anti-Zionism, and the Arab-Israeli conflict. The three sections of the work cover bibliographies and reference works, anti-semitism through the ages, and anti-semitism in literature and the arts. While works in any language are included, an English translation of the title is given in citations to works in foreign languages other than French, German, Italian, or Spanish, a special boon to those who cannot read the many Hebrew titles included.

386.   Crow, Paul A. **The Ecumenical Movement in Bibliographical Outline.** New York, The National Council of Churches in Christ in the U.S.A. Department of Faith and Order, 1965. 80p. LC 65-17940.

Crow takes an historical and thematic approach in this work, covering such reference material as bibliographies, lexicons, and encyclopedias; periodicals; historical surveys; interpretative introductions; works on modern conciliar movements, church union plans, and denominational ecumenism; biographies; and the writings of evangelical critics and antagonists. The books and pamphlets listed are primarily in English, although Crow includes important German, French, and Greek works if untranslated. He excludes periodical articles. The work lacks an index. Now dated, it covers well the postwar period of the ecumenical movement.

387.   Crumb, Lawrence M. **The Oxford Movement and Its Leaders: A Bibliography of Secondary and Lesser Primary Sources.** Chicago, IL, American Theological Library Association and Metuchen, NJ, Scarecrow Press, 1988. 706p. indexes. (ATLA Bibliography Series, no. 24). LC 88-10217. ISBN 0-8108-2141-9.

This lengthy bibliography identifies 5,432 books, pamphlets, theses, chapters in books, periodical articles, manuscripts, microforms, and tape recordings, all part of the "immense literature" on the Oxford Movement (which, Crumb notes was, strictly speaking, a "Catholic movement" within the Anglican Church, beginning with John Keble's Assize Sermon in 1833 and ending with the Gorham Judgment of 1850). Crumb attempts comprehensive coverage of Keble and Edward Bouverie Pusey, two of the leaders. For John Henry Newman, who converted to Roman Catholicism and eventually became a cardinal in that church, Crumb includes materials on the Anglican half of his life, items from his Oxford period, general studies by Anglican authors, and other bibliographies. Crumb excludes general newspaper articles, magazine articles written for a particular diocese, and such primary sources as separately published works of the principals and major collected works. Separately published works of lesser leaders are included. The bibliography is arranged by year, and within each year principally by books and pamphlets, by chapters within books, and then by periodical articles. Some entries are annotated, chiefly with bibliographic information. Separate author, periodical, and subject indexes allow additional entry points to this literature. The author index includes corporate authors, pseudonyms, anonyms and works with titles only. A useful four-page chronology of the movement opens the bibliography; an appendix of bibliographic ghosts indicates the thoroughness with which Crumb carried out this work.

388.   Dahlin, Therrin C., Gary P. Gillum, and Mark L. Grover. **The Catholic Left in Latin America: A Comprehensive Bibliography.** Boston, MA, G. K. Hall, 1981. 410p. indexes. LC 81-778. ISBN 0-8161-8396-1.

After a general chapter on Latin America, the 3,966 unannotated entries here are divided into chapters on individual countries. The compilers provide author and title indexes, but subject access is only through the chapters. Each entry is assigned one to three subject headings; entries with more than one subject heading are repeated under each. Most items are in English, Spanish, or Portuguese, and the few Russian titles are transliterated. An eighteen-page introduction by Berkley A. Spencer details the rise of the Catholic left in Latin America from the early 1950s to the late 1970s.

389.   Day, Heather F. **Protestant Theological Education in America: A Bibliography.** Chicago, IL, American Theological Library Association, and Metuchen, NJ, Scarecrow Press, 1985. 505p. index. (ATLA Bibliography Series, no. 15). LC 85-18300. ISBN 0-8108-1842-6.

To support a history of Protestant theological education in America, Day covers all Protestant denominations. She lists 5,249 unannotated entries in a single alphabet, with subject access through an extensive index covering background materials; materials relating to theological education; association, Bible colleges, and theological seminaries and schools; and individuals significant in theological education. Access is overwhelming for some index entries, such as "Pastors," "Theological education — post-1860," and "Theological students," which list hundreds of entries by accession number. To broaden her scope slightly, Day includes forty-six entries on Roman Catholic theological education, as well as works dealing with situations in Germany and Great Britain.

390.   Dayton, Donald W. **The High Christian Life: A Bibliographical Overview.** New York, Garland, 1985. 207p. index. (The Higher Christian Life: Sources for the Study of the Holiness, Pentecostal, and Keswick Movements, no. 1). LC 85-20764. ISBN 0-8240-6400-3.

Three bibliographic essays, first published with conference proceedings of the American Theological Library Association, are here reprinted: "The American Holiness Movement: A Bibliographic Introduction" by Dayton (1971); "The American Pentecostal Movement: A Bibliographical Essay" by David W. Faupel (1972); and "Keswick: A Bibliographic Introduction to the Higher Life Movements" by David D. Bundy (1975). Dayton is the editor of a projected forty-eight-volume reprint series entitled "The Higher Christian Life: Sources for the Study of the Holiness, Pentecostal, and Keswick Movements," of which this bibliography is the first. In an introduction, he notes that two bibliographies by Charles Edwin Jones (see 407 and 408) cover the material more thoroughly, but he maintains that these three papers "provide a more accessible overview." This literature, particularly fertile for the study of American feminism and other social movements, came out during a century beginning in 1830, and fills the gap between historical material on Methodist origins and attention to Pentecostalism since the 1920s. The editors have eased access through a single author index, and have renumbered the table of contents of each essay to reflect the consecutive pagination of the whole bibliography.

391.   Doohan, Leonard. **The Laity: A Bibliography.** Wilmington, DE, Michael Glazier, 1987. 159p. index. LC 87-45006. ISBN 0-89543-617-6.

In order "to help those insistent on pursuing the reforms of Vatican II" in the Roman Catholic Church, Doohan pulls together bibliographies, official church documents, and works on theology, canon law, lay ministry, work, leadership, social justice, and women.

Most works cited are in English; some are in other European languages. Doohan does not add annotations, and the citations are unnumbered. The bibliography is divided by subject into forty-one chapters; access beyond that is by an author index.

392. Dulles, Avery, and Patrick Granfield. **The Church: A Bibliography.** Wilmington, DE, Michael Glazier, 1985. 166p. index. LC 84-48453. ISBN 0-89453-449-1.

The authors, two prominent Roman Catholic theologians, have attempted to assemble "the more important writings" from the vast amount of materials on ecclesiology published mostly in this century. Only books are included, in English when possible. This is principally intended for Catholic readers, but there are contributions from authors of other denominations, and there are sections on Protestant, Anglican, and Orthodox ecclesiology. The bibliography is divided into fifty-one topics, almost a third of which are historical. Other sections cover basic communities, the Vatican Councils, the papacy, the parish, laity and women in the church, and liberation eschatology. There is an author index.

393. **The Ecumenical Movement: A Bibliography.** Chicago, IL, American Theological Library Association, 1983. 822p. (American Theological Library Association Religion Index Select Bibliography).

This printed subset of the *Religion Index* database (see 476) is divided into a subject index, an author/editor index, and a book review index. In the first part, the subject headings are the descriptors for the *Religion Index* database. Because of the density of the print, the citations are quite difficult to read.

394. Edelheit, Abraham J., and Hershel Edelheit. **Bibliography on Holocaust Literature.** Boulder, CO, Westview Press, 1986. 842p. index. LC 86-9274. ISBN 0-8133-7233-X.

From the growing body of literature on the Holocaust (with 7,000 items identified on Auschwitz alone), the Edelheits choose 9,014 English-language books, periodical articles, booklets, pamphlets, and items identified as being more than a page in length. They add evaluative annotations to the most important. Three chronological periods — "Before the Storm," "The Crucible," and "The Aftermath" — and a focus on "The Perpetrators" form the divisions of the bibliography. Subject access is gained by a lengthy table of contents that gives a detailed breakdown of the four parts. There is also an index of authors.

395. Evans, James H. **Black Theology: A Critical Assessment and Annotated Bibliography.** New York, Greenwood, 1987. 207p. indexes. (Bibliographies and Indexes in Religious Studies, no. 10). LC 87-142. ISBN 0-313-24822-2.

Evans gives full, descriptive annotations to 461 books and articles, cross-referencing each to related entries in three sections: the origin and development of black theology; its relation to liberation movements, feminism, and Marxism; and its place in cultural and global discourse. An introduction offers a brief, critical assessment of each of these areas. Most entries date between 1968 and 1985. Evans states that "black theology is not the product of an intellectual breakthrough by a single theologian, but rather is the naming of the spiritual experience of Afro-Americans." However, fifty of the articles and books listed are by James H. Cone, often credited with the inception of the movement. In addition to the three divisions, Evans provides access through author, title, and subject indexes.

396. Fischer, Clare B. **Breaking Through: A Bibliography of Women and Religion.** Berkeley, CA, Graduate Theological Union Library, 1980. 65p. LC 80-18286.

Fischer breaks out of traditional divisions (women and scripture, Mariology, the writings of saints), which she covers briefly in her second chapter, and lists studies "which consciously target gender roles and propose change." After a first chapter that notes bibliographies, journals, and newsletters, and contains a directory of centers, the organization of her chapters is unclear: women scholars, feminist perspectives (with a multiplicity of subject headings), and "periodicals" (really journal articles concerned with feminist theology). If the organization is unclear, and indexing and annotations are lacking, the material, multidisciplinary and multicultural, is abundant, and browsing this short bibliography is easy.

397. Gill, Athol, comp. **A Bibliography of Baptist Writings on Baptism, 1900-1968.** Ruschlikon-Zurich, Switzerland, Baptist Theological Seminary, 1969. 184p. indexes. (Ruschlikon Seminary Bibliographical Aids, no. 1). LC 71-541921.

Gill identifies 1,250 multilingual books, articles, and book reviews, mostly from Baptist periodicals, arranged as historical, theological, pastoral, and New Testament studies. He briefly annotates some entries, and adds an index of authors and an index of authors of books reviewed.

398. Glanz, Rudolf. **The German Jew in America.** Cincinnati, OH, Hebrew Union College Press, 1969. 192p. indexes. (Bibliographica Judaica, no. 1). LC 68-57048.

Glanz identifies, and occasionally briefly annotates, 2,527 entries on German-Jewish immigrants from German-speaking lands (including Bohemia and Alsace-Lorraine), mainly covering the period between 1820 and 1880. German and Hebrew works are included, though titles in English predominate. There are separate indexes of authors and editors, of other persons, and of places. Glanz especially notes materials on the German-Jew in the broader German-American community, a neglected area.

399. Grimes, Ronald L. **Research in Ritual Studies: A Programmatic Essay and Bibliography.** Chicago, IL, American Theological Library Association, and Metuchen, NJ, Scarecrow Press, 1985. 165p. index. (ATLA Bibliography Series, no. 14). LC 84-23474. ISBN 0-8108-1762-4.

Grimes examines ritual as a universal religious phenomenon which, while not centered on Christianity or Judaism, is essential to understanding them. He offers a thirty-three-page introduction and a bibliography of 1,649 unannotated items, many of which are directly related to the two religions. Drawing on a broad spectrum of contemporary systems of thought, including comparative religions, anthropology, sociology, literature, philosophy, history, communications, psychology, education, and theatre, Grimes divides his entries into chapters on ritual components (action, space, time, objects), ritual types (rites of passage, marriage, funerals, festivals, pilgrimages) and ritual descriptions (rites interpreted with primary reference to specific traditions).

400. Hill, George H., and Lenwood Davis. **Religious Broadcasting 1920-1983: A Selectively Annotated Bibliography.** New York, Garland, 1984. 243p. (Garland Reference Library of Social Science, no. 216). LC 83-20813. ISBN 0-8240-9015-2.

In the light of 1987's controversies over Christian broadcast ministries, this listing of 1,644 entries, including 79 books and 169 theses and dissertations, most annotated, is especially relevant. Coverage for the most part is limited to networks, ministers, producers, directors, and entertainers in the United States. Most citations are to literature on Christian broadcasting; only a tiny percentage covers Jewish, Baha'i, and ecumenical broadcasts. Hill and Davis include a section on religious public relations and advertising. An addendum brings the work up to date through 1983.

401.   Hofmeyr, J. W., and K. E. Cross, comps. and eds. **History of the Church in Southern Africa: A Select Bibliography of Published Material to 1980.** Pretoria, South Africa, University of South Africa Press, 1986. 809p. (Documenta, 37). LC 87-136367. Vol. I: ISBN 0-86981-435-4. Projected set: ISBN 0-86981-457-5.

Using a definition of church history as encompassing the broad development of Christianity, the compilers collect 5,735 books, pamphlets, analytical entries from composite works, theses, and dissertations on that region of Africa lying south of the Cunene and Zambezi Rivers. They exclude periodical articles and archives. The language of listing is English whenever possible. Citations are arranged under four general headings: general; denominations; missions and missionary societies; and topics, which includes the church and race relations. Two indexes are provided, a subject and a name index. The latter includes personal and corporate names, conferences, compilers, editors, biographees, and persons to whom festschriften are dedicated. Additional work is planned; this is designated volume one. For a bibliography of South African theology, see Borchardt and Vorster (299).

402.   Horner, Tom. **Homosexuality and the Judeo-Christian Tradition: An Annotated Bibliography.** Metuchen, NJ, Scarecrow Press, 1981. 131p. indexes. (American Theological Library Association Bibliographic Series, no. 5). LC 81-899. ISBN 0-8108-1412-9.

Horner gives evaluative annotations to many of the 459 books and articles, for the most part published since 1969, that he identifies. He excludes foreign-language materials, book reviews, and newspaper and newsletter articles. The subject index is particularly useful for approaching the list, and an author index is also provided. One appendix lists seventeen definite and twenty-eight possible homosexual references in the Bible; a second lists twenty-two periodicals of gay religious organizations.

403.   Hundert, Gershon David, and Gershon C. Bacon. **The Jews in Poland and Russia: Bibliographic Essays.** Bloomington, IN, Indiana University Press, 1984. 276p. LC 83-49285. ISBN 0-253-33158-7.

In the introduction, Hundert and Bacon note that a more precise title would be "The Jews in Poland, Lithuania, and the Polish Commonwealth to the End of the Eighteenth Century, in the Lands of Partitioned Poland (except Prussia) and the Russian Empire in the Nineteenth and Early Twentieth Centuries, and in Poland and the U.S.S.R. in the Twentieth Century." The work consists of two bibliographic essays, actually two separate works, bound together and consecutively paginated, with a common table of contents and some cross-references. Each essay provides a detailed evaluation of monographs, a survey of reference and general works, and a fifty-page unannotated bibliography of works arranged by author. This thorough, scholarly work lacks a subject index; access is limited to the table of contents and the author index.

404.   Hunt, Thomas C., and James C. Carper. **Religious Colleges and Universities in America: A Selected Bibliography.** New York, Garland, 1988. 374p. indexes. (Garland Reference Library of Social Science, vol. 422). LC 88-14737. ISBN 0-8240-6648-0.

This bibliography follows *Religious Schools in America: A Selected Bibliography* by Hunt and Carper (see 405), who plan a third volume on seminaries. They divide this work into twenty-eight chapters, including an introductory chapter covering major general works on religion and American colleges and universities and two chapters on government aid and government regulation. The remaining twenty-five chapters bring together materials on higher-education institutions pertaining to specific Protestant denominations and to Roman Catholicism and Judaism. In all, 35 contributors provide and often annotate 2,342 citations. Hunt and Carper add an author index, and their extensive subject index includes the proper names of all institutions and persons mentioned in the work.

405. Hunt, Thomas C., James C. Carper, and Charles R. Kniker. **Religious Schools in America: A Selected Bibliography.** New York, Garland, 1986. 391p. indexes. (Garland Reference Library of Social Science, vol. 338). LC 86-12118. ISBN 0-8240-8583-3.

Responding to the resurgent interest in religious schools offering primary and secondary education, the editors have followed up Carper and Hunt's monograph *Religious Schooling in America* (Birmingham, AL, Religious Education Press, 1984) by asking eighteen contributors to identify and annotate books, articles, dissertations, theses, essays, and reports in twenty-three chapters on various aspects of such schools in the United States. The work is divided into several sections: general books; summaries and analyses of court decisions and government aid and regulation; schools operated by seventeen religious groups; and the interaction between public and religious education. Within the section on schools operated by religious groups, Catholicism and Judaism have the most entries. Many chapters are divided into the historical and the contemporary. Subject and author indexes provide access.

406. Jones, Charles Edwin. **Black Holiness: A Guide to the Study of Black Participation in Wesleyan Perfectionist and Glossolalic Pentecostal Movements.** Chicago, IL, American Theological Library Association and Metuchen, NJ, Scarecrow Press, 1987. 388p. index. (ATLA Bibliography Series, no. 18). LC 86-21893. ISBN 0-8108-1948-1.

Jones is the principal bibliographer of the Holiness and Pentecostal movements (see 407 and 408). This new bibliography "on black participation in Wesleyan perfectionist and glossolalic Pentecostal and healing movements in Africa, the West Indies, the United States, Canada and the United Kingdom" includes materials from his two other bibliographies, plus entries on race relations, leader-centered bodies in Africa and North America, and black minorities within white groups. The 2,396 entries are divided into 6 parts: general aspects of the Wesleyan and Pentecostal movements; the Wesleyan-Arminian orientation; the Finished Work of Calvary orientation; leader-centered bodies; schools; and materials by and about prominent figures in the movements. Location symbols are added to citations of monographs. Jones offers much directory information, giving a brief, historical introduction to each body listed in parts two through four. In part five, for schools, he lists names, founding and closing dates, locations, sponsoring organizations, and bibliographic materials. Persons in part five have birth and death dates and locations listed, as well as codes to biographical directories in which they are included.

407. Jones, Charles Edwin. **A Guide to the Study of the Holiness Movement.** Chicago, IL, American Theological Library Association, and Metuchen, NJ, Scarecrow Press, 1974. 918p. index. (ATLA Bibliography Series, no. 1). LC 74-659. ISBN 0-8108-0703-3.

Jones packs 7,300 entries into this scholarly bibliography, covering materials for the study of doctrine, worship, institutional development, related movements, and personalities connected with this outgrowth of Methodist evangelism from 1850 to the present. He divides the work into chapters on three great interdenominational manifestations: the Holiness movement, the Keswick movement, and the Holiness-Pentecostal movement. He also includes a chapter on general works, a directory of schools, and a biographical section, with information on 2,734 persons. He extensively annotates the associations and churches listed with the movements, and provides access to the whole through a combined subject, author, and periodical title index. This, coupled with his *A Guide to the Study of the Pentecostal Movement* (see 408) and his *Black Holiness* (see 406) makes Jones the principal biographer of the Holiness movement.

408. Jones, Charles Edwin. **A Guide to the Study of the Pentecostal Movement.** Chicago, IL, American Theological Library Association, and Metuchen, NJ, Scarecrow Press, 1983. 2 vols. index. (ATLA Bibliography Series, no. 6). LC 82-10794. ISBN 0-8108-1583-4.

Jones (see 406 and 407) here lists 9,883 unannotated entries on the Pentecostal movement, dividing his work into four sections. The first covers articles on the movement as a whole, without regard to doctrine, while the second contains works on the doctrinal traditions: Wesleyan-Arminian and Finished Work of Calvary or Baptistic tradition. The third section enumerates schools and articles written about the schools. The final section lists 3,924 individuals prominent in the movement. Jones provides an extensive, 142-page index to all this material.

409. Kissinger, Warren S. **The Lives of Jesus: A History and Bibliography.** New York, Garland, 1985. 230p. (Garland Reference Library of the Humanities, no. 452). LC 83-48284. ISBN 0-8240-9035-7.

The "life of Jesus" is a genre, based on the principles of historiography and other sciences, that has much occupied religious writers of the nineteenth and twentieth centuries. Starting with the seminal eighteenth-century work by Reimarus, Kissinger offers a solid historical overview of the important examples in the liberal Protestant tradition down to the present. He follows this with a bibliography of almost two thousand unannotated entries, of which slightly under three hundred are meant for juveniles. The major western languages are represented, but the great majority were originally in English or have translations listed. Some entries are films or filmstrips, but these are difficult to locate, as they are not signaled and there is no index. Only full lives or biographies are included; treatments of partial areas, such as the Resurrection, as well as harmonies of the Gospel accounts, are left out.

410. Lagorio, Valerie Marie, and Ritamary Bradley. **The 14th-Century English Mystics: A Comprehensive Annotated Bibliography.** New York, Garland, 1981. 197p. index. (Garland Reference Library of the Humanities, no. 190). LC 79-7922. ISBN 0-8240-9535-9.

Lagorio and Bradley gather together, in 841 descriptive and evaluative annotations, the scholarship of the past one hundred years on (1) the five major figures: Richard Rolle, Walter Hilton, Julian of Norwich, Margery Kempe, and the anonymous author of *The Cloud of Unknowing*; (2) lesser-known mystics and treatises; and (3) an assessment of the ongoing tradition of medieval English spirituality. Lagorio and Bradley list sixteen forthcoming studies in an appendix, and provide access to subjects and authors through a single index.

411. Laska, Vera. **Nazism, Resistance & Holocaust in World War II.** Metuchen, NJ, Scarecrow Press, 1985. 183p. index. LC 84-23586. ISBN 0-8108-1771-3.

With a broad outlook, Laska covers anti-semitism, Nazism in general, war crimes, the Holocaust, art and photography, philosophy and interpretation, and literature. However, her two foci are resistance, both Jewish and non-Jewish, and women, who merit three chapters: "Resistance — Women," "Holocaust — Women," and "Women in Hiding." Indeed, this bibliography is an outgrowth of Laska's earlier *Women in the Resistance and in the Holocaust* (Westport, CT, Greenwood, 1983). In all, she provides 1,907 entries, some with brief annotations, all of books. Most of her subject material is in English, though works in other European languages are included with titles transliterated into the roman alphabet when necessary. The thirteen chapters give broad subject entry, but a specific subject index would have eliminated the stated problem of deciding in which chapter to place works. Laska does add an author index.

412.   Lerski, Jerzy Jan. **Jewish-Polish Coexistence, 1772-1939: A Topical Bibliography.** New York, Greenwood, 1986. 230p. index. (Bibliographies and Indexes in World History, no. 5). LC 86-12119. ISBN 0-313-24758-7.

Lerski, during World War II a courier between Poland and its government-in-exile in London, gathers but does not annotate 2,778 books, brochures, pamphlets, and journal articles. The entries are arranged in thirty-four chapters on all aspects of Jewish life in Poland: demography, economics, culture, art, politics, and so on. Extensive chapters list biographical materials and works on individual towns and shtetls. One chapter covers philo-semitism (with fifty-five entries); another treats anti-semitism (with 141). Author and title indexes give access to the whole, but Lerski has not produced a subject index; the chapter headings offer the only topical access. Eleven languages are represented; Lerski translates all titles into English and standardizes authors' names using the *Encyclopaedia Judaica* (see 25) and the *National Union Catalog* (Washington, D.C., Library of Congress), practices which may make interlibrary loan verification quite difficult. This is, however, a valuable work; if the subject matter seems specialized, it can be argued that the study of Polish-Jewish relations is a prolegomenon to approaching the Holocaust in particular and anti-semitism in general.

413.   Lippy, Charles H. **Bibliography of Religion in the South.** Macon, GA, Mercer University Press, 1985. 498p. LC 85-13575. ISBN 0-86554-161-2.

This thorough work, with 5,175 entries, is an excellent companion to Hill's *Encyclopedia of Religion in the South* (see 35), but is seriously weakened by its lack of indexes. Lippy covers Native American religions; southern blacks; Roman Catholicism; Judaism; Anglicanism; the major Protestant denominations; revivalism; and southern religion and literature, art, architecture, music, and education. In a final brief essay, he recommends areas for future research and analysis. He does not treat the influence of Eastern religions, nor does he pull together material on women or on the influence of the electronic church. The quantity of materials listed is at times disproportionate to the influence of groups: there are 547 entries on Roman Catholicism and only 258 on Baptists. Rather than annotating the entries, Lippy provides extensive, scholarly bibliographic essays at the beginning of each chapter, after the manner of Burr (see 302).

414.   Menendez, Albert J. **Religion and the U.S. Presidency: A Bibliography.** New York, Garland, 1986. 142p. indexes. (Garland Reference Library of Social Science, vol. 334). LC 85-29300. ISBN 0-8240-8718-6.

Noting the emphasis on the religious beliefs of American presidents in recent decades, Menendez cites twenty-eight basic reference sources in an introductory chapter. He then offers a chapter on each president, with notes on his religious beliefs and a bibliography of materials on this, as well as "his relations with various religious communities, and his handling of church-state disputes." Some chapters are short: for example, Menendez is unable to find a single book or article devoted to Millard Fillmore's religious dispositions (apparently there is confusion on the matter). Menendez does, however, cite a total of 696 books and articles, which he indexes by author and by subject. The presidents are arranged in alphabetical rather than the usual chronological order.

415.   Menendez, Albert J. **Religious Conflict in America: A Bibliography.** New York, Garland, 1985. 130p. index. (Garland Reference Library of Social Science, vol. 262). LC 84-13779. ISBN 0-8240-8904-9.

Menendez includes books, periodical articles, law review treatises, doctoral dissertations, master's theses, and some newspaper articles in his 1,408 unannotated entries on this "burdensome truth" of the American religious experience. Though he also includes sociological studies, the scope is primarily historical; seventeen sections, each with an introduction, cover from the colonial experience to the present. Five sections list materials on political conflict along religious lines by examining presidential campaigns. In the last section Menendez covers the Reagan presidency and the New Religious Right. Menendez adds an author index.

416.   Menendez, Albert J. **The Road to Rome: An Annotated Bibliography.** New York, Garland, 1986. 133p. index. (Garland Reference Library of Social Science, vol. 318). LC 85-45110. ISBN 0-8240-8687-2.

Menendez cites 1,461 books and articles, originally in English or translated to it, about the experience of converting to Roman Catholicism, primarily from another western religion or from secularism. He divides these citations into chapters on personal testimonies, autobiographies, biographies, methods and techniques of conversion, and novels of conversion. In spite of the subtitle, the citations are not annotated. However, Menendez does overview the modern conversion phenomenon in his introduction, and he begins each chapter with a lengthy essay. An index provides access by author.

417.   Menendez, Albert J. **School Prayer and Other Religious Issues in American Public Education: A Bibliography.** New York, Garland, 1985. 168p. indexes. (Garland Reference Library of Social Science, no. 291). LC 84-48756. ISBN 0-8240-8775-5.

Menendez lists, without annotation, 1,566 books, periodical and newspaper articles, law journal reviews, dissertations, and theses on a broad range of contexts in which religion and public education have come to crisis points in the United States, including school prayer, Bible reading, the Bible as literature, released time, Christmas break, ceremonies such as baccalaureate services, equal access, textbooks, and religious garb. Menendez devotes a chapter with a short introduction to each controversy. He provides an author index, and a subject index that primarily, and conveniently, lists states and religions. Thus, one can find references on controversies which centered in Ohio or those in which Catholics figured prominently.

418.   Miller, William Charles, comp. and ed. **Holiness Works: A Bibliography.** Kansas City, MO, Nazarene Theological Seminary, 1986. 120p. index. ISBN 0-83-411-1721.

With a narrower focus than Jones (see 407), Miller identifies fourteen hundred books and pamphlets published in America and England since 1800. These he arranges in sections on bibliography, the Bible, general and theological works, sermons and devotionals, and testimonies.

419.   Mills, Watson E. **Charismatic Religion in Modern Research: A Bibliography.** Macon, GA, Mercer University Press, 1985. 178p. indexes. (National Association of Baptist Professors of Religion Bibliographic Series, no. 1). LC 85-127327. ISBN 0-86554-143-4.

Mills's introduction is a fifteen-page bibliographic essay that covers definitions, bibliographies, surveys, charismatic religion in American denominationalism, classification of charismatic groups, glossolalia, and theological studies. Almost nineteen hundred items appear in this bibliography, which covers persons, aspects of the movement, and Pentecostal, Neo-Pentecostal, and mainline churches. Since the whole is arranged by author, use of the subject index is a necessity. There is also an index for editors and joint authors.

420. Mills, Watson E. **Glossolalia: A Bibliography.** New York, Edwin Mellen Press, 1985. 129p. index. (Studies in the Bible and Early Christianity, vol. 6). LC 85-8987. ISBN 0-88946-605-X.

Mills (see also 419) here brings together as many recent and ancient major documents as possible on the phenomenon of glossolalia, or speaking in tongues. The phenomenon, he notes, has occurred sporadically throughout Christian history, has occurred in every major Protestant denomination and in Roman Catholicism, and has become a vital part of Holiness, Pentecostal, and neo-Pentecostal sects of the present day. He divides the work into a bibliographic essay and a list of 1,158 unannotated entries of scholarly and popular books, articles, and dissertations. Most of these are in English, although works from other European languages are included. Mills provides avenues of access through an extensive subject index and through an index of scripture passages.

421. Mills, Watson, E. **The Holy Spirit: A Bibliography.** Peabody, MA, Hendrickson, 1988. 167p. indexes. ISBN 0-913573-91-4.

Christian movements centered on the Holy Spirit have been Mills's specialty for twenty years (see 419 and 420). Here he cites, but does not annotate, 2,098 books, periodical articles, and dissertations from the nineteenth and twentieth centuries that have "shaped the study of the Holy Spirit." The materials reflect a broad range of Protestant and Roman Catholic thinking. The entire bibliography is arranged in a single alphabet by author. Mills gives access to this through subject and scripture indexes, but a division of the material into broad categories would have been helpful.

422. Musto, Ronald G., comp. **The Peace Tradition in the Catholic Church: An Annotated Bibliography.** New York, Garland, 1987. 590p. indexes. (Garland Reference Library of Social Science, vol. 339). LC 86-31950. ISBN 0-8240-8584-1.

This is the second work in a trilogy envisioned by the author. The first, *The Catholic Peace Tradition*, is a monograph published by Orbis in 1986; the third is a projected book of readings. Following a 10-page introduction, Musto lists 1,485 entries in English, French, German, Italian, Spanish, Portuguese, and Latin, and writes evaluative annotations for most. His scope includes materials on Greek, Roman, and biblical concepts of peace; the early church and Middle Ages; the humanist peacemakers of the Renaissance; missionary pacifists; and Catholic plans for world peace and international law from the Middle Ages to the present. Listing both primary and secondary sources, Musto includes theological and philosophical works, canon law, penitential literature, lives of saints, tracts of pacifist missionaries, the writings of humanist and Catholic internationalists, the works of the popular peace movements and liberation theology, and papal statements. His three indexes offer access by title, by author, and by proper name as subject.

423. Peatling, John H., ed. **Annual Review of Research: Religious Education.** Schenectady, NY, Character Research Press and the Religious Education Association, 1980- . index. ISSN 0197-5915. 1980 edition: ISBN 0-915744-23-6.

Peatling reviews research relating to religious education, abstracting eighty-six studies and noting three bibliographies in this work, intended to be an annual but published only once under this name.

424. Pruter, Karl. **Jewish Christians in the United States: A Bibliography.** New York, Garland, 1987. 192p. index. (Sects and Cults in America, Bibliographical Guides, vol. 7, and Garland Reference Library of Social Science, vol. 306). LC 84-48881. ISBN 0-8240-8741-0.

Although Pruter does not annotate his 1,568 entries, he provides extensive historical introductory material to the 7 chapters of this work. Although it emphasizes evangelical and cult missions to the Jews and contemporary Hebrew-Christian messianism (Jews for Jesus), it also covers the historical and theological backgrounds (dating from the first centuries of the common era) and the Jewish reponse to Hebrew Christianity. Although he could have added materials on the efforts toward conversion and dialogue in the mainline Christian churches, Pruter has provided here a good chart for new waters.

425. Puglisi, James F., and S. J. Voicu. **A Bibliography of Interchurch and Interconfessional Theological Dialogues.** Rome, Italy, Centro pro Unione, 1984. 260p. LC 85-119787.

Puglisi and Voicu have attempted to draw together the published proceedings from every dialogue undertaken by fifteen confessional families and churches, as well as two series of dialogues, Faith and Order and Dialogues des Dombes. Every dialogue is signaled by a formula for confessional membership and geographical features. Thus "L-RC/s" stands for a Lutheran-Roman Catholic dialogue in Sweden. Material is arranged by dialogue, and, under this heading, chronologically by meetings; thus, the meetings between two confessions can be traced chronologically. When a meeting is known to have occurred but no published information can be found, this fact is so stated. The authors romanize all Greek and Cyrillic characters. They have not provided an index.

426. Richardson, Marilyn. **Black Women and Religion: A Bibliography.** Boston, MA, G. K. Hall, 1980. 139p. index. LC 80-20457. ISBN 0-8161-8087-3.

Recent commentators have attested to the contributions women have made to American religious development (see, for example, Prince, 359 and Thomas 197), but only recently have those efforts been documented. Richardson supplies 850 entries on black women, most with descriptive annotations, and covering books, journal and magazine articles, reference works, and audiovisual materials. She includes an author/title index, seven photographs, and seventeen biographical sketches of women of achievement whom she wants to rescue from undeserved obscurity. To say that this work fills a gap is classic understatement.

427. Roberts, Richard Owen. **Revival Literature: An Annotated Bibliography with Biographical and Historical Notices.** Wheaton, IL, Richard Owen Roberts, 1987. 575p. index. LC 87-63111. ISBN 0-940033-27-5.

Roberts has spent over forty years gathering materials on revivalism. In this work, following an introduction somewhat devotional in tone, he lists some six thousand books and pamphlets that are either wholly about the phenomenon, have a section on it, or portray its consequences. He excludes materials on Methodism, because the movement is adequately covered elsewhere (cf. Rowe, 331 and 361). This large work is arranged in a single alphabetical sequence by author, but Roberts does provide a subject index and an author index, which includes author's contributions to collections. In addition to regular bibliographic data, Roberts adds at least one location symbol for each work.

428. Robinson, Jacob. **The Holocaust and After: Sources & Literature in English.** Jerusalem, Israel Universities Press, 1973. 353p. (Yad Vashem Martyrs' and Heroes' Memorial Authority [Jerusalem] and YIVO Institute for Jewish Research [New York], Joint Documentary Projects Bibliographical Series, no. 12). LC 78-309835. ISBN 0-7065-1297-9.

This thorough work contains 6,637 entries emanating from English-language countries and covering books and book reviews, articles from Jewish journals of opinion, summaries in English of books and articles in other languages, and scripts from films and television plays. Robinson organizes these into divisions on general information, the background of the Holocaust, persecution and extermination, the Jews in and outside the Nazi regime, the non-Jewish world and the Holocaust, the post-Holocaust years, research and documentation, and imagination and reflection. He includes a comprehensive index of subjects, names, places, institutions, and authors. Although it is an update, for the English-speaking world, of Robinson and Friedman's earlier foundation work (see 429), this very competent bibliography is now itself dated; for more recent works, one must check Cargas (380), Edelheit and Edelheit (394), Laska (411), and Szonyi (438).

429. Robinson, Jacob, and Philip Friedman. **Guide to Jewish History Under Nazi Impact.** New York, Ktav Publishing House, 1973. 425p. indexes. (Joint Documentary Projects Bibliographical Series, no. 1). LC 73-16300. ISBN 0-87068-231-8.

Robinson and Friedman intended this volume to be the foundation of the bibliographic series on the Holocaust, which in the parlance of the late 1950s they call the Catastrophe. Sponsored by the Yad Vashem Martyrs' and Heroes' Memorial in Jerusalem and the YIVO Institute for Jewish Research in New York, and originally published only 15 years after the end of the event, this bibliography contains 3,634 entries, with an additional 4 pages of addenda and 2 of errata. Although the entries are not annotated, the authors often explicate genres (for example, lists of concentration camps and ghettoes). The bibliography is arranged in four major divisions, which are in turn subdivided into a total of twenty-two parts. Part one, on "The Jewish Catastrophe in Historical Perspective," contains sections on comprehensive works, concepts of the Catastrophe, and historical analogies. The second part, "Reference Tools," includes bibliographies, topographical references, chronologies, and biographical and linguistic references. A third part, on research, contains sections on research institutes, archives, libraries, museums, conferences, and methods of research. The last part, "Documentation," includes crimes and trials, anti-Jewish legislation, collections of personal narratives and anthologies, the resistance, the official documentation of Jewish organizations, the non-Jewish world and the plight of the Jews in Nazi-dominated countries, rehabilitation and restitution, periodicals and serials, and audiovisual materials.

This thorough work, citing materials in all the languages of modern Europe, including Hebrew and Yiddish, is fully accessible via six indexes: names, corporate authors, titles, lists of defendants in war-crimes trials, places, and subjects.

Although some areas lack thorough coverage (only four items on the Vatican are listed, and there is nothing on Klaus Barbie), this is the foundation not only for the particular series of which it is the first number, but also for all subsequent bibliographical work on the Holocaust in Europe. Robinson updated this with his English-language bibliography of 1973 (see 428).

430. Ronda, James P., and James Axtell. **Indian Missions: A Critical Bibliography.** Bloomington, IN, Indiana University Press, 1978. 85p. index. (Bibliographical Series, The Newberry Library, Center for the History of the American Indian). LC 78-3253. ISBN 0-253-32978-7.

Ronda and Axtell divide this bibliography on Christian missions to the Indians into two sections. The first is a fifty-page bibliographic essay covering the missionary activities of eight large Christian churches, the goals of the missions, the methods of conversion, and Indian responses. The second section is a list, by author, with complete bibliographic citation of each of the 211 books mentioned in the first part. To link the two sections, each book as it is mentioned in the first is given its citation number in the second; as it is listed in the second, it is given its page number for the first section. The authors list five works for the novice reader and recommend fifteen for a basic library collection.

431. Rudolph, L. C., and Judith E. Endelman. **Religion in Indiana: A Guide to Historical Resources.** Bloomington, IN, Indiana University Press, 1986. 232p. index. LC 84-43186. ISBN 0-253-34960-5.

Indiana, relatively small in population and area, has an enormously rich Jewish and Christian heritage, ranging from the founding of large institutions of mainline denominations to small establishments reflecting the religious creativity of the nineteenth and twentieth centuries. Rudolph and Endelman searched the archives and records of historical societies and institutions, and then queried denominational executives, historians, archivists, and librarians. Although their scope includes all religions, some groups are more heavily represented simply because more records are available. The authors divide this work into three sections. The first, on published works, includes books, periodical articles, theses, and dissertations, arranged by author and including denominational code markings – those developed and used by the Glenmary Research Center (see 180) – and a location code for at least one copy of each. Newspaper articles and county histories are excluded. The second section describes collections of primarily unpublished materials, arranged alphabetically by location symbol. Repositories outside Indiana that have pertinent material are included. The last section is a bibliography of published congregational histories of at least three pages in length, arranged by county and, within county, by town. The index covers the first two parts, and offers access by thirty-three denominational families, personal name, place name, and institution name. Authors are not included, since part 1 is arranged by author. The work lacks any treatment of Native American religion in Indiana. In addition to its value as a resource for the study of religion in Indiana and the Midwest, this fine work is an excellent model for similar work on the remaining forty-nine states.

432. Sable, Martin Howard. **Latin American Jewry: A Research Guide.** Cincinnati, OH, Hebrew Union College Press, and New York, Ktav Publishing House, 1978. 633p. indexes. (Bibliographica Judaica, no. 6). LC 77-18527. ISBN 0-87820-904-2.

Sable includes both scholarly and popular materials in all western languages among the books, reference sources, periodical articles, pamphlets, proceedings, theses and dissertations, government publications, autobiographies, minute books, wills, correspondence, reminiscences, diaries, and legal, religious, organizational, commercial, and personal records listed in his guide, which covers almost every aspect of Latin American Jewish life from 1492 to 1974. This substantial amount of material is arranged by subject and, within subject, by nation or region. The whole collection is accessible through indexes by author, by subject to primary materials, and by subject to secondary materials. A fourth index lists directories. Sable adds two directories of his own, which list periodical titles by nation and general associations. Some entries on Latin American studies in general are included for the novice. Location symbols to eighteen libraries are added to many entries, especially primary sources.

433. Schlesinger, Benjamin. **Jewish Family Issues: A Resource Guide.** New York, Garland, 1987. 145p. index. (Garland Bibliographies in Sociology, vol. 10, and Garland Reference Library of Social Science, vol. 385). LC 86-31854. ISBN 0-8240-8460-8.

Schlesinger has here updated his *The Jewish Family: A Survey and Annotated Bibliography* (Toronto, University of Toronto, 1971). He lists and annotates 524 works under 78 topical headings. Three essays by his wife Rachel have been included. An appendix lists the addresses of publishers. Schlesinger includes seven demographic tables reproduced from the *American Jewish Yearbook 1985* (see 210), and an author index.

434. Shermis, Michael. **Jewish-Christian Relations: An Annotated Bibliography and Resource Guide.** Bloomington, IN, Indiana University Press, 1988. 291p. indexes. LC 87-46365. ISBN 0-253-33153-6.

Shermis has drawn up a useful bibliography and handbook on a field of increasing interest and influence. He cites, for example, 109 congresses on Jewish-Christian relations held in the United States since 1965, 86 of which took place in the 1980s. After an extended essay on the "Educational Aspects of the Jewish-Christian Dialogue," Shermis offers an annotated bibliography of over 550 books, arranged in 18 categories; citations to 25 basic journal articles, as well as lists of other significant articles; a list of journals that deal exclusively with the topic and additional lists of some that occasionally do; the list of congresses, which include symposia, forums, seminars, encounters, meetings, dialogues, colloquia, consultations, and workshops; a media section of films, filmstrips, and videos, and the names and addresses of their distributors; syllabi for courses offered at several colleges; a listing of service groups; and the names, addresses, and telephone numbers of some 120 speakers. Extensive indexes give the reader access to these materials by subject, name and organization, title, and media.

435. Shupe, Anson D., David G. Bromley, and Donna L. Oliver. **The Anti-cult Movement in America: A Bibliography and Historical Survey.** New York, Garland, 1984. 169p. index. (Sects and Cults in America, Bibliographical Guides, vol. 2, and Garland Reference Library of Social Science, vol. 130). LC 82-49028. ISBN 0-8240-9214-7.

Shupe, Bromley, and Oliver have here a bibliography serious in subject matter but flawed in delivery. They divide the anti-cult movement, which they label the ACM, in three: local groups of family members; deprogrammers; and religious groups, including mainline Christians, Jews, and fundamentalists. Chapters, which have extensive if awkwardly written introductions, cover these divisions as well as historical overviews, social science studies, the ACM and the law, and opposition to the ACM by such groups as the American Civil Liberties Union. The types of materials listed change from chapter to chapter: the first, a general historical overview, lists "major sources, principally books," while subsequent chapters list hearings and fugitive materials with no indication of where they can be found. In the introduction to chapter 4, the Jewish ACM is treated; among the 233 citations listed, some cover this subtopic, but one must dig to find them, as they are not grouped together. Although there is an author index, there is no subject index.

436. Spector, Sheila A. **Jewish Mysticism: An Annotated Bibliography on the Kabbalah in English.** New York, Garland, 1984. 399p. indexes. (Garland Reference Library of Social Science, vol. 210). LC 83-48224. ISBN 0-8240-9042-X.

Since Kabbalism is a newly developed field, and Spector could find few scholarly tools, she has undertaken to identify and annotate 1,603 works published in English in the past 400 years, and to arrange them in chapters on reference works, introductory surveys, topics on Jewish mysticism, the history of the Kabbalah, major scholars, and the non-Jewish Kabbalah. She excludes manuscripts, letters, theses and dissertations, and all fiction except for folktales. Her indexes give access by the titles of primary materials; by authors, editors, translators, and festschriften dedicatees; and by subjects. Within each chapter, primary works are listed before secondary, and all entries within a section are in alphabetical order. Hebrew, Aramaic, and Arabic titles are romanized.

437. Swartley, Willard M., and Cornelius J. Dyck. **Annotated Bibliography of Mennonite Writings on War and Peace: 1930-1980.** Scottdale, PA, Herald Press, 1987. 740p. index. LC 87-14932. ISBN 0-8361-1292-X.

An elaborate subject classification system, outlined at the beginning of the work, led to seventeen chapters containing some ten thousand (unnumbered) annotated entries, listing English-language books, theses, dissertations, and articles written by Mennonites in both Mennonite and in non-Mennonite publications, and articles by non-Mennonites in Mennonite publications. A broad definition of *peace* here includes race relations, refugee settlement, law, social action, tax resistance, civil disobedience, justice, labor unions, amnesty, and development. In all, fifty-one Mennonite publications were researched, including *The Mennonite Encyclopedia* (see 13). So few materials were found for the time between the original Anabaptist movement in the sixteenth century and the present century that the editors decided to start with 1930. Interesting is the editors' note on their attempt to use gender-inclusive language throughout the work. A further contemporary touch is the announcement that the Herald Press of Scottdale, PA, and Kitchener, Ontario, will run a computer search of its database for a nominal fee.

438. Szonyi, David M., ed. **The Holocaust: An Annotated Bibliography and Resource Guide.** New York, Ktav Publishing House for The National Jewish Resource Center, 1985. 396p. LC 84-26191. ISBN 0-88125-057-0.
   The field of Holocaust studies is burgeoning, and this enormous and useful compilation attempts to bring materials of many kinds together. There are bibliographies of the extensive fiction and nonfiction literature, audiovisual materials, music, teacher development projects, and oral history, as well as directories of mobile exhibits, centers and research institutes, memorials in the United States and Canada, survivor groups, remembrance day services, speakers, and project and research funding sources. Most entries are given descriptive, commendatory annotations.

439. Von Ende, Richard Chaffey. **Church Music: An International Bibliography.** Metuchen, NJ, Scarecrow Press, 1980. 453p. index. LC 79-23697. ISBN 0-8108-1271-1.
   Von Ende lists 5,445 books, articles, catalogs, and music lists, covering principally the western Christian churches but including some works on Jewish music and on the music of oriental religions. Works are arranged by author under some 284 categories, including genres, personalities, instruments, faiths or denominations, religious orders, publication types, and countries. Each work is listed, on average, under three or four categories, with a full citation under its primary category and a numerical cross-reference under secondary ones. In the category "Personalities," Von Ende arranges the entries by the person featured. He includes works in twenty-five languages, with titles in Cyrillic, Greek, and Gaelic transliterated to the roman alphabet. Authors, editors, and compilers are accessible through an index.

440. Williams, Ethel L., and Clifton F. Brown. **The Howard University Bibliography of African and Afro-American Religious Studies: With Locations in American Libraries.** Wilmington, DE, Scholarly Resources, 1977. 525p. index. LC 76-5604. ISBN 0-8420-2080-2.
   Williams and Brown are "comprehensive ... [but] in no way definitive" in gathering 13,242 entries published from the eighteenth century through the mid-1970s. They include books, periodical articles, and analyticals of books, and divide their entries into five chapters on the "African Heritage," "Christianity and Slavery in the New World," "The Black Man and His Religious Life in the Americas," "The Civil Rights Movement," and "The Contemporary Religious Scene." Each entry includes at least one location symbol from a list of 230 repositories in the United States. When a title does not explain the source, an annotation is added. Appendixes list over one hundred fifty manuscript collections and six thousand biographical and autobiographical sources. Their index lists authors only; subject access is by the subdivisions within chapters.

441. Yassif, Eli. **Jewish Folklore: An Annotated Bibliography.** New York, Garland, 1986. 341p. index. LC 83-48282. ISBN 0-8240-9039-X.

The 1,356 entries, with descriptive and evaluative annotations, are a bibliography of folkloristics rather than folklore; that is, not collections of texts but rather of "scientific attempts to analyze and understand the folkloric phenomenon." Yassif notes that, although his earliest entry is dated 1823, the study of Jewish folklore seriously got under way in the 1870s. He continues coverage through 1980. Yassif does not attempt to cover East European Jewish culture, the Judeo-Spanish culture, or Jews in world folklore where the image is often anti-semitic. Jewish music and art are also excluded. Biblical studies are included when they analyze biblical stories as folk literature. Since he attempts to pick up every folk theme and motif in an annotated book or article, he has provided an extensive index for access.

V. Bibliographies of Religious Serials

442. Bastel, John D., and Lyda K. Bastel. **Union List of Methodist Serials, 1773-1973.** Evanston, IL, Garrett Theological Seminary, 1974. 136p. LC 74-1368.

Adopting the format of the *Union List of Serials* (New York, Wilson, 1965), the Bastels identify periodicals, newspapers, annuals, journals, memoirs, proceedings, and transactions produced by the main branches of American Episcopal Methodism, the Evangelical United Brethren Church, and related groups, and held in 103 libraries in the United States.

443. Cornish, Graham, ed. **Religious Periodicals Directory.** Santa Barbara, CA, ABC-Clio, 1986. 330p. indexes. (Clio Periodicals Directories). LC 83-21366. ISBN 0-87436-365-9.

Cornish identifies 1,763 periodicals, in all languages, published throughout the world and covering religion in its broadest sense. He includes periodicals "which publish articles dealing with original research," but excludes "newsletters, general magazines, parochial publications, edificatory and proselytizing publications, and devotional material," as well as monographic series. The whole is arranged alphabetically by title within six geographic regions: Canada and the United States, Latin America, Europe, Africa, the Middle East, and Asia and the Pacific. Within geographic regions, countries are separate. Each periodical can also be accessed through the title and subject-geographic index.

For each entry, Cornish notes the title, International Standard Serial Number (ISSN), year of first publication, frequency, publisher, subscription address, sponsoring institution, contents annotation, self-indexing, languages of articles, coverage in indexing and abstracting services, and former titles.

444. Dawsey, James. **A Scholar's Guide to Academic Journals in Religion.** Metuchen, NJ, Scarecrow Press, 1988. 290p. (American Theological Library Association Bibliography Series, no. 23). LC 88-18104. ISBN 0-8108-2135-4.

To assist potential writers in getting published, Dawsey examines and annotates 530 journals, based on surveys sent to their editors and on information published in the journals themselves. The entry for each journal includes its subject matter; type of articles sought; topics of special interest; audience; possibilities for unsolicited articles, simultaneous submissions, research notes, and review articles; advertising policy; style; languages accepted; length requirements; number of copies of a submission required; selection process and its length; proportion of manuscripts accepted; correct mailing addresses; subscription costs. Information on indexing and abstracting services covering each journal and parent organizations is garnered from *Ulrich's International Periodicals Directory* (New York, Bowker, 1932-). The entries are organized into thirty-three broad subjects within the field of religion, and there are extensive cross-references at the end of each chapter. The chapter on Judaism, for example, lists twenty-one journals primarily on that subject, but an additional seventy-seven are also cross-listed because they print articles on Judaism, although it is not their primary focus. An appendix gives complete bibliographic citations to thirteen style manuals. Three essays on writing practices in general, on first getting into print, and on writing book reviews introduce the work, and Dawsey adds an index of journal titles to complete it.

445.   Fieg, Eugene C., comp. **Religious Journals and Serials: An Analytical Guide.** New York and Westport, CT, Greenwood, 1988. 218p. index. (Annotated Bibliographies of Serials: A Subject Approach, no. 13). LC 87-32276. ISBN 0-313-24513-4.

Fieg cites and extensively annotates 328 popular and academic periodicals. Although he purports to cover all religions, 242 pertain to Christianity and 9 to Judaism. His citations are arranged by chapters with broad subject headings, including indexes and abstracts, history of religions, primal religions, spiritualism, religion and society, Eastern religions, Near Eastern religions, Judaism, Christianity, Islam, and modern faiths. The chapter on Christianity is further subdivided into nine categories. Fieg provides five indexes for the work: title, publisher, place of publication, subject, and intended readership.

Each entry includes complete bibliographic information, including title, date of foundation, title changes, mergers, frequency, prices, publisher, editor, illustrations, self-indexing, advertising policy, circulation figures, basis of manuscript selection, microform availability, reprint availability, policy on book reviews, special issues, indexing and abstracting services, database citation, target readership, and policy on sample copies. This information is followed by a lengthy descriptive and evaluative annotation.

446.   Lippy, Charles H., ed. **Religious Periodicals of the United States: Academic and Scholarly Journals.** New York and Westport, CT, Greenwood, 1986. 609p. index. LC 85-9861. ISBN 0-313-23420-5.

Lippy's introduction is a history, with a bibliography attached, of religious publishing in the United States, where, he notes, over twenty-five hundred religious periodicals are currently being published. He singles out over one hundred for extensive study, often of several pages, wherein he covers the history of the periodical, its outstanding editors, and the general themes it has pursued. Together with a bibliography on each publication, Lippy includes a publishing history in outline form which includes name changes, volume and issue data, publisher and place of publication, editors, and circulation. Entries are extensively cross-referenced from commonly known earlier names. Some of the journals included have ceased publication, but were very influential in their day. All relate to Christianity, Judaism, or religion in general; none are specific to any other world religion.

Although "academic and scholarly" is the scope of the subtitle, some general, large-circulation magazines are included such as *America, Ave Maria, Christianity Today, Christianity and Crisis, The Christian Science Monitor, Commentary, The Christian Century,* and *Commonweal.*

A first appendix is a ten-page time line linking the first publishing dates of major religious journals to significant events in American religious history. A second lists journals by sponsoring organization and religious orientation. An extensive index covers all names of persons and periodicals, and all subjects covered in the work.

447. Regazzi, John J., and Theodore C. Hines. **A Guide to Indexed Periodicals in Religion.** Metuchen, NJ, Scarecrow Press, 1975. 314p. LC 75-22277. ISBN 0-8108-0868-4.

This guide covers 2,700 periodicals indexed 3,545 times in 17 indexing and abstracting services. There are four parts: a list of the services, the periodical titles, an inverted-entry (key word in context) listing by every important word in the titles, and a list by service of the periodicals indexed in each. This is a very useful tool, but is unfortunately poorly reproduced in the archaic computer printoff style of the early 1970s.

448. Rogow, Yitzhak, publisher and ed.-in-chief. **Directory of World Jewish Press and Publications.** Jerusalem, Directory of World Jewish Press and Publications, 1984. 134p. index.

Rogow provides access to 866 Jewish publications worldwide, including bulletins, newsletters, newspapers, journals, and magazines. First divided by continent, entries are then arranged alphabetically by country, and, in the United States, by state. Some thirty-one irregular publications are included. Each entry includes title, address, telephone number, editor, founding date, publisher, language, frequency, circulation, how printed, content, readership, principal contributors, affiliation, and advertising information. There is an index. Himmelfarb (see 210) lists more Jewish publications in the United States, but Rogow's scope is, of course, worldwide.

449. Singerman, Robert, comp. **Jewish Serials of the World: A Research Bibliography of Secondary Sources.** New York, Greenwood, 1986. 378p. indexes. LC 86-344. 0-313-24493-6.

Singerman's objective is to identify pertinent sources for writing a world history of the Jewish press. To this end, he lists 3,041 books, articles, dissertations, and theses in a geographic arrangement of the world by 1939 boundaries. He includes three general chapters on the Hebrew, Yiddish, and Judezmo (Ladino) press. He does not include indexes to periodical literature, which can be found in Brisman (see 338) and Shunami (see 364). Access is enhanced by an author index and a subject index that covers analyzed titles, editors named in studies, and topics, such as "juvenile serials."

7
Abstracts, Indexes, and a Database

I. Abstracts

450. **Abstracts of Research in Pastoral Care and Counseling, 1972- .** Richmond, VA, Joint Counsel on Research in Pastoral Care and Counseling. Annual. ISSN 0733-2599.

The articles from some sixty periodicals are here abstracted and arranged according to subjects pertinent to the pastoral ministry: adolescence, aging, AIDS, alcohol, chaplaincy, childhood, and the like. While not all the periodicals are religious, each is useful to ministry, as, for example, the *Journal of Divorce* and the *Journal of Psychology.* Besides the topical arrangement, the editors offer access by author, title, and subject indexes. With the 1988 edition, citations to relevant entries in *Dissertation Abstracts International* (Ann Arbor, MI, University Microfilms, 1938-) are included.

451. **Current Christian Abstracts, 1985- .** Sue Job and Betty Gibb, eds. Columbia, MO, the editors. Monthly. ISSN 0883-1440.

Principally the work of the two librarian-editors, this work now indexes thirty religious periodicals; the religion sections of *The Christian Science Monitor*, the *Los Angeles Times*, and *The Washington Post*; and religion notes in *Time, Newsweek*, and the *Saturday Evening Post.* The editors provide monthly and annual cumulated subject indexes, but no other indexes.

452. **Missionalia Abstracts, 1973- .** Pretoria, South Africa, South African Missiological Society. Three issues yearly. ISSN 0256-9507.

The editors regularly cover 150 periodicals and produce, in English, some 900 abstracts of articles and some books. They add annual subject and author indexes. The South African Missiological Society was formed in 1968, has members from the Reformed, Anglican, Congregational, Presbyterian, and Baptist churches, and is affiliated with the International Association of Mission Studies in Oslo, Norway.

453. **Religious and Theological Abstracts, 1958- .** Moyerstown, PA, Religious and Theological Abstracts. Quarterly, with annual cumulation. ISSN 0034-4044.

Providing about 800 abstracts per issue, the editors cover some 225 scholarly periodicals, and arrange the abstracts in four major fields: biblical, theological, historical, and practical, each with further subdivisions. They provide indexes by author, subject, and scriptural reference. With a strong ecumenical bent, the editors have covered Protestantism, Roman Catholicism, Eastern Orthodoxy, and Judaism from the beginning of the publication.

454.   **Science of Religion, 1976- .** Amsterdam, The Netherlands, Institute for the Study of Religion, Free University. Quarterly. ISSN 0165-8794.

The purpose of this work is "to provide a systematic bibliography of articles contributing to the academic study of religions." It offers lengthy abstracts, in English, of articles on phenomenology, comparative studies, the sociology and anthropology of religion, Hinduism, Buddhism, other Asian religions, antiquity, Judaism, Christianity, Islam, and new religious movements. Each issue contains a cumulative author and subject index for the year. The abstracts are numbered consecutively and, with the 1988 edition, have reached 8,293.

455.   **Theology in Context: Information on Theological Contributions from Africa, Asia, Oceania, and Latin America, 1984- .** Aachen, Germany, Institute of Missiology-Missio. Semiannual. ISSN 0176-1439. (English edition of *Theologie im Kontext*).

In order to foster communication among theologians of the Third World, and between those of the Third and the First, *Theology in Context* reprints the tables of contents of over one hundred journals, summarizes selected articles, surveys books, and reports on theological conferences. The titles of articles are left in the original languages but, if in a non-western language, a translation of the title is given.

II. Serial Indexes

456.   Berlin, Charles, comp. and ed. **Index to Festschriften in Jewish Studies.** Cambridge, MA, Harvard College Library, and NY, Ktav Publishing House, 1971. 326p. indexes. LC 72-138460.

Taking up the work of Marcus and Bilgray (see 467), Berlin provides the key to 6,700 articles from 243 *Festschriften*, all available at Harvard and published between 1935 and 1970. He includes works, in all scholarly languages, on Jewish history and literature of all periods and places. An extensive subject index with 13,200 entries, as well as an author index, allow easy access to this vast collection. Berlin romanizes authors' names from the Hebrew, but does not transliterate book or article titles.

457.   **The Catholic Periodical and Literature Index, 1930- .** Haverford, PA, Catholic Library Association. Bimonthly, with biennial cumulations. ISSN 0008-8285.

International in scope, this author and subject index has a single alphabet of matters by or of interest to Catholics or scholars concerned with Roman Catholicism. Since 1968 and the merger with *The Guide to Catholic Literature* (see 460), books are listed by author, title, and subject (an exception: books not in English are not listed by subject). The popes are listed by papal name, and their entries have three subdivisions: collected works; texts of encyclicals and letters, speeches, and commentaries on them; and biographical and general works about the popes. Within the single alphabetical sequence, the editors have sections for "Book Reviews," wherein books under study are listed by author, "Motion Picture Reviews," wherein films are alphabetized by title, and "Theater—Criticism, Plots, Etc—Single Works," wherein plays are also entered by title.

458.   **Christian Periodical Index (A Selected List): An Index to Subjects and Authors and to Book and Media Reviews, 1956- .** Cedarville, OH, Association of Christian Librarians. Quarterly, with annual cumulation and five-year cumulations through 1975. ISSN 0069-3871.

The editors began indexing twenty, and are now up to eighty-five, periodicals, primarily titles with a conservative, evangelical, Protestant bent. Some are scholarly; most are for the general reader. In addition to a subject index, there is a section of book reviews, arranged by author of books reviewed.

459. Elenchus Bibliographicus in **Ephemerides Theologicae Lovanienses, 1924-** . Leuven-Louvain, Belgium, E. Peeters. Quarterly. ISSN 0013-9513.

Beginning in 1977, the *Elenchus Bibliographicus* separated from the journal *Ephemerides Theologicae Lovanienses.* Reflecting but not limited to Roman Catholic interests and the Catholic ordering of theology, this unannotated bibliography covers general matters, history of religions, Hebrew Scriptures, New Testament, fundamental theology, dogmatic theology, theology of the sacraments and liturgy, ascetic-mystical theology, moral theology, and canon law. Although the division headings are in Latin, enough English-language books, articles, and dissertations from around the world are picked up by this international resource to merit continuing examination by students who read only English. The editors provide access through an index of authors and an index of theological history, wherein the reader can find an issue or a theologian.

460. The Guide to Catholic Literature, 1888/1940-1968. Detroit, MI, W. Romig.

In all, eight volumes of this series were published, covering the years 1888-1940, 1940-44, 1944-48, 1948-52, 1952-55, 1956-59, 1960-63, and 1964-67. The early volumes were edited and published by Romig, and the final three by the Catholic Library Association, which in 1968 merged this with *The Catholic Periodical Index* to form *The Catholic Periodical and Literature Index* (see 457). In a single alphabet, Romig enters books by title, by subject, and by the main entry or author. The main entry, in addition to bibliographic information on the book in question, often contains biographical information on the author and notes reviews of the book. Romig created an international bibliography by listing works in French, German, Italian, and Spanish.

461. Guide to Social Science and Religion in Periodical Literature, 1970- . Flint, MI, National Periodical Library. Quarterly, with multiannual cumulations. ISSN 0017-5307.

Articles from approximately one hundred periodicals, mostly Christian but some Jewish or general, are indexed under broad subject headings ("Education," "Old Testament," "Spiritual Life") which are not always subdivided. There are no annotations or abstracts, but the number of words in each indexed article is included after the citation.

462. Index of Articles on Jewish Studies, 1969- . Jerusalem, Magnes Press. Annual. ISSN 0073-5817.

This extensive, scholarly bibliography now lists some four thousand books and articles in the European languages (and roman alphabet) as well as in Hebrew and Yiddish (in the Hebrew alphabet). Beginning in 1969, the editors have attempted to cite every book and article on Judaism published during and after 1966. Items missed in earlier volumes are added in later years. Thousands of periodicals are perused for studies on bibliography; the Hebrew Scriptures; the Apocrypha; the Dead Sea Scrolls and early Christianity; law; spirituality; liturgy; language and literature; Jewish history, culture, and society; and Israel. Indexes list works by author and by subject, and there is a separate index for book reviews. Each index is divided in two, with the first part giving listings in the European languages and the second in Hebrew and Yiddish. Entries are numbered from the Hebrew front of each volume, which readers of European languages see as the back.

463. Index to Book Reviews in Religion, 1986- . Chicago, IL, American Theological Library Association. Bimonthly, with annual cumulations. ISSN 0887-1574.

An enlarged and enhanced version of the *Book Review Index* contained in *Religion Index One* (see 470) through 1985, this work indexes book reviews and review essays and articles from approximately five hundred journals and some annuals. The 1986 annual cumulation contains references to 9,134 books, with many more reviews, since some books were reviewed by more than one source. Over three quarters of the books reviewed are in English. The editors provide access to the reviews through author/editor, title, series, reviewer, and classified subject indexes. Translators, joint authors, and joint editors are cross-referenced to the author/editor index. As with all indexes issued by the American Theological Library Association, all material in this is accessible by online search of the database *Religion Index* (see 476).

464. **Index to Jewish Periodicals, 1963- .** Cleveland Heights, OH, Index to Jewish Periodicals. Semi-annual. ISSN 0019-4050.

The editors provide an author and subject index to Jewish topics in some four dozen special and general interest journals in English. Not all the journals indexed are specifically Jewish in content (for example, the *Journal of Biblical Literature*).

465. **International Bibliography of the History of Religions/Bibliographie internationale de l'histoire des religions, 1952- .** Leiden, The Netherlands, E. J. Brill. Annual. ISSN 0538-5105.

Supported by UNESCO and produced under the auspices of the International Association for the Study of the History of Religions, this work lists scholarly books and originally indexed three hundred journals, a figure which has grown through the years. With a special, though not exclusive, emphasis on antiquity and the ancient Near East, its offerings on Judaism and Christianity were lean in early years but have grown to constitute approximately a third of each issue. Difficulties of production have caused recent volumes to appear as much as five or six years after the years they cover.

466. Marcus, Jacob Rader, ed. **An Index to Scientific Articles on American Jewish History.** Cincinnati, OH, American Jewish Archives, and New York, Ktav Publishing House, 1971. 240p. (Publications of the American Jewish Archives, no. 7). LC 72-138460. ISBN 0-87068-139-7.

Marcus collects essays, from thirteen periodicals, on the life, culture, and history of the American Jew, and lists each by author, title, and subject heading. He indexes six periodicals not covered by the 1972 edition of the *Index to Jewish Periodicals* (see 464).

467. Marcus, Jacob Rader, and Albert Bilgray. **An Index to Jewish Festschriften.** Cincinnati, OH, Hebrew Union College, 1937. 154p. LC 37-15143. Reprint: New York, Kraus Reprint, 1970.

This classic bibliography lists four thousand articles in fifty-three festschriften with full citations under author, title, and subject. The subject headings, spelling, and transliteration practices follow those used in *The Jewish Encyclopedia* (see 26). Hebrew titles are listed in a separate alphabet. Coverage is broad, but essays limited to biblical and semitic philological materials are not included.

468. O'Brien, Betty A., and Elmer J. O'Brien. **Religion Index Two: Festschriften 1960-1969.** Philadelphia, PA, American Theological Library Association, 1980. 741p. LC 81-126147. ISBN 0-9604960-0-9.

A *Festschrift* is "a collection of studies presented to a scholar or institute or in celebration of an occasion or event" (Introduction). It may be a separate volume or a journal issue. The O'Briens include volumes dealing with religion and topics closely related to religion, such as art. All the great religions provide subject matter, but Christianity predominates since most Festschriften come from western Europe or America. Many titles are in German, since the idea for Festschriften originated in Germany in the mid-nineteenth century. Following a title list and a series list, the material is separated into an author/editor index and a subject index that uses Library of Congress subject headings. The fullest citation to materials is under the editor's name, where a list of authors of articles in a Festschrift is included. The O'Briens identify 13,241 author and editor entries from 783 Festschrift titles.

469. Parker, Harold M., Jr., comp. **Bibliography of Published Articles on American Presbyterianism, 1901-1980.** Westport, CT, Greenwood Press, 1985. 263p. index. (Bibliographies and Indexes in Religious Studies, no. 4). LC 85-7987. ISBN 0-313-24544-4.

Parker identified 2,981 articles published in this century in secular and religious journals on 25 Presbyterian denominations. The unannotated entries are arranged by author without break in a single alphabet; hence the importance of the fifty-page topical index, which Parker recommends be read first. For the most part, the journals are scholarly, in English, and exclude house organs. There is no list of titles covered, but all are spelled out in citations.

470. **Religion Index One: Periodicals, 1949- .** Chicago, IL, American Theological Library Association. Twice yearly, with second issue a cumulation. ISSN 0149-8428.

Known through 1976 as the *Index to Religious Periodical Literature*, and ecumenical though somewhat Protestant in orientation, this is now a subject index (using Library of Congress subject headings) and an author/editor index to the material in over four hundred periodicals from throughout the world. Since 1986, a scriptural passage index, arranged by the canonical order of books in the Bible rather than alphabetically, has been available as well. Because this index's readership includes scholars, teachers, students, clergy, religious leaders, and the general public, it aims at comprehensive inclusion of articles on religion, with an emphasis on western religions, and can be used for research on the social sciences and ethics as well. This is perhaps the most important element in *Religion Index*, the database produced by the American Theological Library Association. Its entries for the years 1949 through 1959 and 1975 to the present can be searched by computer online (see 476).

471. **Religion Index Two: Multi-Author Works.** Evanston, IL, American Theological Library Association, 1976- . Annual. LC 78-645074. ISSN 0149-8436.

471.1. Dickerson, G. Fay, ed. **Religion Index Two: Multi-Author Works 1970-1975.** Chicago, IL, American Theological Library Association, 1982. 2 vols.

471.2. Treesh, Erica, ed. **Religion Index Two: Multi-Author Works 1976-1980.** Evanston, IL, American Theological Library Association, 1989. 2 vols. ISBN 0-9604960-3-3.

As a companion to *Religion Index One*, which indexes periodical literature, the annual *Religion Index Two* (*RIT*) covers separately published collections of essays that are scholarly treatments of religious or theological subjects, in the western languages, by more than three authors. These include conference proceedings, festschriften, and issues of regular or irregular series or annuals. Classroom readers, journals, and single or joint author monographs are excluded. After a title and a series list, each volume has an author/editor index and a subject index with the fullest entry, including the table of contents, for a book under the editor's name.

Religion Index Two: Multi-Author Works 1970-1975 includes 30,154 articles from 2,612 books which were published between 1970 and 1975 inclusive, and replaces the *RIT* volumes for those years.

Religion Index Two: Multi-Author Works 1976-1980 adds indexing for 1,250 books not included in the annual volumes for 1976 to 1980, and has a total of 37,392 articles in 2,864 books. Some books indexed were published during 1970 to 1975, but missed in the earlier compilation. The titles and series lists at the beginning of the first volume include the titles and series from the 1970-75 volumes, to create a single decade-long list.

Religion Index Two: Festschriften 1960-1969 (see 468) offers indexing for the 1960s for a single one of the types of multi-author works covered by later indexing.

All the indexing in these volumes is available by searching the *Religion Index* database (see 476).

472. **Research in Ministry, 1981- .** Chicago, IL, American Theological Library Association. Annual.

This bibliography cites project reports and theses submitted for the doctor of ministry degree at the twenty-eight schools accredited by the Association of Theological Schools. The editors add subject and author indexes. As with other publications of the American Theological Library Association, the citations listed here are included in the *Religion Index* database, and can be accessed by online search (see 476).

473. Schwab, Moise. **Index of Articles Relative to Jewish History and Literature Published in Periodicals, from 1665 to 1900, Augmented Edition.** With an Introduction and Edited List of Abbreviations by Zosa Szajkowski. New York, Ktav Publishing House, 1971. 613p. indexes. LC 74-114721. ISBN 0-87068-163-X.

Versions of this work were printed between 1899 and 1923, sometimes in the form of a lithographed manuscript. The current edition is a reprint that contains Szajkowski's introduction; a list of periodical abbreviations; Schwab's introduction (in French) to his 1899 edition; the 1914-23 edition, which contains the articles listed alphabetically by author, by roman initial, and by Hebrew initial or Hebrew pseudonym when only those are available; two handwritten indexes: by subject (in French) and by Hebrew word; and two lists of errata. Schwab (1839-1918), a prolific scholar of Judaica who himself is listed for 112 articles, brought together in this still-much-used bibliography the seminal periodical literature in the major European languages, especially French, German, and English, on Jewish history and literature.

474. **Southern Baptist Periodicals Index, 1965- .** Bolivar, MO, Estep Library, Southwest Baptist University. Annual. ISSN 0081-3028.

Originated by the Historical Commission of the Southern Baptist Convention and taken over by Estep Library in 1984, this work now indexes fifty Baptist periodicals. Book reviews were added with the 1987 volume. A thesaurus of subject headings in use in the index was developed by the Baptist Information Retrieval System in 1984.

475. **Theological and Religious Index, 1972- .** Harrogate, Yorkshire, England, Theological Abstracting and Bibliographic Services. irregular. ISSN 0306-087X.

Edited by Graham Cornish (see 443), and started in 1971 in mimeographic form as *Theological and Religious Index*, this now covers twenty-one broad subject divisions, and includes citations to some American and British theses.

III. A Database

476. **Religion Index.** Evanston, IL, American Theological Library Association.

477. Treesh, Erica, ed. **Religion Indexes: Thesaurus**, 5th ed. Evanston, IL, American Theological Library Association, 1989. 356p.

Religion Index is the database that includes the material published in paper format in *Religion Index One* (see 470) between 1949 and 1959 and from 1975 to the present (a project is under way to fill in the years 1960 through 1974); *Religion Index Two* (see 471) from 1960 to the present; *Research in Ministry* (see 472) from 1981 to the present; and *Index to Book Reviews in Religion* (see 463) from 1986 to the present. The full scope of the database can best be appreciated by reading the descriptions in this bibliography of these four serial bibliographies and their cumulations. All bibliographic citations and abstracts in these publications can be searched, for the years included, by author, subject headings, or by key words from titles or abstracts. The subject headings most frequently used are published in Treesh's thesaurus.

The database can be searched by Boolean operators, that is, subjects can be linked together or purposely set apart. Searches can be limited to a single journal title, a single language, or a span of years. Individual biblical verses can be searched.

The database is widely available in academic and public libraries through the following database vendors:

Dialog Information Services
3460 Hillview Avenue
Palo Alto, CA 94304
800/334-2564 or 415/858-3785

(Dialog makes the database available as its File 190.)

BRS Information Technologies
1200 Route 7
Latham, NY 12110
800/345-4277 or 518/783-1161

H. W. Wilson Co.
950 University Avenue
Bronx, NY 10452
212/588-8400

Wilson publishes the database online through its WILSONLINE and also on a CD/ROM retrieval system, WILSONDISC, which can be used on a library's own personal computer equipment.

8
Quotation Dictionaries

478. Alcalay, Reuben. **Basic Encyclopedia of Jewish Proverbs, Quotations and Folk Wisdom.** Bridgeport, CT, Hartmore House, 1973. 587p. index. LC 73-83991. ISBN 0-87677-153-3.

With quotations from the Hebrew Bible, the Apocrypha, the Mishnah, the Babylonian and Jerusalem Talmuds, the Jewish literature of Spain, the Qabbala, Hassidic writings, modern Hebrew literature, and Yiddish and Ladino wit, Alcalay forms a more academic collection than Rosten (see 485), giving the quotation in Hebrew and in English and sometimes adding an equivalent English proverb to the translation. Thus the Hebrew-to-English translation "company in distress makes sorrow less" is followed by "trouble shared is trouble halved." Arrangement is alphabetical by subject, with cross-references. Alcalay purports to offer an "index of authors and books and glossary of Hebrew words," but the list of authors is really a biographical dictionary, with birth and death dates for each but no references to quotations in the text. Thus, one cannot find all the phrases uttered by, for example, Sholem Aleichem or Theodor Herzl which Alcalay has included.

479. Baron, Joseph L., ed. **A Treasury of Jewish Quotations,** new rev. ed. New York, J. Aronson, 1985. 623p. indexes. LC 85-3857. ISBN 0-8766-8894-6.

Baron collects aphorisms, maxims, proverbs, and comments on Jewish history, languages, and lands. His arrangement is topical and within topic, alphabetical by author, with biblical passages first. Non-Jewish authors are signaled by an asterisk. His definition of *Jews* is broad, and includes Spinoza, Marx, and the New Testament authors. In this most scholarly of Jewish collections, Baron has included date and page number (where possible) for each source, an index of authors, an index of two thousand of the most familiar quotations arranged by first line, a glossary of Hebrew and Yiddish words, a bibliography, and a detailed subject index.

480. Castle, Tony, comp. **The New Book of Christian Quotations.** New York, Crossroad, 1982. 293p. index. LC 82-25253. ISBN 0-8245-0551-4.

Castle offers 4,110 quotations under 450 subject headings. In trying to strike a balance between ancient and modern sources, he includes quotations from every century of the common era. An author index includes each author's dates; there are no anonymous materials. Castle's subject headings cover more practical matters than Mead's (see 482); one can look to Castle for statements on death, manners, lying, superstition, and work. There is evidence of changing times: Mead relates nothing about sex, while Castle gives seven quotations.

481.   Chapin, John, ed. **The Book of Catholic Quotations: Compiled from Approved Sources Ancient, Medieval and Modern.** New York, Farrar, Straus and Cudahy, 1956. 1,075p. indexes. LC 56-11061.

The 10,400 quotations Chapin assembles here include maxims, proverbs, definitions, ecclesiastical pronouncements, and statements from saints, church doctors, mystics, and poets. The vast majority stem from Catholic publications, but some are from sources antagonistic to the church. Statements from the church hierarchy are carefully differentiated from the rest, as are those from sources which were on the "Index of Prohibited Books" (suppressed just after Vatican II). The latter are marked with an asterisk and accompanied by explanatory notes. Chapin draws from American and English Catholic culture and literature; except for the popes and canon law, continental sources are excluded, by design. Biblical verses are also left out. The work is evidence of the mentality of anglophone Catholicism just before Vatican II, both in its care to identify "correct" statements, and in its claim to be comprehensive while at the same time excluding input from Europe and all other cultures of the world.

482.   Mead, F. S., ed. and comp. **Encyclopedia of Religious Quotations.** Westwood, NJ, Fleming H. Revell, 1965. 534p. indexes. LC 65-23623.

Finding no contemporary book of religious quotations, Mead compiled his own. From "Adversity" to "Zeal," he offers short quotations from all major religions, although he draws predominantly from Christianity. He reports working assiduously at the difficult process of attributing thoughts correctly to their original authors, but he also includes anonymous material. Mead provides access through an author index, and through an index of topics that gives cross-references to many more quotations than are grouped under the general subject headings.

483.   Neil, William, comp. **Concise Dictionary of Religious Quotations.** Grand Rapids, MI, Eerdmans, 1974. 214p. indexes. LC 74-17470. ISBN 0-8028-3451-1.

Neil's religious quotations are somewhat exalted and offer little help with day-to-day living. Unlike most other quotation dictionaries, he does include biblical verses (see also Simcox 486), taken from the New English Bible. A subject index lists extensive cross-references for quotations which might have been placed under many subject headings. Although infused by a Christian outlook, the work includes some quotations from non-Christian sources.

484.   Proctor, F. B., comp. **Treasury of Quotations on Religious Subjects: From the Great Writers and Preachers of All Ages.** London, Hodder and Stoughton, 1887. Reprint: Grand Rapids, MI, Kregel Publications, 1977. 816p. indexes. LC 76-15741. ISBN 0-8242-3500-5.

This basically Protestant (with some anti-Roman polemics) collection shows its scope and its nineteenth-century origins with its charming sub-subtitle: "Treasury of Things New and Old: Illustrations, Readings, Papers, Sermons, Notes, Suggestions, Condensed Narratives, Adaptions, Analogies, Analyses and Digests of Topics from Many a Learned Volume." What need for aught else? Arrangement is alphabetical by author, with access by subject through a general index. Proctor, unlike many later religious quotation gatherers, does include biblical passages. He lists his sources by name, but does not note in which of an author's works a quotation can be found.

485. Rosten, Leo. **Leo Rosten's Treasury of Jewish Quotations.** New York, McGraw-Hill, 1972. 716p. index. LC 72-298. ISBN 0-0705-3978-2. Reprint: Northvale, NJ, J. Aronson, 1988. 716p. index. LC 88-16739. ISBN 0-8766-8891-1.

Rosten has collected quotations for a lifetime, and here provides 4,352, including folk sayings, aphorisms, and treasures from the Torah, the Talmud, and rabbinical literature. His aim is personal: to make the reader laugh, smile, and think. To this end, he includes the wise and the humorously wise: "If God lived on earth, people would break all his windows" and "God, if you don't help me, I'll ask my uncle in America." He signals his favorites with a fleuron. Rosten provides an introduction on collecting and translating proverbs and on the nature of Yiddish proverbs. His explanatory essay on the Torah, the Talmud, the Mishnah, the Midrash and Haggada, the Gemara, and the Responsa is valuable to Jew and gentile alike. Extensive appendixes include a list of English spellings of Hebrew and Yiddish words, an essay on translating Hebrew, a biographical directory of authors quoted, a glossary with many Hebrew and Yiddish words, and a select bibliography with books and articles in English and books in Yiddish, Hebrew, and German. For the non-Jew, this is a welcome invitation to the heart of Jewish culture.

486. Simcox, Carroll E. **A Treasury of Quotations on Christian Themes.** New York, Seabury Press, 1975. 273p. indexes. LC 75-2229. ISBN 0-8164-0274-4.

Simcox arranges his material under very broad subject headings – "God," "Creation," "Man," "Life in the Spirit" – and then subdivides each. Thus, under "God" there is "Atheism," "Attributes," "Belief," "Bible," and so on. Since many subdivisions are unexpected ("Bible" under "God"), the indexes by sources and subjects are important keys. Simcox includes biblical passages and adds an index to them as well. Not all his sources are Christian, and he ranges far afield to include the clever and original (W. C. Fields on sex, for example).

487. White, David Manning. **The Search for God.** New York, Macmillan, 1983. 372p. index. LC 83-9427. ISBN 0-02-627110-9.

White collected three thousand statements in the course of thirty years of reading Jewish, Christian, and other authors whom he calls the "God seekers." Fully indexed by author, title, and subject, the statements, usually a few lines in length, are arranged by broad categories: what God could be, God the unknowable, seeking God, the attributes of God, faith in God, evil, suffering and God, and God's governance. This thoughtful collection makes an excellent bedside-table companion.

488. Wirt, Sherwood Eliot, and Kersten Beckstrom, comps. and eds. **Living Quotations for Christians.** New York, Harper & Row, 1974. 290p. indexes. LC 73-6330. ISBN 0-06-069598-6. Reprint: **Topical Encyclopedia of Living Quotations.** Minneapolis, MN, Bethany House, 1982. 290p. indexes. LC 82-4503. ISBN 0-87123-574-9.

From 350 Protestant, Catholic, and Jewish sources, Wirt and Beckstrom drew together 3,500 quotations on a wide variety of very practical matters: taxes, sex, boredom, conservatism (but not liberalism), war, and so forth. Theology is left for other collections; here there are no entries for Trinity, incarnation, or resurrection, although there is "God," "Jesus Christ," and "Depravity." Biblical passages are excluded. There is an author index and a topical index. This is more useful than Mead (see 482) or Castle (see 480) for comments on matters of daily life.

489.   Woods, Ralph Louis, comp. and ed. **The World Treasury of Religious Quotations.** New York, Hawthorn Books, 1966. 1,106p. index. LC 66-15355.

Woods compiles sayings from Buddhist, Hindu, Taoist, Confucian, Islamic, Zoroastrian, Jewish, and even Marxist sources, but, as with Mead (see 482), Christianity predominates. Biblical sayings are excluded. Woods made an effort to date the quotations, which are arranged chronologically under fifteen hundred subject headings. There are few clichés in this high-quality gathering.

9
Core Journals

The number of magazines and journals treating religions in general, or the branches of Judaism and Christianity in particular, is great. Directories published in the mid- and late 1980s describe and evaluate this literature in a comprehensive manner (see the section on serials in chapter 6). I have here identified those scholarly journals which are widely indexed and most frequently found in libraries, and which are sources of additional bibliographic information through their extensive book reviews.

490. **ADRIS Newsletter, 1971- .** The Bronx, NY, Association for the Development of Religious Information Systems (Department of Theology, Fordham University). Quarterly. ISSN 0300-7022.

This newsletter, edited by the Jesuit R. F. Smith, carries an enormous amount of information about current events, publishing, and automation of religious studies. The scope is limitless, but in practice most of the sources reviewed concern Jewish or Christian materials. An extensive, worldwide list of conferences emphasizes North America. Information about religious organizations is contained in the section on "News, Organizations, Announcements, Directories." There are reviews of new reference books, bulletins of recent books, summaries of important periodical articles, reports of ongoing research, and reviews of the automation of information on religion. With its copious, high-quality information, and a very low subscription price, this is one of the most useful and cost-effective bibliographic sources for librarians and scholars interested in religion.

491. **American Jewish History, 1893- .** Waltham, MA, American Jewish Historical Society. Quarterly. ISSN 0164-0178.

The organ of the American Jewish Historical Society (see 535), this journal carries learned articles on any aspect of American Jewish history, often linked in theme issues, and with occasional special reports. Each issue offers book reviews and often bibliographic essays. In a regular bibliographic essay, the librarian of the society covers Judaica Americana. Affairs of the society, such as the presidential address and reports of annual meetings and lists of members, are carried. There is a general conference calendar on Jewish studies as well as lists of recent dissertations in the field.

492. **Anglican Theological Review, 1918- .** Evanston, IL, Anglican Theological Review (Seabury-Weston Theological Seminary). Five numbers per year. ISSN 0003-3286.

This "unofficial organ of the theological seminaries and colleges of the Episcopal Church" offers scholarly contributions, primarily from Episcopalians, but has evolved into a general theological journal with input from thinkers of other religious traditions. Each issue contains several articles meant for the generally educated reader, poetry, numerous book reviews, and often a bibliographic review article.

493. **Baptist History and Heritage, 1965- .** Nashville, TN, Historical Commission of the Southern Baptist Convention and Southern Baptist Historical Society. Quarterly. ISSN 0005-5719.

Each number begins with an editorial stating the theme of the issue, which is then covered by several scholarly articles. Bibliographic essays may be included. Five or six book reviews and "News Notes" on Baptist history normally follow. The official business of the sponsoring organizations appears as needed, and includes reports on meetings, membership lists, annual reports, and presidents' reports.

494. **Brethren Life and Thought, 1955- .** Oakbrook, IL, Brethren Journal Association and Bethany Theological Seminary. Quarterly. ISSN 0006-9663.

The journal contains articles examining Brethren history, and presenting biblical exegesis and theological and moral themes from the Brethren perspective (the Brethren Churches advocate pacifism). In addition to the scholarly articles, each issue contains poetry and reviews of books on Brethren topics. Occasionally, an issue will have a single theme.

495. **The Catholic Historical Review, 1915- .** Washington, DC, Catholic University of America Press. Quarterly. ISSN 0008-8080.

This journal presents scholarly articles on the worldwide history of Catholicism, and an extensive array of book reviews. Books received but not reviewed are listed. Significant periodical articles on Catholic history are cited by broad subject division, but are not abstracted. A "Notes and Comments" section offers news of the Catholic Historical Association; reports on conferences, symposia, seminars, and lectures; prizes and grants; and other news of interest to scholars.

496. **Christian Jewish Relations, 1968- .** London, Institute of Jewish Affairs. Quarterly. ISSN 0144-2902.

Reporting on the broad range of relations between Christians and Jews, from ecumenical outreach to historical disasters, this journal contains scholarly articles, news reports from around the world, documentation of Christian-Jewish encounters, and a model "list of books received" that includes a brief statement of contents for each book.

497. **Church History, 1932- .** Wallingford, PA, American Society of Church History. Quarterly. ISSN 0009-6407.

This is the primary scholarly journal published in the United States for the global history of Christianity. It offers articles by America's premier church historians, including John Tracy Ellis, Henry Warner Bowden, Ernest R. Sandeen, Martin Marty, and Jaroslav Pelikan, most of whom have written reference books listed in this bibliography. In addition to articles, the affairs of the society are noted, including minutes of council meetings, agendas for conferences, and membership lists. Book reviews are numerous, and, since 1979, shorter book notices are included. The editors also include abstracts of doctoral dissertations on church history.

498. **Cross Currents, 1951- .** West Nyack, NY, Convergence. Quarterly. ISSN 0011-1953.

A half-dozen articles, as well as shorter "perspectives" and "communications," in each issue "explore the implications of Christianity for our times." This is one journal in which female theologians and other thinkers have traditionally been published. An issue will often be devoted to a theme. About ten books are reviewed at some length in each issue, and a few are given short notices. Early contributors included many of the progressive thinkers of the 1950s, such as Hannah Arendt, Jean Danielou, Nicholas Berdyaev, Oscar Cullmann, and Paul Ricoeur.

499. **Dialogue: A Journal of Mormon Thought, 1966- .** Salt Lake City, UT, Dialogue Foundation. Quarterly. ISSN 0012-2157.

A note on the inside cover states that the purpose of this journal is "to express Mormon culture and to examine the relevance of religion to secular life." Coverage is extended to all the divisions within Mormonism. With editors and contributors from throughout the United States and beyond, it offers scholarly articles, notes and comments, personal narratives, fiction, poetry, photography, book reviews, and brief notices. Until recently, the column "Among the Mormons" appeared in every issue, providing bibliographies of books, dissertations, and articles on Mormon matters.

500. **The Ecumenical Review, 1948- .** Geneva, Switzerland, World Council of Churches. Quarterly. ISSN 0013-0796.

Begun in 1948 by the founders of the European postwar ecumenical movement, this journal contains articles on current ecumenical topics, including foundational thinking, practical applications, observations and the reporting of events. There is often a bibliographic review article. Book reviews, when included, are lengthy. The "Ecumenical Forum" contains extended statements emanating from joint working groups, while the "Ecumenical Chronicle" contains shorter statements and reports resulting from conferences and meetings. The "Ecumenical Diary" offers chronological notes on events. A list of books received gives titles predominantly in English, while the "Bibliographica Oecumenica" lists new titles available in the World Council of Churches library in Geneva.

501. **The Ecumenist, 1962- .** Ramsey, NJ, Paulist Press, and Montreal, Canada, Faculty of Religious Studies of McGill University. Bimonthly. ISSN 0013-080X.

This short journal (sixteen pages each issue), edited by Gregory Baum, a leading Roman Catholic ecumenist, was intended from its inception as a forum for Roman Catholic ecumenical effort. Its premier issue is dated the same month, October 1962, that the Second Vatican Council opened in Rome. Scholarly pieces on current ecumenical topics are offered by contributors from a variety of religious traditions. Conferences are reported. Baum's frequent articles are often reviews of books of ecumenical interest.

502. **Harvard Theological Review, 1908- .** Cambridge, MA, Harvard Divinity School. Quarterly. ISSN 0017-8160.

With an emphasis on the Judeo-Christian tradition, this journal presents highly scholarly articles that eschew technical vocabulary and often link religious themes to philosophy or literature. The last issue of each year offers summaries of doctoral dissertations in religious studies accepted by Harvard. There are occasional short "Notes and Observations," and a list of books received, but no book reviews. Some articles contain valuable bibliographic appendixes.

503. **Immanuel: A Bulletin of Religious Thought and Research in Israel, 1972- .** Israel, Ecumenical Theological Research Fraternity, and New York, Anti-Defamation League of B'nai B'rith. Semiannual. ISSN 0302-8127.

The purpose of this journal is "to present recent developments in Israel with the areas of religious studies and theology." This is carried out in original articles, and in translations and summaries of the works of Israeli scholars that have already appeared in Hebrew. There are sections on the Hebrew Bible, the New Testament and First Centuries Judaism, Jewish thought and spirituality, Jewish-Christian relations, and contemporary religious life and thought in Israel. The editor is a French Dominican (Catholic) priest; on the editorial board, each section is represented by a Jewish and a Christian scholar. Book announcements cover Israeli theological publishing.

504. **Journal for the Scientific Study of Religion, 1961- .** Washington, DC, Society for the Scientific Study of Religion (Catholic University of America). Quarterly. ISSN 0021-8294.

The Society for the Scientific Study of Religion, founded in 1949, promotes the methods of the social sciences for the study of religion in general. The scope of the journal is not limited to Judaism and Christianity, but an overview indicates a predominance of Jewish and Christian subject matter, if only because these are the religions the contributors, mostly American scholars, have at hand to study. Hence, there is objective, academic study of many contemporary Jewish and Christian phenomena and problems. Each issue contains seven or eight articles, sometimes addressing a theme, as well as research notes, comments, and perspectives, and a dozen or so book reviews.

505. **The Journal of Ecclesiastical History, 1950- .** New York, Cambridge University Press. Quarterly. ISSN 0022-0469.

Covering the "universal church," east and west, Catholic, Protestant, and Orthodox, from the New Testament period to the present, this journal contains several learned articles in each issue. It also carries a section on "Notes and Documents," a bibliographic review article, and a plenitude of full-length book reviews and short notices, as well as a list of books received (organized by publisher). The quality is unmatched; even the shorter book notices are often by scholars of international repute. While the articles are broadly applicable, this journal is especially valuable for the bibliography of church history.

506. **Journal of Ecumenical Studies, 1964- .** Philadelphia, PA, Temple University. Quarterly. ISSN 0022-0558.

This journal was initially published in 1964, with an emphasis on Protestantism, Catholicism, and Orthodox Christianity, at the Roman Catholic Duquesne University in Pittsburgh. With the editors drawn from among the leaders in the Christian and Jewish ecumenical movements, it now covers the entire movement within and between these two religions, as well as their contacts with other world religions. Each issue contains scholarly articles on theological aspects of ecumenism; explorations of practical problems, including discussions and responses; several dozen book reviews; abstracts of periodical articles from a broad, international range of journals; and a list of ecumenical events. The latter includes reports on meetings, interfaith statements, visits, conferences, interfaith studies, formal dialogue sessions, and institutes.

507. **Journal of Jewish Studies, 1948- .** Oxford, England, Oxford Centre for Postgraduate Hebrew Studies. Semiannual. ISSN 0022-2097.

Similar in format to Oxford's *Journal of Theological Studies* (see 511), this periodical is "designed to foster Hebrew and Jewish studies from the biblical period to the present time" (inside cover). Each issue contains eight to ten articles of the highest scholarship, as well as two to four book reviews, an occasional bibliographical survey, and a list of books received. Early editors and contributors included some of the greatest Jewish scholars of this century, among them Leo Baeck, Martin Buber, Cecil Roth, and Gershom Scholem.

508. **The Journal of Religion, 1921- .** Chicago, IL, University of Chicago Press. Quarterly. ISSN 0022-4189.

The University of Chicago Press publishes both *History of Religions*, which has little to do with the Jewish and Christian traditions, and this journal, which ranges over contemporary and historical Judaism and Christianity and the broad cultures which have grown out of these religions. Each issue contains approximately eight articles and often a lengthy review article on an author or subject. Of particular note are the numerous book reviews and shorter book notes, as well as the occasional bibliographic article.

509. **The Journal of Religious Ethics, 1973- .** Decatur, GA, Scholar's Press. Semiannual. ISSN 0384-9694.

The contributors to this journal include the foremost scholars of ethics in America. Theme issues are common, with the theme introduced by an editorial. Bibliographic studies are sometimes included among the articles. In recent years, issues have contained a small number of book reviews.

510. **Journal of the American Academy of Religion, 1933- .** Atlanta, GA, Scholars Press. Quarterly. ISSN 0002-7189.

This journal, the official publication of the Academy (see 534), has offerings on all religions, but there is a heavy emphasis on matters Christian and Jewish. The editorial board is made up of ranking American religion scholars. Each issue contains several articles, often a lengthy essay reviewing the work of a scholar, an idea, or a book, and sometimes a discussion and response. There are extensive book reviews and a list of books received.

511. **Journal of Theological Studies, 1899- .** Oxford, England, Oxford University Press. Semiannual. ISSN 0022-5185.

Edited by leading Oxford Christian theologians, each issue of this journal offers five to eight articles of high scholarship on a full range of biblical, historical, and theological topics, as well as shorter "Notes and Studies" and a half-dozen full-length book reviews. The more plentiful shorter book notices, characterized by masterful evaluations, cover much continental theological publishing not always in ready circulation in the United States.

512 **Judaism: A Quarterly Journal of Jewish Life and Thought, 1952- .** New York, American Jewish Congress. Quarterly. ISSN 0022-5762.

Each issue contains thoughtful essays on Jewish history, philosophy, and theology, and on the Jewish response to the contemporary world, as well as poetry, and extended reviews, often of a single book. Citations to received books are collected in a lengthy list divided by subject.

513. **The Mennonite Quarterly Review, 1927- .** Goshen, IN, The Mennonite Historical Society. Quarterly. ISSN 0025-9373.

This "journal devoted to Anabaptist-Mennonite history, thought, life, and affairs" (inside cover) contains theological and historical essays by scholars of this rich tradition, which includes the Amish and Hutterite movements. Each issue also contains research notes, book reviews, and shorter book notices. All materials are in English, but there is much evidence of scholarly connections with the traditions in German-speaking countries.

514. **Religious Studies, 1965- .** New York, Cambridge University Press. Quarterly. ISSN 0034-4125.

A great majority of the articles, and an even greater number of the book reviews, in this journal deal with materials from the Jewish and Christian traditions. The writing is consistently very scholarly and highly readable. The editors and contributors are some of the most internationally reknowned thinkers on world religions, though most have a Judeo-Christian heritage. All books mentioned, even limited editions, are reviewed, sometimes at length, sometimes with short notices.

515. **Religious Studies Review, 1975- .** Macon, GA, Council of Societies for the Study of Religion (Mercer University). Quarterly. ISSN 0319-485X.

This review offers scholarly examination of the extensive publication in the broad field of religion for the American discipline of religious studies. Christianity and Judaism weigh heavily in this scope. Each issue contains several extensive bibliographic review essays on a single author or theme, and review notes on more than three hundred books. Each year there is a listing of dissertations in progress in religious studies. The work of numerous contributors is brought together by editors grouped in the divisions of methodological studies, social scientific study of religion, theology and philosophy of religion, ethics, religions of the ancient Near East, the history of Christianity, modern European Christianity, and the history of Judaism.

516. **Review of Religious Research, 1959- .** Washington, DC, Religious Research Association (Catholic University of America). Quarterly. ISSN 0034-673X.

Articles in this journal report the rigorous use of social scientific methods to analyze religious phenomena such as the transmission of values and the growth of cults. As with the *Journal for the Scientific Study of Religion* (see 504), although the scope is unlimited, in practice much of the research concerns the Christian and Jewish phenomena in America. Where *JSSR* leans to the theoretical, this journal stresses the practical and applicable. Members of the Religious Research Association include not only social scientists and theologians, but also "church researchers and planners, ...teachers, administrators, clergy, editors, city planners, [and] market researchers." Theme issues are common. Each issue contains one to two dozen book reviews; each year a scholarly lecture to the Association is printed.

517. **Studies in Formative Spirituality, 1980- .** Pittsburgh, PA, Institute of Formative Spirituality (Duquesne University). Triannually. ISSN 0193-2748.

The aim of this journal is "to study and foster the art and discipline of foundational human and Christian formation." Its international list of contributors often come from the Roman Catholic tradition, but the direction of the journal is ecumenical: the theme for a recent issue was "Contemporary Jewish Perspectives." Until 1988, each issue was structured around a theme with several articles, a translation, a bibliography (often annotated), and summaries of selected works on the theme. Future issues will not necessarily be limited to a single theme. The editor, Adrian Van Kaam, director of the institute, contributes a regular article on "the Terminology of the Science of Foundational Formative Spirituality." In brief, this journal is of interest to those of all religious traditions who are interested in the psychology of the spiritual life.

518. **Theological Studies, 1940- .** Baltimore, MD, Theological Studies. Quarterly. ISSN 0040-5639.

Published "for the theological faculties of the Society of Jesus [Jesuits] in the United States," but including the work of contributors from a wide range of academic institutions, this journal is a major vehicle for contemporary American Catholic thought. Each issue contains five or six articles, overviews of current theological topics, and over thirty book reviews. An extensive list, in each issue, of unreviewed books is divided into scriptural studies; history; morality and law; pastoral, spiritual, and liturgical studies; and philosophical works.

519. **Theology, 1920- .** London, Society for Promoting Christian Knowledge. Six times yearly. ISSN 0040-571X.

In keeping with the purpose of the society — widely known in the English-speaking world as the SPCK — to spread Christian thought throughout the world, this journal features lively essays by Christian, often Anglican, theologians on contemporary issues. Letters to the editor are included, as are approximately a dozen book reviews, in each issue. An extensive list of received books, divided into eleven sections, is an excellent survey of current British religious publishing.

520. **Theology Digest, 1953- .** St. Louis, MO, Theology Digest (St. Louis University). Quarterly. ISSN 0040-5728.

The editors of this unique publication scan four hundred theological journals in eight languages, and present three- to six-page English digests of articles in periodicals not generally available in the United States. Each digest is first sent to the original author for approval before publication, and an abstract of the article is prepared by the editors. A book survey, which attempts to include "all important religious books published in the United States," features a nonevaluative annotation as well as cost and full bibliographic description for each book. Each survey is extensive; one recent issue had just under three hundred entries. Originally reflecting Roman Catholic thought, especially as expressed in European publications, *Theology Digest* has since the mid-1960s included many authors from other traditions and places.

521. **Theology Today, 1944- .** Ephrata, PA, Theology Today. Quarterly. ISSN 0040-5736.

In addition to academic articles on biblical and theological subjects, this journal includes editorials, poetry, and original essays, and has such regular features as "Critics Corner" and "Theological Table Talk," all by leading American theologians from various denominations and traditions. Contributors have included James Cone, Avery Dulles, Martin Marty, Monika Hellwig, David Tracy, and Gregory Baum. Over a dozen and a half books are fully reviewed in each issue, and another dozen receive shorter evaluative and descriptive notes.

522. **Tradition: A Journal of Orthodox Jewish Thought, 1958- .** New York, Rabbinical Council of America. Quarterly. ISSN 0041-0608.

In this journal, called "Orthodoxy's entree into intellectual and scholarly circles" (Louis Bernstein), scholars of the Orthodox Jewish tradition apply the Torah to contemporary situations which call for ethical responses, in articles such as "Judaism and Animal Experimentation," "Orthodoxy and Women's Changing Self-perception," and "Preemptive War in Jewish Law." Most issues contain a "Survey of Recent Halakhic Literature," that is, writings on the application of Jewish Law to life situations. Book reviews, a few in each issue, are lengthy evaluations.

10
Principal Research Centers, Institutes, Scholarly and Professional Organizations, and Library Associations

The information for this chapter is based on a survey taken in August and September of 1989. Quotations about the purpose and scope of organizations are taken from these groups' literature. Along with other groups, I have attempted to identify the historical societies of most large churches.

I. Research Centers and Institutes

523. **American Baptist Historical Society.** 1106 South Goodman Street, Rochester, NY 14620-2532. 716/473-1740.

Founded in 1853, and now the official depository of the American Baptist Churches in the U.S.A., the ABHS collects materials of all kinds relating to Baptist history. It supports two centers, the American Baptist-Samuel Colgate Historical Library on the campus of Colgate-Rochester Divinity School, at the above address, and the American Baptist Archives Center, P.O. Box 851, Valley Forge, PA 19482-0851 (215/768-2378). The centers respond to written and telephoned questions on Baptist history and family records. An extensive publishing program includes the *American Baptist Quarterly*, the *Baptist Bibliography* by Edward C. Starr (see 366), and other reference works, some authored by William H. Brackney (see 134).

524. **American Institute for Patristic and Byzantine Studies.** R.R. 1, Box 353-A, Minuet Lane, Kingston, NY 12401. 914/336-8797.

The institute promotes research on and translation of the Eastern Church Fathers and other historical figures of the Orthodox Church of the Byzantine and later eras. In 1982, it began publication of *The Patristic and Byzantine Review*, which features articles by an international and ecumenical group of scholars.

525. **Center for Applied Research in the Apostolate.** Georgetown University, P.O. Box 1601, Washington, DC 20057. 202/687-8080.

A Roman Catholic research institute using the extensive facilities at Georgetown University, this organization has since 1964 employed the tools of the social sciences to produce attitudinal surveys, institutional planning and organizational development documents, demographic data, and directories for Catholic dioceses, religious communities, and institutions.

526. Center for Reformation Research. 6477 San Bonita Avenue, St. Louis, MO 63105. 314/727-6655.

526.1. Society for Reformation Research. Same address.

Founded in 1957 and supported by private donors, a friends organization, and the four main bodies of the Lutheran Church in the United States, the Center for Reformation Research "exists to promote the study of the sixteenth century, a period vital to our understanding of western religious and cultural traditions." It maintains a library and sponsors seminars, conferences, and programs, as well as a newsletter and the Sixteenth Century Bibliography series. It also serves as the administrative office of the Society for Reformation Research.

The society, founded in 1947, promotes the study of the Reformation and Counter-Reformation and is affiliated with the German Verein für Reformationsgeschichte. In addition to its own conferences, it sponsors scholarly sessions at meetings of the American Historical Association. With the German organization, it co-sponsors the Archive for Reformation History and the *Literature Review*.

527. Center for Research in Faith and Moral Development. Candler School of Theology, Emory University, Atlanta, GA 30322. 404/727-4155.

Founded in 1980, this center has undertaken funded research on such topics as religious education, the faith development of Israeli kibbutz founders, and the public church (that is, the church which is actively involved in public life). The center sponsors fellows in residence who wish to work in developmental research.

528. Leo Baeck Institute. 129 East 73rd Street, New York, NY 10021. 212/744-6400.

"Founded in 1955, [the institute] is devoted to the history of German-speaking Jewry, from early times until its tragic destruction by the Nazis." It has offices in London and Jerusalem, but hosts a library in New York with 60,000 volumes and 750 periodical titles dating from the eighteenth to the twentieth century. The archives hold an extensive collection of family and commmunity histories, a thousand memoirs from Jews of all walks of life written between 1790 and 1945, and 30,000 photographs. The institute offers lectures and exhibits, and supports seminars, symposia, and doctoral fellows.

529. Office of History. Presbyterian Church (U.S.A.). 425 Lombard Street, Philadelphia, PA 19147. 215/627-1852.

529.1. Presbyterian Historical Association. Same address. 1,100 members.

The association was created from the 1988 merger of the Presbyterian Historical Society (founded in 1852) and the Historical Foundation of the Presbyterian and Reformed Churches, to provide a voluntary support group for the Office of History. The Office of History was established in 1988 as the archives and research center for the Presbyterian Church (U.S.A.). It maintains a library of 200,000 titles, dating from the fifteenth century to the present, as well as collections of nonprint media, including photographs, slides, films, filmstrips, sound recordings, and databases. The archives contain 10,000 cubic feet of records on the church and on other Presbyterian organizations and "ecumenical partners," such as the National Council of Churches, the American Sunday School Union, the American and Foreign Christian Union, the Gray Panthers, and the American Society of Church History. The organization has supported the publication of *American Presbyterianism: the Journal of Presbyterian History* since 1901, as well as monographs and microform publications. It also maintains an oral history program.

530. **Religion and Public Life.** 156 Fifth Avenue, Suite 400, New York, NY 10010. 212/627-2288.

Presided over by the Lutheran pastor Richard John Neuhaus, the institute, whose purpose is "to advance a religiously informed public philosophy for the ordering of public life," publishes *First Things: A Monthly Journal of Religion and Public Life*, and "sponsors scholars conferences, consultations, research projects, public education events, and a fellows program."

531. **YIVO Institute for Jewish Research.** 1048 Fifth Avenue, New York, NY 10028. 212/535-6700. FAX 212/879-9763.

The YIVO Institute "is a center of study, research and publishing dedicated to documenting and understanding the experiences and creativity of East European Jewry." Founded in Vilna, Lithuania, in 1925, its center there was destroyed by the Nazis. The New York center, established in 1940, received many of the publications of the Vilna library after the war. It now has a library of 330,000 books and periodicals, and archives of 10,000 linear feet arranged in over 1,200 collections, with 10,000 photographs of Russian and Soviet Jewry as well as video materials. YIVO sponsors research through scholarships, and supports an extensive monograph publishing program. It has worked with the Yad Vashem Memorial in Jerusalem to document extensively the destruction of European Jewry by the Nazis, and has published much of the most important scholarship on this subject.

II. Scholarly and Professional Organizations

532. **Academy of Homiletics.** Lincoln Christian Seminary. P.O. Box 178, Lincoln, IL 62656. 217/732-3168. 150 members.

The purpose of the academy is "to bring together professors and teachers of homiletics for the study of the place of preaching in theological education, for the discussion and sharing of ideas and methods, and for the fostering of scholarly research in this and other related areas and disciplines." The academy meets annually and publishes the papers presented.

533. **American Academy of Jewish Research.** 3080 Broadway, New York, NY 10027. 212/678-8864. FAX 212/678-8947. 500 members.

Organized in 1919, the academy promotes Jewish learning and research by holding annual meetings (last week of December), supporting Jewish scholars studying abroad, and distributing annual grants-in-aid for the publication of scholarly works. The academy publishes the proceedings of the annual meeting, a monograph series, and a texts and studies series.

534. **American Academy of Religion.** Department of Religion, 501 Hall of Languages, Syracuse University, Syracuse, NY 13244-1170. 315/443-4019. FAX 315/443-5390. 6,000 members.

The largest American scholarly organization in the field of religious studies, the AAR is currently linked to the Society of Biblical Literature (see 763) (one can hold joint membership). It brings together scholars of all religious traditions, methods of study, and religious subject areas. Its publications include the *Journal of the American Academy of*

Religion (see 510), the *Critical Review of Books in Religion*, and several series. AAR offers research grants, group project grants, travel grants, and awards for excellence in publication.

535. **American Jewish Historical Society.** 2 Thornton Road, Waltham, MA 02154. 617/891-8110. FAX 617/899-9208. 3,500 members.

Founded in 1982, the society "is dedicated to the collection, preservation, and dissemination of information on the history of Jews on the American continent." It maintains a library with eighty thousand volumes and seven million manuscripts on the campus of Brandeis University, and publishes *American Jewish History* (see 491) as well as a newsletter and reference works.

536. **Association for Jewish Studies.** Widener Library M, Harvard University, Cambridge, MA 02138. 1,300 members.

From 1969, this learned society has sought "to promote, maintain, and improve teaching, research, and related endeavors in Jewish Studies in colleges, universities, and other institutions of higher learning." An annual conference in December brings the membership together. The association publishes the *AJS Newsletter* and the *AJS Review*, a scholarly journal, as well as volumes of proceedings from conferences it has sponsored.

537. **Association for Religion and Intellectual Life.** College of New Rochelle, New Rochelle, NY 10805-2308. 914/654-5425. 1,000 members.

This ecumenical association, heavily influenced by Roman Catholics, is dedicated to advancing the integration of spiritual and intellectual life, and to facing contemporary ideologies with in-depth study to find commonality in the Jewish and Christian traditions. The membership holds an annual conference on a single theme, and publishes the quarterly *Religion & Intellectual Life*, with articles by leading American religious thinkers.

538. **Association for the Sociology of Religion.** Continuing Education, Lebanon Valley College, Annville, PA 17003-0501. 717/867-6336. FAX 717/867-6124. 600 members.

This scholarly association seeks "to advance theory and research in the sociology of religion," including "comparative, historical and theoretical contributions." To achieve its ends, the association holds an annual meeting and publishes *Sociological Analysis* as well as a newsletter. It works in particular to strengthen graduate studies, and offers research grants for the study of women in religion.

539. **Association of Disciples for Theological Discussion.** Division of Higher Education Christian Church (Disciples of Christ), 11780 Borman Drive, Suite 100, St. Louis, MO 63146-4159. 314/991-3000. 25 members.

The association is comprised of active members of the Disciples of Christ who are involved in religious studies at the undergraduate and graduate levels. The members meet yearly to discuss papers on themes pertinent to the church. They also serve as the editorial board of *The Disciples Theological Digest*, an annual containing abstracts of works about the church or by its writers.

540. **Association of Statisticians of American Religious Bodies.** National Ministries, American Baptist Churches USA, P.O. Box 851, Valley Forge, PA 19482-0851. 215/768-2480. FAX 215/768-2470. 29 members.

Since 1935, this body has brought together the statisticians of Jewish, Catholic, and Protestant bodies, furnished a forum for the exchange of ideas and methods, and worked toward standardization for the correlation of religious statistics. In recent years, the association has emphasized analysis and utilization of statistics. Annual programs explore population studies, and forms, methodologies, definitions, and categories of religious statistics. The association maintains a liaison with the United States Census Bureau (see 181).

541. Catholic Commission on Intellectual and Cultural Affairs. P.O. Box 21, Notre Dame, IN 46556. 219/277-1053. 340 members.

Founded in 1946, the commission provides "a forum for the interchange of ideas, the development of mutual intellectual cooperation, and for the discussion of significant issues of intellectual and cultural life in our times." The commission brings together Catholic intellectual and cultural leaders to discuss contemporary themes at annual meetings and publishes the contributions in the *CCICA Annual*.

542. Catholic Theological Society of America. Loyola University, Chicago, IL 60626. 312/274-3000. 1,300 members.

Founded in 1946, the society is comprised of American and Canadian Catholic theologians in seminaries, colleges, and universities. It seeks "to promote studies and research in theology, to relate theological reflection to current problems, and to foster a more effective theological education by providing a forum for an exchange of views among theologians and with scholars in other disciplines." The society holds an annual convention each June. In addition to its proceedings, it commissions special publishing projects.

543. Concordia Historical Institute. 801 De Mun Avenue, St. Louis MO 63105. 314/721-5934. 1,800 members.

Founded in 1847 and affiliated with the Lutheran Church — Missouri Synod, the institute maintains records from the early days of Lutheranism in Germany, although it specializes in Lutheran history in the United States. An extensive library contains books, pamphlets, periodicals, microfilm collections, and over two-and-one-half million manuscripts, documents, and letters. Films, photographs, and artifacts are also included. The institute publishes *The Concordia Historical Institute Quarterly*, actively helps local congregations preserve historical records, provides extensive help in preparing congregational histories and biographies of church leaders, and answers reference questions.

544. Council of Societies for the Study of Religion. Mercer University, Macon, GA 31207. 912/741-2376.

Ten constituent societies and two affiliate societies make up the council, which publishes the quarterly *Religious Studies Review* (see 515) and the *CSSR Bulletin*, a clearinghouse of information of the societies sent to the entire collective membership. In addition, the council publishes the *Directory of Departments and Programs of Religious Studies in North America* (6th ed. 1989) (see 187) and the *Directory of Faculty of Departments and Programs of Religious Studies in North America* (1988).

545. Disciples of Christ Historical Society. 1101 Nineteenth Avenue, South, Nashville, TN 37212. 615/327-1444. 5,300 members.

The society was founded in 1941 to collect materials on the Campbell-Stone movement in the nineteenth century and to serve as the historical institute for the Christian Church (Disciples of Christ), the Christian Churches, and the Church of Christ. The society maintains a library of 29,000 volumes as well as biographical files, congregational records, audiovisual items, and collections of personal papers and microforms. It assists with research questions and publishes the historical quarterly *Discipliana*.

546. Evangelical Theological Society. Reformed Theological Seminary, 5422 Clinton Boulevard, Jackson, MS 39209. 601/922-4988. 2,000 members.

Founded in 1947, the society seeks "to foster conservative biblical scholarship by providing a medium for the oral exchange and written expression of thought and research in the general field of the theological disciplines as centered in the Scriptures." Coming from a variety of denominations, the membership has produced a single credal statement as the sole condition for membership: "The Bible alone, and the Bible in its entirety, is the Word of God written and is therefore inerrant in the autographs." The society meets annually, encourages the publication of monographs, and produces the *Journal of the Evangelical Theological Society*.

547. Fellowship of Catholic Scholars. Gannon University, Erie, PA 16541. 814/871-7220. 800 members.

Scholars of various disciplines who uphold the teachings of the Catholic Church join in supporting each other through this fellowship, which publishes a quarterly newsletter and the proceedings of its annual convention.

548. General Commission on Archives and History of the United Methodist Church. P.O. Box 127, Madison, NJ 07940. 201/822-2787. 1,200 members.

The main historical resource for the United Methodist Church, the commission publishes *Methodist History*, a quarterly, and *The Historian's Digest*, a newsletter to its members.

549. Historical Commission of the Southern Baptist Convention. 901 Commerce Street, Suite 400, Nashville, TN 37203-3620. 615/244-0344.

549.1 Southern Baptist Historical Society. Same address. 1,100 members.

Formed in 1951, the Historical Commission supports ongoing publications, conducts research projects, microfilms historical materials, produces audiovisual materials, conducts history workshops, operates an oral history program, organizes conferences, and advises local churches and Baptist associations. It maintains the Southern Baptist Historical Library and Archives, which contain some twenty-one thousand books, seventy thousand annuals of Baptist associations and conventions, microfilmed eighteenth- and nineteenth-century Baptist records from England, papers of Southern Baptist leaders, transcribed oral history interviews, audiovisual materials, and Baptist periodicals and newspapers from throughout the world.

The commission sponsors *Baptist History and Heritage* (see 493), the newsletter *Baptist Heritage Update*, and *Southern Baptist Periodical Index* (see 474), and led in developing the *Encyclopedia of Southern Baptists* (see 17).

550. Historical Committee of the Mennonite Church. 1700 South Main Street, Goshen, IN 46526. 219/535-7477.

The Historical Committee encourages research leading to publication on the Anabaptist and Mennonite movements in general. It maintains the archives of the Mennonite Church, with 1,800 collections of personal papers dating back to 1525, Mennonite Church records, and the papers of inter-Mennonite organizations.

551. Jewish Chautauqua Society. 838 Fifth Avenue, New York, NY 10021-7064. 212/570-0707. FAX 212/570-0960. 15,000 members.

Sponsored by the National Federation of Temple Brotherhoods, the society has for almost a century fought anti-semitism by supporting college lectureships, chapel services, secondary school presentations, book grants, film and video production, and interfaith institutes.

552. **Jewish Publication Society.** 1930 Chestnut Street, Philadelphia, PA 19103-4599. 215/564-5925 and 800/234-3151. 12,000 members.

Founded in 1888, the society has sponsored almost nine hundred titles, some of the most prominent of which are *TANAKH, The JPS Torah Commentary,* and the *American Jewish Yearbook* (see 210). Other books have included "biographies, histories, novels, art, poetry, holiday anthologies, children's books, religious and philosophical studies, [and] translations of scholarly and popular classics."

553. **Lutheran Historical Conference.** Valparaiso University, Valparaiso, IN 46383.

The conference is an umbrella organization that coordinates "the archival, microfilm and historical activities of the Lutheran church bodies in North America." It supports an Essays and Reports series, based on its annual meetings, and a monograph series, as well as the *LHC Newsletter.*

554. **Mormon History Association.** P.O. Box 7010, University Station, Provo, UT 84602. 801/378-4995. 800 members.

Organized in 1965 as an independent scholarly organization, the association is "dedicated to the understanding, research, and publication of Mormon history." It holds annual meetings at sites significant to Mormon history, and sponsors both a newsletter and *The Journal of Mormon History*, which includes articles by Mormon and non-Mormon scholars alike.

555. **National Association of Baptist Professors of Religion.** Mercer University, Macon, GA 31207. 912/744-2880. 650 members.

The association, open to teachers of religious studies in accredited institutions, has an extensive publishing program with a Festschriften series, a Special Studies series, and a Dissertation series. It sponsors the quarterly *Perspectives in Religious Studies*, edited by the association's chief officer, Watson E. Mills, who is also executive officer of the Council of Societies for the Study of Religion and author of several reference works (see 419-421, and 710).

556. **North American Academy of Liturgy.** Room 120, Huegli Hall, Valparaiso University, Valparaiso, IN 46383. 219/464-5340. 380 members.

The two-fold purpose of the academy, founded in 1974, is "to promote liturgical scholarship among its members ... [and] to extend the benefits of this scholarship to the worshipping communities to which its members belong." Members, who meet annually, include scholars and artists from Judaism and many Christian churches. The June issue of the periodical *Worship* includes the papers of the annual meeting.

557. **Religious Education Association.** 409 Prospect Street, New Haven, CT 06511-2177. 203/865-6141. 2,900 members.

Founded in 1903 by William Rainey Harper, first president of the University of Chicago, the association exists "to promote religious and moral education." Though predominantly Protestant in the beginning, it now counts Eastern Orthodox, Jewish, and Catholic teachers for half its membership. It sponsors international conferences, supports the quarterly journal *Religious Education* and the newsletter *REACH*, and organizes workshops and special projects.

558. Society for Pentecostal Studies. P.O. Box 2671, Gaithersburg, MD 20886. 301/990-2060. 600 members.

This ecumenical society proposes to encourage and publicize the work of Pentecostal scholars, to study the relation of Pentecostal theology to other disciplines, and, from its academic viewpoint, to support the purposes of the World Pentecostal Fellowship. It convenes an annual meeting, and sponsors the journal *Pneuma* and the society's *Newsletter*, which contains extensive book notices.

559. United Society of Shakers. Sabbathday Lake, Poland Spring, ME 04274. 207/926-4597.

The society, quartered with one of two remaining Shaker communities, sponsors conferences and supports the publication of books, booklets, and *The Shaker Quarterly*, "a journal of scholarly investigation into Shaker art, architecture, biography, history, industries, music, literature and theology." The society also maintains a Shaker library and museum.

560. United States Catholic Historical Society. 3 Downing Drive, East Brunswick, NJ, 08816. 201/613-1051. FAX 201/613-9002. 1,200 members.

Organized in 1884, by preeminent American Catholic historians John Gilmary Shea and Charles Herbermann (see 21) among others, the society sponsors seminars and has an extensive publishing program, which has included the quarterly *U.S. Catholic Historian* a monograph series, and a Historical Records and Studies series. The society emphasizes the history of the Catholic Church in America.

III. Library Associations

561. American Theological Library Association. 820 Church Street, Third Floor, Evanston, IL 60201. 708/869-7788. 640 members.

Founded in 1947, this premier association for religion librarians of all persuasions has particularly strong publishing and book preservation programs. *Religion Index one* (see 470), *Religion Index Two* (see 471) with its cumulations, *Research in Ministry* (see 472), and *Index to Book Reviews in Religion* (see 463), as well as the online database *Religion Index* (see 476), which combines all of the above, are published by ATLA, as is a lengthy bibliographic series, many of the volumes of which are annotated in these pages. The association's preservation program currently offers on microfiche 14,000 books on religion published between 1850 and 1915; it has a 50-year goal of 250,000 titles. Other major purposes of ATLA are the professional growth of its members through annual conferences and continuing education; the improvement of theological libraries, especially through the development of standards; and the promotion of research and development projects.

562. Association of Christian Librarians. P.O. Box 4, Cedarville, OH 45314. 513/766-2211. 300 members.

Founded in 1957, the association, which grants full membership to evangelical librarians working in academic libraries, and associate membership to librarians in other types of libraries, proposes "to address the professional and spiritual needs of Christians committed to excellence in librarianship, to promote high standards of professionalism in the practice of librarianship, [and] to promote service to the academic library community worldwide." Toward this last purpose, it is developing a procedures manual for libraries in developing countries.

The association meets annually, and publishes *The Christian Librarian* quarterly as well as the *Christian Periodical Index* (see 458). Members must agree to a doctrinal statement.

563. **Association of Jewish Libraries.** c/o National Foundation for Jewish Culture, 330 Seventh Avenue, 21st floor, New York, NY 10001. 900 members.

The association was created in 1965 from the merger of the Jewish Librarians Association (1946), primarily concerned with academic collections, and the Jewish Library Association (1962), concerned with synagogue and community libraries. The two divisions of the current association continue to serve the needs of these libraries and their staffs. The association publishes the *AJL Newsletter* and *Judaica Librarianship*.

564. **Association of Seventh-day Adventist Librarians.** Union College Library, Lincoln, NE 68506. 402/486-2514. FAX 402/486-2678. 120 members.

The association serves "to enhance communications between Seventh-day Adventist librarians; to serve as a forum for the discussion of mutual professional concerns...; and to promote librarianship and library services to Seventh-day Adventist institutions." It holds an annual meeting and publishes *ASDAL Action*, a newsletter. Members publish the *Seventh-day Adventist Periodical Index.*

565. **Catholic Library Association.** 461 West Lancaster Avenue, Haverford, PA 19041. 215/649-5250. 2,500 members.

The goal of the association is "to promote the development and improvement of libraries, especially the development of religious-oriented libraries as centers of Christian thought." To this end, it sponsors sections on library education and on academic, children's, high school, and parish libraries, as well as on archives. It also supports round tables on cataloging and bibliographic instruction, and twenty-nine geographical chapters. Among its publications are *The Catholic Periodical and Literature Index* (see 457), the association journal, *Catholic Library World*, and a series of bibliographies and monographs on librarianship.

566. **Church and Synagogue Library Association.** P.O. Box 19357, Portland, OR 97219. 503/244-6919. 2,000 members.

Formed in 1967, the association assists individual members (many of whom are volunteers and not professional librarians) with guides, bibliographies, video rentals, individual assistance, and a promotional kit on how to set up a local library. The guides cover promotion, selecting materials, cataloging, standards, subjects, archives, bulletin boards, and the like. The association publishes a bimonthly bulletin.

567. **Council of Archives and Research Libraries in Jewish Studies.** c/o National Foundation for Jewish Culture, 330 Seventh Avenue, 21st Floor, New York, NY 10001. 212/960-5400. FAX 212/629-0508. 40 institutional members.

The council serves as an umbrella organization for the principal libraries of Judaica in the United States, including those of the Spertus College of Judaica, Hebrew Union College-Jewish Institute of Religion, YIVO Institute for Jewish Research (see 531), and the Leo Baeck Institute (see 528), as well as the Judaica divisions of such research libraries as the New York Public Library, the Library of Congress, and the National Library of Canada.

568.   **Evangelical Church Library Association.** P.O. Box 353, Glen Ellyn, IL 60138-0353. 708/668-0519. 450 members.

The association exists to provide professional help and advice to local members who lead church libraries, and to provide a forum for the staff of such libraries. It holds an annual meeting and publishes *Librarians World* each quarter. National and local officers must subscribe to a doctrinal statement.

Part II

The Reference Literature
on the Bibles of
Judaism and Christianity

11
Biblical Encyclopedias and Dictionaries

569.   Achtemeier, Paul J., general ed. **Harper's Bible Dictionary.** San Francisco, CA, Harper & Row, 1985. 1,178p. index. LC 85-42767. ISBN 0-06-069862-4.

Under the double aegis of Harper & Row and the Society of Biblical Literature (see 763), 179 scholars representing "the spectrum of religious thought within the Judeo-Christian heritage" (Preface) produced this substantial work to bring contemporary scholarship on biblical matters to the educated general reader. Articles cover persons and places mentioned at least three times in the Bible, or, if mentioned fewer times, are nevertheless important; all theological terms; every book in both testaments and the Apocrypha; all important words; the biblical languages; kinds of biblical literature; music and art; the geography of the Holy Land; and the social and economic structures and religious practices of the peoples of the biblical world. Major articles treat the Temple in Jerusalem, Moses, Jesus, Paul, manuscript texts and English translations of the Bible, and ancient Jewish and Christian writings not in the Bible. A special attention to archaeology results in articles on its history, methods, and results as well as notes on all major sites and recent finds at Ebla, Nag Hammadi, Nuzi, Mari, and Tell el-Amarna.

Keeping the general reader in mind, the writers avoid technical language, or define it when use is necessary. Cross-references appear at the end of many articles. Bibliographies appended to longer articles note scholarly English-language works dating through the mid-1980s. Illustrations in the form of black-and-white and color photographs and line drawings are frequent and well chosen in reflecting modern finds. The lists of abbreviations, useful for a wide range of reading on biblical topics, cover languages, the books of the Bible, the Apocrypha and Pseudepigrapha, early Christian and Rabbinic works, the Dead Sea Scrolls, Targums, Mishna, and the Nag Hammadi tractates. Even the endpapers are well wrought, containing in the front lists of the biblical books, as understood by Hebrew and Septuagint Jews and Protestant, Catholic, and Orthodox Christians, and in the back a time-line of the biblical period from 3000 BCE to 200 CE. Eighteen multicolor maps with their own index complete the work.

Although Jewish scholars have made contributions, this work tilts toward Christianity. Minor matters such as retention of the designations "B.C." and "A.D." aside—the editors note that they are conventions and not confessional statements—it is observable that more space is devoted to matters of Christian interest. The treatment of Greek, the language of the New Testament, is more thorough and detailed than that of Hebrew, for example. This work is meant to be a companion to the more recently published *Harper's Bible Commentary* (see 630); notwithstanding the above criticism, together these two works succeed beyond others in their goal of presenting the wealth of contemporary biblical scholarship to the lay reader.

570. Alexander, Pat, organizing ed. **The Lion Encyclopedia of the Bible**, new rev. ed. Batavia, IL, Lion Publishing, 1986. 352p. index. LC 86-7226. ISBN 0-7459-1113-7.

Alexander's work is reminiscent of the many Eerdmans handbooks and encyclopedias, and reflects a conservative Protestant outlook. It is divided into twelve parts, such as land; archaeology; history of the Bible as a written book; understanding the Bible; religion and worship in the Bible; key teachings; home and family life; people, work and society; places, nations, and peoples; and an atlas of biblical history. Those sections on people, places, and words are arranged alphabetically, while the others are organized by theme, with a single index to all the nonalphabetical sections. Visual emphasis is strong, with some five hundred color photographs and line drawings included.

571. Bauer, Johannes B., ed. **Encyclopedia of Biblical Theology: The Complete Sacramentum Verbi.** New York, Crossroad, 1981. 1,139p. indexes. LC 81-626. ISBN 0-8245-0042-3. Reprint of **Sacramentum Verbi.** New York, Herder and Herder, 1970. 3 vols.

Comparable to but much shorter than Kittel (see 589), this is the product of fifty-three European Roman Catholic scholars, many from Germany, including many who had worked as expert theologians supporting bishops taking part in Vatican II. The emphasis is on theological concepts; the editors leave out the historical, the biographical, and the archaeological. The words are defined in signed essays that run into several pages and have full bibliographies of works in the scholarly European languages. A supplementary bibliography lists works published between the third German edition (1967) and the first English one (1970). The editors have added a subject index, as well as indexes of biblical references and Hebrew and Greek words.

572. Blaiklock, Edward M., and R. K. Harrison, general eds. **The New International Dictionary of Biblical Archaeology.** Grand Rapids, MI, Zondervan, 1983. 485p. (Regency Reference Library). LC 82-13552. ISBN 0-310-21250-2.

Signed articles by twenty scholars cover principal sites and discoveries in the Holy Land. The reader can find the sites among the thirty-three maps, mostly in color. Black-and-white photographs are abundant, and the editors add striking color photographs as well. Selective bibliographies are appended to the articles.

573. Botterweck, G. Johannes, and Helmer Ringgren, eds. **Theological Dictionary of the Old Testament.** Grand Rapids, MI, William B. Eerdmans, 1974- . 5 vols. to date. LC 73-76170. ISBN 0-8028-2338-6.

A number of translators are bringing the volumes of the monumental *Theologisches Wörterbuch zum Alten Testament* into English almost as soon as they appear in German. Twelve volumes are projected for the set, and in many ways this is a companion to Kittel on the New Testament (see 589). The emphasis of each entry is on the Hebrew word, but attention is given to the Septuagint Greek, Qumran texts, and extrabiblical literature in the ancient Near East. The signed essays are learned, contain extensive bibliographic notes to periodical and monographic scholarly literature, and are structured according to the nature of each word. The nineteen pages on "abh" ("father") contain an etymology of the Hebrew, notes on *father* in the ancient Near East outside the Old Testament, and twelve pages on the Old Testament use of the term, including linguistic usage, explanation of the role of the father among the Hebrews, theological usage, and notes on God as father.

To date, without indexes, there is little hope for those who have no knowledge of Hebrew. Words are listed in and according to the Hebrew alphabet and are transliterated to the roman alphabet. All Hebrew references within the essays are in the roman alphabet, but translations come only in the course of the essays, making even browsing difficult.

574.   Bromiley, Geoffrey W., general ed. **The International Standard Bible Encyclopedia.** Grand Rapids, MI, Eerdmans, 1979-88. 4 vols. LC 79-12280. ISBN 0-8028-8160-2.

The importance of new developments in archaeology is stressed by the structure of the editorial staff for the latest edition of this encyclopedia: there is an editor for the Hebrew scriptures, an editor for the New Testament, and an editor for archaeology. Scrapping the original plan to keep much of the material from the 1915 and 1929 editions, these editors developed essentially a whole new encyclopedia, avowedly more scholarly and more conservative than its predecessors. Signed articles cover all personal and place names from the Bible as well as all words having theological or ethical meaning. The Apocrypha are covered as well as the canonical books. The predominance of biblical references are to the Revised Standard Version, although readings from the New English Bible and the Authorized Version are sometimes included. The format for each entry includes the word, its pronunciation, the word in its original language (transliterated to the roman alphabet), variant renderings, biblical references, and definition. Major articles are preceded by outlines. Cross-references link related terms. Bibliographies have been appended to articles, but they are not as abundant as those in the *Interpreter's Dictionary of the Bible* (see 576), with which this set is comparable. It is of course more up-to-date than the *IDB*, and generally more conservative in outlook. Photographs and drawings are plentiful, with 275 in the first volume alone, and a section of color photographs in each volume takes full advantage of contemporary high-quality printing techniques. Stressing the dictionary format, as does the *IDB*, the editors have eliminated the indexes present in earlier volumes.

575.   Brown, Colin, general ed. **The New International Dictionary of New Testament Theology.** Grand Rapids, MI, Zondervan, 1975-78. 3 vols. indexes. LC 75-38895. ISBN 0-310-21928-0.

This work is based on the German *Theologisches Begriffslexikon zum Neuen Testament*, but Brown has added seventy major articles, enlarged the glossary of technical terms, and built extensive new bibliographies for each entry. Each bibliography is composed of two parts, one of English-language books and articles and one of foreign-language materials, predominantly in German. The scope is theological; historical, geographical, and archaeological words are included only when they have theological meaning. The emphasis is on words, not on broad concepts such as Paul's theology. The words are arranged alphabetically in English. Each article includes one or more Greek words of which the English is the translation, and each Greek word is studied in three parts: its classical (nonbiblical) use, its Old Testament use (in the Greek Septuagint translation of the Hebrew Scriptures), and its New Testament use. The third volume contains cumulative indexes of all three volumes, covering Hebrew and Aramaic words, Greek words, and theological subjects. This last volume also contains ten excellent survey articles, such as that by Brown accompanying the listing for "Resurrection" entitled "The Resurrection in Contemporary Theology."

576.   Buttrick, George Arthur, ed. **The Interpreter's Dictionary of the Bible: An Illustrated Encyclopedia Identifying and Explaining All Proper Names and Significant Terms and Subjects in the Holy Scriptures, Including the Apocrypha, with Attention to Archaeological Discoveries and Researches in the Life and Faith of Ancient Times.** New York and Nashville, TN, Abingdon Press, 1962. 4 vols. LC 62-9387.

> 576.1.   Crim, Keith, general ed. **The Interpreter's Dictionary of the Bible: An Illustrated Encyclopedia.... Supplementary Volume.** Nashville, TN, Abingdon Press, 1976. 998p. LC 62-9387. ISBN 0-687-19269-2.

Meant to be a companion to *The Interpreter's Bible* (see 636), the original four-volume set is the distillation of the best post-World War II biblical scholarship, taking account especially of the newly discovered treasure hoards of papyri and extensive archaeological work done since the publication of Hastings' great work at the turn of the century (see 586). Achieving its goal of wide distribution in public, academic, school, church, and personal libraries, the dictionary has an intended readership ranging from scholar to pastor to student to layperson. The 253 contributors include leading Protesant and Jewish (but not Catholic) scholars from fifteen countries. The subtitle is not often listed in bibliographies, but accurately states – even understates – the scope. All proper names in both the Hebrew and Christian scriptures are entered, in signed articles, as are all words having special biblical meaning. Making the work encyclopedic are studies of the Bible's literary environment, history, and archaeological sources, as well as studies of methods of transmission and schools of interpretation through the ages. Each entry includes biblical language (in the Hebrew or Greek alphabet), variants in the King James and Revised Standard versions, multiple full definitions, and biblical quotations. Abundant cross-references link related articles. Bibliographies with citations to major books and articles in the modern scholarly languages complete most entries. Black-and-white photographs, drawings, and maps are frequent. A collection of color photographs is found in each volume, and twenty-four clear, color maps are appended to the first volume.

The 1976 supplement turns the work into a five-volume set, updates articles in the earlier work, adds entries on new aspects of biblical theology and new archaeological finds, and looks afresh, through a deepened consciousness of social history, at some topics. There are eight new pages of color photographs, abundant black-and-white photographs, sketches, and maps, and new bibliographic material. Cross-references to articles within the supplement and within the original set are frequent, and articles that are updates are cross-referred to the entry in the original dictionary (recent printings of the earlier four-volume work contain references to this supplement). Crim notes that Roman Catholic scholars, as well as Protestant and Jewish, contributed to the supplement.

The original edition, with this supplement, is comparable in scope and purpose to the *International Standard Bible Encyclopedia* (see 574).

577.   Cheyne, Thomas Kelly, and J. Sutherland Black. **Encyclopaedia Biblica: A Critical Dictionary of the Literary, Political, and Religious History, the Archaeology, Geography, and Natural History of the Bible.** New York, Macmillan, 1899-1903. 4 vols. Single-volume edition, 1914. 5,444 columns. LC 02-705.

In gathering the considerable fruits of serious late nineteenth-century biblical studies, Cheyne and Black describe new developments as "advanced" and "progressive," especially in the areas of archaeology and literary criticism. They were spurred by their mentor William Robertson Smith, who wrote the biblical articles for the *Encyclopaedia Britannica*, and who brought in as contributors the chief German biblical scholars of the day. Smith and the editors did not conceive of the work as a miscellaneous collection, but rather a comprehensive survey of the whole Bible, with articles linked by many cross-references.

578.   Cornfeld, Gaalyahu, ed. **Pictorial Biblical Encyclopedia: A Visual Guide to the Old and New Testaments.** Tel Aviv, Israel, Hamikra Baolam, and New York, Macmillan, 1964. 720p. index. LC 65-12852.

Cornfeld offers the general reader developments in biblical scholarship that have taken place since the First World War. Throughout the work, which contains major articles on ancient cities, the religion and culture of Canaan, Assyria, Babylonia, early Christianity, the Dead Sea Scrolls, Egypt, and aspects of Israelite culture and history, the contributions of prominent biblical scholars are given notice. There are, however, no bibliographic references, and the articles are not signed. Maps are included, as well as over eight hundred black-and-white pictures from archaeological institutes and private collections. Cornfeld has added an index to subjects, biblical names, and some of the references to scholars.

579.   Corswant, Willy. **A Dictionary of Life in Bible Times.** Completed and illustrated by Edouard Urech. Translated by Arthur Heathcote. New York, Oxford University Press, 1960. 308p. LC 60-4719.

Corswant and Urech have arranged their material in the alphabetical format of a dictionary, but they have also provided a classification scheme, thus allowing the work to be used as a handbook, and breaking the material up under three headings: secular life, religious life, and animals, plants, and minerals. They include "the outward and visible aspects of the personal, social, and religious life of the Israelites and early Christians" (Preface) as well as the flora, fauna, and minerals. References to the Bible are added to the end of each article. Where newer works have photographs, Urech has provided line drawings, often more useful than the former in that they highlight what is being discussed. A listing of contents by article title is superfluous.

580.   Douglas, James Dixon, organizing ed., and Norm Hillyer, revision ed. **New Bible Dictionary.** Wheaton, IL, Tyndale House, 1982. 1,326p. index. (International Christian Handbooks). LC 81-86052. ISBN 0-8423-4667-8.

580.1.   Hillyer, Norm et al. eds. **The Illustrated Bible Dictionary.** Wheaton, IL, Tyndale House, 1980. 3 vols. index. LC 79-92540. ISBN 0-8423-7575-2.

A product of more than 160 evangelical scholars, mostly from the British Isles, the useful *New Bible Dictionary* work has undergone various revisions for two decades. Hillyer stresses that the present edition takes account of new archaeological discoveries. It has over two hundred black-and-white maps and diagrams taken from *The Illustrated Bible Dictionary*. A full index covers the maps and diagrams as well as the text. All articles are initialed by their writers, and longer articles are followed by short, up-to-date bibliographies that list works from a variety of scholarly traditions. There is no index of scripture references—it would have had to be massive. This work is often cited by others as one of the better single-volume biblical dictionaries.

The *Illustrated Bible Dictionary* has the same text as the *New Bible Dictionary*, but contains copious illustrations, including color and black-and-white photographs, time lines, genealogies, maps, and reconstructions of buildings. Pictures illustrate plants, artifacts, birds, insects, jewelry, stelle, manuscripts, and architecture. There is a particular focus on illustrating recent archaeological discoveries.

581. Douglas, James Dixon, revising ed., and Merrill C. Tenney, general ed. **The New International Dictionary of the Bible, Pictorial Edition.** Grand Rapids, MI, Zondervan, 1987. 1,162p. indexes. LC 87-2220. ISBN 0-310-33190-0.

With an emphasis on the persons, places, and books of the Bible, this work is the product of sixty-five conservative scholars, most from North America. Seventeen color maps are appended, and there are frequent black-and-white photographs and line drawings as well as sixteen pages of color photographs. The photography in general does not capture the spirit of the Holy Land in the same manner as the better biblical atlases or handbooks. There is a map index and a sixty-five page scripture index, a device lacking in Douglas's *New Bible Dictionary* (see 580).

582. Gehman, Henry Snyder, ed. **The New Westminster Dictionary of the Bible.** Philadelphia, PA, Westminster Press, 1970. 1,027p. index. LC 69-10000. ISBN 0-664-21277-8.

Gehman updated *The Davis Bible Dictionary* to create the 1944 edition of *The Westminster Dictionary of the Bible.* This current work is completely redone rather than updated, and takes account of the widespread developments in the biblical sciences since the Second World War. With detailed articles, many of them quite lengthy, it is largely the work of Gehman. No list of contributors is given, and the articles are unsigned. Gehman is a Hebraist and, although the Christian view is dominant throughout, materials on the Hebrew Scriptures predominate. The black-and-white photographs that accompany many articles seem inadequate when compared to the resplendent color of recent bible dictionaries. Sixteen small color maps with an index were appended by the scholars who published *The Westminster Historical Atlas to the Bible* (see 670).

583. Gentz, William H., general ed. **The Dictionary of Bible and Religion.** Nashville, TN, Abingdon Press, 1986. 1,147p. LC 85-15011. ISBN 0-687-10757-1.

Gentz has produced for the general reader an "expanded Bible dictionary" to include the history of Christianity, Christian doctrine, and materials relating to other major world religions and new religions. The result is of mixed value. What one finds here among the 2,800 entries is excellent; whether one expects to find it or would look here first is another matter. An extreme example is an entry on Dwight D. Eisenhower, wherein mention of his father's Mennonite background is the only religious point made. Article length does not always reflect the importance of the subject: Hans Kung, the Catholic scholar, is treated to a relatively lengthy biography, while Native American religion merits only two paragraphs. Nevertheless, the sketches of modern biblical scholars and modern theological movements are especially good and not always available elsewhere. Extended overview articles on such topics as bible translations and biblical criticism are also excellent. Cross-references are extensive. Gentz makes an effort to be ecumenical—that is, he enlists contributors from several branches of Protestantism and includes at least one Catholic and one Jew—and he attempts a balance between liberal and conservative viewpoints.

584. Harris, R. Laird, Gleason L. Archer, and Bruce K. Waltke, eds. **Theological Wordbook of the Old Testament.** Chicago, IL, Moody Press, 1980. 2 vols. index. LC 80-28047r842. ISBN 0-8024-8631-2.

Forty-six evangelical scholars collaborated to produce this wordbook. Since the general reader and pastor constitute its intended readership, it is less exhaustive than Botterweck's *Theological Dictionary of the Old Testament* (see 573). Names of biblical characters and places, for example, are not included unless they have theological import, such as Abraham and Jerusalem. Words are studied "from biblical usage, etymological background, comparision with cognate languages, translations in the ancient versions, synonyms, antonyms, and theological significance" (Introduction). The bibliographies have many entries. The arrangement of entries is by the consonants of the Hebrew alphabet. Words with the same roots are treated together; nouns with prefixes are therefore treated out of alphabetical order, but are cross-referenced from the alphabetical position.

585. Hartman, Louis F. **Encyclopedic Dictionary of the Bible.** New York, McGraw-Hill, 1963. 2,634 columns. LC 63-9699.

Hartman has adapted rather than just translated A. van den Born's *Bijbels Woordenboek* (2d edition: The Netherlands, Roermond, 1954-57), with the result that this edition reflects both the American and Dutch Roman Catholic state of biblical scholarship in the 1960s. It is noteworthy that, while this American edition was being published, Vatican II was taking place, and the influence of liberal Dutch theologians on that council was considerable. The writers offer detailed information on biblical persons, places, flora and fauna, societies, and culture. Some black-and-white photographs and line drawings are found throughout the work, but not as abundantly as in the earlier Steinmueller (see 596) or as in Gehman (see 582). The scholarship is solid; the articles are initialed by the Dutch writer and often, where extensive revision has been done, by the American translator/writer. Biblical references are very abundant; longer articles have sometimes-lengthy bibliographies of English-language and continental sources. Cross-references are seldom used.

586. Hastings, James, ed. **A Dictionary of the Bible Dealing with Its Language, Literature, and Contents Including the Biblical Theology.** Edinburgh, Scotland, T. & T. Clarke, and New York, Scribner's, 1898-1902. 4 vols. LC 99-1974.

586.1. Hastings, James, ed. **A Dictionary of the Bible ... Extra Volume: Containing Articles, Indexes, and Maps.** New York, Scribner's, 1919. 936p. indexes.

586.2. Hastings, James, and John A. Selbie. **Dictionary of the Bible.** New York, Scribner's, 1929.

586.3. Hastings, James, ed. **Dictionary of the Bible,** rev. ed. Edited by Frederick C. Grant and H. H. Rowley. New York, Scribner's, 1963. 1,059p. index. LC 62-21697.

Hastings here captures the best in late nineteenth-century biblical scholarship, reflecting decades of valuable work in Britain and America and on the continent. He covers "all persons and places, the antiquities and archaeology of the Bible, ...its ethnology, geology, and natural history, ...biblical theology and ethics, and even ... the obsolete or archaic words occurring in the English Versions" (Preface). Articles are signed, except when very brief, and were each reviewed by three scholars as well as the editors. The Hebrew or Greek words (not transliterated to the roman alphabet) are given for all proper and many common names. Fourteen maps accompany the articles, as do color illustrations. Bibliographies, now very much dated, are appended to longer articles. Biblical quotations are taken from the Authorized Version and the Revised English Version. The fifth volume, published after World War I, contains thirty-seven new articles on such extra-biblical matters as the discovery of Hammurabi's Code, as well as additional biblical topics. Six indexes to the whole five-volume set cover authors, subjects, scripture texts, Hebrew and Greek words, illustrations, and maps. The four maps in this fifth volume reflect the knowledge of the Middle East gained by British expeditions.

The 1929 single-volume dictionary is based on the subjects listed in the index of the five-volume set, but here all signed and most unsigned articles of the larger set are written afresh by different authors, with new materials reflecting the scholarship of the 1920s. Intended for the general reader, this volume eschews Hebrew and Greek words except in transliteration. The 1963 dictionary edited by Grant and Rowley proves the lasting popularity of Hastings, and is perhaps the last revision possible without a wholly new reworking of the material. While leaving some articles untouched, the editors incorporated materials from the study of biblical languages and archaeological finds in particular. References are now to the Revised Standard Version. Eleven maps, originally published by Thomas Nelson in *Peake's Commentary* (see 622) are also included.

587.   Huey, F. B., Jr., and Bruce Corley. **A Student's Dictionary for Biblical and Theological Studies.** Grand Rapids, MI, Academie Books (Zondervan), 1983. 208p. LC 83-16701. ISBN 0-310-45951-6.

The compilers define some fourteen hundred grammatical terms and literary devices, for the student "who tackles the Hebrew and Greek texts" of the Bible; add a biblical reference for each definition; include many cross-references to link related terms; and append a four-page bibliography of useful reference works. Words more properly found in the many theological and biblical dictionaries are excluded. This unique and handy paperback is an excellent value for the theological student and practicing religious professional who first comes across (or has forgotten) such words as *paraenesis, dysteleology, colometry,* and *formal correspondence.*

588.   Inglis, James. **A Topical Dictionary of Bible Texts.** Grand Rapids, MI, Baker Book House, 1985. 524p. index. LC 70-3371. ISBN 0-8010-5038-3.

The original title of this reprint is *The Bible Text Cyclopedia*, published by Fleming H. Revell in 1859. It is a combination dictionary and concordance, with all persons of note and historical events defined and given a multitude of references in the Bible. The editor notes that its strength is its references to passages where the meaning is found though the exact word in question is not.

589.   Kittel, Gerhard, and Gerhard Friedrich, eds. **Theological Dictionary of the New Testament.** Translated and edited by Geoffrey W. Bromiley. Index volume compiled by Ronald E. Pitkin. Grand Rapids, MI, Eerdmans, 1964-76. 10 vols. LC 64-15136. ISBN 0-8028-2404-8.

Translated from the German *Theologisches Wörterbuch zum Neuen Testament*, and referred to simply as "Kittel" or "TDNT," this massive dictionary offers an extended etymological and theological definition of every word of religious significance in the New Testament, including proper names from the Hebrew Scriptures and prepositions of theological importance. Kittel began the work in 1928, with the plan that fifteen scholars could finish it in three years. It was actually completed in 45 years by 105 contributors, 50 of whom, including Kittel, died during the process. Among those contributors are some of the greatest German biblical scholars of the twentieth century.

The reader should have a rudimentary knowledge of Greek, although, with the use of the index volume, those lacking Greek can make useful headway. Entries are listed by the Greek alphabet; words, phrases, and more extensive quotations are neither transliterated to the roman alphabet nor translated to English.

The essays on each word are extensive, sometimes running to several pages. Organization is clear, and varies according to the nature of each entry. That for "agathos" ("good") has four sections: agathos in Greek philosophy, in Hellenism, in the Old Testament and Judaism, and in the New Testament. References to periodical and monographic scholarly literature are extensive; the first volume contains a twenty-four page list of abbreviations of the scholarly support material.

The organization of the whole set is uniform, but the nature and content of the essays changed over the course of time. Friedrich took over editorship with volume five (Kittel on his deathbed thus charged him), and notes in his preface to the last volume that in later essays etymological discussion is reduced, more account is taken of the differences in the literature in the New Testament, closer attention is paid to the contexts of words, and discussion of gnosticism plays a bigger role.

The final volume contains indexes by English key words, by Greek key words, by Hebrew and Aramaic key words, and by biblical references. It also contains a splendid fifty-page essay by Friedrich on the prehistory of the *TDNT* going back to the Reformation.

What the *TDNT* does for the New Testament, Botterweck (see 573), not yet complete, accomplishes for the Hebrew scriptures.

590. Leon-Dufour, Xavier, ed. **Dictionary of Biblical Theology**, 2d ed. Revised and enlarged. Translated by P. Joseph Cahill. New York, Seabury Press, 1973. 712p. indexes. LC 73-6437. ISBN 0-8164-1146-8.

As Bauer's *Sacramentum Verbi* (see 571) is a product of postwar German Catholic scholarship, so this work is the reflection of the recent French school, and many of its contributors were, like Bauer's, influential theologians during Vatican II. The Catholic foundations of the dictionary are clearly stated in a cerebral introductory essay by Leon-Dufour on biblical theology and the place of a dictionary in it. The emphasis of the extensive essays is not on semantic analysis, but on the doctrinal expression of themes through a variety of words. The seventy collaborators worked more closely with each other than is common, reading and altering each other's drafts with the end of creating a communal work. Indeed, many of the essays have two signatures. The editor holds down the number of biblical references, for which he refers the reader to the many concordances available; he also excludes bibliographic references. However, cross-references at the end of each article are numerous, and an analytic table at the end of the work lists article titles and many subjects cross-referenced in the work. The revised edition contains forty new articles and even fuller cross-references than its predecessor.

591. Leon-Dufour, Xavier. **Dictionary of the New Testament.** Translated by Terence Prendergast. San Francisco, CA, Harper & Row, 1980. 458p. index. LC 79-3004. ISBN 0-06-062100-1.

Leon-Dufour is a leading French Catholic scripture scholar, who earlier produced the *Dictionary of Biblical Theology* (see 590). This work, based on the second French edition of 1978, offers a unique two-part structure: the dictionary proper, including more than 1,000 of the 5,500 separate words in the New Testament, is preceded by a 58-page introduction packed with information on the cultural milieu out of which the Christian scriptures sprang. The purposes of this introduction are to give the modern reader the "mental furniture" of the period and to gather together the content of separate dictionary entries. There are many cross-references from the introduction to the word entries and from the words to the introduction. The dictionary lists all words which require historical, geographic, archaeological, literary, or theological explanation, and includes basic critical concepts and some modern terms. Each entry consists of a definition and references, often to the Hebrew scriptures as well as to the New Testament. Leon-Dufour appends an index of Greek words (written in the roman alphabet), each of which is translated into an English word that is entered in the dictionary. He also includes fourteen charts, tables, and timelines. This work is singularly successful in bringing the fruits of high scholarship to the educated reader.

592. McKenzie, John L. **Dictionary of the Bible**. Milwaukee, WI, Bruce, 1965. 954p. LC 65-26691.

McKenzie, a first-rank Roman Catholic biblical scholar, single-handedly produced, over an eight-year period, this now-dated dictionary, which reflects a new Roman Catholic appreciation for the scientific study of the Bible. It is meant for the educated reader. While no single scholar can capture the totality of current biblical studies, McKenzie succeeds in offering thousands of learned articles on persons, places, events, literary devices, and themes in both testaments. The scope is for the most part limited to the Bible itself, with no attention to transmission and translation of the scriptures, or to the history of the communities which revered the Bible. McKenzie does, however, include articles on the Trinity, explaining briefly the development of its post-biblical theology, and he covers the discovery of the Qumran scrolls. No bibliographical references appear with the articles; instead, McKenzie provides a four-page bibliography of scholarly resources at the beginning. Black-and-white photographs are plentiful, and McKenzie adds fifteen color maps of the biblical lands at various stages of their history. There is, however, no gazetteer or index for the maps.

593. Myers, Albert C., ed. **The Eerdmans Bible Dictionary**. Grand Rapids, MI, Eerdmans, 1987. 1,094p. LC 87-13239. ISBN 0-8028-2402-1.

Based on the *Bijbelse Encyclopedie* edited by W. H. Gispen (Kampen, The Netherlands, J. H. Kok, 1975), this American edition revised and expanded major articles, especially to take account of recent archaeological discoveries. Although its focus is primarily evangelical, it reflects the varied viewpoints of a wide range of Protestant writers as well as Catholic, and Jewish scholars. There is a major entry for each book of the Bible, including the apocryphal and deuterocanonical, as well as for literary genres, geographical regions, and civilizations. The five thousand entries cover all persons and places and many animals, plants, and objects named in the Bible. Also covered are biblical theology, the text and transmission, the early church, and extrabiblical writings. Words in Hebrew, Greek, and other ancient languages are transliterated to the roman alphabet. Pronunciation is added. Black-and-white photographs, charts, and line drawings are frequent, and there is a twelve-page color map section produced by Hammond. Cross-references link smaller entries to larger. Bibliographies, appended to important articles, are current through 1986, and reflect ecumenical scholarship. The Revised Standard Version is the text of preference, though attention is paid to alternative renderings in the King James Version, New International Version, and the Jerusalem Bible.

594. Pfeiffer, Charles F., ed. **The Biblical World: A Dictionary of Biblical Archaeology**. New York, Bonanza Books, 1966. 640p. index. LC 66-19312. ISBN 0-5171-1922-6.

Building on initial work in the nineteenth century, archaeology has become one of the great methods for understanding the Bible in the twentieth. This dictionary focuses on the immense amount of information uncovered—literally—by this science and the places where the information was found. Persons and places are mentioned only when they have archaeological significance. Some forty-four experts contributed to the work, but the articles remain unsigned. They range in length from a few paragraphs to a few pages, and the longer have bibliographies of journal articles and books, most often in English. Black-and-white photographs illustrate finds and vistas, but there are no maps locating ancient cities and modern digs. Blaiklock's work (see 572) has more recent information, but Pfeiffer's remains quite useful.

595. Richards, Lawrence O. **Expository Dictionary of Bible Words.** Grand Rapids, MI, Zondervan, 1985. 720p. indexes. LC 85-3330. ISBN 0-310-39000-1.

In covering significant concepts expressed in the English Bible, Richards provides a work for the general reader similar to what Kittel (see 589) and Brown (see 575) have produced for the advanced student and scholar. The words listed are often abstract. There are few entries for the names of persons of places; even "Jesus" and "Christ" have remarkably short notes, and there are no entries for Moses, Isaiah, or John. Definitions are twofold, giving first the Hebrew or Greek meaning of the word in biblical times and second the manner in which the word develops a biblical concept. Conservative in tone, there is no attempt at new scholarship, and bibliographic references are wholly absent. Quotations are usually taken from the New International Version. Cross-references link related terms, and four indexes greatly expand the usability: Hebrew words, transliterated to the roman alphabet; Greek words, also transliterated; subjects; and scripture references.

596. Steinmueller, John E., and Kathryn Sullivan. **Catholic Biblical Encyclopedia.** New York, Joseph F. Wagner, 1956. 2 vols. in one. 1,845p. LC 50-4611.

Modern, critical biblical studies, long a staple in Protestant centers of learning, received impetus in the Catholic community from the publication by Pope Pius XII of the encyclical letter *Divino afflante spiritu* in 1943. Steinmueller and Sullivan produced the first modern biblical dictionary in the English language emanating from the Catholic tradition. With 4,600 articles on the Hebrew Scriptures, and 1,700 on the New Testament, they cover biographical, geographical, archaeological, and dogmatic matters relating to the scriptures. Largely the work of these two scholars, the articles are not signed. The two eschew bibliographies for reasons of space, and refer the reader to other works for references. Black-and-white photographs, many taken by Steinmueller, are frequent. This attempt to provide the educated nonspecialist reader with a biblical resource reflecting high scholarship is a clear foreshadowing of the creative mentality associated with Vatican II.

597. Vine, William Edwyn. **An Expository Dictionary of Old Testament Words.** Edited by F. F. Bruce. Old Tappan, NJ, Fleming H. Revell, 1978. 176p. LC 78-7564. ISBN 0-8007-0930-6.

Vine died in 1949, leaving this manuscript work, much smaller than his New Testament study (see 598). Taking words from the King James Version, he gives the Hebrew from which the English is translated, and follows with an explanation on how the word is used in biblical passages. The publisher added an eight-page bibliography on linguistic tools for Old Testament study and a long essay on "How, When, and By Whom the Bible Was Written."

598. Vine, William Edwyn, Merrill F. Unger, and William White, Jr. **An Expository Dictionary of Biblical Words.** Nashville, TN, Thomas Nelson, 1985. 319p. and 755p. indexes. LC 84-3359. ISBN 0-8407-5387-X.

598.1. Vine, William Edwyn. **The Expanded Vine's Expository Dictionary of New Testament Words.** Edited by John R. Kohlenberger III with James A. Swanson. Minneapolis, MN, Bethany House, 1984. 1,349p. LC 84-21591. ISBN 0-87123-619-2.

598.2. Unger, Merrill F., and William White, Jr., eds. **Nelson's Expository Dictionary of the Old Testament.** Nashville, TN, Thomas Nelson, 1980. 509p. indexes. LC 80-24092. ISBN 0-8047-5179-6.

The Vine, Unger, and White dictionary joins two separate works between its covers: *An Expository Dictionary of New Testament Words*, edited by Vine, and *Nelson's Expository Dictionary of Old Testament Words*, edited by Unger and White. What both have in common is that "the most significant biblical words are illustrated by Scripture passages, comments, cross-references, ancient and modern meanings, precise etymologies, historical notes, and clearly defined technical information" (Publisher's Preface). Both provide an in-depth study of biblical word usages for the serious reader who lacks a command of Hebrew or Greek.

White opens the Old Testament section (319 pages) with an extensive introduction detailing the history and characteristics of the Hebrew language. Each English word is followed by the Hebrew of which it is a translation, with the Hebrew rendered in both the roman and Hebrew alphabets. Following a thorough definition, principal uses in the Old Testament are cited. Unger and White provide an index of the English words, and a Hebrew word index that refers the searcher to the Hebrew section of Strong (see 727) and Brown, Driver, and Briggs (*Hebrew and English Lexicon of the Old Testament*, Oxford, England, Clarendon Press, 1978, 1907) as well as to their own treatment.

Vine's New Testament dictionary (755 pages) is similarly arranged: each English word is followed by its Greek equivalent, written in both roman and Greek alphabets. The definition and a list of principal (and often all) uses in the New Testament follow. The publishers add an index of the original Greek words (romanized) with citations to *The New Strong's* (see 727).

Vine's work, first published in 1939, has been reprinted by a variety of publishers. Kohlenberger and Swanson correct errors and omissions and add cross-references to Strong (see 727), to Brown, Driver and Briggs, and to Arndt and Gingrich's *Greek-English Lexicon of the New Testament and Other Early Christian Literature* (Chicago, IL, University of Chicago Press, 1979).

599. Watson, Francis. **A Guide to the New Testament.** Totowa, NJ, Barnes & Noble, 1987. 198p. index. LC 87-14531. ISBN 0-389-20767-5.

Informed in historical-critical scholarship, and contemporary in outlook, Watson has produced a short, readable guide to the New Testament. He has kept the number of entries limited so they can be treated at greater length, and indeed they range from fulsome paragraphs ("Demons," "Decapolis") to several pages ("Romans, Paul's Letter to"). Prominent persons, places, events, ideas, and each New Testament book merit entries. Sixteen pages of topics are listed, with cross-references, at the end of the work. Watson does not include bibliographic references; he does add a map of Palestine and a brief chronological table.

600. Wigoder, Geoffrey, general ed. **Illustrated Dictionary & Concordance of the Bible.** New York, Macmillan, 1986. 1,070p. LC 86-16318. ISBN 0-02-916380-3.

Under Wigoder's direction, a team of international scholars, many of them Jewish, but some from the highest ranks of Catholic and Protestant scholarship, produced this dictionary, first published in Israel. Like similar comprehensive dictionaries, every person and place mentioned in both testaments is entered. Also like other contemporary works, special attention is given to reporting new information from recent archaeological work. Striking color photography is abundant. A general article on plants includes seventy-nine photographs of various species, truly informative to the reader who has never seen hyssop or saffron. Maps are frequent but uneven in quality; that locating Bythynia is clear, that on

Cappadocia is confusing in the extreme. In spite of the weighty credentials of the contributors, the articles are not signed. The "concordance" of the title is not comprehensive, but rather is a series of biblical references printed in the margins for almost every article. An additional six pages of references arranged by subject form an appendix. There are no bibliographic materials beyond these Bible references. The combination of color photography, solid information, and lack of bibliographic information indicate that this text will find its best use on family bookshelves.

12
Biblical Handbooks

601.   Alexander, David, and Pat Alexander, eds. **Eerdmans' Handbook to the Bible.** Grand Rapids, MI, Eerdmans, 1973. 680p. indexes. LC 73-7638. ISBN 0-8028-3436-1.

Meant for the general reader, this handbook packs in a good deal of information, but skirts the findings of modern scholarship. For example, the editors take a negative view of a two- or three-author theory for the Book of Isaiah. The handbook's four parts consist of an introduction on the times of the Old and New testaments and on the English Bible; two parts consisting of book-by-book commentaries on the Old and New testaments; and a catch-all section with key themes, a who's who, a gazetteer of places, and an index. Color and black-and-white photographs are plentiful; there are maps, but no bibliographic references.

602.   Alter, Robert, and Frank Kermode. **The Literary Guide to the Bible.** Cambridge, MA, Harvard University Press, 1987. LC 86-32172. ISBN 0-674-87530-3.

For the general, well-educated reader, Alter and Kermode offer an alternative to technical biblical criticism: analysis of the books of the Bible as literary creations. After a general introduction and introductions to each of the testaments, they collect the work of an international and ecumenical group of literary scholars, mostly from secular universities, who present essays on every major book and groupings of smaller books ("The Twelve Prophets," "The Pauline Epistles"). Seven additional essays cover special topics such as the characteristics of Hebrew poetry, the English translations of the Bible, and relating biblical writing to other ancient literatures. No single critical method is espoused, but some, such as Marxist and psychoanalytic, are excluded. The tone is conservative: the phrase "Old Testament" is used, and the King James Version is preferred for its literary quality. Under the editorship of two established literary critics, this handbook gathers some of the best thinking from the movement in modern universities to teach the Bible as literature.

603.   Bailey, Lloyd R., ed. **The Word of God: A Guide to English Versions of the Bible.** Atlanta, GA, John Knox Press, 1982. 228p. index. LC 81-85335. ISBN 0-8042-0079-3.

Eleven established biblical scholars offer evaluations and historical introductions to the Revised Standard Version, the New English Bible, the New Jewish Version, the New American Standard Version, the Jerusalem Bible, Today's English Version (The Good News Bible), the Living Bible, the New International Version, and several study Bibles. A brief historical evaluation of the King James Version follows in an appendix. Bailey also offers a set of tables noting the available editions of the translations, their clarity, and their accuracy as measured by a comparison of their treatment of a single but very theologically important verse, Isaiah 7:14. A briefly annotated, seven-page bibliography includes citations to reviews of each translation and general articles on biblical translation into English. Bailey's work treats fewer translations than that published a year later by Kubo and Specht (see 612), but each translation is treated in more depth. Kubo and Specht often take a different tack in their evaluations, and offer more bibliographic information. Bailey alone adds an index to his work.

604. **The Bible Companion.** Nashville, TN, Abingdon Press, 1985. 493p. LC 85-1215. ISBN 0-687-03148-6.

The editors, anonymous except for a preface written by one William Barclay, produce here for the general reader a broad base of information divided into four general areas: an introduction to ancient books and the making of the Old and New Testaments; a 1,300-entry dictionary of persons, places, events, birds, plants, and animals found in the Bible; a concordance, based on the New International Version, to 4,600 topics; and helps for Bible study, including a chronology of events, lists of measures and money, the Hebrew calendar, and a program for reading. Decided weaknesses are the lack of a bibliography and an index. A note acknowledges the borrowing from *The Interpreter's Dictionary of the Bible* (see 576).

605. Blair, Edward P. **Abingdon Bible Handbook.** Nashville, TN, Abingdon Press, 1975. 511p. index. LC 75-6774. ISBN 0-687-00169-2.

This handbook combines scholarship and devotional material for the general reader. The first part is introductory, reviewing names and major characteristics of the Bible, the various canonical lists of books, and translations into English. The second part offers a historical background for each book in the Bible, including an outline of the contents, discussion of authorship, and a review of the basic scholarly discussions of the book. A last section treats basic teachings to be drawn from the Bible. Reflecting the evangelical Protestant tradition, this work does include liberal Protestant and Roman Catholic scholarship in the bibliographies spread throughout. One wishes for lengthier treatment of scholarly discussions and more extensive bibliographies.

606. **Cambridge History of the Bible.** Cambridge, England, Cambridge University Press, 1963-70. 3 vols. indexes. LC 63-24435. Vol. 1: **From the Beginning to Jerome.** Edited by P. R. Ackroyd. ISBN 0-521-07418-5. Vol. 2: **The West from the Fathers to the Reformation.** Edited by G. W. H. Lampe. ISBN 0-521-04255-0. Vol. 3: **The West from the Reformation to the Present Day.** Edited by S. L. Greenslade.

There is a slant in these fine volumes toward the transmission of the Bible in the western world. Nevertheless, so much information can be accessed from the bibliographies, and by the indexes from the essays, written by leading British and continental scholars, that they are often placed in reference collections. The first volume covers language and scripture, books in the ancient world, the Old Testament, the New Testament, and the Bible in early Christianity. The second treats texts and versions of both testaments, early Christian book production, Jerome's contributions, medieval exegesis and exposition, medieval illustration, and the coming of vernacular translations. The last volume covers the Bible in the Reformation, modern English versions, modern continental versions, the rise of scientific biblical scholarship, modern missionary use of the Bible, and the printing of the Bible. As is often the case with British productions, high scholarship is combined with eminent readability.

607. Eissfeldt, Otto. **The Old Testament: An Introduction Including the Apocrypha and Pseudepigrapha, and Also the Works of Similar Type from Qumran.** Translated by Peter R. Ackroyd. New York, Harper & Row, 1965. 861p. indexes. LC 65-15399.

The genre of introductions to the Bible or its parts is ancient, and works of this sort are generally not put in reference collections. However, Eissfeldt is widely cited as a basic resource, offers many concise explanations of much that has been worked out by scholarly endeavor in the past hundred years, and lists many bibliographic references; thus, it does well for even a small library to have a copy in reference along with one for circulation. The five parts cover the preliterary stage of the Old Testament, the literary prehistory of its books, an analysis of the books, the canon, and the text. Hebrew words, when quoted, are generally translated to English. In addition to the numerous bibliographic references in the text, there is a section of additional literature and notes that parallels the entire work. Indexes to scripture passages and to authors offer useful paths of access.

608. Fee, Gordon D. **New Testament Exegesis: A Handbook for Students and Pastors.** Philadelphia, PA, Westminster Press, 1983. 154p. indexes. LC 82-24829. ISBN 0-664-24469-6.

Fee was inspired by the first edition of Stuart (see 618), and has organized this work in similar fashion. His first two chapters include a guide for full exegesis and illustrative material on exegeting the original text. The third chapter, original to Fee and copied by Stuart for his second edition, is a shorter guide for sermon preparation. The fourth chapter is a bibliography of aids and resources for New Testament exegesis; Fee also includes bibliographic materials in his earlier chapters. Both Fee and Stuart produced their works to assist pastors in writing text-based sermons, and both stress the importance of and give instructions on relating biblical passages to the present situation of the audience.

609. Harpur, James. **Great Events of Bible Times: New Perspectives on the People, Places and History of the Biblical World.** Garden City, NY, Doubleday, 1987. 199p. index. LC 86-24155. ISBN 0-385-23678-6.

"Of the many books on Bible themes this one really does offer something entirely new" (Foreword); and so it does. Each age has its own devices, and the current period is known for satellite photographs and computer graphics. In addition to actual photographs, the maps in this atlas often are created from the unusual perspective (though see Pritchard 666) of the satellite's eye, and battles and journeys are shown on terrain mapped in three-dimensional grids by computer. More traditional illustrations include archaeological photographs and examples of painting and sculpture. There is much color, especially in artists' renderings of battles and cutaways of structures. The work is historical in arrangement, covering the development of Judaism, the life of Jesus Christ, and the rise of early Christianity. About two-fifths of it concerns the period before the common era; the remainder treats New Testament subjects. The results of careful scholarship are here supplied to the general reader.

610. Harrison, R. K., ed. **Major Cities of the Biblical World.** Nashville, TN, Thomas Nelson, 1985. 292p. index. LC 85-10508. ISBN 0-8407-7520-2.

Twenty-seven ancient cities, often the seats of important Jewish and early Christian communities, are highlighted in nine- to nineteen-page essays by biblical scholars, which cover for each its physical description, history, and religious significance. At the beginning of each essay, a general map of the eastern Mediterranean locates the city in question and other major centers. Much from modern archaeological finds is included here. Some cities, such as Ebla, Mari, and Nuzi, are not mentioned in the Bible, but flourished contemporaneously with biblical events, and are of great importance to an understanding of ancient civilizations and languages. A short bibliography is appended to each essay, and an index offers subject access to the whole work.

611. Hughes, John Jay. **Bits, Bytes & Biblical Studies.** Grand Rapids, MI, Zondervan, 1987. 643p. index. LC 87-6163. ISBN 0-310-28581-X.

After a treatment of personal computers in general, Hughes introduces word processing, concordance, and database management programs; reviews language-learning programs for Hebrew, Greek, Latin, Sumerian, and Egyptian; offers information on projects creating machine-readable versions of the Masoretic (Hebrew) and Septuagint (Greek) texts of the Hebrew Scriptures and the Greek New Testament; describes major online services; and provides overviews of thirteen English-language Bible texts. Hughes adds extensive bibliographies of books, articles, and software.

612. Kubo, Sakae, and Walter F. Specht. **So Many Versions? Twentieth-Century English Versions of the Bible**, rev. and enlarged ed. Grand Rapids, MI, Zondervan, 1983. 401p. LC 82-21965. ISBN 0-310-45691-6.

Sixteen of the chapters of this work cover individual Protestant, Roman Catholic, Jewish, and ecumenical translations of the Bible. A beginning chapter takes account of four translations done in the first decade of the century; another treats the Readers Digest Bible, a condensation of the Revised Standard Version; and one contains notes on colorful translations such as the Cotton Patch Version, in the English of the southern United States, and The Gospels in Scouse, the dialect of Liverpool, England. A final chapter offers guidelines for selecting a version. Very useful for scholars and lay readers alike is a thirty-page annotated list of twentieth-century English versions; the ten-page glossary is important mainly for the general reader. A lengthy bibliography concludes the work. Kubo and Specht offer detailed analysis and historical introductions to the translations they treat. Since they personally wrote the whole work, they cannot produce the inside information that the essays gathered by Bailey (see 603) reflect, but Bailey covers fewer translations and offers a less extensive bibliography.

613. Packer, James I., Merrill C. Tenney, and William White, Jr., eds. **The Bible Almanac.** Nashville, TN, Thomas Nelson, 1980. 765p. index. LC 79-23475. ISBN 0-8407-5162-1.

The editors intend here to expand the horizons of lay readers. In forty-six chapters, they pack much information into this volume covering history, coinage, weights and measures, clothing, food, means of travel, architecture, flora and fauna, minerals, tools, warfare, diseases, poetry, languages, economics, pagan religions, manners and customs, music, laws, marriage and divorce, childhood, and the Jews in New Testament times. There is a who's who, "All the People of the Bible," and a gazetteer, "All the Places of the Bible." The photographs are not always well chosen—one wonders at the need to show the modern canal at Corinth. The editors have added a subject index to access this mass of information.

614. Preminger, Alex, and Edward L. Greenstein, comps. and eds. **The Hebrew Bible in Literary Criticism.** New York, Crossroad/Ungar/Continuum, 1986. 619p. index. LC 86-16069. ISBN 0-8044-3266-X.

Preminger and Greenstein gather passages of one hundred to one thousand words in length from writers who have touched on the literary merits of the Hebrew Bible and who represent a wide variety of schools and times. Here are Nietzche and Goethe, and also representatives from "new criticism, formalist poetics, psychoanalysis, structuralism, and even the recently blooming deconstruction" (Preface). They include otherwise untranslated works. The material is grouped in three main areas: the Hebrew Bible in general; its literary features, such as characters, diction, humor, imagery, lyric, metaphor, and meters; and the texts, the treatment of which is arranged alphabetically by person or event (Abraham, Amos, Babel, Balaam, Creation) rather than by the order reflected in the canonical arrangement of biblical books. A small fourth section covers the Apocrypha. An enormous amount of fresh material is included here for writers and speakers at all levels, and the work also serves as a bibliography for in-depth exploration of authors whose works have been culled. A useful index lets the reader find all the passages of a given author.

615.   Richards, Lawrence O. **The Word Bible Handbook.** Waco, TX, Word Books, 1982. 864p. index. LC 81-22007. ISBN 0-8499-0279-7.

This work, composed in the main of 130 theological essays, is knowledgeable but very conservative, rejecting in some instances the consensus of twentieth-century biblical scholars of all persuasions on such matters as the dual or triple authorship of the Book of Isaiah and the non-Pauline authorship of some letters under Paul's name. There are thirteen maps and twenty-nine useful charts, pictures, and line drawings, and a full index.

616.   Ryken, Leland, comp. and ed. **The New Testament in Literary Criticism.** New York, Frederick Ungar, 1984. 349p. index. LC 84-129. ISBN 0-8044-3271-6.

To assist readers studying the Bible as literature, Ryken gathered excerpts, from literary critics and biblical scholars, ranging from short paragraphs to a page and treating the "plot, character, setting, point of view, and diction" of New Testament books. After a fifteen-page introduction on the nature of literary criticism of the New Testament, and a group of critical passages on the New Testament as a whole, Ryken arranges the excerpts according to individual books or groups of books in the New Testament and to literary forms such as parables and satire.

617.   Soulen, Richard N. **Handbook of Biblical Criticism**, 2d ed. Atlanta, GA, John Knox Press, 1981. 239p. LC 81-1674. ISBN 0-8042-0045-9.

Soulen prepared extensive but not encyclopedic explanations of methodologies and critical movements, definitions of theological terms, and biobibliographies of major ancient and modern biblical theologians. The second edition of this handbook is thus the best inexpensive desk reference in English for both the beginning student and the advanced reader.

Biblical references supplement definitions, and bibliographic references are added to explanations of schools of criticism. A list of abbreviations and common Latin terms used in textual criticism, a list of abbreviations of periodicals and scholarly works, and a bibliography of works Soulen consulted complete the handbook, along with a short guide for writing an exegetical paper.

618.   Stuart, Douglas K. **Old Testament Exegesis: A Primer for Students and Pastors**, 2d ed. Philadelphia, PA, Westminster Press, 1984. 142p. indexes. LC 84-10431. ISBN 0-664-24559-5.

"An exegesis," Stuart writes, "is a thorough, analytical study of a biblical passage done so as to arrive at a useful interpretation of the passage" (Introduction). He offers this fine, step-by-step handbook to students and pastors who have little or no acquaintance with modern scholarly languages beyond English or the biblical languages (especially, in this case, Hebrew). The four chapters cover the format for full exegesis; illustrations for the steps of a full exegesis; a shorter format for sermon preparation; and an extensive, annotated list of aids and reference resources. Specific works are accessible through an author index, and Stuart also adds a scripture index.

619. Turner, Nicholas. **Handbook of Biblical Studies.** Philadelphia, PA, Westminster Press, 1982. LC 82-7111. ISBN 0-664-24436-X.

Turner, proposing not to teach but to remind, gives very short definitions for some fifteen hundred terms, used as tools of biblical scholarship, which are not yet regularly included in dictionaries and handbooks of the Bible, and are often brought into English unchanged from foreign languages, such as *Sitz im Leben, Geonim, crux interpretum,* and *peirasmos.* Turner adds lists containing essential dates, archaeological periods, dynasties, the dating of biblical books, English translations of biblical books, the Greek and Hebrew alphabets, the Jewish calendar, samples of scripts, and a theological who's who. The work is more useful for its lists than for its short definitions and explanations. If a critical school or term is not found in larger biblical reference works, where is one to find more than these minimal definitions? This question remains unanswered and the reader unsatisfied, for Turner gives no bibliographic references.

620. Woude, A. S. Van der, general ed. **The World of the Bible.** Grand Rapids, MI, Eerdmans, 1986. 400p. index. Translated by Sierd Woudstra. (Bible Handbook, vol. 1). LC 86-2214. ISBN 0-8028-2405-6.

The currency, scholarship, and readability of this translation from the Dutch *De Wereld van de Bijbel* make it an important contemporary contribution for the general, perceptive reader. A four-volume series is envisioned, with books in addition to the present one covering the Old Testament, the intertestamental period, and the New Testament. This first work is divided into sections covering geography, archaeology, systems of writing and languages of the biblical world, textual witnesses and the text histories of the Old and New testaments, a history of the ancient Near East, and biblical institutions. Bibliographic references accompany the articles, and presentation is enhanced by abundant black-and-white and color photographs. Maps are included on the end papers.

621. Zohary, Michael. **Plants of the Bible.** Cambridge, England, Cambridge University Press, 1982. 223p. indexes. LC 82-4535. ISBN 0-521-24926-0.

The beauty of this book, with its many detailed photographs, cannot be overstated. Zohary has spent his life as a botanist in the Holy Land, and writes with the direct inspiration of the flora. An extended essay on the identification of plants in the Bible (often difficult), topography, cultivated lands and deserts, seasons and climate, agriculture, trade, and plants in religious and artistic use is followed by a classification of the plants into nine categories: fruit trees, field crops, wild herbs, forest trees, river and marsh plants, wilderness plants, thorns and thistles, flowers, and plants used for drugs, spices, incense, and perfume. A color photograph of each plant named accompanies one or more biblical verses mentioning the plant and several paragraphs on the theories of plant identification. The work is completed by a glossary, a two-page bibliography, an index of plant names, and an index of biblical references. Few other reference works can make the reading of biblical passages so vivid for readers in every category, from children to advanced scholars.

13
Biblical Commentaries

I. Single-volume Commentaries

622. Black, Matthew, general ed. and New Testament ed., and H. H. Rowley, Old Testament ed. **Peake's Commentary on the Bible.** London, Thomas Nelson, 1962. 1,126p. index. LC 62-6297.

Peake's commentary first appeared in 1919 (and was supplemented in 1936) with the purpose of presenting modern biblical scholarship to the general reader. With the same purpose, the editors of this 1962 edition assembled the work of sixty-two contributors, including the best minds in post-World War II, Protestant, English-language, biblical scholarship. Though mostly British, they also include the Americans William Foxwell Albright and John Bright and the Swede Krister Stendahl. The new edition uses the Revised Standard Version (RSV) of the Bible as its base of reference.

It follows the format of the older edition, with social and political background and historical and religious development dealt with in eight general introductory articles. There follow sixteen articles introducing the Old Testament, a commentary on each Old Testament book, sixteen articles on the New Testament, and a commentary on each of its books. Each Old and New testament book is given its own introduction dealing with special questions, such as authorship, as well as the paragraph-by-paragraph commentary. Bibliographies at the end of each article and commentary are international in scope, but cite English editions of works when they are available.

Sixteen color maps are provided, based on Nelson's *Atlas of the Bible* (see 659) but "checked, revised and updated," and these are accessible through an index of place names.

There is an extensive index to the entire work, utilizing a special indexing system: the entire work is divided into 930 sections, with paragraphs in each section marked by lower-case letters. For example, "Day of the Lord" is covered in 115a, 124d, 128g, 135f, and 513a. Nonscriptural names such as those of modern theologians are included, and cross-references are plentiful. Thus, one can negotiate this commentary either by looking up a biblical book and tracing it line by line, or through the index by proper name or subject.

Peake's original work is the model for subsequent single-volume commentaries meant to bring the findings of biblical scholarship to the general reader. The format and the indexing system have not only been retained by Black, but also were adopted by Brown (see 623), Fuller (see 626), and Bruce (see 624).

Black's reworking of Peake must now be supplemented by more recent works, such as Fuller (see 626) and Mays (see 630), but for scholarly excellence and readability it should not be overlooked.

623. Brown, Raymond E., Joseph A. Fitzmyer, and Roland E. Murphy. **The Jerome Biblical Commentary.** Englewood Cliffs, NJ, Prentice-Hall, 1968. index. 2 vols. in one. 1,527p. LC 68-9140.

This work is the first major English-language, Roman Catholic, biblical commentary to be published reflecting that church's expanded interest in scientific biblical criticism, which was given strong impetus by Vatican II, but which the editors correctly trace to Pope Pius XII, whose encyclical *Divino afflante spiritu* laid out the blueprint for the movement. A scholarly work, this book is meant to go well beyond the popular pamphlet commentaries that proliferated in the 1960s. It is not, as many previous Catholic efforts were, a commentary on an English translation of the Latin Vulgate Bible, long considered the official Bible of the Roman Catholic Church. Contributors could use any scholarly contemporary English translation of the Bible that correctly reflected the sense of the Hebrew and Greek originals.

The fifty contributing scholars, all Catholics, produced eighty articles, twenty-five on topics of biblical study such as overviews of hermeneutics, canonicity, and Old Testament themes. The remaining fifty-five articles are detailed, paragraph-by-paragraph commentaries on individual books or groups of books in the two testaments. Bibliographies are abundant, gathering materials in all major scholarly languages. A thorough, lengthy index provides access to the whole work. Cross-references from one article to another are frequent. Four single-color maps are included, as is a short list of "suggested basic books."

Found in American Catholic schools, parishes, colleges, and universities, as well as in public libraries, this commentary has been the workhorse of Catholic biblical studies for the past twenty years. Because of its evident scholarship and heavy reliance, "cheerfully acknowledged," on non-Catholic scholarship, it has proven useful to a broad range of Christian and Jewish students. Since the pace of biblical scholarship has quickened in recent decades, the serious reader should turn from this to Fuller (see 626) or Mays (see 630), or to a multivolume commentary for more contemporary material. A second edition, *The New Jerome Biblical Commentary*, with the same editors and publisher, will gather together much recent scholarship and was due to appear in late 1989.

624. Bruce, Frederick Fyvie, general ed. **The International Bible Commentary with the New International Version.** Grand Rapids, MI, Zondervan, 1986. 1,629p. LC 86-234. ISBN 0-310-22020-3.

This single-volume commentary, aimed at the educated nonspecialist reader, is conservative in viewpoint, but takes into account a wide range of contemporary biblical scholarship. Its 43 contributors, all seemingly male Protestants, are from throughout the English-speaking world. In the British tradition of scholarship, some of the contributors have backgrounds in nonacademic professions such as civil service or accounting.

The organization of the work is modeled on the earlier *Peake's Commentary on the Bible* (see 622), although there are no general articles introducing the whole Bible. There are, however, fourteen articles introducing the Old Testament, followed by a commentary on each book, and fourteen introducing the New Testament, also followed by a commentary on each book. Twenty-nine maps accompany the Old Testament section, but the New Testament is cartographically served only by four small maps, in an essay on environmental backgrounds. These are not listed in the table of maps in the front of the book. The line-by-line commentaries list parallels among books of the Bible. There is much annoying use of boldface type to highlight words the commentators think important. Bibliographies at the end of each essay and commentary contain only English-language titles, although some of these are translations from French and German, and the selections represent a broad range of Protestant, Roman Catholic, and Jewish classic scholarship from the nineteenth century and recent contributions from the late twentieth. The work contains no index.

625. Dummelow, John Roberts, ed. **A Commentary on the Holy Bible: Complete in One Volume, with General Articles.** New York, Macmillan, 1908. 1,091p. Reprint: New York, Macmillan, 1984. LC 84-20085. ISBN 0-02-533770-X.

Macmillan has often reprinted this early twentieth-century "textual, doctrinal, and moral" commentary for the general reader, because it incorporates the fertile Protestant scholarship of the time. Its introductory articles treat the Hammurabi Code, then recently discovered, and include an enlightened essay on "The Creation Story and Science," which creationists and scientists of the 1980s would do well to read. The fifty-seven commentators are mostly British, but also include Americans and Canadians. Dummelow uses the King James Version of the Bible for reference in the commentary.

626. Fuller, Reginald C., Leonard Johnston, and Conleth Kearns, eds. **A New Catholic Commentary on Holy Scripture.** London, Thomas Nelson, 1975. 1,363p. index. LC 81-210577. ISBN 0-1712-2010-2.

The original edition, *A Catholic Commentary on Holy Scripture*, published by Thomas Nelson in 1953, was influenced by, although conceived before, the encyclical *Divino afflante spiritu*, issued by Pope Pius XII in 1943, which gave the impetus to scientific biblical scholarship in the Roman Catholic Church. This edition, said by the editors to be four-fifths new, reflects the resurgence of Roman Catholic biblical studies following the Second Vatican Council (1962-65). Its sixty-four contributors are all Roman Catholic scholars, mostly British and Irish, although at least six are Americans who also contributed to the earlier *Jerome Biblical Commentary* (see 623).

Following the plan of Peake's single-volume commentary (see 622), first published in 1922, there are thirteen general introductory articles, five introductory articles to the Old Testament, a chapter-by-chapter commentary on each book of the Old Testament, twelve introductory articles to the New Testament, and commentaries on the New Testament books. Since it is Roman Catholic in provenance, it contains commentaries on books considered apocryphal by Jews and Protestants. Each book of both testaments receives a thorough introduction and initial bibliography, covering important works in English and often other European languages, written by scholars of many denominational backgrounds. Additional bibliographic citations, often to articles, are inserted in the commentary when pertinent. The Revised Standard Version of the Bible (RSV) is the translation favored by the editors, though individual commentators sometimes used others; thus, the numbering of chapters and verses follows RSV practice, although that of the Masoretic has been added in brackets when different.

A single eighty-page index leads the reader to subjects mentioned anywhere in the commentaries or introductory essays. In the manner of Peake, the entire commentary is divided into 975 sections, with the paragraphs of each section signaled by the letters of the alphabet. Fourteen clear, two-color maps, some noting recent archaeological findings, complete the work.

Much of the biblical scholarship of the mid-1970s is packaged for the general reader in this intense and valuable book; comparison with the *Jerome Biblical Commentary* (see 623) forces the conclusion that such an effort, by one group or another, is needed in every decade.

627. Guthrie, Donald, and J. A. Motyer, eds. **The New Bible Commentary**, rev. Grand Rapids, MI, Eerdmans, 1970. 1,310p. LC 71-111346.

In the standard format of single-volume commentaries, this work is arranged with twelve general introductory essays and commentaries on the individual books of the Bible. Five of the essays and thirty-seven of the sixty-six commentaries were entirely rewritten from the first edition (1953). The editors used the Revised Standard Version for biblical referral, whereas the earlier edition was linked to the King James Version. A conservative Protestant commentary, it includes among its fifty-one contributors some of the weightiest scholars of that tradition, including F. F. Bruce and G. W. Bromiley.

628. Howley, G. C. D., F. F. Bruce, and H. L. Ellison. **The New Layman's Bible Commentary in One Volume.** Grand Rapids, MI, Zondervan, 1979. 1,712p. LC 79-14838. ISBN 0-310-22010-6.

Based on a multivolume effort, this commentary sets aside devotional elements and emphasizes a close examination of the text. Its contributors reflect conservative Protestant scholarship, and include the prolific Scottish biblicist Frederick Fyvie Bruce. As with most single-volume commentaries, this is organized like Peake (see 622). While it offers no general introductory essays to the whole Bible, fourteen articles precede the commentary on the Hebrew Scriptures and fourteen more precede the commentary on the New Testament. Each book of the Bible receives a brief introduction, an outline, a verse-by-verse commentary, and a bibliography. No Bible text is printed, but the Revised Standard Version is used for reference purposes.

The section on the New Testament is a reprint of Howley's *A New Testament Commentary* (Grand Rapids, MI, Zondervan, 1969).

629. Laymon, Charles M., ed. **The Interpreter's One-Volume Commentary on the Bible: Introduction and Commentary for Each Book of the Bible Including the Apocrypha, with General Articles.** Nashville, TN, Abingdon Press, 1971. 1,386p. index. LC 71-144392. ISBN 0-687-19299-4.

Although the name is similar, and the intended readership and the publisher the same, this is not a shorter version of *The Interpreter's Bible* (see 636). Laymon assembled a new group of contributors, including Protestant scholars from many denominations, as well as Jews and Roman Catholics, to produce this commentary. The Apocrypha are covered, evidence of the increased recognition of their importance. Thirty-nine well-conceived general articles are divided into groups covering biblical interpretation; the geographical and historical setting; the making of biblical literature; the religion of the Bible; and text, canon, and translation. Each book of the Bible receives an introduction and a passage-by-passage commentary. Black-and-white photographs are abundant, as are boldly drawn, small maps of limited areas, which unfortunately do not give the reader a feel for the relation of the area covered to the larger regions of the Middle East.

630. Mays, James L., general ed. **Harper's Bible Commentary.** San Francisco, CA, Harper & Row, 1988. 1,344p. index. LC 88-45148. ISBN 0-06-065541-0.

As is its companion work, *Harper's Bible Dictionary* (see 569), this is a joint venture between the publisher and the Society of Biblical Literature (see 763), and is meant to bring contemporary biblical scholarship to the generally educated reader. The dictionary deals with the Bible in terms of subjects, the commentary in terms of its books. Eighty-two well-known scholars from the Jewish, Catholic, and Protestant traditions contribute commentaries on the books of the full scriptural canon of Judaism, Roman Catholicism, Protestantism, and Orthodoxy.

Four integrative essays cover the Bible as a whole, and deal with its historical context, a comparison with other literature of antiquity, its interpreters, and its communities. More specific introductory material is given for seven parts: Old Testament history, the Psalms and Wisdom literature, the Prophetic books, the Apocrypha, the Gospels and Acts, the Pauline letters, and the general letters to the Christian churches. Finally, each book receives its own introduction, a section-by-section commentary, and a short, up-to-date bibliography. In addition, some thirty-two short essays cover topics of special interest ("The Women in Genesis," and "The Miracles of Jesus in Mark.").

Cross-references signalled by an arrow refer the reader to appropriate articles in the companion *Harper's Bible Dictionary*. Occasional black-and-white photographs and two sections of color prints enhance the work, and sixteen full-color maps, eleven of them imported directly from the *Dictionary*, along with their accompanying index, complete it.

More than its companion *Dictionary*, this commentary gives fair quantitative treatment to the Hebrew Scriptures, designated throughout as the Old Testament. Its careful and clever design, and useful drawing together of contemporary Anglo-North American biblical scholarship, make it the leading commentary of the late 1980s for the general reader, and the update for earlier single-volume commentaries such as Black (see 622), Brown (see 623), and Fuller (626).

631. Plaut, W. Gunther. **The Torah: A Modern Commentary.** New York, Union of American Hebrew Congregations, 1981. 1,787p. LC 80-26967. ISBN 0-8074-0055-6.

The Torah consists of the first five books of the Hebrew Scriptures. Plaut provides commentaries on four of them: Genesis, Exodus, Numbers, and Deuteronomy. Bernard J. Baumberger supplied a commentary on Leviticus. The commentators are liberal in outlook, and take account of contemporary scientific biblical scholarship. This work is meant for both synagogue and personal reading. Each Torah book receives a general introduction and an essay linking it to other Near Eastern literature; for Genesis, Exodus, and Deuteronomy, a map on which their main activities are traced appears. The Hebrew Masoretic text and the New Jewish Version in English are given for each book.

In addition to introduction and the biblical text in the two languages, the commentary consists of six parts: textual notes, arranged by verse, which explain the text; commentary, in the form of brief, interpretative essays on broader sections of text; "the gleanings," passages from world literature including Midrash (Jewish lore) as well as Christian and Moslem literature; footnotes with further explanation; references to a vast body of Jewish and Christian scholarly literature listed on over eighty pages at the end of the volume; and Haftarot, that is, additional readings from the prophetic books of the Hebrew Scriptures established to be read in the synagogue.

632. Wesley, John. **Wesley's Notes on the Bible.** Edited by G. Roger Schoenhals. Grand Rapids, MI, Francis Asbury Press (Zondervan), 1987. 612p. LC 86-26678. ISBN 0-310-36410-8.

John Wesley (1703-1791), with his brother Charles a founder of Methodism, wrote extensively on the Bible. Schoenhals took Wesley's three volumes on the Hebrew Scriptures and two on the New Testament (3,682 pages altogether), and condensed them into the present work by using such principles of selection as eliminating biblical quotations; taking something on every chapter of the Bible; selecting comments proportionally (where Wesley wrote much or little, Schoenhals selected much or little, respectively); excluding technical comments on language and geography; and including all Wesley's personal references as well as his theological, pastoral, and "colorful" expressions.

II. Multivolume Commentaries

633. Albright, William Foxwell, and David Noel Freedman, general eds. **The Anchor Bible.** Garden City, NY, Doubleday, 1964- .

Albright and subsequent editors assembled leading Protestant, Catholic, and Jewish scholars of recent decades to produce the individual commentaries in this series, which, having reached volume 44, is still in production. The format of each volume is similar. The author produces a new translation of the text under study, adds notes on the text, and offers an exposition of the meaning. "[I]ts method is to arrive at the meaning of biblical literature through exact translation and extended exposition, and to reconstruct the ancient setting of the biblical story, as well as the circumstances of its transcription and the characteristics of its transcribers" (Series Preface). It is aimed at the general reader, "yet it is written with the most exacting standards of scholarship." Greek and Hebrew words are transliterated to the roman alphabet. Generally, the volumes do not contain bibliographies as thorough as those in the *Hermeneia* (see 637) or *Word* (see 640) commentaries.

634.   Allen, Clifton J., general ed. **The Broadman Bible Commentary.** Nashville, TN, Broadman Press, 1969-72. 12 vols. LC 78-93918.

The editors offer general articles on the whole Bible in the first volume, on the Hebrew Scriptures in the eighth, and on the New Testament in the twelfth. Short, scholarly, ecumenical bibliographies follow each general article. Bringing solid but now-dated scholarship to ministers and lay persons, this is a conservative Protestant commentary whose fifty-seven contributors, all apparently males, were "carefully selected for their reverent Christian faith and their knowledge of Bible truth" (Introduction). For Biblical quotations, the editors have chosen the Revised Standard Version.

635.   Briggs, Charles Augustus, Samuel Rolles Driver, Alfred Plummer. **The International Critical Commentary on the Holy Scriptures of the Old and New Testaments.** Edinburgh, Scotland, Clark, and New York, Scribner's, 1895-1937. 45 vols.

Engaging the best British and American scholars of the day, the editors brought together the wealth of high scholarship of early twentieth-century biblical studies, including philological, exegetical, literary, and archaeological matters. In answer to the great German commentaries, often translated into English, this is the first multivolume English-language commentary "based on a thorough critical analysis of the original texts of the Bible and upon critical methods of interpretation" (Editor's Preface). Each book of the Bible receives an introduction, critical comments on the body of the text, philological commentary, and general commentary. No practical or homiletic exegesis accompanies the effort. Though quite dated, these authoritative volumes are still widely used by scholars as well as students and clergy.

636.   Buttrick, George Arthur. **The Interpreter's Bible.** Nashville, TN, Abingdon Press, 1952-57. 12 vols. indexes. LC 51-12276.

This classic commentary is one of the best produced for the general reader and practicing minister. Over the years, it has found a place on the reference shelves of almost every college and public library in English-speaking North America. The editors and 125 contributors, including many renowned mid-century biblical scholars, strove to produce a commentary noted for "honest scholarship within the Protestant evangelical faith" (prefatory notes: "How to Use the Interpreter's Bible"). Each passage of the Protestant canonical books receives three-fold treatment, evident in the layout of the pages of the commentaries. First, two English translations of each passage are printed at the top of the page: the King James Version and the Revised Standard Version. Midway on the page is the exegesis, the explanation of "what a word or phrase meant for its original speaker in the original time and occasion" (prefatory notes). Last is the exposition, meant to spur a minister's thoughts for homiletic preparation. Each book of the Bible also receives an introduction, which includes an overview of the entire book, an outline, and a bibliography. The Apocrypha are not treated.

The general articles are particularly strong, eleven for the whole Bible, eleven for the Old Testament in the first volume, and fourteen for the New Testament in the seventh volume. When the editors came to publish the last volume in 1957, they felt the development of biblical studies over the decade merited an additional three articles, including one on the Dead Sea Scrolls. The editors have also included a black-and-white map for almost every book in the Bible, as well as four color maps (two for the Old Testament and two for the New Testament) which serve as the endpapers in the volumes of the commentary.

The original plan included massive indexing, which was to take a projected 350 pages of the last volume. This was cut to 140 pages that include a short index of scripture references cited out of context in the commentary, and a full index of subjects. There is no index of illustrations, as originally planned; indeed, illustrations are minimal. A series of twenty-nine color plates of ancient Biblical texts in the final volume continues to be striking after thirty years.

Though dated, the exegetical scholarship is authoritative, and the juxtaposed translations are very convenient for the librarian and the general reader.

637. Cross, Frank Moore, and Helmut Koester, eds. **Hermeneia: A Critical and Historical Commentary on the Bible.** Philadelphia, PA, Fortress, 1971- .

Meant for the serious student (which may be the general reader if he or she intends to work hard), the *Hermeneia* utilizes "the full range of philological and historical tools including textual criticism…, the methods of the history of tradition, and the history of religion" (Series Foreword). The full range of Semitic and classical languages are brought into play, but always with English translations. Many of the volumes are translations into English. Those published to date represent the work of international scholars of the highest critical level; the great German theologian Rudolf Bultmann, for example, did the Johannine Epistles. Accordingly, the extensive bibliographies list materials in all scholarly languages. The editors intend an extensive process of revisions to keep the series up to date. In addition to the canonical books of the Hebrew Scriptures and the New Testament, the series will include commentaries on apocryphal and gnostic texts.

638. Gaebelein, Frank E. **The Expositor's Bible Commentary.** Grand Rapids, MI, Zondervan, 1979- . 12 vols. (Regency Reference Library). LC 76-41334.

As of this writing, the editors have brought out nine volumes of this commentary, which includes the New International Version of the Bible. The seventy-eight contributors are evangelical scholars from a wide range of chiefly English-speaking, Protestant denominations. The chief principle of interpretation is the grammatico-historical method: "the primary aim of the exegete is to make clear the meaning of the text at the time and in the circumstances of its writing" (Preface). The first volume is a collection with nine general introductory essays, eleven studies on the Hebrew Scriptures, and fifteen studies on the New Testament. Bibliographies appended to the treatment of each book of the Bible are a special strength; for instance, a nine-page list of books, articles, and commentaries accompanies the Gospel of Matthew.

639. Henry, Matthew, and Thomas Scott. **Commentary on the Bible.** Nashville, TN, Thomas Nelson, 1979. 3 vols. ISBN 0-8407-5163-X.

"Enduring work" takes on new meaning here: Henry, twenty-five years a Presbyterian pastor in Chester, England, first published this commentary in 1710. It was much republished in the nineteenth century, often with the notes Scott first brought out in 1792. The King James Version is published with the commentary. Untouched by scientific biblical scholarship, which began in late eighteenth-century Germany, Henry nevertheless attempts serious understanding, adding notes on the authenticity of each book and reasoning, for example, that the Gospel of Matthew must have been written in 37 CE or shortly thereafter (the twentieth-century consensus is the mid-80s CE).

640. Hubbard, David A., and Glenn W. Barker. **Word Biblical Commentary.** Waco, TX, Word Books, 1982- . 52 vols. LC 81-71768.

Forty-six American, Canadian, British, and Australian contributors from the evangelical tradition of contemporary Protestantism are producing a new translation from the original Hebrew and Greek biblical texts for this commentary. Each individual commentary is originally in English; none are translations, as is the case with the *Hermeneia* commentary (see 637). Each volume contains an extensive bibliography; the original translation; notes on the text; a section on the form, structure, and setting of the biblical book; a commentary that relates the book to other parts of the Bible; a broader explanation; and special notes, when appropriate. The commentators append bibliographies to individual passages. If all volumes equal those published to date, of contemporary commentaries this will be the richest in bibliography.

641. Stonehouse, Ned, and Frederick Fyvie Bruce, general eds. **New International Commentary on the New Testament.** Grand Rapids, MI, Eerdmans, 1951- . 17 vols.

Although they began this work almost four decades ago, the editors have attempted to keep the scholarship as up to date as possible through planned revisions of the individual commentaries. F. F. Bruce, for example, first published his commentary on the Acts of the Apostles in 1954, but came out with a revision in 1988. The commentators are New Testament scholars from Europe, North America, and South Africa.

14

Biographical Sources for the Bible and Biblical Studies

I. Biographical Sources for Biblical Characters

642. Barr, George. **Who's Who in the Bible.** Middle Village, NY, Jonathan David, 1975. 177p. LC 74-1965. ISBN 0-8246-0179-8.

Barr offers no scope notes, introduction, or preface to this who's who. He does include root meanings for his names and limited references to biblical passages for each name he includes. The entry on "Peter," for example, includes two references to the Gospel of Matthew, and one to Luke, but none to Mark, John, or Acts. For the general reader, the combination of Brownrigg (see 643) and Comay (see 646), or the individual works of Coggins (see 645) or Calvocoressi (see 644), are preferable.

643. Brownrigg, Ronald. **Who's Who in the New Testament.** New York, Holt, Rinehart and Winston, 1971. 448p. LC 75-153654. ISBN 0-0308-6262-0.

Brownrigg opens this companion to Comay (see 646) with an extensive introduction on the backgrounds of the New Testament. He lists all named persons in the New Testament, and for each gives the root meaning of the name; a summary, often extensive, of biographical information; an assessment of the significance of the person; and a list of references. Brownrigg offers more details—his entry on Jesus is sixty-two pages—than Barr (see 642) or Sims and Dent (see 650), but his work remains highly readable. Photographs, black-and-white and color, are abundant throughout.

644. Calvocoressi, Peter. **Who's Who in the Bible.** New York, Viking Penguin, 1987. 269p. index. 87-50540. ISBN 0-670-81188-2.

After a brief introduction to the Bible, its languages, and its dates, Calvocoressi gives selected coverage of the famous, the infamous, and the obscure from both the Hebrew Bible and the New Testament. He does not mention his principles of selection. In addition to the biographical facts for each entry, he also offers an appraisal and, for some, a note on the impact, especially artistic, of the person through the ages. Among his entries are some without names (the Prodigal Son); some families, tribes, and nations; and a few subjects (Apocrypha, Egypt) which, given the title of this book, no knowledgeable reader would expect to find here. He includes a glossary of seventeen terms and five well-drawn, black-and-white maps. Unlike many another editor of biblical biographical dictionaries, he includes an index. A useful genealogical appendix outlines six families: Adam to Noah, Abraham's extended family, the children of Israel, Ruth and the line of Jesse, the Maccabees, and the Herods. For a comparison of this and a work of similar quality, see Coggins (645).

645. Coggins, Richard. **Who's Who in the Bible.** Totawa, NJ, Barnes & Noble, 1981. 232p. LC 81-140183. ISBN 0-389-20183-9.

Coggins begins with a brief introduction to the geography and history of the Hebrew Bible and the New Testament. For each entry, he includes what can be known about the person, as well as an assessment. Like Calvocoressi (see 644), he has produced one of the better works of this genre, and the two authors merit comparison. Coggins adds no index, while Calvocoressi's is extensive and detailed. They both include about the same amount of entries. Calvocoressi includes maps; Coggins does not. Both offer chronological tables. Although Coggins shows a deeper acquaintance with contemporary biblical scholarship, the works of both are weakened by the lack of bibliographical references.

646. Comay, Joan. **Who's Who in the Old Testament: Together with the Apocrypha.** New York, Holt, Rinehart and Winston, 1971. 448p. LC 79-153655. ISBN 0-0308-6263-9.

Like the companion volume to the New Testament (see Brownrigg, 643), this begins with extensive introductory essays on the backgrounds of its part of the Bible. Comay lists the persons of the Hebrew Bible and, for each name, gives the Hebrew meaning, a biographical account, and references to biblical passages. She includes ten maps prepared by Karta of Jerusalem, prominent Israeli mapmakers (see 269 and 284). She also offers introductory material on the Apocrypha, fifteen Jewish books written between 200 and 100 BCE, and a separate alphabet of who's who entries on persons in the Apocrypha. Comay encapsulates the consensus of modern scholarship for the general reader. Isaiah, for example, is identified as three persons: the prophet who inspired the original thirty-nine chapters of the book bearing his name, and Second Isaiah and Third Isaiah who authored the next two sections of the book. Monochrome and color photographs, often of artistic representations of biblical figures, are abundant.

647. Cook, Madison Dale. **Biographical Concordance of the New Testament.** Neptune, NJ, Loizeaux Brothers, 1985. 216p. LC 84-7164. ISBN 0-87213-089-4.

This very useful resource identifies every person mentioned in the New Testament; gives the contemporary English pronunciation; the meaning of the name; a brief biographical note; and a citation to book, chapter, and verse in the King James Version from which the biographical information, however slight, emanated. The citation is also summarized. Multiple persons with the same name are numbered separately. Cook maintains an avowedly conservative position, which means he accepts some positions challenged by other contemporary biblical scholars, such as the notion that the Apostle John, the brother of James, was in fact the Beloved Disciple in the fourth Gospel and also that this John is the author of the fourth Gospel, the three epistles named for John, and the Book of Revelation at the end of the New Testament. Because he refers to the King James Version, Cook maintains some awkward spellings; "Esaias" is used rather than "Isaiah," and there is no cross-reference from the more common spelling. He includes persons from the Hebrew Bible who are mentioned in the New Testament, noting a major reference to a passage in the Hebrew Bible for each.

648. Deen, Edith. **All the Women of the Bible.** New York, Harper & Row, 1955. 409p. index. LC 55-8521.

Deen divides her work into three sections: extended studies of the more prominent women in the Bible; an alphabetical list of named women; and a chronological listing of nameless women in the background, often in groups. Her index of names consolidates these lists. Her bibliography includes general reference books on the Bible and a list of fifty-one nineteenth- and twentieth-century books treating women in the Bible. Her style is flowery yet readable, and her meditative essays are backed by solid, if now dated, scholarship. In some cases, for example, for Delilah, she traces artistic representations down through the ages.

649.   Lockyer, Herbert. **All the Men of the Bible: A Portrait Gallery and Reference Library of More than 3000 Biblical Characters.** Grand Rapids, MI, Zondervan, 1958. 381p. LC 58-4616. ISBN 0-310-28080-X.

Lockyer has written a series of reference books, all with the formulaic title "All the ... of the Bible." His work is characterized by a conservative notion of inspiration and a homiletic tone, and is uncluttered by the notions of contemporary biblical scholarship.

This volume begins with an essay on the importance of names from the Bible (wherein Lockyer takes note of the abiding practice among Anglo-Saxon peoples, especially Protestants, of choosing biblical names for their children, a practice which began with the publication of the Geneva Bible in 1560). For each name entered Lockyer gives a modern pronunciation, a translation from Hebrew to English, a description, and citations to biblical verses. There are no bibliographic references to extra-biblical materials, a common failing in books of this type. Coverage is mixed. The entry on Paul is only two pages; that on Jesus is six, and includes genealogical materials and treatment of names applied to him, such as Lord, Emmanuel, etc. There is a brief essay on anonymous men, a superfluous index of major characters, and a very short bibliography at the end of the work. Although the publishers are different, this work is obviously the partner to Deen's (see 648). The works of Comay (see 646) and Brownrigg (see 643), or of Coggins (see 645) or Calvocoressi (see 644), are currently the best in this genre.

650.   Sims, Albert E., and George Dent, comps. and eds. **Who's Who in the Bible: An ABC Cross Reference of Names of People in the Bible.** New York, Philosophical Library, 1960. 96p. LC 60-16209.

For the general reader, Sims and Dent treat the major personalities in the two sections of the Bible. Their approach is biased toward Christianity, and sometimes their explanations are theological, such as that for Jesus Christ. They add a pronunciation guide.

II. A Biographical Source for Biblical Studies

651.   **Who's Who in Biblical Studies and Archaeology, 1986-1987.** Washington, DC, Biblical Archaeology Society, 1986. 272p. LC 86-072710. ISBN 0-9613089-3-1.

This valuable work, with a scope wholly different from the other biographical works herein cited, lists 1,500 biblical specialists with traditional who's who entries: birth, parents, spouse, children, education, professional position, publications, avocations, and current work and home addresses. The editors have included a geographical index, as well as a specialization index that lists archaeology; the Hebrew Bible; the New Testament; semitic languages, texts, and epigraphy; the Apocrypha; and post-biblical studies.

15
Biblical Atlases

652. Aharoni, Yohanan, and Michael Avi-Yonah. **The Modern Bible Atlas**, rev. ed. London, George Allen & Unwin, 1979. 184p. index. LC 78-40879. ISBN 0-04-220008-3. Published in the United States by Macmillan in 1977 as **The Macmillan Bible Atlas.**

This is the best atlas to have on hand when reading the Bible, not just because of the excellence of the maps, but also because of their sheer quantity—264 in all. As with all Bible atlases, this records the epic sweeps of history, but, better than most, it also displays details of events recorded in both the Hebrew Scriptures and the New Testament. Thus, there are separate maps for "The Deployment for the Battle of Gilboa" (map 95), "The Death of Saul" (96), and "The Burial of Saul" (97). The history of the Jews is covered through the second revolt against the Romans in 135 CE, an event little known even to educated Christians, but of immense importance in the development of the early church as well as Judaism.

This is essentially the fruit of Israeli scholarship, but Christianity is covered by twenty-four maps ranging from "The Birth of Jesus and the Flight into Egypt" to "The Church in the First Century A.D." and "The Church in the Second Century A.D."

The maps are monochromatic with light green on dark green. Throughout the work, there are line drawings of artifacts, sites, buildings, and architectural parts.

One feature not found in other atlases is the "Key to Maps According to the Books of the Bible." In this, for example, fifteen references to thirteen maps are noted for I Samuel, and twenty-eight references to twelve maps for the Gospel of Matthew. Two chronological tables are included. A general table covers the years from 2800 BCE to 135 CE; a more detailed layout covers 1640 BCE to 150 CE. The editors have indexed all place names on the maps.

653. Baly, Dennis, and A. D. Tushingham. **Atlas of the Biblical World.** New York, World Publishing, 1971. 208p. indexes. LC 71-107641.

Baly is an authority on biblical geography, having written the standard work, *The Geography of the Bible* (2d ed.: New York, Harper & Row, 1974). In this atlas, he and Tushingham write on six topics, moving from the broad to the specific: archaeology and ancient environments, the world of the Bible, some effects of Middle Eastern climate, the natural regions of the Middle East, the natural regions of the Levant, and Jerusalem. To accompany the text, they produce fourteen color and thirty-five monochromatic maps, and intersperse sixteen color and fifty-two black-and-white photographs. The color maps are well detailed and easily read. The bibliography is divided in two: the first part covers atlases, maps, and books consulted in the production of this atlas, and the second is a basic bibliography on the geography of the Middle East, the Arabian peninsula, Northeast Africa, Iran and Afghanistan, Mesopotamia, Palestine and the Levant, Jerusalem, and Turkey. Baly and Tushingham have produced the most geographically technical biblical atlas which can be studied by both the lay reader and the biblical scholar for whom geography is a lacuna. The text of the work is sometimes interrupted by pages of maps and their accompanying explanations, a minor inconvenience. The editors add indexes to the text and to the maps.

654. Beitzel, Barry J. **The Moody Atlas of Bible Lands.** Chicago, IL, Moody Press, 1985. 234p. indexes. LC 85-675158. ISBN 0-8024-0438-3.

Ninety-five multicolor maps and thirty-nine "figures," most of which are carefully chosen color photographs, cover the physical geography of the Holy Land, its historical geography, and a short history of biblical mapmaking. Beitzel espouses an "avowedly evangelical standpoint," and interprets for the general reader the scholarly discussion of possible locations for biblical places and events. A thirty-six-item bibliography contains materials by scholars from a range of religious backgrounds. A unique feature is the special attention to the needs of the color-weak and the color-blind, and Beitzel has chosen the map colors accordingly. Place names and geographic features are printed in boldface, making this one of the more visually understandable atlases. A four-page time line, insufficient in detail, covers the years 10,000 BC to 100 AD. A map citation index provides access to all geographical data appearing on maps in the atlas, and Beitzel also includes indexes for biblical passages and "extra-biblical literature," by which he means the Apocrypha and Old Testament Pseudepigrapha.

655. Blaiklock, Edward M., ed. **The Zondervan Pictorial Bible Atlas**, 2d ed. Grand Rapids, MI, Zondervan, 1972. 505p. indexes. LC 78-95273.

Blaiklock arranges eighty-five maps, seventeen in color, into sixteen chronological chapters, covering events from Genesis through the expansion of the early Christian church. The maps are often small and lack detail. There are, however, many line drawings and photographs, and the extensive text accompanying the maps helps this atlas serve as a biblical handbook as well. Indexes allow for access to the whole work by scripture reference and by persons, places, and subjects, and to the color maps by place name. Four appendixes treat the archaeology of the biblical lands, their languages, their geology, and their cities. Blaiklock includes only a few bibliographic references. Aimed at the general reader, this book with its larger print will be attractive to those with vision difficulties.

656. **Eerdmans' Atlas of the Bible: With A-Z Guide to Places.** Grand Rapids, MI, William B. Eerdmans, 1983. 68p. LC 83-175648. ISBN 0-8028-3583-X.

This work combines and republishes sections nine and ten of the *Eerdmans' Family Encyclopedia of the Bible* (Grand Rapids, MI, Eerdmans, 1978). The multicolor maps are for the general reader, and do not represent careful scholarly cartography. They are accompanied by color photography of the Holy Land, and the editors have added time lines and a short gazetteer of prominent places, with descriptions and references to biblical passages as well as coordinates to the maps.

657. Frank, Harry Thomas, ed. **Atlas of the Bible Lands.** Maplewood, NJ, Hammond, 1984. 48p. index. LC 83-675795. ISBN 0-8437-7056-2.

Unlike other atlases cited here, which most often contain extensive texts, this is made up almost solely of its fifty-eight well-designed maps, most of which are in color. There is an accompanying time chart and an occasional photograph. The "gazetteer index" leads the student to the places noted on the maps. Covering history from the age of the patriarchs to the spread of Christianity throughout the Mediterranean region, this has more maps on specific events and times, but less on technical geography, than most of the larger atlases.

658.   Gardner, Joseph L. **Reader's Digest Atlas of the Bible: An Illustrated Guide to the Holy Land.** Pleasantville, NY, Reader's Digest, 1981. 256p. index. LC 80-53426. ISBN 0-89577-097-0.

Like Blaiklock's biblical atlas (see 655), this well-illustrated, well-designed, and well-written work serves a dual purpose: atlas and handbook. An introduction treats people, animals, plants, weights and measures, and the history of the biblical lands. The atlas proper is arranged historically from the time of the patriarchs to the spread of Christianity. The multicolor maps are printed with good contrast. A thirty-two-page gazetteer includes description of places and the principal biblical references for them. Throughout the work, in addition to color photographs of locations and monuments, there are artists' renditions of subjects no longer available for the camera such as clothes, the Temple, and animals. The work closes with a chronology, a list of citations, an index, and a too-brief bibliography.

659.   Grollenberg, Lucas Hendricus. **Atlas of the Bible.** Translated and edited by Joyce M. H. Reid and H. H. Rowley. London, Nelson, 1956. 166p. index. LC 56-14320.

This most scholarly of biblical atlases, the product of the best Roman Catholic pre-Vatican II biblical research, is a translation from the Dutch *Atlas van de Bijbel.* It contains a foreword by Rowley and the great American Protestant scholar William Foxwell Albright, and a preface by the French Dominican Roland de Vaux, who during the 1940s and 1950s headed the École Biblique in Jerusalem. Rogerson (see 667) considers it "probably the best Bible atlas ever produced."

Thirty-seven maps in yellows and browns have legible on-map texts in red. A multitude of black-and-white photographs have long been superseded by the excellent color photographs of later works, but these midcentury photographs show sites and panoramas unchoked by automobiles and tour buses.

There is an emphasis on the Hebrew Scriptures, about which five of the six sections of the work are concerned, reflecting the mature thinking of the time on such topics as the wanderings of the patriarchs. Only the three maps in section six concern Christian events, and the endpaper surveys the journeys of Paul. The editors add an index of places and persons.

660.   Hurlbut, Jesse Lyman. **Bible Atlas: A Manual of Biblical Geography and History Especially Prepared for the Use of Teachers and Students,** rev. ed. New York, Rand McNally, 1954. 168p. LC 39-3543.

Kraeling (see 661) notes that the original edition of this, published in 1884, was the first biblical atlas to contain printed photographs. Despite this technological promise, and a revision carried out in 1938, the use of color in its ninety maps, charts, and diagrams is primitive in comparison with the fine early twentieth-century British production by Smith (see 668). The general arrangement is historical, and each chapter contains teaching outlines. Because it was published in the same decade as Grollenberg (see 659), its photographs, though black-and-white, are uncluttered by modern vehicles and buildings.

661.   Kraeling, Emil Gottlieb Heinrich. **Rand McNally Bible Atlas.** Chicago, IL, Rand McNally, 1966. 487p. indexes. LC 66-20881.

An extensive text, valuable for its detailed attention to geography, is accompanied by twenty-two color and fifty monochromatic maps, as well as tables, plans, and black-and-white photographs. The indexes are equal in depth and breadth to the text: a geographical index lists all places named on maps and in the text, and a subject index includes all persons mentioned. In general, the maps are inferior to subsequently published atlases, but the continuing strength of this work lies in its details.

662.   May, Herbert G., ed. **Oxford Bible Atlas**, 3d ed. Revised by John Day. New York, Oxford University Press, 1984. 144p. LC 84-10052. ISBN 0-19-143452-3.

The twenty-six maps are sandwiched between two extensive essays, "Introduction: Israel and the Nations" and "Archaeology and the Bible." The maps are printed in two or three colors, and are clear and readable, although at times crowded because this work is not in the large folio size favored by atlas publishers. Photographs are abundant but in black-and-white, unusual for an atlas published in the 1980s. The text accompanying each map offers detailed historical information on the period covered. The gazetteer is arranged according to the spelling of place names used in the Revised Standard Version, and each entry includes, when applicable, an alternative ancient name and a modern name, some explanatory notes on the importance of the place, and map coordinates. This is handy, readable, and scholarly, but does not contain as much information as the equally recent works by Pritchard (see 666) or Rogerson (see 667).

663.   Monson, J., general consultant. **Student Map Manual: Historical Geography of the Bible Lands.** Jerusalem, Pictorial Archive (Near East History) Est., 1979. [168]p. LC 84-675065.

This work is the result of the Wide Screen Project, a comprehensive audiovisual aid on the historical geography of the Bible lands, which includes an archive of 2,500 slides. With this atlas, the cartographers attempt in accurate and detailed manner to reflect the configuration of these lands. This can be the most useful of atlases once its heterodox design is appreciated: all maps have an eastern rather than a northern orientation, that is, it is as if each map were created by a cartographer suspended over the Mediterranean and looking eastward over Israel. The reason for this is that the work is based on a series of wall maps which understandably are broader than they are high. The divisions of the atlas include sixteen regional maps; ten maps summarizing archaeological work in the Holy Land from the Stone Age to the Byzantine period; historical maps from the Canaanite to Byzantine periods; the archaeology of Jerusalem; and indexes of 865 place names on the maps, including an index of main names with Arabic or Hebrew modern names, an index of alternative names, and an index of grid references. The index of main names is cross-indexed to the *Encyclopedia of Archaeological Excavations in the Holy Land* (see 90). Also, for each site, a reference number is given to specific slides in the Pictorial Archive.

Each section begins with a summary of the contents and a list of bibliographic references. The maps are carefully drawn, with geographical features and road systems clearly shown. A special technique of contour-based relief shading was developed for the mapping, which makes for maximum clarity and detail. A list referencing biblical verses to the maps begins the atlas, and references to the Bible, to other primary sources, to archaeology, to the archive of slides, and to the scholarly *Macmillan Bible Atlas* (see 652) are frequent. This is a unique work, a companion to rather than a competitor of other scholarly atlases.

664.   Negenman, Jan H. **New Atlas of the Bible.** Edited by Harold H. Rowley; translated by Hubert Hoskins and Richard Beckley. Garden City, NY, Doubleday, 1969. 208p. index. LC 69-11566.

Like the earlier and more scholarly Grollenberg (see 659), which Rowley also had a hand in editing, this is a translation of a Dutch atlas, *De Bakermat van de Bijbel*. For the general reader, Negenman offers almost forty color maps, in eleven chapters, as well as chronologies, boxes containing specialized information, color and black-and-white photographs, tables, and samples of ancient writing. The maps are visually attractive and printed in several colors, but lack reference lines that would simplify locating places from the index.

665.   Pfeiffer, Charles F. **Baker's Bible Atlas**, rev. ed. Grand Rapids, MI, Baker Book House, 1979. 340p. indexes. LC 60-15536. ISBN 0-8010-6930-0.

In addition to nineteen color and nineteen black-and-white maps, Pfeiffer provides extensive geographic and historical materials in the twenty-seven chapters of this work. To them he adds a lengthy gazetteer with references to maps, a too-brief time line, and indexes to biblical persons and places and to modern place names. This information, interspersed with eighty-seven black-and-white photographs and drawings, makes this work comparable to the biblical handbooks (see chapter 12). The maps, prepared by Hammond, are generally readable, though the pages are smaller than in most atlases; the attempt to separate the colors into as many as fifteen shades to indicate differences in vegetation is not completely successful.

666.   Pritchard, James B., ed. **The Harper Atlas of the Bible.** New York, Harper & Row, 1987. 254p. index. LC 86-675550. ISBN 0-06-181883-6. In UK: **The Times Atlas of the Bible.** London, Times, 1987. LC gb87-32425. ISBN 0-7230-0295-9.

Pritchard led a team of almost fifty internationally known scholars, predominantly Christian but some Jewish, in producing this atlas, which incorporates the results of current biblical studies and the most recent archaeological and textual findings. There are 134 maps. An eight-page time line, the fullest in any English-language biblical atlas, records period names, culture, sites, subsistence, climate, technology, social organization, and architecture for the earliest periods to 2850 BCE; for later periods, it lists events influencing Palestine, dominant foreign powers, archaeological eras, and biblical books (strangely, omitting the letters of Paul).

The 450 photographs and illustrations, most in color, are creatively construed: in some cases photographs are retouched to eliminate modern structures, thereby giving the reader/viewer a truer sense of the period in question. Some of the artists' renderings are so realistic as to appear to be high-altitude photographs of scenes. The many cutaways of buildings and hills are based on the latest archaeological information and theories.

The atlas is arranged by the main divisions of the Bible as it is understood by Christians: the Old Testament, the Inter-Testamental Period, and the New Testament. The 134 maps are all in color. Many are arranged as though viewed from a satellite, with the curvature of the earth apparent. Some defy convention, and do not orient toward north at maptop; these can be disconcerting, but one must understand that Ramses II cared more about covering the flanks of his army than about where north was. Few of the maps included are designed in the traditional flat Mercator style. Rogerson (see 667), with which Pritchard begs comparison, uses more traditional map styles, though he also includes a few satellite viewpoints since readers are now accustomed to such actual photographs of earth scenes.

Pritchard addresses new interests such as the spread of non-Pauline Christianity in the first century and the condition of the Jewish Diaspora in that same era.

A directory of "People of the Bible" is a detailed but selective list, with chapter and verse treatment of each person. Thus, we can learn of the life of Baruch the scribe through reference to the four passages in the book of Jeremiah which treat him.

A full index includes most of the place names shown on the maps, and is arranged by the spelling of the names in the Revised Standard Version of the Bible. Variant spellings are listed, as are earlier Egyptian and Akkadian, later Greek and Latin, and modern Arabic and Hebrew versions. Place names are given location designations for the endpaper maps, according to the Palestinian Grid Reference, an ordnance survey developed under the British Mandate and still in use.

There is no bibliography as such, but books are occasionally noted by the contributors. Although Jewish scholars took part in the project, the text is decidedly Christian in orientation, with the words "Old Testament" and "New Testament" used throughout.

667. Rogerson, John William. **Atlas of the Bible.** New York, Facts on File, 1985. 237p. index. LC 84-25980. ISBN 0-8160-1206-7.

Rogerson emphasizes geography rather than history in this fine atlas, which is easily compared with the slightly newer and more scholarly Pritchard (see 666). Rogerson divides the work into three parts, relating the Bible to its literature, its history, and its geography. For geography, thirteen regions of biblical lands are studied in detail with maps, photographs, and illustrations.

The forty maps are mostly traditional flat projections with north at the top, although Rogerson has arranged some from satellite viewpoints which show the curvature of the earth. This is particularly felicitous in showing the journeys of Paul where Rogerson's mapmaker has captured the sense of the man's moving out from Palestine to the greater Roman world. Pritchard, with 137 maps to Rogerson's 40, has many more nontraditional projections and orientations. A clever device Rogerson employs is to supply a mini-gazetteer on the page opposite the main map for a region. This supplies coordinates for place names, and cites biblical verses which mention the places.

A particular strength is Rogerson's inclusion of thirteen special-feature articles on such topics as the Codex Sinaiticus, animals, plants, warfare, everyday life (also a strength in Pritchard), Jerusalem as the Jews knew it, other contemporary religions, and the topography of the passion of Jesus. He has also brought in treatments of thirteen archaeological sites, which include outlines of the communities under investigation and photographs of artworks and objects found.

Rogerson's two-page chronological table is too brief to be worthwhile; Pritchard's has far more detail. Rogerson does add an excellent short bibliography on Palestinian geography, a gazetteer, and an index of the biblical names mentioned in the atlas. Like Pritchard and many another atlas — but not like Aharoni (see 652) — this work is Christian-oriented.

668. Smith, George Adam, ed. and designer. **Atlas of the Historical Geography of the Holy Land.** London, Hodder and Stoughton, 1915. 60 plates. index. LC m16-6.

For its time, this was a superior and scholarly cartographic achievement for biblical studies, covering times from the earliest biblical age through the period just before World War I, and taking into account the recent advances in the location of place names in the Bible. Smith divides the work into sections covering general physical features; economic geography; political geography; and a unique section on conceptions of the Holy Land prevalent at former periods, such as "Palestine according to Eusebius" and "The World and Its Races according to the Old Testament." A section of notes on the maps cites ancient and modern authorities. The superiority of British mapmaking is evidenced in the delicate use of color on the maps that foreshadows *The Times Atlas of the Bible* (see 666). Smith includes a twelve-page index of place names.

669. Wood, D. R. W., organizing ed. **New Bible Atlas.** Wheaton, IL, Tyndale House, 1985. 128p. index. LC 84-52722. ISBN 0-8423-4675-9.

The maps, plans, and photos in this atlas are arranged in four general chapters covering the biblical lands (including terrain, climate, vegetation); the Old Testament and

Intertestamental periods; the New Testament and early Christian church periods; and the empires and the peoples of the biblical world. This work grew out of research for *The Illustrated Bible Dictionary* (see 580.1), but contains unique material. Sometimes taking a cue from satellite photography for orientation and design, the maps, most multicolored, are plentiful. Occasional pages are padded with superfluous photographs of modern scenes. Time charts and summaries of biblical history accompany the maps. An index allows the finding of locations first by ancient, then by modern, name.

670.   Wright, G. Ernest, and F. V. Filson, eds. **The Westminster Historical Atlas to the Bible**, 5th ed. Philadelphia, PA, Westminster Press, 1956. 130p. indexes. LC 56-9123.

Published in the same year as Grollenberg's atlas (see 659), and like it including an essay by William Foxwell Albright, this work contains eighteen maps and eighty-eight black-and-white photographs. The umber maps are not as clear as Grollenberg's. However, the great strength of the work is its exhaustive attention to place names: all mentioned in the Bible are contained in its topical concordance, along with their modern names and, when shown, their locations on the maps. Approximate locations are given, if known, for those not shown on maps. As with Grollenberg, the emphasis is on the Hebrew Scriptures; two-thirds of the maps deal with the pre-Christian era, and the remainder with the period from Jesus's life through the fourth century of the common era. Now quite dated, a final map and its accompanying text note excavation sites in the twentieth century. Additional indexes give access to the text, and, unique in this genre, note contemporary Arabic names for biblical places.

16

Biblical Literature Guides
and Bibliographies

I. Guides to Biblical Literature

671. Allison, Joseph D. **The Bible Study Resource Guide.** Nashville, TN, Thomas Nelson, 1982. 223p. index. LC 82-18800. ISBN 0-8407-5814-6.

Allison, a pastor, provides both a handbook and an annotated bibliography for the beginning adult student. He includes chapters on English versions; study Bibles; topical Bibles; a buyer's guide; concordances; commentaries; dictionaries, encyclopedias and handbooks; atlases; introductions; language study aids; and miscellaneous study aids. Each chapter includes an explanation and history of the genre and a selective annotated bibliography of the items in question. Additional helpful lists include a general bibliography, binderies that will rebuild overwrought Bibles, and out-of-print book dealers. A full index of authors and topics offers access to the many citations. Quite useful for its purpose, this work does not cover as many tools or offer such trenchant evaluations as Hort's *The Bible Book* (see 677), which, however, is limited to the New Testament.

672. Childs, Brevard S. **Old Testament Books for Pastor and Teacher.** Philadelphia, PA, Westminster Press, 1977. 120p. index. LC 76-52457. ISBN 0-664-24120-4.

Aiming primarily at the pastor and also the scholar, Childs collects and annotates serious Bible study tools, among them bibliographies, English translations of the scriptures, dictionaries and encyclopedias, introductions and histories, theologies, histories of exegesis, commentary series, single-volume commentaries, and, the major part of the book, commentaries on individual books of the Hebrew Scriptures. An established biblical theologian, Childs holds strong opinions and is unafraid to state them; works that he finds praiseworthy should receive serious consideration.

673. Cully, Iris V., and Kendig Brubaker Cully. **A Guide to Biblical Resources.** Wilton, CT, Morehouse-Barlow, 1981. 153p. LC 81-80625. ISBN 0-8192-1286-5.

With the aim of introducing the general reader to Bible study, the Cullys briefly trace the history of the transmission of the written Christian Bible to the English-speaking world. They then develop bibliographic essays on popular as well as scholarly resources, Bible study courses for adults and for children, the Bible in public and in personal devotion, and the Bible in literature and art. The editors append an extensive and useful list of publishers' addresses. The work is useful not for its expository, unevaluative annotations—there is no competition here for Hort (see 677) or Martin (see 680)—but for its lists of popular and didactic materials, including books, pamphlets, films, filmstrips, teaching packets, and games. It is best used by the general reader or by the professional in support of teaching activities.

674.   Danker, Frederick W. **Multipurpose Tools for Bible Study**, 3d ed. St. Louis, MO, Concordia Publishing House, 1970. 295p. indexes. LC 59-15554.

Though now dated, Danker's work has received wide recognition. He offers a thorough historical overview and evaluation of biblical reference materials, and often takes a genre (for example, encyclopedias) and traces its development from the Renaissance through the 1960s. He covers concordances, the Scriptures in Hebrew and in the Greek Septuagint, dictionaries and encyclopedias, commentaries, English versions, materials on Judaism, archaeological works, and the Dead Sea Scrolls. The whole is accessible both by subject and by author indexes.

675.   Fitzmyer, Joseph A. **An Introductory Bibliography for the Study of Scripture**, rev. ed. Rome, Italy, Biblical Institute Press, 1981. 154p. index. (Subsidia Biblica, no. 3).

Fitzmyer has chosen and carefully annotated 551 works which he deems basic for the student about to begin coursework on the study of the scriptures. He divides these into twenty-four chapters covering bibliography, periodicals, series, biblical texts, ancient versions, English versions, lexica, grammars, concordances, dictionaries, introductions, commentaries, biblical theology, archaeology, geography, history, literature of the intertestamental period, New Testament apocrypha, gnostic materials, literature of the rabbinic period, works on the Greek and Roman religious milieu, hermeneutics, and others. He signals important works with a single asterisk and the most important with two. Since the bibliography of biblical studies is characterized by heavy use of standard abbreviations, he gives the abbreviation for periodicals, series, and reference works in the margin to the left of an annotation. This work, a new edition of a 1961 version, is widely cited for its introductory value.

676.   France, R. T., ed. **A Bibliographical Guide to New Testament Research**, 3d ed. Sheffield, England, JSOT Press, 1983. 56p. ISBN 0-9057-7419-1.

France has put together a short bibliographic guide for beginning students, wherein he emphasizes English-language publications in general and British imprints in particular. His twenty-seven sections include coverage of British library facilities, the study of modern languages for biblical research, reference books, and narrow subjects such as the Targums, the intertestamental period, and Qumran. Although shorter, with less citations, this is similar in outline and purpose to the somewhat older Scholer (see 682), who covers American publications.

677.   Hort, Erasmus. **The Bible Book: Resources for Reading the New Testament.** New York, Crossroad, 1983. 209p. index. LC 83-14446. ISBN 0-8245-0557-3.

Taking a cue from *Consumer Reports*, Hort has produced a buying guide for New Testament resources. He reviews introductions, English translations, concordances, Greek grammars and study aids, dictionaries and encyclopedias, atlases, handbooks, almanacs, and commentaries. Each entry is evaluated for reliability, filling the needs of at least one level of readership (beginner, advanced, professional), and being the best edition available. Resources of each type are divided into "The Best" and "The Rest." An evaluative summary of "Best Buys" is found at the end of major sections and chapters.

Hort has competently produced an unusual and inexpensive reference book useful to New Testament students of all levels and theological backgrounds. He is a master of concise and witty annotations; for example, "Worth its weight in gold, it can be purchased for about that much in cloth, and considerably less in paper" (p. 73).

The scope of the work is occasionally, and to everyone's benefit, stretched, as when a section of the Old Testament in Greek is included. A quick reference guide of all works annotated includes for each the author's last name, short title, publisher, type of binding, ISBN, date of publication, and 1983 list price. Hort also adds an index of authors.

678. Kerr, Ronn, comp. **Directory of Bible Resources: A Comprehensive Guide to Tools for Bible Study.** Nashville, TN, Thomas Nelson, 1983. 240p. LC 83-13244. ISBN 0-8407-5876-6.

On behalf of the National Committee for the Year of the Bible (proclaimed by President Reagan for 1983), Kerr attempted to gather "nearly all of the Bible study and Bible reading resources available in North America" (Introduction). The materials gathered for annotation were in print at the time of publication, reflect Protestant, Eastern Orthodox, Catholic, and Jewish traditions, and range from fundamentalist to liberal and from popular to scholarly. Some are in languages other than English. The annotations are provided by the publishers and are therefore not objective; they generally include title, author, price, order information, description, and codes that signify religious slant and kind of readership targeted. The work is divided into twelve chapters which group materials by types. Pictures of covers of books abound, but offer little information. There is a useful name-and-address list of publishers, but the book, sadly, lacks an index.

679. Marrow, Stanley B. **Basic Tools for Biblical Exegesis: A Student's Manual.** Rome, Italy, Biblical Institute Press, 1978. 75p. index. (Subsidia Biblica, 2). Reprint of the 1976 edition with addenda and corrigenda. LC 78-316658.

In this widely recommended work for the serious beginning student, Marrow lists and selectively evaluates 215 scholarly tools. Eight sections cover bibliographies, Hebrew and Septuagint texts of the Hebrew Scriptures and Greek texts of the New Testament, lexicons (dictionaries of Hebrew, Aramaic, or Greek), dictionaries, concordances, works on the Apocrypha and Pseudepigrapha, and subsidiary materials on Jewish and Hellenistic sources. Where possible, Marrow notes an English translation of a major tool, but many are only available in German, French, or Latin. Subjects and authors are accessible by an index. This short bibliography is especially useful for finding what many agree are the major twentieth-century scholarly sources for biblical research.

680. Martin, Ralph P. **New Testament Books for Pastor and Teacher.** Philadelphia, PA, Westminster Press, 1984. 152p. LC 83-21654. ISBN 0-664-24511-0.

Unlike Childs (see 672), Martin limits his selection to contemporary, available works. The first two-thirds of this book contain a series of bibliographic essays meant to provide religious professionals with choices for their personal libraries, and bibliographies, basic exegetical tools, English translations of the Bible, dictionaries and encyclopedias, New Testament introductions and histories, theology, series commentaries, single-volume commentaries, and commentaries on individual books. The essays are followed by a forty-eight-page bibliography, which gives in one alphabet full citations to all the works mentioned in the essays. The value of this work lies in its ecumenical perspective, its unflinching and informed evaluations and recommendations, and its treatment, making up half of the bibliographic essays, of commentaries on individual New Testament books.

681. Osborne, Grant, ed. **An Annotated Bibliography on the Bible and the Church.** Deerfield, IL, Trinity Evangelical Divinity School, 1982. 127p.

As an aid to local pastors, the faculty of Trinity Evangelical Divinity School plans to compile a new edition of this bibliography every five years. The current edition covers the Bible, missions, the philosophy of religion, systematic theology, church history, Christian education, pastoral counseling, and practical theology. Since its contributors are many, the work is uneven, with some citations receiving extensive evaluative and descriptive annotations and others treated only briefly. Although most of the books cited are from Protestant sources, the ecumenically inclined editors list the works of a fair number of Roman Catholic and Jewish scholars. Browsing is necessary since there is no index.

682. Scholer, David M. **A Basic Bibliographic Guide for New Testament Exegesis,** 2d ed. Grand Rapids, MI, Eerdmans, 1973. 94p. LC 72-94610. ISBN 0-8028-1503-0.

Scholer cites and briefly explains 434 reference works and monographs on 16 aspects of New Testament study, including bibliographies, texts, concordances, lexicons, grammars, introductions, dictionaries and encyclopedias, English translations, commentaries, and the literatures of the cultures of the New Testament period. The format is similar to France (see 676), but Scholer usually notes American imprints, whereas France predominantly offers British.

II. Bibliographies of Biblical Literature

683. Aune, David Edward. **Jesus and the Synoptic Gospels: An Introductory Bibliographical Study Guide and Syllabus.** Madison, WI, Theological Students Fellowship, 1980. 93p. index. (Theological Students Fellowship-Institute for Biblical Research Bibliographic Study Guides).

The synoptic gospels are the first three, attributed to Matthew, Mark, and Luke, and similar enough to each other (and different from the fourth gospel), that they are often studied or "seen together," that is, "syn-optic." Aune collects 990 entries in English for intermediate and advanced students. Scholarly materials are emphasized, and all traditions of study, including Catholic, Protestant, and Jewish, are represented. Five general divisions include introductory materials, literary criticism, tradition criticism, historical criticism, and biblical theology. Aune subdivides these sections and explains the basic concepts of each approach in introductory material. He enhances access with an author index. For a more thorough bibliography on the synoptic problem, with listings in other languages, see Longstaff and Thomas (703).

684. **British Museum General Catalogue of Printed Books.** London, Trustees of the British Museum, 1959-66. Vols. 17-19.

684.1. **British Museum General Catalogue of Printed Books: Ten-Year Supplement 1956-1965.** London, Trustees of the British Museum, 1968. Vols. 4-5.

684.2. **British Museum General Catalogue of Printed Books: Five-Year Supplement 1966-1970.** Vol. 3.

684.3. **British Museum General Catalogue of Printed Books: Five-Year Supplement 1971-1975.** Vol. 2.

684.4. **The British Library General Catalogue of Printed Books 1976-1982.**
London, K. G. Saur, 1983. Vol. 5.

The first work, based on earlier book catalogs of the British Museum, includes 263 volumes and lists almost six million separate books. Volume 17 lists, with full bibliographic descriptions, complete Bibles and Old Testament editions, arranged under the headings "Old Testament," "Pentateuch," "Historical Books," "Prophets," and "Hagiographa." Volume 18 offers New Testament editions, arranged under "New Testament," "Gospels," "Epistles," and "Liturgical Epistles and Gospels." Volume 19 contains an appendix listing works "upon the Bible and its separate parts," and an index listing all the Bibles first under the headings used in volumes 17 and 18, then by language, and last by title.

The subsequent supplements use the same categories for listing Bibles, but do not include indexes. The British Library edition, published in 1983, uses an arrangement similar to the catalogs produced by the Library of Congress. These immense British catalogues are comparable in scope to the *National Union Catalog of Pre-1956 Imprints* (see 711) and subsequent National Union catalogs in the United States, but the British entries tend to have more thorough bibliographic descriptions, and catalog only the holdings of the one national library (albeit great in size) and not the nation as a whole.

685. **Catalogue de la Bibliothèque de l'École Biblique et Archeologique Française** (Catalog of the Library of the French Biblical and Archeological School), Jerusalem, Israel. Boston, MA, G. K. Hall, 1975. 13 vols. LC 76-452906. ISBN 0-8161-1154-5.

This is an author and subject listing (with subject headings in French) in a single alphabet of books and periodical articles on the Hebrew scriptures, the New Testament, Judaism, Christian antiquity, papyrology, linguistics, epigraphy, numismatics, archaeology, Assyriology, Egyptology, geography, oriental history, and biblical theology. Some fifty-five thousand books in all scholarly languages are included. The researcher is told that the library subscribes to over three hundred periodicals, but these are nowhere listed. Each book of the Bible and the Dead Sea Scrolls is listed as a subject heading, with chapters and verses as subdivisions.

686. Charlesworth, James H. **The New Testament Apocrypha and Pseudepigrapha: A Guide to Publications, with Excursuses on Apocalypses.** Chicago, IL, American Theological Library Association, and Metuchen, NJ, Scarecrow Press, 1987. 450p. index. (ATLA Bibliography Series, no. 17). LC 85-18350. ISBN 0-8108-1845-0.

Charlesworth, a much published authority on extracanonical biblical literature, defines the New Testament apocrypha and pseudepigrapha (NTAP) as "a modern collection of Christian extra-canonical writings, dating from the early centuries, perhaps from around 125 to 425, or from the decades in which the latest writings in the New Testament were composed until one century after Christianity became the state religion of the Roman Empire and the New Testament was widely considered closed." He notes that "the main characteristic ... is that they purport to be apostolic and spiritually equal to the NT documents" (Introduction, p. 6). He enunciates eight goals for this work: to clarify the nomenclature, to order and describe the NTAP, to publish a full bibliography, to point out the vast number of publications and lack of consensus on this area, to intimate the significance of the NTAP, to draw attention to the apocalyptic genre, to facilitate research, and to lay the basis for an edition of the NTAP similar to his two-volume critical edition of *The Old Testament Pseudepigrapha* (Garden City, NY, Doubleday, 1983-85). His four divisions include an introduction defining the writings; an extensive essay on the canonical Apocalypse of John (the Book of Revelation), its theology, and its impact on subsequent apocalypses; a bibliography of the texts and translations of Jewish and Christian apocalypses; and a bibliography of publications on the NTAP, arranged according to the name of the New Testament figure appearing in the title, thus bringing together almost a hundred gospels, acts, letters, and apocalypses. Charlesworth annotates many entries, transliterates Russian and Greek periodical titles, and translates exotic scripts, and provides an index to this seminal work.

687.   Fitzmyer, Joseph A. **The Dead Sea Scrolls: Major Publications and Tools for Study.** Missoula, MT, Scholars Press for the Society of Biblical Literature, 1975. 177p. indexes. (Sources for Biblical Study, no. 8). LC 75-5987. ISBN 0-88414-053-9. A 1977 reprint includes an addendum.

It is a cliché to state that the Dead Sea Scrolls are the most important body of new material for biblical study in centuries, but it is startling to be told by Fitzmyer that "we are still waiting for publication of about 95 per cent of the texts from Qumran Cave 4 alone" (Foreword). There has indeed been an enourmous body of scroll literature published since the initial finds in 1947, and Fitzmyer attempts to sort out the myriad publications for the student, explain the sigla used by English-language writers for the scrolls, summarize the contents of the texts, and introduce the student to the tools. He includes lists of sites, full bibliographic information on the publications, bibliographies of the scrolls, survey articles, concordances, dictionaries, secondary collections of Qumran texts, translations into modern languages, outlines of the more important texts, and bibliographies on selected topics of scroll study, with access through an index of modern authors and an index of biblical passages. He is exhaustive in listing sites and published texts which came from them, but not exhaustive in secondary materials.

688.   Forestell, J. T. **Targumic Traditions and the New Testament.** Chico, CA, Scholars Press, 1979. 137p. index. (Society of Biblical Literature: Aramaic Studies, no. 4). LC 79-19293. ISBN 0-89130-352-9.

Forestell supplements Nickels (see 712) with ten years of additional materials on the Targums, Aramaic translations of the Hebrew Scriptures. Although Forestell lists studies from the period 1930 to 1955, his emphasis is on 1956 to the publication date. Like Nickels, he adds a New Testament index that lists studies by book and chapter and verse. He also provides access through a subject index, and lists in an appendix recent editions of the Targums and their translations.

689.   Freitag, Ruth S. **The Star of Bethlehem: A List of References.** Washington, DC, Library of Congress, 1979. 44p. LC 79-16434. ISBN 0-8444-0292-3.

After a brief discussion of the various serious theories put forth to explain the star mentioned at the beginning of St. Matthew's Gospel, Freitag cites and sometimes abstracts popular and scholarly materials gathered from history, astronomy, and biblical studies. Most of the works are in English, but all major scholarly languages are represented.

690.   Gottcent, John H. **The Bible as Literature: A Selective Bibliography.** Boston, MA, G. K. Hall, 1979. 170p. index. (A Reference Publication in Literature). LC 79-17450. ISBN 0-8161-8121-7.

The study of the Bible as literature is a growing phenomenon (cf. Alter and Kermode, 602). Gottcent defines the field, and upholds the validity of it as a discipline in itself apart from the scientific theological analysis usually associated with the Bible. In eight chapters, he descriptively annotates hundreds of books and articles examining the field—arguing both for it and against it—and applying the techniques of literary criticism to the Bible and its individual books. He interfiles subjects and authors in a single index, and provides cross-references in the text.

691.   Grossfeld, Bernard. **A Bibliography of Targum Literature.** Cincinnati, OH, Hebrew Union College Press, and New York, Ktav Publishing House, 1972, 1977. 2 vols. indexes. (Bibliographica Judaica, nos. 2 [i.e., 3], 8). LC 78-184306. Vol. 1: ISBN 0-87068-192-3. Vol. 2: ISBN 0-87820-905-0.

Targums are Aramaic translations and paraphrases of the Hebrew Scriptures dating from before the common era. Grossfeld's first volume lists scholarly materials (books, chapters in books, articles in periodicals, encyclopedias, and dictionaries) on Targums in general, Targum Onqelos, the Palestinian Targum, Targum Jonathan, special aspects of Targum literature (for instance, Targum and the New Testament), translations, and a section on lexicons, chrestomathies, concordances, grammars, and book reviews. The second volume adds literature published since 1972, and goes back to pick up nineteenth-and twentieth-century literature not covered in the first. Grossfeld includes both Jewish and Christian sources, and makes the whole accessible through an author/editor index.

692.   Harrington, Daniel J. **The New Testament: A Bibliography.** Wilmington, DE, Michael Glazier, 1985. 242p. index. LC 85-45447. ISBN 0-89435-535-8.

Harrington, editor of *New Testament Abstracts* (see 722) since 1972, chooses what he feels to be the best books and articles cited in that abstracting journal, and arranges them under 103 subject headings broadly grouped into six categories: texts and tools, interpretation, Gospels and Acts, epistles, New Testament theology, and the world of the New Testament. The citations are not annotated, nor are the abstracts reprinted. The entries are not numbered, but there appear to be just under two thousand of them. What Harrington considers the best works he signals with an asterisk. The value of this bibliography lies in its subject access, a feature *New Testament Abstracts* lacks. Harrington also provides an author index.

693.   Herbert, Arthur Sumner. **Historical Catalogue of Printed Editions of the English Bible: 1525-1961.** London, British and Foreign Bible Society, and New York, American Bible Society, 1968. 549p. indexes. LC 70-350005. ISBN 0-564-00130-9.

In this revision and expansion of a 1903 edition by T. H. Darlow and H. F. Moule, Herbert identifies and arranges chronologically 2,524 editions of the Bible in English, from the 1525 edition of Tyndale's New Testament (the entire Bible in English, including the Old Testament, was not printed until the 1535 edition of the Coverdale translation) to the publication of the New English Bible in 1961. Herbert begins the work with essays on Bible translation prior to Tyndale, and then descriptively catalogs each entry, including the date, title, size, printer, place of printing, and location symbol for any of six Bible libraries in Great Britain and five in the United States. Every identifiable edition in English is included through 1824; thereafter, reprints are excluded. Registers of signatures are added for the earliest editions. Each entry also includes the catalog number of Darlow and Moule, the Short Title Catalog number through 1640, and from 1771 the reference number from *The English Bible in America* (see 694). Each edition published after 1611 is assumed to be the King James Version unless otherwise stated. Two appendixes cover commentaries that have new translations and versions in English provincial dialects. Four indexes provide access by translator, reviser and editor; by printers and publishers; by place of printing and publication; and through general subjects. A short bibliography on translation of the English Bible completes this scholarly bibliography, the definitive guide to British editions.

694. Hills, Margaret Thorndike, ed. **The English Bible in America: A Bibliography of Editions of the Bible & the New Testament Published in America 1777-1957.** New York, American Bible Society and New York Public Library, 1961. 477p. indexes. LC 61-12303.

Hills's original purpose was to prepare a list of American editions for a new edition of Darlow and Moule (see 693). The work became so extensive that, in this separate publication, following an introductory essay on "The English Bible in America," she identifies and catalogs 2,573 items, arranging them chronologically and including full title, pagination, measurement, location in a North American library, description, note on inclusion of the Apocrypha, note on reprints, and material on illustrations. Unless otherwise stated, each edition is the King James Version. Six indexes give access to the material by state and town; by publisher and printer; by translation and translator; by editor and commentator; by edition title; and through general subjects.

695. Hospers, J. H., ed. **A Basic Bibliography for the Study of the Semitic Languages.** Leiden, The Netherlands, E. J. Brill, 1973-74. 2 vols. LC 73-181086. Vol. 1: ISBN 90-04-03623-7. Vol. 2: ISBN 90-04-03870-1.

With an emphasis on materials published in western languages, this work lists, but does not annotate, bibliographies, handbooks, grammars, lexicons, and text editions, intending to gather everything the student of semitic languages will need. The first volume, of most use to the biblical scholar, covers the languages of the ancient Near East: Akkadian, Sumerian, Anatolian, Hurrian, Urartian, Elamitic, Ancient Persian, Ugaritic, Phoenician-Punic, Amarna-Canaanite, Hebrew (which occupies a quarter of this bibliography), Syriac and Aramaic, Epigraphic South Arabian, and Ethiopian. There is also a section here on comparative semitics. The second volume is given over to pre-classical, classical, and modern literary Arabic as well as modern Arabic dialects. All semitic words are romanized. There is no index.

696. Hultgren, Arland J., comp. **New Testament Christology: A Critical Assessment and Annotated Bibliography.** New York, Greenwood, 1988. 485p. indexes. (Bibliographies and Indexes in Religious Studies, no. 12). LC 88-24645. ISBN 0-313-25188-6.

Hultgren annotates 1,917 scholarly studies on Christology, which G. E. Gorman (see 308) defines in the foreword as "the study of the person, nature, and work of Jesus Christ." Hultgren divides his bibliography into five general sections including introductions, studies on Christological foundations, Christological titles, the Christologies of the New Testament writers, and Christological themes. His extensive indexes allow access to the material by author, editor, and compiler, by title, and by subject.

697. Humphrey, Hugh M. **A Bibliography for the Gospel of Mark, 1954-1980.** New York, Edwin Mellen Press, 1981. 163p. index. (Studies in the Bible and Early Christianity, no. 1). LC 81-18717. ISBN 0-88946-916-4.

Humphrey here lists 1,599 citations culled from *Elenchus Bibliographicus Biblicus* (see 719), *New Testament Abstracts* (see 722), and the *Elenchus Bibliographicus* section of *Ephemerides Theologicae Lovanienses* (see 459). Since this is a repetition of these listings, the value of Humphrey's work lies in bringing all the citations on Mark together and setting up a classification system, with sections on commentaries, studies on the composition of the gospel, manuscript evidence, patristic witness, surveys of literature, textual studies, and theological studies. Humphrey also adds cross-references, arranges citations under a topic in chronological sequence, with most recent first, and indicates when an abstract or book review is available. In all, materials from 231 journals have been brought in for the time period covered.

698.　Hurd, John Coolidge, Jr., comp. **A Bibliography of New Testament Bibliographies.** New York, Seabury Press, 1966. 75p. LC 66-16653.

　　Hurd's bibliography of bibliographies opens up access to earlier twentieth-century biblical studies. He includes monographic bibliographies, bibliographic articles published in periodicals, and other works with extensive bibliographic appendixes, and divides these into four sections: book lists, historical and chronological surveys, comprehensive research bibliographies, and the biographies and bibliographies of New Testament scholars. Hurd gives the dates covered by each entry so that the reader can note, for example, that an article published in 1965 contains a bibliography of materials published between 1950 and 1964. Hurd has not provided an index.

699.　Kissinger, Warren S. **The Parables of Jesus: A History of Interpretation and Bibliography.** Chicago, IL, American Theological Library Association, and Metuchen, NJ, Scarecrow Press, 1979. 439p. indexes. (ATLA Bibliography Series, no. 4). LC 78-23271. ISBN 0-8108-1186-3.

　　As the subtitle indicates, Kissinger's work has two distinct parts. The first, a monograph in itself, is a history of the interpretation of the parables in the first three gospels, from the earliest Christian writers (Irenaeus, Tertullian) to the present. The second part, the bibliography, a little less than half the book, is itself divided in two: a bibliography of parables in general and bibliographies of forty-seven individual parables. Kissinger includes books and articles from periodicals and encyclopedias in the major scholarly languages as well as audiovisual materials. Entries are not numbered and are not annotated. Kissinger provides an index of subjects, and one of names, which includes the authors listed in the bibliographies and the interpreters covered in the first part of the book.

700.　Kissinger, Warren S. **The Sermon on the Mount: A History of Interpretation and Bibliography.** Chicago, IL, American Theological Library Association, and Metuchen, NJ, Scarecrow Press, 1975. 296p. indexes. (ATLA Bibliography Series, no. 3). LC 75-29031. ISBN 0-8108-0843-9.

　　In the first of two parts of this work, Kissinger offers a history of the interpretation of the Sermon on the Mount, from the early Christian church to the present. The bulk of this treatment is given to Protestant theologians — twenty pages go to Martin Luther — but other traditions are covered, including Jewish interpretations and notes on Leo Tolstoy. The second part is a bibliography, divided into three sections, on texts of the Sermon; criticism, interpretation, sermons, and meditations on the Sermon; and criticism, interpretation, sermons, and meditations on the Beatitudes. The bibliography includes articles in all major European languages, and reflects work from all Christian denominations as well as Judaism and other world religions. An appendix lists the Sermon in sixty-one languages, and Kissinger adds a general index to both parts and to biblical references by chapter and verse.

701.　Langevin, Paul-Emile. **Bibliographie Biblique. Biblical Bibliography. Biblische Bibliographie. Bibliografia Biblica. Bibliografia Biblica. 1930-1975.** 1,586p. 2 vols. Quebec, Canada. Presses de l'Université Laval, 1972, 1978. LC 72-225363. ISBN 0-7746-6793-1.

　　The first volume of this work lists articles from 70 Roman Catholic periodicals, published between 1930 and 1970 in French, English, German, Italian, and Spanish, and from 286 books published in French, English, and German. Five general headings on the introduction to the Bible, the Old Testament, the New Testament, Jesus Christ, and biblical themes are divided into a thousand subdivisions. Some articles are cited in more than one place in the schema. Tables in this volume include abbreviations used, lists of periodicals and works, authors cited, and headings employed in the five languages.

The second volume brings coverage of the seventy Catholic periodicals to 1975 and includes coverage of fifty additional journals of Protestant, Jewish, or transdenominational outlook. In addition, another eight hundred books, including festschriften, are analyzed for articles. The five general sections are in this volume subdivided into two thousand precise subdivisions.

702.   LaSor, William Sanford. **Bibliography of the Dead Sea Scrolls, 1948-1957.** Pasadena, CA, Fuller Theological Seminary, 1958. 92p. index. (Fuller Library Theological Seminary Bibliographical Series, no. 2). (Issued as Fuller Library Bulletin, no. 31, Fall, 1958). LC 59-4991.

LaSor cites, but does not annotate, 2,711 items, and groups them in three divisions: general works, the texts of Qumran, and interpretations of Qumran literature. Each division is further divided into approximately two dozen subheadings, thereby giving a measure of subject access to this collection. There is also an author index. LaSor has orchestrated a comprehensive bibliography here, pulling in the earliest Associated Press dispatches regarding the finds in the caves southeast of Jerusalem, as well as later, more reflective popular and scholarly treatment. One can trace here the growing realization of the immense value of the finds to biblical studies.

703.   Longstaff, Thomas Richmond Willis, and Page Allison Thomas, comps. and eds. **The Synoptic Problem: A Bibliography, 1716-1988.** Macon, GA, Mercer University Press, 1988. 235p. index. (New Gospel Studies, no. 4). LC 88-21575. ISBN 0-86554-321-6.

The synoptic Gospels, the first three, are similar enough for the reader to conclude that the work of one of the writers may have influenced the others; the synoptic problem is the question of which was written first, and consequently influenced the others, and whether there were additional written or oral sources such as collections of the sayings of Jesus. William R. Farmer's foreword to this work gives a fine short overview of the synoptic question, and Longstaff and Thomas list 1,967 items, twice as many as Aune (see 683), on all aspects of it. They include English, French, and German books, articles, dissertations, and book reviews, and add an author/title index, a key-word index, and an index by date of publication, the latter important for quick identification of eighteenth- and nineteenth-century works.

704.   Malatesta, Edward, comp. **St. John's Gospel 1920-1965: A Cumulative and Classified Bibliography of Books and Periodical Literature on the Fourth Gospel.** Rome, Italy, Pontifical Biblical Institute Press, 1967. 205p. indexes. (Analecta Biblica, no. 32). LC 70-386588.

Malatesta's 3,120 entries are drawn largely from the section of *Elenchus Bibliographicus Biblicus* (see 719) on St. John's gospel, as well as other sections, and include original research as well as popular presentations. He lists books, articles from some four hundred periodicals, sections of books, and some eighteen hundred book reviews. Material in all modern scholarly languages is included. Translations of books and articles are noted. The bibliography is arranged in sections on the history of modern Johannine research, introductions to the study of the fourth gospel, its texts and versions, literary criticism, exegesis, theology, and the fourth gospel in the church's life. A detailed table of contents covers all major areas of Johannine studies, and Malatesta provides indexes of authors and of reviewers.

705. Mattill, A. J., and Mary Bedford Mattill. **A Classified Bibliography of Literature on the Acts of the Apostles.** Leiden, The Netherlands, E. J. Brill, 1966. 513p. index. (New Testament Tools and Studies, vol. 7). LC 66-6106.

With 6,646 unannotated entries, the Mattills have attempted to identify every scholarly book, journal article, and dissertation on the Acts from the period of the Church Fathers up to 1961, in 20 languages. They divide the bibliography into nine sections covering bibliographical, general, textual, philological, literary, form-critical, historical, theological, and exegetical studies. This last group, arranged by biblical chapter and verse, includes works on individual passages, and constitutes nearly one third of the Mattills' work. They exclude New Testament introductions, book reviews not in the form of articles, homiletic and devotional works, and articles in dictionaries and encyclopedias. An author index provides access to this massive work.

706. Metzger, Bruce M. **Annotated Bibliography of the Textual Criticism of the New Testament, 1914-1939.** Copenhagen, Denmark, Ejnar Munksgaard, 1955. 133p. index.

Metzger here gathers 1,188 books, dissertations, and articles, from 236 periodicals and serials in 17 languages, and adds brief summary notes. His citations are arranged in nine sections: handbooks, Greek manuscripts, the versions of the New Testament, the church fathers, Tatian's *Diatesseron* and medieval harmonies, families of texts, textual criticism of specific passages, paleography, and personalia. To these subject divisions he adds an author index. He has chosen the inclusive dates because several German bibliographies came to a halt at the outbreak of the First World War, and many periodicals ceased publication with the beginning of the Second.

707. Metzger, Bruce M. **Index of Articles on the New Testament and the Early Church Published in Festschriften.** Philadelphia, PA, Society of Biblical Literature, 1951. 182p. index. (Journal of Biblical Literature Monograph Series, vol. 5). LC 51-3190. Supplement, 1955. 20p.

Metzger checked over twelve hundred festschriften and found pertinent materials in half of them. He first lists these, and then arranges the 2,150 articles, in 20 languages, in broad divisions on the New Testament and on the ancient church. The first part covers New Testament background, criticism, individuals, and the apostolic church, as well as philology, geography, archaeology, textual criticism, and theology. The second treats individuals in the early church and its history, philology, councils and synods, relations with the state, art, and rites. See-also references often complete each subdivision, and Metzger provides an index of the authors of articles.

708. Metzger, Bruce M., comp. **Index to Periodical Literature on Christ and the Gospels.** Leiden, The Netherlands, E. J. Brill, 1966. 602p. index. (New Testament Tools and Studies, vol. 6). LC 66-6136.

Over a 3-year period, Metzger and 35 graduate students combed 160 periodicals from the periodicals' years of inception through 1961 (or their cessation of publication, if before that). Sixteen European languages are represented. The compilers bring together here 10,090 unannotated entries, and arrange them in 6 parts: bibliographical articles; historical studies on the life of Jesus; critical studies on the Gospels, divided according to schools of criticism; articles on related noncanonical literature; theological studies; and articles on the influence and interpretation of Jesus Christ and the Gospels in worship, the arts, and culture in general. Subject access is through the classification scheme within each division; Metzger adds cross-references when an article falls in two or more categories. An author index completes the work. Like Metzger's other biblical bibliographies (see 706 and 707), this work is now dated, but serves as a foundation for subsequent bibliographical work.

709. Metzger, Bruce M., comp. **Index to Periodical Literature on the Apostle Paul**, 2d ed. Leiden, The Netherlands, E. J. Brill, 1970. 185p. index. LC 75-888624.

Metzger and 20 graduate students examined 110 periodicals in 14 European languages, identifying 2,987 articles on Paul. Each periodical was examined from its inception through 1957, or the date of cessation of publication if before that. The entries are arranged in a six-part classification scheme, including bibliographical articles, historical studies on the life of Paul, critical studies on the Pauline literature, Pauline apocrypha, theological studies, and the history of the interpretation of Paul and his work. Metzger includes cross-references when an article merits more than one location; he also provides an author index.

710. Mills, Watson E. **A Bibliography of the Periodical Literature of the Acts of the Apostles 1962-1984.** Leiden, The Netherlands, E. J. Brill, 1986. 115p. indexes. (Supplements to Novum Testamentum, vol. 58). ISBN 90-04-08130-5.

Mills arranges, by author, citations to 991 journal articles on Acts in the major scholarly languages. His intent is to supplement Mattill and Mattill (see 705), but, as he himself notes, he covers some of the same territory as Wagner (see 718.1). However, he provides far more access points than Wagner by including indexes by journal title, by biblical verse, and by subject, and by using abundantly a simple cross-reference system: articles on the same topic are linked at each citation by lists of citation numbers. Mills includes articles alone, and not books, and therein he differs from the two previous bibliographies. His exactitude is attested by his twenty-two-page list of journals, printed alphabetically by spelled-out title and repeated alphabetically by abbreviation.

711. **National Union Catalog, Pre-1956 Imprints.** Vols. 53-56. London, Mansel, 1980. LC 67-30001.

The total work, often called simply "Pre-'56 Imprints" or "Mansel," is "a repertory of the cataloged holdings of selected portions ... of the major research libraries of the United States and Canada, plus the more rarely held items in the collections of selected smaller and specialized libraries" (Introduction). With its supplement, it comprises 754 volumes published between 1968 and 1981, and is found in most larger public and academic libraries in North America.

The four volumes given over to the Bible contain sixty-three thousand entries, in some seven hundred languages and dialects, arranged according to the order of the English Authorized Version (AV), also known as the King James Version (KJV). In general, the schema includes 129 sections· (1) Bible manuscripts, (2) Bibles by languages, (3) the whole Old Testament, (4) multilingual editions of the Old Testament, (5 to 60) individual Old Testament books, (61 to 80) Old Testament apocryphal books, (81) the whole New Testament, (82 to 127) individual New Testament books, and (128 and 129) New Testament apocryphal books. Within each category, the arrangement is by language and date of publication; thus, one will find the entry "Bible. English. 1611. Authorized Version." for the first references to the King James Version (KJV) and "Bible. O.T. Jeremiah. English. 1870." for an 1870 English printing of the book of Jeremiah alone.

Of special value is the inclusion of materials from the great collection of the American Bible Society in New York. Unlike the rest of the Mansel collection, the Bible volumes include materials printed in alphabets other than the Latin, Greek, or Gaelic. A location symbol, often of the location supplying the cataloging information, is given for each entry.

712.   Nickels, Peter. **Targum and New Testament: A Bibliography Together with a New Testament Index.** Rome, Italy, Pontifical Biblical Institute Press, 1967. 88p. index. (Scripta Pontificii Instituti Biblici, no. 117). LC 73-505376.

Targums are taken from the early Jewish liturgy, and this bibliography reflects the growing awareness of the commonality between first-century Jews and Christians. Nickels lists studies which "use Targumic material in treatment of a New Testament text or theme" (Introduction). Works solely on the Targums are excluded, as are essays from encyclopedias. Nickels first lists linguistic, form critical, thematic, and dogmatic studies, and then provides an index of New Testament texts "whose translation or interpretation has been related to the Targums." See Forestell (688) for additional materials on the Targums and the New Testament.

713.   Noll, Stephen F. **The Intertestamental Period: A Study Guide.** s.l., Inter-Varsity Christian Fellowship of the United States of America, 1985. 92p. index. (Theological Students Fellowship-Institute for Biblical Research Bibliographic Study Guides).

Noll lists 483 studies in English on the period between the writing of the last books of the Hebrew Scriptures and the first of the Christian, and arranges these into introductions and works on the history, institutions, language and literature, and distinctive theological motifs of the period. Since this is prepared primarily for students, Noll notes whether a work is considered basic or advanced. He adds an author index.

714.   Oster, Richard, comp. **A Bibliography of Ancient Ephesus.** Chicago, IL, American Theological Library Association, and Metuchen, NJ, Scarecrow Press, 1987. 155p. index. (ATLA Bibliography Series, no. 19). LC 87-12617. ISBN 0-8108-1996-1.

Oster's purpose in compiling this is to correct a neglect in current scholarship of Ephesus as a center of early Christianity. He arranges by author, and provides a subject index to, 1,535 citations to books and periodical articles chiefly on the early Christian period, with representative materials on the earlier archaic and classical and the later Byzantine periods.

715.   **A Periodical and Monographic Index to the Literature on the Gospels and Acts: Based on the Files of the École Biblique in Jerusalem.** Pittsburgh, PA, The Clifford E. Barbour Library, Pittsburgh Theological Seminary, 1971. 336p. (Bibliographia Tripotamopolitana, no. 3). LC 78-27276.

As the subtitle makes clear, the notations here listed are drawn from the shelf list of the École Biblique (see 685), and include materials missed in the first filming of the card catalog. In addition to books, the catalog of the École Biblique contains citations to periodical articles reflecting publication back to 1890, the year of its foundation. The introduction to this bibliography, by R. Thomas Schwab, offers a short history of the library of the École. The arrangement of materials is by New Testament book, and by chapter and verse within each book. The editors have provided no other means of access. In spite of bibliographies which cover similar ground, such as *Elenchus Bibliographicus Biblicus* (see 719), *New Testament Abstracts* (see 722), *Internationale Zeitschrift* (see 721) and *Mattill for Acts* (see 705), the editors found enough original material in the shelf list to warrant this international bibliography.

716.   Peterson, Paul D., ed. **Paul the Apostle and Pauline Literature: A Bibliography Selected from the ATLA Religion Database,** 4th rev. ed. Chicago, IL, American Theological Library Association, 1984. 551p. (ATLA Religion Index Select Bibliographies).

This work is produced from the *Religion Index* database (see 476), and therefore contains material already available in the four hardcopy indexes produced from that database (see 463, 470, 471, and 472). However, pulling together citations on Paul and the Pauline literature is valuable to any researcher on this most popular area of New Testament studies. To buy a printout of this from ATLA (see 561) is to pay a fraction of the expense of a thorough search of the database. Like the hardcopy products, it is arranged in three parts: a subject index, the largest part at 339 pages; an author and editor index comprising 185 pages; and a short index of book reviews. The complete entries for books are in the author/editor index.

717.   Purvis, James D. **Jerusalem, the Holy City: A Bibliography.** Chicago, IL, American Theological Library Association, and Metuchen, NJ, Scarecrow Press, 1988. 499p. indexes. (ATLA Bibliography Series, no. 20). LC 87-4758. ISBN 0-8108-1999-6.

Purvis assembles unannotated citations to, and provides subject and author indexes for, almost six thousand books and articles in scholarly journals and popular magazines. The majority of the material surveyed is in English, but some is in French, German, Italian, or Spanish; all is available in North America. The first section of the work lists general materials and studies of the geography, archaeology, water systems, walls, and tombs of Jerusalem. Three chapters follow the chronology of biblical periods; the final four chapters cover the history of the city from the biblical period to the present.

718.   Wagner, Gunter, ed. **An Exegetical Bibliography of the New Testament: Matthew and Mark.** Macon, GA, Mercer University Press, 1983. 667p. LC 83-969. ISBN 0-86554-013-6.

718.1.   Wagner, Gunter, ed. **An Exegetical Bibliography of the New Testament: Luke and Acts.** Macon, GA, Mercer University Press, 1985. 550p. LC 83-969. ISBN 0-86554-140-X.

718.2.   Wagner, Gunter, ed. **An Exegetical Bibliography of the New Testament: John and 1, 2, 3 John.** Macon, GA, Mercer University Press, 1987. 350p. LC 83-969. ISBN 0-86554-157-4.

The eight books of the New Testament in the titles are given line-by-line bibliographic treatment. If one is interested, for example, in Matthew 5:18, Wagner has twenty-seven entries on the verse.

Since 1958, Wagner and his students have gathered references to periodical articles, parts of monographs, and commentaries reflecting mid- and late-twentieth century literature on biblical studies in all scholarly languages. Citations are brief for books, with early entries containing author, title, and date of publication. Place of publication was added for later entries. Citations for articles are standard. Wagner provides no indexes; entry to the material is solely by biblical verse. One can find bibliographies listing periodical articles, but Wagner's listing of sections of commentaries and monographs is unique. A volume on the major Pauline letters is planned.

17
Biblical Abstracts and Indexes

719. **Elenchus Bibliographicus Biblicus, 1961- .** Rome, Italy, Pontifical Biblical Institute Press. Annual. Robert North, comp. ISSN 0392-7423.

From 1920 til 1960, this was published in the journal *Biblica* (see 746). Since its independence in 1961, it has been considered the premier bibliographic device for biblical scholarship, pulling in journal articles, books, dissertations, and essays in festschriften in all scholarly languages. Some thirteen hundred periodicals are regularly checked, and the 1984 edition included the contents of 154 festschriften. In all, this edition contains 14,295 unannotated entries. The contents are divided into twenty categories covering bibliography; introductions; critical texts; exegesis of the whole Bible; of the historical, didactic, and prophetic books of the Old Testament; New Testament general exegesis; commentaries on the Gospels and the Acts of the Apostles; on the Johannine corpus; on Paul; on the Catholic epistles; biblical theology; biblical philology; the Apocrypha, Qumran, and Judaism; gnosis and other religions; history of the Middle East; archaeology; geography; and history of biblical science. Until 1981, division headings were only in Latin; since 1982, they are in both Latin and English. To make the materials in this massive work accessible, North provides indexes of authors, of Greek and Hebrew words, and of scripture references. Publication generally runs several years late. It can be difficult to use, because of its size, and because its continental bibliographic methods may be unfamiliar to Americans, but it is comprehensive and what it can yield is worth any effort.

720. Hupper, William G., comp. and ed. **An Index to English Periodical Literature on the Old Testament and Ancient Near Eastern Studies.** Chicago, IL, American Theological Library Association, and Metuchen, NJ, Scarecrow Press, 1987. 2 vols. to date. (ATLA Bibliography Series, no. 21). LC 86-31448. Vol. I: ISBN 0-8108-1984-8. Vol. 2: ISBN 0-8108-2156-5.

In the first of a projected multivolume work, Hupper identifies approximately seventy-five hundred articles from six hundred periodicals dating from the eighteenth century up to 1970. Many nineteenth-century articles are identified here which would otherwise not be available to the English-language reader. Hupper's plan is for seven general sections, of which two appear in the first volume: bibliographical articles—general studies, and Ancient Near Eastern civilization—general studies. The second volume carries the second schema forward with sections on Ancient Near East history and modern scientific studies on the Ancient Near East. Volumes four and five will deal directly with the Hebrew Scriptures, both critically and exegetically. A detailed classification schema in the table of contents is at present the only form of access to this massive work; a subject and author index will appear in the future.

721. **Internationale Zeitschriftenschau für Bibelwissenschaft und Grenzgebiete/ International Review of Biblical Studies/Revue Internationale des Études Bibliques, 1951- .** Düsseldorf, Germany, Patmos. Biennial. F. Stier, comp. ISSN 0074-9745.

The more than three thousand abstracts in the 1986-87 edition are arranged in broad subject categories with German subject headings, but this work can be of great use to the English reader, as many English-language books and periodical articles from around the world are entered. Each abstract is in the language of the original article or book. This ranks with *Elenchus Bibliographicus Biblicus* (see 719), *Old Testament Abstracts* (see 723), and *New Testament Abstracts* (see 722) as an essential device for scholarly biblical studies.

722. **New Testament Abstracts, 1956- .** Cambridge, MA, Weston School of Theology and the Catholic Biblical Association of America. Three times yearly. ISSN 0028-6877.

Over 1,400 periodical articles are abstracted each year, and approximately 250 books receive descriptive notices as well. Among the articles abstracted are evaluative book reviews and literature surveys. The abstracts are divided into five categories covering the New Testament in general, the Gospels and Acts of the Apostles, the Epistles and Revelation, biblical theology, and the New Testament world. This arrangement is repeated for the book notices. The third issue each year has indexes for the whole year, covering authors of articles and book reviews, book notices, and scriptural passages.

723. **Old Testament Abstracts, 1978- .** Washington, DC, Catholic Biblical Association. Three times yearly. ISSN 0364-8591.

Almost three hundred journals are examined for relevant articles, which are abstracted by scholars of the Hebrew Scriptures who represent many confessions, including Judaism. Book notices, over a hundred each year, are short, evaluative descriptions, not full reviews. The abstracts are arranged in broad subject areas covering archaeology, epigraphy, and philology; history and geography; the Pentateuch; the historical books; the wisdom literature (the Writings); the major prophets; the minor prophets; biblical theology; and intertestamental and apocryphal literature. The third issue each year has an author index, a scriptural passage index, and an index to words in Hebrew and other ancient languages, including Greek.

724. **Society for Old Testament Study. Book List, 1946- .** Manchester, England, University of Manchester. Annual. ISSN 0081-1440.

724.1. Rowley, H. H., ed. **Eleven Years of Bible Bibliography: The Book Lists of the Society for Old Testament Study 1946-56.** Indian Hills, CO, Falcon's Wing Press, 1957. 804p. index. LC 57-7079.

724.2. Anderson, G. W., ed. **A Decade of Bible Bibliography: The Book Lists of the Society for Old Testament Study 1957-1966.** Oxford, England, Basil Blackwell, 1967. 706p. index. LC 68-103190.

724.3. Ackroyd, Peter Runham, ed. **Bible Bibliography 1967-1973. Old Testament: The Book Lists of the Society for Old Testament Study.** Oxford, England, Basil Blackwell, 1974. 505p. index. LC 75-327642. ISBN 0-631-16071-1.

The *Book List* was begun before World War II and circulated among members of the society. After the war, it became more comprehensive and was published, with the 1946 edition containing notes on books published since 1940. The notices indicate the contents and quality of books, but are not full reviews; they are arranged by broad subject area, including general treatments, archaeology and epigraphy, history and geography, texts and versions, exegesis and modern translations, literary criticism and introductions, law and religion and theology, life and thought of surrounding peoples, apocrypha and post-biblical studies, and philology and grammar. Although books from throughout the scholarly world are listed, all abstracts are in English. The three large volumes are reprints of the years covered rather than cumulations, although each does have a cumulated author index.

18
Bible Concordances

I. Concordances to the King James Version

725. Cruden, Alexander. **A Complete Concordance to the Holy Scriptures of the Old and New Testaments.** New York, Fleming H. Revell, 1916. 757p. LC 20-191.

This much-reprinted concordance to the King James Version was first published in 1737. Many common words, such as prepositions, are omitted, but are nowhere listed, so the reader does not know what not to look for. It is not analytical, that is, word entries do not give the original Hebrew or Greek word from which they are translated. The publication of Strong in 1894 (see 727) corrected Cruden's shortcomings and rendered it obsolete, but publishers have continued to find a niche for it.

726. Gibson, John C. L., and Ian A. Moir, eds. **Reader's Digest Family Guide to the Bible: A Concordance and Reference Companion to the King James Version.** Pleasantville, NY, Reader's Digest, 1984. 832p. LC 84-13261. ISBN 0-89577-192-6.

For the general reader (the "family"), this is a limited concordance to the King James Version (KJV), based on Strong (see 727), with seven thousand key words followed by one hundred thousand context lines. The editors attempt a middle path between the exhaustive, scholarly concordances and the small, inadequate versions sometimes found at the end of Bible editions. Here much additional material is included in attractive and novel packages. Introductory essays cover the history of the Bible, a synopsis of each book, the biblical cosmos, prophecy, the parables of Jesus, and the Apostles. Tables after the concordance treat words that have changed their meanings since the writing of the KJV ("goodman" and "prevent"), biblical chronology, the Jewish calendar, weights and measures, and genealogies and dynasties. Throughout the concordance proper, the editors have interspersed "theme-boxes" with quotations on such matters as baptism, ministry, music, peace—collectively a kind of quotation dictionary. Monochromatic reproductions of the masters of painting on biblical subjects also appear throughout the work.

727. Strong, James. **The New Strong's Exhaustive Concordance of the Bible.** Nashville, TN, Thomas Nelson, 1984. 1,793p. LC 84-16562. ISBN 0-8407-5360-8.

In 1894, at the end of a thirty-five year effort, with input from some one hundred collaborators, Strong first published this concordance to the King James Version (KJV). The most popular concordance in the English-speaking world, it has been reprinted with great regularity since. This current edition is newly typeset, and the editors have added new sections and corrected existing materials. Strong set the pace for usable analytical concordances. Every word in the English Bible, with the exception of forty-seven so common that no one would seek a reference by means of them (a, an, and, are, ... he, her, him, his, ... the, thee, their), is listed with quotations of each of its scripture references and, for each such reference, a referral number to the original word, of which it is a translation, in the Hebrew and Greek dictionaries at the end of the work. This system of referral numbers for Hebrew and Greek originals has become something of a standard, and is used by some other concordances, such as Young (see 729). An appendix lists the forty-seven common words, with every scripture reference listed by reference number but not by quotation; thus, here it is possible to locate every "the" used in the KJV. The Hebrew dictionary has 8,674 words and the Greek 5, 624, the total number of words in these languages used in the Bible.

A unique feature of this particular edition of Strong is a "Key Verse Comparison Chart," in which eighteen hundred verses, emanating from every book in the Bible, are listed as they appear in six major contemporary translations: KJV, New King James Version, New American Standard Bible, New International Version, Revised Standard Version, and Today's English Version. The edition is completed by a short list of "the teachings of Christ," with scripture references, and, more importantly, tables covering the Jewish calendar and feasts; biblical money; and liquid, dry, weight, and length measures.

728. Walker, James Bradford Richmond. **Walker's Comprehensive Bible Concordance.** Reprint: Grand Rapids, MI, Kregel Publications, 1976. 968p. LC 76-15841. ISBN 0-8254-4010-6.

Like many another reference book done in the pre-computer nineteenth century, this, first published in 1894, is said to have sent its compiler to an early grave. Walker stresses that it is a text-finder to the King James Version; that is, it leads to biblical passages by most key words, but does not include every word, as does Strong (see 727). Walker has not listed the words he has not treated. The arrangement is "rigidly alphabetical"; thus, derivative words are not included with their primaries, and, unlike the earlier Cruden (see 725), names of persons and places are included in the single alphabet. There is no attempt to connect entries with their Hebrew and Greek originals. Most readers will prefer Strong (see 727) or Young (see 729) for the King James Version, but Walker retains a following.

729. Young, Robert. **Young's Analytical Concordance to the Bible.** Nashville, TN, Thomas Nelson, 1982. 1,425p. indexes. LC 82-14203. ISBN 0-8407-4971-6.

Young first published this concordance to the King James Version in England in 1879, thus preceding the American Strong (see 727), who also took the KJV as his text. However, the two compilers offer different approaches. Strong notes each English word, and then lists every use of it, arranged by the biblical canon (Genesis first, Revelation last) and not differentiating by parts of speech or Hebrew and Greek originals, although he adds a reference number to his Hebrew and Greek lexicon for each use. Young notes the English word, but then gives meanings under separate lists for variant Hebrew and Greek originals. Thus, Strong has *love* with an enormous list of occurrences after it. Young has it first as a noun, with five lists under it for the four Hebrew words and one Greek in the original texts; a second entry for *love* as a verb has nine lists for nine originals. Young therefore is more useful for serious word study and whenever words of frequent occurrences are of interest. Unlike Strong, Young does not list all words, and this edition contains no mention of those which, however common, are left out. Young has added lexicons to Hebrew and Greek, with each word printed first in the roman and then the original alphabet, and this edition adds Strong's reference number to each word in the lexicon. The edition also contains a "universal subject guide" of over two hundred pages which lists themes, persons, and places and gives important biblical references to each. This subject guide is useful to readers of versions other than the King James. A list of every proper name in the Bible, with its accent, is present but nowhere mentioned in the introduction, and a table of contents is nonexistent. British scholar Donald Guthrie has offered an excellent introduction to the work, which outlines the various ways in which a concordance can be a help to the biblical student.

II. A Concordance to the Douay-Rheims Version

730. Thompson, Newton, and Raymond Stock. **Complete Concordance to the Bible (Douay Version).** St. Louis, MO, B. Herder, 1945. 1,914p. LC 45-8426.

The Douay or Douay-Rheims Version was produced by expatriate English Catholics in Belgium and France at a time when Roman Catholicism was outlawed in Britain. While the King James Version (KJV) became the Protestant standard for several centuries, the Douay became the Catholic. While the KJV is based on the Greek original, such as it was understood in the "textus receptus" of the sixteenth century, the Douay is translated from the Latin Vulgate, produced by St. Jerome in the fourth century. Thompson and Stock here offer a simple concordance, with a single alphabet for all English words including proper names. After each word, every occurrence is listed by chapter and verse in the Catholic canonical arrangement of books. There is no linking of the words to the Latin original of the Vulgate. Common words are omitted, but there is no list to tell the reader what the omissions are. While interest in the King James Version is likely to be eternal, because of its influence on literature and speech patterns, the Douay Version, replaced in Roman Catholic liturgical usage by the New American Bible, seems destined to obscurity.

III. Concordances to the Revised Standard Version

731. **A Concordance to the Apocrypha/Deuterocanonical Books of the Revised Standard Version: Derived from the Bible Data Bank of the Centre Informatique et Bible (Abbey of Maredsous).** Grand Rapids, MI, Eerdmans, 1983. 479p. LC 82-16310. ISBN 0-8028-2312-2.

The "Apocryphal" books of the Old Testament are those which are not accepted into the canon of Jewish and most Protestant bibles. All but a few are accepted by the Roman Catholics and Eastern Orthodox, and are then called "Deuterocanonical." A revision of the Apocryphal/Deuterocanonical books was completed for the Revised Standard Version in 1957. This concordance includes 155,875 word occurrences. Over half of these, or 83,235, are applications of 77 common words (*to* appears 4,356 times), and these are only listed with the number of their occurrences. The other words are given brief quotations. This concordance is not analytical, that is, it does not lead from English back to the original language, usually Greek. Each word listed is accompanied by two numbers: the first is its total occurrences and the second is its usage as a percentage of the total usage of all words.

732. Ellison, John William, comp. **Nelson's Complete Concordance of the Revised Standard Version Bible,** 2d ed. Nashville, TN, Thomas Nelson, 1984. 1,136p. LC 84-27256. ISBN 0-8407-4954-6.

Ellison worked with a Univac I at Remington Rand in 1956 to produce this concordance to the Revised Standard Version. It is exhaustive in that it indexes all words except 131. Two points about these 131 words: Ellison himself notes they make up 59 percent of the Bible; also in the 1890s, without a computer, Strong (see 727) completed a concordance to the King James Version which indexed all words except 47 (these he indexed in an appendix). Ellison's concordance is not analytical, in that it does not lead the student back to the words used in the original Hebrew, Aramaic, or Greek. This is the best concordance that could be produced in a primitive age of computers. For more advanced output, see Whitaker (734).

733. Morrison, Clinton. **An Analytical Concordance to the Revised Standard Version of the New Testament.** Philadelphia, PA, Westminster Press, 1979. 770p. LC 77-26210. ISBN 0-664-20773-1.

Morrison has produced a more sophisticated concordance than the earlier Ellison (see 732) because he has analyzed each English word in the Revised Standard Version (RSV) by relating it to its Greek original. By adding a Greek index lexicon, he has enabled the user to find each use of a specific Greek word in the New Testament as well. By arranging this lexicon according to the transliteration of the Greek words into the roman alphabet, he assures that any reader can use the concordance profitably, even if he or she does not read Greek. Whitaker (see 734) is not so indulgent. As Young did for the King James Version, Morrison has separated the meanings of the English words according to the Greek originals and, again, given the Greek originals in both the Greek and roman alphabets. For each separate Greek original under the English word, he has listed context lines for every occurrence in the New Testament. He bases his choice of words on the Greek text, and eliminates only four words from consideration: *ho* (the); *kai* (and); *de* (but); and *autos* (self). (The thirty-seven thousand occurrences of these four make up a quarter of the New Testament.) As the King James Version is well served by both Strong and Young, the Revised Standard Version will be best served when the Hebrew Scriptures are given a companion to Morrison's New Testament treatment and these two are then offered along with Whitaker.

734. Whitaker, Richard., comp. **The Eerdmans Analytical Concordance to the Revised Standard Version of the Bible.** Grand Rapids, MI, Eerdmans, 1988. 1,548p. indexes. LC 88-19217. ISBN 0-8028-2403-X.

Even with more sophisticated use of computers than Ellison's early effort (see 732), the production of this concordance took seven years; the reason is its careful analysis of each English word used in the Revised Standard Version, that is, the identification of the Hebrew, Aramaic, Greek, or Latin word or phrase from which it is translated. Whitaker arranges his English words as Strong did for the King James Version (see comparison of Strong and Young in Young, 729), and includes every occurrence of an English word in the canonical order of the books of both testaments, with Strong's reference number after each to lead to the Hebrew, Aramaic, Greek, or Latin original.

The preface and introduction, read together, give an idea of the complexity of biblical translation and consequently of concordance production. The more than four hundred thousand entries include all words and phrases in the RSV except for many prepositions and conjunctions, most subordinating and demonstrative pronouns, and all forms of *have* and *be* except *being* as a noun and *am* in the self-identification of God as "I am." Inflections of words are listed under a main entry; thus, *filling* and *filled* are under *fill*. Of special convenience are the separate listings for numbers and proper names. The editors are careful to note that the lists of Hebrew, Aramaic, Greek, and Latin words at the end of the concordance are not dictionaries, but contain only the words of the Bible and no others; hence, they consider these lists indexes. They have arranged these indexes according to the Hebrew and Greek alphabets, thus rendering helpless anyone who cannot read these alphabets. The RSV, which undergoes continuous examination by a committee for accuracy of translation according to developments in scholarship, is considered among the most careful of translations. This well-constructed concordance is a valuable scholarly companion to it.

IV. A Concordance to the New English Bible

735. Elder, E., comp. **Concordance to the New English Bible: New Testament.** Grand Rapids, MI, Zondervan, 1965. 401p. LC 65-4322.

This must be used in conjunction with a concordance to the King James Version of the New Testament, as it includes words only when they are not used at all or not in the same verse as the King James Version. It is not analytic, that is, it does not give the original Greek word from which the English is translated.

V. Concordances to the New King James Version

736. **The Complete Concordance to the Bible: New King James Version.** Nashville, TN, Thomas Nelson, 1983. 1,083p. LC 83-13271. ISBN 0-8407-4959-7.

This is definitely meant for the general reader, as 363 words are not indexed, a rather large number when compared with Strong's 47 (see 727). The preface notes that there are "over 265,000 biblical references for the 13,331 words in the NKJV vocabulary." (A different age would have found significance in the palindromic 13,331.) Words are signalled by an asterisk when they are spelled the same as nonindexed words. For example, *leaves* as the plural of *leaf* is indexed, but it is not indexed as the verb in "he leaves." Cross-referencing is particularly well done, relating words to larger families, linking variant spellings of proper names, and variant names for the same persons or places. The same publishers have produced a second concordance for the New King James Version that is arranged by phrases rather than individual words (see 737).

737. **The Phrase Concordance of the Bible.** Nashville, TN, Thomas Nelson, 1986. 741p. index. LC 86-16314. ISBN 0-8407-4948-1.

Fifty-two hundred phrases from the New King James Version (NKJV) rather than individual words are the entry points for this concordance. One can therefore look up uses of "word of God," "spirit of God," "day of the Lord," "kingdom of heaven," or "Lord of Lords." There are cross-references for common phrases from four other English translations: the King James Version, the Revised Standard Version, the New American Standard Bible, and the New International Version. Thus, "abounding in love" from the New International Version is referenced to "abundant in mercy." This system of cross-reference somewhat overcomes the lack of analytics in this work: there are no references to the Hebrew, Aramaic, or Greek original words or phrases, and thus the reader can never be quite sure of identifying all the occurrences of a single phrase. A fifty-six-page key word index aids the reader who cannot remember the first word of a phrase. Although two scholars are acknowledged in the introduction for their contributions, curiously no other editor or compiler is credited for this useful device for the lay reader.

VI. A Concordance to the
New American Bible

738. Hartdegen, Stephen J., general ed. **Nelson's Complete Concordance of the New American Bible.** Collegeville, MN, Liturgical Press, and Nashville, TN, Thomas Nelson, 1977. 1,274p. LC 77-22170. ISBN 0-8407-4900-7.

The *New American Bible*, translated by a team of mostly Roman Catholic scholars, was published in 1970. This concordance to it lists three hundred thousand entries for eighteen hundred key words. About one hundred fifty common words, including most articles, prepositions, and auxiliary verbs, are not indexed. References to book, chapter, and verse for each word are included, as well as short quotations to capture the sense of the word. However, the concordance is not analytical; there is no attempt to lead the reader back to the original Hebrew, Aramaic, or Greek words. Hartdegen suggests that readers look for these words in concordances of the Bible in its original languages, but Whitaker's work (see 734), and the much earlier Young (see 729) and Strong (see 727), do make the connection between the English translation and the original languages for the serious reader. This is especially helpful for pastors and students who seek a high level of accuracy.

VII. A Concordance to the
New American Standard Version

739. Thomas, Robert L., general ed. **New American Standard Exhaustive Concordance of the Bible: Hebrew-Aramaic and Greek Dictionaries.** Nashville, TN, A. J. Holman, 1981. 1,695p. LC 80-39626. ISBN 0-87981-197-8.

This work, computer-generated as all now are, is exhaustive, in that its four-hundred-thousand-plus entries include all but fifty-one words in the New American Standard Version. It is analytical in that it refers the reader to the Hebrew, Aramaic, or Greek word from which each word is translated. In fact, Thomas has used the same number referencing system as Strong (see 727), but has reworked the definitions in his dictionary sections.

VIII. A Concordance to the
New International Version

740. Goodrick, Edward W., and John R. Kohlenberger, eds. **The NIV Complete Concordance: The Complete English Concordance to the New International Version.** Grand Rapids, MI, Zondervan, 1981. 1,044p. LC 80-28401. ISBN 0-310-43650-8.

With this concordance to the *New International Version*, the editors say they strive to find a middle ground between an exhaustive concordance, containing references to every word in the Bible, and an abridged work such as might be found printed in the back of a Bible. Accordingly, they omit references to almost 950 words, including all articles and most prepositions and adverbs. One might argue that *courageously, slanderously,* and *sparingly* should not have been sidestepped. The "complete" in the title is apparently justified by the editors' note that they add all references for each word that is listed. The work is not analytical, that is, it does not list the original Hebrew or Greek word the English translates. Each entry is followed by a one-line contextual quotation. The editors add cross-references between variant spellings of a word.

IX. A Concordance to All
English New Testaments

741. Darton, Michael, ed. **Modern Concordance to the New Testament.** Garden City, NY, Doubleday, 1977. 786p. LC 77-365063. ISBN 0-385-07901-X.

Based on but greatly modified from a French original, this complex concordance is an attempt to provide a single resource to resolve the following problems: there are many English translations of the New Testament; various English words or phrases can translate one Greek word; and a single English word can translate many Greek words.

It is a concordance of all English translations and at the same time of the Greek New Testament. Words are grouped in 341 thematic concepts; thus, the entry for *beginning* includes "(1) Begin, Beginning; (2) Begin to cry – Burst into tears; and (3) Alpha and Omega." Under each section, the possible Greek words are listed, transliterated into the roman alphabet; following these are the phrases from any current (1977) translation of the New Testament wherein the word is used. An English index includes every English word used in contemporary translations, and refers the reader to the thematic section in which the word is treated. A Greek index with the words written in the Greek alphabet accomplishes the same task. Thus, the reader can use the work as an analytical concordance by studying the Greek New Testament words behind the English translations, can skip the Greek entirely, or, in a halfway stage, can read the Greek roots in roman transliteration. Additionally, the editors provide an index to proper names and an index of Greek roots.

This unique concordance rises to its task well, but has several weaknesses. Lists of symbols used as marginal references and symbols used within the text are printed on a separate card, a kind of bookmark, and nowhere else in the book. Lose the card and you lose the explanation of the symbols. Although this concordance addresses the problem of an abundance of English translations, no list of the studied translations is given. Finally, given the complex nature of the project, the explanatory material at the beginning of the concordance and at the beginning of each index is unnecessarily confusing.

Overlooking these minor problems, the experienced reader will turn to this concordance before all others.

19
Biblical Quotation Dictionaries

742.   Levine, Mark L., and Eugene Rachlis, eds. **The Complete Book of Bible Quotations.** New York, Pocket Books, 1986. 568p. index. LC 88-134630. ISBN 0-671-49864-9.

After searching the entire King James Version for passages that meet their criterion of "quotability," that is, "how the phrase sounds in speech and on paper" (indeed, how does a phrase sound on paper?), the editors have chosen five (according to the cover) or six (according to the preface) thousand quotations and classified them into eight hundred categories. Quotations are taken from all books of the Bible, and each is listed under at least two categories. A very useful key-word index lists every important word in every quotation except "Jesus," "God," and "Lord." The outlook of the editors is indicated by the category "Sex," which is given only cross-references: "See Adultery, Carnality, Celibacy, Fornication, Homosexuality, Immorality, Incest, Lust." Celibacy and homosexuality aside, one concludes that everyone from the prophets to ordinary folk like us must have come to earth through one of the remaining unholy choices. The *Interpreter's Dictionary of the Bible* and its *Supplement* (see 576) treat this topic in a more wholesome and balanced manner.

743.   McLeish, Kenneth, and Valerie McLeish. **Longman Guide to Bible Quotations.** Harlow, Essex, England, Longman, 1986. index. 415p. LC 87-103514. ISBN 0-5825-5573-6.

The McLeishes choose and print in full sentences the key verses of the entire King James Version, and then add a feature unique to this collection, a short explanation or commentary for each verse. An index of key words leads to each quotation.

744.   Speake, Jennifer, ed. **Biblical Quotations.** New York, Facts on File, 1983. 203p. index. LC 83-1511. ISBN 0-87196-241-1.

Speake has published a kind of short Bible by printing what she feels to be quotable passages from the entire King James Version, except for the Psalms, for which she uses the Coverdale translation, since that is what was printed in the Anglican Book of Common Prayer. The index—almost half the work—consists in the main of key words from the culled passages, but also includes well-known phrases not actually in the Bible (prodigal son), and theme headings (peace, justice).

745.   Stevenson, Burton Egbert. **The Home Book of Bible Quotations.** New York, Harper, 1949. 645p. index. LC 49-11832.

Stevenson placed verses from the King James Version under some fifteen hundred subject headings. Under a heading, each verse is quoted completely and cited by book, chapter, and verse. An index then repeats each verse by at least one key word, and gives the page and position on the page of the main entry. Stevenson includes Old Testament and New Testament apocrypha as well as such early Christian literature as the epistles of Clement and Barnabas and the Apostles' Creed. Stevenson sometimes explains an obscure reference. Though older than Levine's (see 742) or Speake's (see 744), Stevenson's biblical quotation dictionary is still the best. All three are based on the King James Version, which has not changed since 1611.

20
Core Biblical Journals

746. **Biblica, 1920-** . Rome, Italy, Pontifical Biblical Institute. Quarterly. ISSN 0006-0887.

The Pontifical Biblical Institute draws some of the best Roman Catholic biblical scholars and students, and its development reflects the considerable progress of biblical studies in this church since the beginning of the century. Articles in the journal have been published in Italian, German, French, Spanish, and Latin as well as English; but, reflecting the increased influence of British, American, and Commonwealth biblical scholarship, English now seems to predominate. Scholars who are not Catholic now make contributions. Each issue is divided into lengthy essays, shorter notes, and book reviews. Because of the international scope of the Institute, books are sometimes received for review from areas of the globe not usually touched by other journals. The comprehensive *Elenchus Bibliographicus Biblicus* (see 719) was published as a section of *Biblica* until 1960, but is now separate.

747. **Biblical Archaeologist, 1938-** . New Haven, CT, American Schools of Oriental Research. Quarterly. ISSN 0006-0895.

The purpose of this glossy quarterly is "to provide the general reader with an accurate scholarly yet easily understandable account of archaeological discoveries and their bearing on the biblical heritage" (cover). Much colorful photography, as well as line drawings and maps, accompanies the articles, which are written by major international scholars involved in digs in the Middle East. Articles cover not only archaeological findings, but also secondary subjects, such as biblical museums and leading scholars themselves. Book reviews appear in each issue, and the editors at times include reviews of the reference literature. A particular feature is the "Colophon," on the last page, which may be a poem, a particularly meaningful photograph, or a translation from an ancient text.

748. **The Biblical Archaeology Review, 1975-** . Washington, DC, Biblical Archaeology Society. Bimonthly. ISSN 0098-9444.

Practicing archaeologists and biblical scholars write for the general reader; fine color photography accompanies the articles. Treatment of work in Israel is particularly generous. The editors include news notes on the Biblical Archaeological Society. Of special interest is the "Queries and Comments" column, which usually contains several dozen letters whose writers range from advanced scholars to school children.

749. The Catholic Biblical Quarterly, 1939- . Washington, DC, Catholic Biblical Association of America. Quarterly. ISSN 0008-7912.

This has evolved from a periodical linking a small circle of seminary professors from a single religious tradition to a major international journal with Protestant, Catholic, and Jewish writers. Recent years have seen the growth of contributions from female biblical scholars. Each issue has seven or eight essays, which may be written by established scholars or young scholars publishing for the first time. "Biblical News" reports on the Catholic Biblical Association and notes seminars, conferences, and the publications of its members. The editors include over four dozen full-length book reviews and shorter notices, as well as up to a dozen reviews of "Collected Essays."

750. Interpretation: A Journal of Bible and Theology, 1947- . Richmond, VA, Union Theological Seminary. Quarterly. ISSN 0020-9643.

Some of America's best biblical scholars contribute five to eight articles for each issue, often relating biblical thought to major contemporary issues. A half-dozen major book reviews, often several pages in length, precede some two dozen shorter reviews. The editors include a list of books received.

751. Journal for the Study of the Old Testament, 1976- . Sheffield, England, JSOT Press. Three times yearly. ISSN 0309-0892.

First published in typescript, this journal is academic in the most literal sense: a note on the inside cover announces, "copyright is waived where reproduction of material from this Journal is required for classroom use or course work by students." While some renowned British and American scholars sit on the editorial board, articles are often by lesser-known writers who occupy academic posts and parishes. Most issues contain a lengthy book review, followed by a short book list with descriptive paragraphs. The editors also arrange for review of computer software of interest to biblical students.

752. Journal of Biblical Literature, 1881- . Decatur, GA, Scholars Press. Quarterly. ISSN 0021-9231. Sponsored by the Society of Biblical Literature.

Recent issues of this influential American biblical journal, sponsored by the Society of Biblical Literature (see 763), have averaged nine essays each, all in English. Contributors are leading Protestant, Catholic, and Jewish world scholars in biblical studies. Approximately five dozen books are reviewed in each issue, of which one dozen are collections of essays.

753. New Testament Studies, 1954- . Cambridge, England, Cambridge University Press. Quarterly. ISSN 0028-6885.

Full-length articles and shorter studies by high-level scholars characterize this journal. English predominates, but French and German are also found. No book reviews are included, but the editors do list the books they have received. The journal is sponsored by the Studiorum Novi Testamenti Societas (Society for Studies of the New Testament), a world-wide ecumenical association of some eight hundred biblical scholars.

754. Semeia: An Experimental Journal for Biblical Criticism, 1974- . Decatur, GA, Scholars Press. Quarterly. ISSN 0095-571X.

The product of American scholars, and supported by the Society of Biblical Literature (see 763), this "is an experimental journal devoted to the exploration of new and emergent areas and methods of biblical criticism.... Studies employing the methods, models, and findings of linguistics, folklore studies, contemporary literary criticism, structuralism, social anthropology, and other such disciplines and approaches, are invited" (cover). The articles for each issue are arranged around a central theme, and the issues are numbered consecutively from the beginning.

755.   **Vetus Testamentum, 1951-** . Leiden, The Netherlands, E. J. Brill. Quarterly. ISSN 0042-4935.

Sponsored by the International Organization for the Study of the Old Testament, this journal has from its beginning offered the highest level of international scholarship on the "Old Testament," a translation of its Latin title. Several essays of fifteen to twenty pages in each issue are followed by essay-length book reviews. An extensive "Book List" offers short, evaluative descriptions of scholarly books, arranged by authors' names in a sequence that takes two years of publishing to complete the alphabet. A 1989 issue notes a book published in 1982. Most articles are in English; some are in French.

21
Principal Biblical Research Centers and Institutes, and Professional Biblical Associations and Societies

I. Biblical Research Centers and Institutes

756. **American Schools of Oriental Research.** 711 West 40th Street, Suite 354, Baltimore, MD 21211. 301/889-1383. FAX 301/889-1157.

Founded in 1900, this institute now sponsors research centers in Cyprus, Jordan, and Israel. Its original purpose, to "encourage research about the geography, history, archaeology and ancient and modern languages and literatures of Palestine, Mesopotamia and other Oriental countries, by affording education opportunities to graduates of American Colleges and Universities and to other qualified students, and by prosecution of original research, excavations, and explorations," was long carried out under the leadership of William Foxwell Albright, preeminent American archaeologist and biblical scholar. The society publishes the *Bulletin* and *Biblical Archaeologist* (see 747), as well as the *Journal of Cuneiform Studies* and many monograph series.

757. **Institute for Biblical Research.** Wheaton College, Wheaton, IL 60187. 312/260-5000. 300 members.

Founded in 1970, this academic institute holds annual meetings, sends out a newsletter to its membership, sponsors research and publication by its members, and supports regional study groups. Its purpose is "to foster the study of the Scriptures within an evangelical context; to establish facilities for the furtherance of biblical studies; [and] to encourage university and college students toward a vocation of biblical scholarship."

II. Professional Biblical Associations and Societies

758. **American Bible Society.** 1865 Broadway, New York, NY, 10023. 212/581-7400. FAX 212/408-1512. 500,000 members.

Far and away the largest American-based organization promoting the reading and study of the Bible, the American Bible Society publishes the King James Version (KJV), Today's English Version (TEV), the New King James Version (NKJV), and the Revised

Standard Version (RSV) in English; scholarly editions in Greek and Hebrew; and translations into Spanish, Apache, Navajo, Cherokee, Hawaiian, Khmer, Chinese, Japanese, Korean, Vietnamese, Arabic, French, German, Haitian French, Italian, and Polish. The society also supports an extensive publishing program of related materials, including large-print, cassette, and braille Bibles; Bible-based devotional works; children's Bibles and study materials; and materials for those with learning difficulties. As an affiliated society of the United Bible Societies, it supports extensive, worldwide, translation programs and reported at the end of 1988 that 310 languages and dialects have the complete Bible, 695 additional have the New Testament, and another 902 have at least one complete book of the Bible. This eminently ecumenical society, originally and still predominantly Protestant (and reflecting input from every shade of Protestantism), has in recent decades welcomed Roman Catholic and Eastern Orthodox members.

759. **Catholic Biblical Association of America.** Catholic University of America, 620 Michigan Avenue, N.E., Washington, DC 20064. 202/635-5519. 1,140 members.

Since the Second Vatican Council and the renaissance of biblical studies in the Catholic Church, the association's members come from public and non-Catholic universities as well as church institutions. The association meets yearly, and its publishing program includes *The Catholic Biblical Quarterly* (see 749), *Old Testament Abstracts* (see 723), and a monograph series. It supported the original *Jerome Biblical Commentary* (see 623), as well as a new edition scheduled to appear in late 1989.

760. **International Bible Society.** P.O. Box 62970, Colorado Springs, CO 80962-2970. 719/488-9200. FAX 719/488-3840. 30,000 supporters.

Founded in 1809, the society has produced the New International Version (NIV) of the Bible in English and a Spanish equivalent, has worked with evangelical religious groups worldwide, and has sponsored translations of the Bible into more than 350 languages.

761. **International Organization for Septuagint and Cognate Studies.** Department of Philosophy and Religion, Clemson University, Clemson, SC 29634-1508. 803/656-5358. 375 members.

The Septuagint is the Greek version of the Hebrew Scriptures, translated in Alexandria, Egypt, in the third century BCE. This scholarly society, founded in 1968, publishes the *IOSCS Annual Bulletin* and a monograph series, and meets annually. Its purpose is "to carry out critical study of Jewish Greek Scriptures and related subjects."

762. **International Society of Bible Collectors.** 1260 Orchard Lane, Lansdale, PA 19446. 215/368-8455. 200 members.

In addition to serving Bible collectors, the society, founded in 1964, also aids librarians in identifying new translations of the complete Bible, either one of the testaments, and individual books. Its quarterly, *Bible Collectors' World*, disseminates information on new translations, editions, and versions.

763. **Society of Biblical Literature.** 819 Houston Mill Road, N.E., Atlanta, GA 30329. 404/636-4744. 5,500 members.

Founded in 1880, the SBL is the major academic society encouraging "the critical investigation of biblical literature, together with other related literature, by the exchange of scholarly research both in published form and in public forum." It is affiliated with and holds joint annual meetings with the American Academy of Religion (see 534); members of SBL have the option of joint membership with AAR. *Religious Studies News*, published five times yearly, is a joint newsletter of both the SBL and the AAR. The SBL also works cooperatively with the American Schools of Oriental Research (see 756) and the International Organization for Septuagint and Cognate Studies (see 761). The SBL publishes the *Journal of Biblical Literature* (see 752) and *Semeia* (see 754), as well as many monograph series. It has produced *Harper's Bible Dictionary* (see 569) and *Harper's Bible Commentary* (see 630).

Author/Title Index

The numbers in this index refer to entries, not to pages. Titles of all works annotated are indexed as well as the titles of organizations in chapters 10 and 21. Authors, editors, compilers, and translators are indexed. Writers and titles mentioned within annotations are signalled by an "n." Where titles are very short or are the same for different works, I have clarified the matter by including the author's last name in parentheses.

Subject Index

The numbers in this index refer to entries, not pages.

William Jessup University
Library
333 Sunset Blvd.
Rocklin, Ca 95765